CHASING LOVE

KAT T. MASEN

Kat T. Masen

Chasing Love

A Billionaire Love Triangle
The Dark Love Series Book 1

Copyright 2020 Kat T. Masen
All Rights Reserved

Disclaimer: The material in this book contains graphic language and sexual content and is intended for mature audiences, ages 18 and older.

ISBN: 979-8654418876
ISBN: 979-8755757355

Editing by Nicki at Swish Design & Editing
Proofing by Kay at Swish Design & Editing
Cover design by Outlined by Love Designs
Cover Image Copyright 2020
First Edition 2020
All Rights Reserved

PROLOGUE
CHARLIE

I wrapped my arms around myself to shelter my body from the sea breeze. The evening air was cool yet humid—the lingering smell of rain mixed with salt. A sudden flash of lightning brightened the dark sky, a beautiful sight followed by the inevitable. I placed my hands over my ears, burying my head between my legs. The crash of thunder startled me. Slowly, I raised my head and uncovered my ears, then I listened to the low rumble disappear into the night.

I hated storms, they terrified me, but here I sat, waiting patiently as I had always done.

This was our special place, but tonight, with the moon obscured behind the thick dark clouds, this no longer felt like our safe haven. Anxiously, I pulled out a weed that stood between the rocks and tore it apart until there was nothing left. The lightning struck once again, and the threat of thunder forced me to bury my head. I rocked back and forth as I hugged my knees. Unwillingly, my mind returned to the night my fear of storms began...

. . .

"He's the most beautiful man you'll ever see. His soul will capture you but don't be fooled, Mi Corazon. He'll use all his powers to draw you in when there's nothing left to do but take the one thing you've been holding on to."

It was past my bedtime, but I couldn't sleep. A storm was rolling in, and the thunder was getting louder. I pulled the covers over me, frightened by this creature Momma spoke about. With my heart racing and my voice shaking, I dared ask the question that haunted me.

"Who is he, Momma?"

Momma paused, staring out of the large window. Fear passed over her classically beautiful face. I wasn't sure why. Daddy would protect her. Daddy had a gun and said if anyone would ever hurt us, he'd hunt them down like hungry wolves.

"The big bad wolf," she whispered.

The big bad wolf was scary. I didn't understand what I'd be holding on to. I was only eight. This fairy tale was nothing like the others. Where was the happy ending? Momma told this story as if she memorized it by heart.

"Will he come for me, Momma?"

The thunder shook the house, and I clutched her arm as tight as I could. I was scared, the roar was so loud, and I didn't want the big bad wolf to come for me. He scared me. I wanted to stay with Daddy, Momma, and Sissy. As the noise became louder, I buried my head under Momma's arm, trying to shut out the horrible sound.

"Momma, I'm scared."

"Sleep, Mi Corazon."

Humming my favorite lullaby, she stroked my hair to calm me down until I fell asleep in her arms.

. . .

I never believed the myth about the big bad wolf, but for some reason, it stuck with me, and unfortunately, so did my fear of storms. Just poor timing, I kept telling myself. Frustrated, I looked down at my watch. *You've got to be kidding me.* He's an hour late. Like I had nothing better to do than wait around for him. I could've finished my English assignment I had been putting off for days because *he* was more important. My grades were already slipping, and Principal Stephens could smell my fear of failure a mile away.

Just as I was about to get up and leave, his masculine arms wrapped around me, warming my body. Placing soft kisses along my neckline, the stale smell of some alcoholic beverage lingered on his breath. My heart sank. I knew something was wrong, but I wasn't in the mood to be sympathetic. I was sick and tired of all this sneaking around.

"Rough night? Haven't you heard of a cell?"

I could see the lie coming. "Rough doesn't even cut it. I'm sorry, my cell is acting up."

Distracted, he moved his hands underneath my jacket and ran them along my stomach.

"You smell like you've been to a frat party," I spat, frustrated.

Unable to hide my annoyance any longer, I moved his hands away, but he stopped me immediately. He tightened his grip around my waist and buried his head in my hair.

"Your hair... it's so... I miss you..." he mumbled words that made no sense, and I grew even more irritated. I pulled away and stood up, the blood in my veins beginning to pump vigorously from anger.

"What's this? I know you better than you know yourself. You're drunk for a reason." Without hesitation, I blurted out the words that plagued my mind. "You're going to tell me it's over. The signs are here, you've been acting weird all week. Let's see... Sammy cried so much you felt sorry for her, and you owe it to your marriage to make it work."

He stood up fast, unsteady on his feet. I half-expected him to laugh it off, but even in his intoxicated state, he seemed to understand what I meant. The hesitation alone was enough for me to think the worst, but I stood and waited without taking a breath. His eyes fixated on me, a trance I tried not to get pulled into, but slowly I felt drawn in, cast under his spell without any hope of climbing out.

"*Over?* I can't fucking breathe without you, Charlotte. This is torture. Us, not being able to be us in front of everybody. Don't do this, okay? Don't fucking make it out like it's over."

He was trying to blow off steam, equally frustrated with our constant battle to hide our relationship. I got it, I did, but he was the one to blame here, not me. I was just the girl who fell in love with her best friend's brother who happened to be married.

The wind shifted and so did his mood. He ran his finger down my cheekbone just as he had always done, then slowly and reassuringly he placed his lips on mine.

"Look at me, Charlotte," he begged.

My eyes found their way back to his, and just like they had done a million times before, the emerald green shone back at me. In their reflection, I saw only us.

Him, me—together against the world.

He placed my hand over his heart. "As long as this beats, it's for you. I'll find a way for us to be together. Don't give up on us. We happened for a reason. The rest are obstacles we can overcome. As long as you place your trust in me, I promise never to break you. I love you... only you. I swear, it'll be us for life, baby. Ride or die, 'til death us do part."

I gave into him that night because I loved him more than life itself, but it was soon afterward that I realized what Momma tried to tell me all along.

The big bad wolf had come for me. Taken all that was mine, then left me alone in the dark. He'd emptied me of everything good and pure, leaving me hollow and unable to love, wandering alone in the darkness like a tortured soul. I prayed that he wouldn't come for me, but he did. His name was Alexander Edwards, and that night he filled me with promises, made me believe it was only us in this world, that we only needed each other.

"Ride or die, 'til death us do part."

And that was the last time I saw him.

ONE

CHARLIE

Present

It's day two of my mission to create balance in my life.

I made the mistake of reading this article about living the best life possible and why our bodies need self-care. I run every second day or so, but according to this journalist, being a member of a gym motivates you to work out and increases social activity.

Two areas I'm failing at miserably.

Standing here in front of this machine with two handles side-by-side and a chair meant for sitting, I'm dumbfounded. I assume you pull the handles together which works your arms.

Placing my towel on the bench, I take a seat and latch onto the handles, reining them in. The handles don't budge, making me look stupid for even trying this.

And this is why I don't do machines.

Or the gym.

Frustrated and barely breaking a sweat, I step away and walk toward the cross-trainers. This can't be too difficult.

There are five cross trainers, and three of them are taken. A young guy is going hard, sweating profusely with no towel in sight to wipe his dripping forehead. A girl, attractive with cute workout wear, is beside him with a cell in hand taking selfies.

Then there's granny beside me. Gray permed hair cut short with a white sweatband sitting on her head to hold it back. She wears an oversized sweatsuit in baby pink, made of that same material people wear when parachuting off a plane.

Her speed is slow, yet consistent, looking easy enough for me to keep up with.

Flinging my towel over the rail and nestling my earphones into my ears, I follow the instructions and press the button to start the machine. Okay, move feet like walking and swing arms. Easy.

My body unwillingly moves too fast, whacking the front and forcing me to grip tight not to fall off.

"Doll, are you all right?"

Great, granny feels sorry for me.

I hate the gym so much.

"Um, yeah. Just getting my bearings."

"I'm Susan. I haven't seen you around. New to the joint?"

Moving my feet slower this time, I gain momentum and try to hold this conversation.

"Charlie, but it's short for Charlotte," I tell her, coordinating my movements. "Yes, first time here. I read this article, and I'm trying to be nicer to my body, especially since I love anything carbs, donuts, you know... the food that kills you."

Susan smiles, nodding her head in agreement. "Doll, you look fantastic. Let me tell you a story. I've got eight children and fifteen grandbabies. My body has seen it all, carried a few ten pounders, too. But nothing, and I mean nothing, can prepare you for being seventy-two and chasing little ones around. That's why I come here every morning."

I have to give it to Susan, she doesn't look in her seventies, early sixties at best.

"I also heard that gyms are great for socializing. Look, Susan, it's not like I'm desperate to meet a guy, but you know... it's kinda been a while, and I'm pushing thirty in a few years. I just don't know where the time has gone. Okay, wait, I lie. I focused on my career so much and opening our small firm that I didn't have time for anyone. Now look at me, I can't even use a cross-trainer without almost falling off," I ramble, oversharing way too personal information.

Susan slows down her movements until she hits a complete stop. Stepping off the machine, she grabs her towel and water bottle. "I don't do this all the time, but you strike me as a lady who can use some help. I have a son, Jesse Junior. He's from out of town but never settled down with a woman. I think he'd be a good match. I could pass on your number."

The humiliation just doesn't stop. Jesse Junior certainly doesn't seem like my type. An out-of-towner means country boy on some isolated farm expecting me to raise his kids and bake pies every day.

"You know what?" I say, keeping a smile and the conversation amicable. "If the next time you see me, I'm still single, you pass me Jesse's number."

"Junior, doll, Jesse Junior," she corrects me. "Jesse is my husband, and Lord knows he'd eat you up like a hungry wolf." Susan waves goodbye, and walks toward the restroom, disappearing behind the red door marked *Ladies*.

I manage to use the cross trainer for another twenty

minutes, listening to Olivia Newton-John's 'Let's Get Physical' in hopes of inspiring my newfound hobby. All I can think of for twenty minutes is whether or not anyone will judge me if I wear spandex to the gym.

Slowing down my pace, I hit stop and step off the machine, knees shaking and unbalanced. I wonder how many Hershey bars I just worked off. God, I need chocolate so bad.

In an effort to forget about my sweet tooth, I decide to try another workout, casually walking past a man sitting at the machine I previously attempted to use. He's lifting his arms, making grunts, then I realize how stupid I look since I didn't use the machine that way, hence my abandonment earlier.

That's it, I'm making the gym my bitch. I refuse to be a pawn in its sick and twisted game.

Spotting another machine by the corner, I make my way over and get comfortable, placing my towel on the chair. This one looks easy. All I have to do is pull the lever-looking thing and work on my arms.

I'm about five minutes in, and I am certain my limbs will need to be amputated tomorrow. Grabbing my towel, I stand, bumping into a man, accidentally resting my hands on his chest.

"Oh my God. I'm so sorry. I just wasn't looking," I apologize, out of breath.

He rests his hands on my shoulders, pushing me away but kindly and in a non-offensive way. Baring a grin, his expression is amusing rather than annoying.

"Hey, it's cool. My fault." He pulls one of his earbuds out, "Lost in some Bon Jovi... you know, gym music."

"'Livin' on a Prayer'?"

He laughs, cute dimples gracing his perfectly sculpted

face. Gosh, he's gorgeous. He reminds me of someone, but I can't figure out who.

"'Keep the Faith,'" he answers. "But I'll do some sets to 'Livin' on a Prayer' occasionally."

My eyes wander toward his chest, surrounded by his toned arms. His tank is white, dripping in sweat but not in the gross way that makes you scrunch your nose. No, more like the I-want-my- milkshake-to-bring-you-to-my-yard type sweat.

He extends his hand. "I'm Julian... Julian Baker."

"Charlie Mason." I shake his hand, relishing in how masculine his hands are and why they do something to me I haven't felt in a long time.

"So, the machine. Are you done?"

I turn around, unwillingly, then realize my unwarranted lust over this man is pathetic since he only wants the machine.

"Um, yeah, go for it. I've wiped it down and everything, so like you don't have to worry about sweat or rashes. Wait, is a sweat rash why we're supposed to wipe it down, or can you catch like herpes?" The words are like verbal diarrhea, and my temperature rises from sheer embarrassment. "Look, I don't know anything about herpes, so can we forget I ever mentioned that?"

Slight creases form around Julian's hazel-colored eyes. His smile, warm and friendly, turns into a small laugh.

"I trust you, but thanks for the lesson on body rashes."

"I'm mortified," I admit, laughing at my own stupidity. "It was nice meeting you. Maybe we can do this again sometime... the awkward rash talk. Have fun."

My attempt to walk away is to pick up any dignity that's left behind.

"Wait," Julian calls.

I turn around to face him, waiting for him to tell me how stupid I was back then.

"Maybe we could do this again, but somewhere else like over coffee. And we could leave the rash talk behind, only if it's okay with you?"

His flirty grin is hard to ignore, my cheeks rising slowly into a joyous smile. Maybe this gym business isn't so bad. Kill two birds with one stone—workout and meet a gorgeous man.

"Sure." I motion for him to follow me to the counter where I steal a pen from the receptionist. I grab Julian's arm, writing my number across it.

"I'll call." He smiles, flashing that grin one more time for me. "And you better answer."

"Oh, I will," I respond with a flirtatious wink, letting go of his arm. "See you later, Julian."

TWO

CHARLIE

The oddest thing about me is that I love Monday mornings. I don't suffer from the so-called 'Mondayitis' like everyone else I know. There's something about a new week, a fresh start, which excites me. The possibilities are endless.

Lately, I've kept myself busy by listening to podcasts to try to nurture my brain. That, and I have been single for a year straight. According to many of my close friends, a year is the slippery slope to crazy cat lady syndrome. So, I have one cat, Coco. She's a great cat—obedient, cuddly, and doesn't leave dead mice in my apartment.

I do, however, feel sorry for having to leave her alone for several hours and often contemplate getting another cat so they can chill and have cat-type fun.

My phone sits on the boardroom table in front of me. Taking a deep breath, I text back Julian. He messaged me late last night, a day after my embarrassing stint at the gym. We texted for hours about trivial topics, but nevertheless, I really enjoyed his online company and equally witty banter.

So, I'm seizing the day. According to this podcast, if I don't act, I won't receive good things in my life.

And I don't want to become a crazy cat lady.

The temptation to check my phone to see if he responds is too great, so I place it face down on the table and stare at my surroundings, waiting for our meeting to start. My train of thought has so easily gone from cats to an episode of *Grey's Anatomy* where George died, and I sobbed like a baby.

"Monday, can you believe it?"

The voices enter the room, my colleagues looking less than pleased by the early Monday morning meeting. After quickly taking a seat, all heads are down, fingers busily typing away on their phones. In a room full of people, there's nothing but the sounds of tapping and the constant ping or chirp followed by more tapping.

Aside from loving Mondays, I also love my job. If I could, I'd never leave this place. Some call me a workaholic. I prefer the word 'passionate.' It helps that I adore my co-workers. Over time, they have become good friends, and our office has become like a close-knit family.

While waiting for the last person to arrive, I focus my attention on my new shoes. Okay, so I have a problem, and I have no doubt in my mind I'm a shoe addict. These new Louboutins are fresh off the fall line, and I'm a woman possessed by my need for shiny new patent leather and a heel that could poke your worst enemy's eye out. As I cross my legs admiring my new guilty pleasure, I catch sight of Eric taking a photograph with his phone.

"Absolutely gorgeous, Charlie. Let's hashtag this." Fingers busily typing away, Eric smiles. Moments later, he flashes me the picture.

"How nice of you, Eric. Did that interrupt your busy Candy Crush schedule? You have a problem, you know that, right? I'd like to see you live one day... actually, no... make that half a day without your phone."

"I did, remember?"

"Taking it back to the shop and getting a loaner phone does not count."

"Well, for your information, I'm now using my phone to order lunch."

Now that catches my attention. Lunch, and it's only eight fifty-five in the morning. Please be the sushi rolls from the Japanese place that just opened around the corner. My stomach rumbles at the thought, and, embarrassed, I let out a loose cough and make a mental note to eat more breakfast in the morning. Clearly, my stomach and I aren't in harmony with this let's-just-have-a- cup-of-coffee diet, which has become a terrible lazy habit.

"Charlie, the people all the way in Africa can hear your thoughts as well as your belly. And yes, I'm ordering from that new Japanese place. And no, you aren't eating those salmon rolls that make you puke up more than Linda Blair in *The Exorcist*."

"Disgusting, but you do have a point."

Suddenly, I feel queasy. That was one hell of a bad salmon roll. How is it possible that I'm not scarred enough that my body still craves it? The problem is, I remember how mouth-watering it was when I took the first bite and failed to remember the aftermath. I shudder at the thought, and mentally scold myself for craving it again. I'm so weak.

"Of course, I have a point," Eric continues, confidently. "I'm your personal assistant and BFF. It's my job to steer you away from danger, and that includes bad sushi rolls."

He buries himself in his phone again, looking up for only a moment to show me some picture of a dog wearing a Halloween costume. I have to chuckle because it's beyond pathetic someone's gone to these lengths, yet cute at the same time.

Eric always makes me laugh. He brings out the fun in everyone, plus he reminds me every day that we're Generation Y, living in a world that can no longer function without social media and ridiculous abbreviations such as BFF, LOL, and YOLO.

Like a whirlwind, Nikki, who's my partner at the firm, throws her stuff on the large mahogany table creating a loud bang, startling the others. Her usual perfect copper hair looks disheveled as she blows it out of her face, annoyed it strayed. Her bright blue eyes have dark circles underneath them. I can't help but worry as I take in her appearance.

"Nikki, are you okay?" I ask quietly, trying not to attract attention.

"No, not really. I spent most of the night sick from that Italian place we love to order the seafood marinara from. My new Dior dress is ruined because Rocky couldn't wait to reach the toilet or basin. It was the most disastrous anniversary in the history of bad anniversaries like a scene from one of those cheesy movies."

"The ruby-colored Dior dress?"

"Yes, Eric. The ruby-colored Dior dress, which is at the dry cleaners being cleaned of any traces of projectile seafood marinara," she answers in a huff.

"Thank God, Nikki. That dress is to die for."

It's totally Eric to worry about the dress more than the person. He's fashion-obsessed, and if you're his best friend, it's impossible not to feel the same. It is the main reason why I designated him as my personal shopper when I don't have time to shop for myself. We're a lethal combination, but American Express seems to love us.

"Okay, seriously, let's get this meeting underway before I projectile vomit over all of you," she quickly interjects.

With a look of disgust, she starts the meeting, and I follow her lead. We talk about our schedules for the week, an upcoming workshop Eric and Emma, Nikki's assistant, will be attending tomorrow, and lastly, my long-awaited trip to Hawaii for my cousin's wedding.

When the meeting finishes, I find myself alone with Nikki, giving us a few minutes to catch up before we're inundated with work for the rest of the day.

"So, I'm guessing your anniversary didn't have a happy ending?"

"Honestly, Charlie, you know I love Rocky, but there's seriously nothing more unattractive than seeing your husband covered in vomit, bent over the toilet bowl crying while calling his mom and asking her to come over."

"He called his mom?" I question, trying to hold back my laughter.

"Yes, and she arrived exactly an hour later with what could only be described as the entire drugstore."

I'm not surprised. Rocky is such a momma's boy. Poor Nikki, she doesn't exactly dislike his mom but hates being the second person he asks for in a crisis.

"Enough bitching about my sookie-la-la-momma's-boy husband and back to work."

"You sure you don't want to go home and rest for the day?"

"Charlie, you've known me what, eight years? Since when do I ever go home sick?"

"True. We'll catch up later," I say as I walk out of the room and head toward my office.

I sit at my desk and start thinking about what Nikki said. Eight years seems like a lifetime. I do a mental calculation of the years in my head. I can't believe how long it has been since we first met in college.

Nikki and I were designated roommates. Both of us were studying law, which was why they dumped us together. The only problem was that Nikki was a bitch, the mean-girl type, the type who made your life a living hell. She thought she ruled the world, gave no one the time of day except for her college boyfriend, Rockford Romano.

Rocky was a burly Italian guy, huge muscles, and he was the quarterback on the college football team. Women threw themselves at him, men wanted to be him, but students were generally scared of his tough ego. There were rumors that his family was part of the Mafia, but in truth, he was nothing but a pussycat. The kindest, sweetest guy you could ever meet who worshiped the ground Nikki walked on.

They began dating, would break up every week only to get back together again.

I mean, Nikki has always been beautiful. She puts Victoria's Secret models to shame. Her long, lean legs made her supermodel tall, and her body's toned as a result of the Pilates she did every day in our dorm room.

Despite her being a total glamour-puss, she still remained the campus bitch. If you had a pair of tits and a vagina, she watched you like a hawk around her man.

One night during the end of our first year, I found her lying on the bathroom floor, sobbing, surrounded by pregnancy tests. She needed a friend, so I was there to console her, but that night we became more like sisters than friends.

I did everything I could at the time to support Rocky and Nikki during the pregnancy, mainly covering her shifts at the local pizza joint when she was too tired to work.

And seven months later, they welcomed William Nicholas Romano into the world at exactly 11:34 p.m. I watched him being placed on his mother's chest, not a dry eye in the room. I still remember the moment Rocky handed him to me, and I held my godson for the first time. Leaning down, I placed a soft kiss on his wrinkly forehead and inhaled his baby scent. I fell in love with the boy the moment I laid eyes on him, but holding him, that broke me, in a good way. There was this unconditional love for him I couldn't explain, and it has only grown since.

"Okay, settle a bet. Who wears it better? Jennifer Aniston or J Lo?"

Eric is waiting impatiently, tapping his foot as I analyze the image in front of me, breaking me away from my past reflection.

"J Lo. Now seriously, don't you have anything better to do like making sure everything's wrapped up before I go to Hawaii?"

"I'm in denial about you going because I'm a jealous best friend who still doesn't understand why you're not taking me," Eric asserts with an envious stare.

"I'm not going to justify my need for a holiday since I've worked for two years straight with no break. Now, get back to work and make sure you order me the salmon rolls."

Eric leaves my office and closes the door behind him. Sitting in my plush chair, I take a moment to refocus. I have a lot to do and will need to haul some serious ass before next Friday.

There's no time for being lazy or unorganized. Focus, regroup, and get your shit together, Charlie.

My cell beeps loudly, breaking my zen. It's a text from Julian.

Julian: *I'm glad you finally texted me. I wasn't sure how long a gorgeous woman like yourself would leave me hanging. I'm free today at two if you are? I promise to behave if you want me to.*

The text follows with the address of a café. I'm unable to hide the smile which so easily graces my face from his cute text. Even through a message, he still has this charm about him. My fingers type back quickly, letting him know I'm free and how much I love the café he suggests because of the peanut shop next to it, accidentally hitting send and realizing that peanuts autocorrected to penis.

Me: *Duck, I'm sorry. Penis.*

Me: *Argh! I mean Penis.*

Me: *PEANUTS.*

I yell loudly in frustration. Stupid autocorrect. Did it not understand no one gives a flying fuck not duck? How difficult is it for the companies to realize and fix the problem? Once again, I have managed to embarrass myself in front of an unbelievably sexy guy which is probably why I have been single for a year. Taking a deep breath, I close my eyes only to open them when my phone pings.

Julian: *Charlie, relax. All the ducks in the world*

couldn't change how happy you've made me today.
I'll see you at 2 next to the penis store.

This time, I manage to laugh instead of yell. It's been a long time since I've flirted with a guy, and if there's anyone worth flirting over it's Julian Baker.

I have a good feeling about this.

THREE

CHARLIE

If there's a list of top ten things people are terrified of doing, first dates has to be one of them.

Throughout my lifetime, I've done many things outside my comfort zone like bungee jumping off the High Steel Bridge in Washington. It's the biggest adrenaline rush I have ever experienced, yet not one I'll likely repeat in this lifetime.

I've gotten a tattoo, although I'm terrified of needles, and held a snake on a wildlife tour even though they petrify me.

Each time I experienced a level of discomfort for trying out something different, I always try to remind myself why I push my boundaries.

And right now, I need to remind myself of how nice Julian is and what we're doing could be something *amazing*.

The café isn't overly busy. The lunch rush has been and gone, and the only people lingering are the afternoon coffee addicts and people like me.

I choose a table close to the exit, just in case it all goes pear-shaped, and I need a quick getaway. On the plus side, it has a window and view of some construction workers. They are cute, whistled at me when I walked past, then went back to their grueling job of repairing the sidewalk.

Breathing out, my nerves ease but only slightly. I pull out my compact for the hundredth time to check my lipstick isn't smudged all over my teeth. Biting down, I quickly examine, happy with the clean results, then put my compact away.

It's not like I haven't dated before. There have been others subjected to my awkward first dates. Some even made it past several rounds. A couple of lucky ones made it to the bedroom, and that's where it ended. Nikki and Eric often tell me I'm too picky, a detriment to my quest to find the one. Both of them believe I have this imaginary man in my mind, he sits on this pedestal, and no one has a chance of bumping him off his so-called throne.

I hate that part of them is right.

And I especially hate that the thought of him even crosses my mind right now.

"Hey."

Julian is standing beside where I sit, looking incredibly handsome in a pair of dark jeans and maroon polo top. I'm quick to stand, leaning my body over the table to kiss his cheek. As my skin caresses his freshly-shaven cheekbone, my stomach flutters, making my entire body hyper-aware. His scent, a masculine aftershave, lingers in the air delightfully.

With his hand resting on my hip, we both pull away at the same time, our gaze connecting through the sheer force of a simple touch. His playful grin instantly relaxes my nervous energy as we both sit down on the wooden chairs.

Julian scans the café, looks at the door, then shakes his head with a knowing smile.

"I promise I'm not an ax-wielding murderer."

The door. This guy knows all the single tricks.

"I know," I casually say, grabbing the menu. "I like the view."

"Of the construction workers?"

"Um, no... well, maybe."

Julian slides his hand forward, resting it on top of mine. My imagination is running wild, wondering why I allow myself to put up a guard when in front of me, Julian couldn't care less.

"Relax, please. I won't kill you, and if you get off on watching sweating men jackhammer concrete, I'll still find you gorgeous."

My shoulders fall, relieved he's broken the awkward tension. I don't know what's wrong with me around him. It's almost like I'm desperate to make this work somehow, scared if I don't, I'll fall into a familiar spiral and struggle to break free, again.

"We should order," he suggests. "How long do I have you?"

"Me? For however long you want."

Shit. Another lie. The pile of work on my desk is astronomical, and about an hour before walking in here, Nikki dumped a new case on my desk she wants me to review before I leave. I'm expecting to pull an all-nighter, the only way I can stay on top of my workload and life.

"Um, okay, sorry, maybe long enough for a latte?"

The waitress makes her way over and takes our order. Julian orders an espresso, and then gives me a brief explanation how he became addicted during his last trip to Sicily.

"Wow, so you travel a lot. What is it you do?" I ask.

"Journalism. I write pieces for a few magazines and

occasionally some of the well-known newspapers, depends on what the trend is at the time."

The waitress returns, placing our beverages on the table, then leaves quickly.

"And you?"

"Family law," I reply, wrapping my hands around the hot cup in front of me.

"I didn't peg you for a lawyer but admire your tenacity." Bringing the small glass toward his lips, he drinks the espresso in almost one go. "Tell me how you became a lawyer? Is there a reason behind it? And where did you study?"

This question isn't one I haven't been asked before. Truth be told, I've explained it more than I can count, nailed the story to a tee, leaving out various components which are deemed unnecessary to relive, especially to a stranger.

I begin to explain to him how it all started, and how my childhood felt like a turbulent rollercoaster ride from my mother's repeated absences until she left for good, serving my father with divorce papers.

"Explains why you chose family law," Julian says, sympathetically.

"I'd seen the worst side of them come out. They didn't think I could understand their adult conversations, but I knew what was going on."

"Then Yale, impressive and hard to get into?"

"Says the Harvard graduate," I tease, welcoming the change of topic. Julian raises his brow, watching curiously until I realize I gave away my secret. "Fine, I may have stalked your Facebook profile."

His soft chuckles ease my embarrassment. Raising my

cup toward my lips, I take another sip, relishing in the caffeine fix my body so desperately needs.

"What can I say? I'm a woman of many talents," I gloat with a smile.

We both laugh, and though the light-hearted banter is a refreshing change, I push away the feelings which crawl their way to the surface every time my mind wanders to a time in my past where darkness prevailed, and nothing, absolutely nothing, could take away the pain which had consumed me.

I clear my throat, hoping Julian doesn't notice my change in demeanor.

"I met my good friend, Nicole, or Nikki as I call her, at Yale. We were both studying law, and after years of working for some awful employers, we took the plunge and opened Mason & Romano, a boutique law firm."

"That's quite some risk and at such a young age."

"Yes, I know. I studied nonstop. It's all I did for pretty much most of my twenties," I tell him, reflecting on the long hours with my eyes on textbooks which led to compromised eyesight and having to wear glasses when I read. "Nikki and her husband were raising a young child. The juggling act of parenthood and thriving careers was harder than each of them expected."

I go on to tell Julian about the decision to move to the city. Rocky was fortunate to have had a contact in the media industry and got a job almost immediately as a sports commentator. He can talk all day about sports, something I've now grown accustomed to.

Nikki and I both found jobs at separate firms. The first year was grueling, and I had questioned my decision several times. But somewhere along the way, I realized I was making a difference. I was passionate about working in law and loved my job, except for my seedy boss. I ignored his inappropriate comments about my attire and the way he said my hair smelled good when I walked past him. It was all kinds of wrong, and it made me uncomfortable.

"Fortunately enough, a solution presented itself late one Sunday afternoon while hanging in the playground. It came from Nikki at her wits end juggling motherhood," I tell him, reliving the memory.

"Will called his nanny Mommy the other day," Nikki spoke softly as she watched Will play in the sandpit with the other children. "Charlie, I can't do this anymore, work twelve-hour days and never see my son."

"We opened with a small client base, and as we grew, we both hired personal assistants— Eric and Emma. Business is booming. We even hired another attorney, Tate, and extra interns to run the office."

"Quite an amazing journey," he praises. "I can tell you're passionate about what you do."

Julian has this face that instantly calms you. Throughout telling my story, I felt my heart racing at times. But just looking into his eyes, everything I'd been holding on to which I hadn't realized, slowly began to ease. He listens attentively, staring with an inquisitive gaze. A true gentleman unlike some of the jerks I dated who would just stare at my chest while licking their lips.

"I didn't want to end up like my mother... miserable with this unwarranted chip on her shoulder, stuck in a small town making hot tamales every day. I was out to prove a point."

"We have a lot in common. I, too, was always trying to prove a point. And well, here I am with the most gorgeous woman in Manhattan."

I smile and touch his hand with ease. This dating thing isn't so bad, not when the man is as handsome as Julian Baker.

Quickly glancing at my phone, I notice the time. With a disappointed smile, I finish the last of my latte. I don't want to end this quick date of ours, and unlike anything I have ever done before, I muster up all my confidence to ask for a second date. "So, dinner. My place? I can make a mean tamale," I half-joke.

The corner of Julian's mouth curves upward into a cocky grin before he bites down, teasing me softly. "Tonight?"

"Wow, um... tonight." I mentally run through my work-load again. The old Charlie would've kindly tried to reschedule. Work has always come first, but I'm sick of the rules I created for myself.

Out with the old, in with the new.

"You know what? Yes. Tonight will be perfect."

"Your place or mine?"

"How about mine?" I suggest selfishly, knowing I can cram in a few more hours of work after he leaves. "I'll text you my address.

"Perfect." Julian looks at his watch but is quick to apolo-gize for being rude.

"No, I get it. I've got a ton of work to do, too."

I stand at the same time as Julian. His hands wrap around my waist, and gently, he grazes his thumb down my cheek and across my bottom lip. My pulse begins to race again toward my hammering heart echoing beneath my chest. My gaze shifts away from his deep stare and toward his lips, desperate to taste them on my own. Slowly, Julian leans down, brushing his lips against mine as I close my eyes and relish in the warm feeling consuming me.

Pulling away in an agonizing pace, we both catch our breaths.

For the longest time, I didn't think it was possible to feel all the things Julian has made me feel with just one kiss. Perhaps I'm crazy, allowing myself to fall prey to his charm.

But I am no longer eighteen.

No longer a foolish kid.

"Tonight?"

"Tonight," I whisper back, tilting my head to kiss him one more time.

FOUR

CHARLIE

The knock on my door echoes through the apartment.

Wiping my hands on my apron, I walk toward the door and open it to a very dashing Julian dressed in a pair of navy chinos and a white buttoned-collared shirt. With a grin smothering his already handsome face, I struggle to hold back my desire to touch and explore his body in ways my single-woman mind has imagined the past few nights.

"Well, hello, gorgeous."

Julian hands me a bottle of wine, making it a perfect addition to the meal I've prepared. Taking it from him, I grab his hand and close the door behind him.

"So, this is your place?" He scans the living room, taking it all in with a curious smile. "Very nice."

"By nice, do you mean small?"

"It's Manhattan. In perspective to other apartments I've seen, it's a comfortable size."

"Would you like a tour? Though, I'm warning you, it'll take zero-point-two seconds."

"Yes, but first..." He takes the bottle from my hand, placing it on the coffee table. Sliding his hands around my back, he pulls me in, bringing his hand back up to my chin. With a quickening breath, he drags my face to be closer to his, so close I can almost taste him. Tilting my head slightly, I painfully wait for him to kiss me. Our breaths mingling together in such an intimate space, heighten our desperate need to kiss.

I wrap my hands around the back of his neck, coercing him to kiss me deeply. Our lips touch, barely, and with lust driving our bodies, I press harder against his mouth, releasing the long-awaited moan which has built up inside of me.

Julian instantly reacts, tightening his grip on my ass as his body presses against mine. My mind, shallow in its thoughts, immediately notices his rock hard cock pressing between us.

Pulling away, I attempt to catch my breath. "Did you still want the tour?"

"Yes," he murmurs, placing his lips on mine again. "Lead the way, Miss Mason."

Coco purrs on the couch, desperate for attention.

"This is Coco."

"A ragdoll?" He gently pats Coco's fur and, of course, she's lapping up all the attention. "We had one growing up."

I grab the bottle of wine and his hand as well, then show him the two bedrooms, bathroom, the kitchen and dining area at a quick pace. The apartment, purchased twelve months ago, is a true testament to my hard work over the last few years. I love Manhattan and don't expect to move anywhere else anytime soon.

"It's a beautiful place you've made for yourself," he

compliments before his eyes gravitate toward the countertop where I have attempted to make tamales. "This all smells delicious."

"If there's one thing my mom taught me well, it's this. Shall we eat?"

We sit at the small dining table inside the cozy kitchen. A candle is burning between us—some romantic scent Eric gave me to bring love into my life. He's a believer of all things kooky, strikingly similar to my mom who believes in spirits, the universe, and stars aligning if you're lucky enough.

We speak about work, mainly Julian and his passion for journalism. He's a very cultured man, having traveled to the remotest of countries to maintain the integrity of the pieces he writes. I love the fire in his soul when he speaks with such conviction. I could listen to him for hours, and rarely, has anyone captured my attention in this way.

"I love how passionate you are. You're a rare breed, Mr. Baker."

"I could say the same for you." He grins, lifting the glass toward his lips as he finishes the remnants of his wine. "You graduated from Yale, own a business, can cook mean tamales, and..."

He pauses, parting his lips while staring into my eyes.

Leaning forward, I rest my elbows on the table, inching closer to him while we kiss gently.

Pulling back, only just, I croon, *"And?"*

"Your kiss makes me want to strip you down to nothing right here, right now."

I can feel my heart beat every single pound in my chest. Biting the corner of my lip, I stare into his eyes.

How can it be, a man so beautiful and pure, is single in

a city where millions of women roam the streets looking for someone as perfect as him?

And he's here, with me.

I don't want to take any more chances, and throwing every single bit of caution that I've held onto for the last eight years, I throw it all out the window in a split second.

My hands move toward his collar, guiding him back to me for a passionate kiss. Our tongues battle feverishly, moans escaping in tiny breaths as we juggle to stand. Julian lifts me, prompting my legs to wrap around his waist. Our kisses continue as he walks us down the hall and toward my bedroom.

With the light off, yet the glow from the living area illuminating our faces enough to see, he places me on the bed and hovers above me.

The weight of his desire is staring back at me in an intense gaze.

There's a magnetic force between us, one pulling me so fast that I'm unable to stop and think. Everything I can have possibly imagined in a man who can please my unconventional world is standing over me unbuttoning his shirt. Bare-chested, with a shirt thrown carelessly to the ground, I admire the most perfectly sculpted chest before me. Unable to control my urges, my hand grates his abs, stopping just shy of his belt buckle.

"Do you know how beautiful you look beneath me, gorgeous?"

I love the way he calls me *gorgeous*, sounds almost like I belong to him and no one else.

You don't belong to anyone else.

You never did.

Shaking my head, I drown out the irrelevant noise and undo his belt, yanking his zipper down.

Julian drops his body forward, hands gripping my face. His lips press firmly against mine, desperately tasting every inch of my mouth. Hard and forcefully, his tongue rolls against mine, sending a stream of sensations to every part of my body and making me ache everywhere for him.

My hands move to the back of his head, clutching his hair in my fists as we fight to get closer to one another.

I pull away, out of breath. "Julian... is this too soon?"

He doesn't say a word but rather tries to show me in his actions. In a slow, agonizing pace, he unbuttons my dress, removing the straps over my shoulders as I lay beneath him. With only my black lace bra and panties remaining, my chest begins to rise and fall rapidly, waiting in anticipation for him to make his next move.

The desire in his eyes, the raw, animalistic hunger, is staring back at me. God, I want to combust lying here as I stare back at this sexy man, a man who has walked into my life at the perfect time.

I sit up, pulling him closer to me as he leans down and places his mouth on mine, again. Every kiss becomes harder, more aggressive, and demanding. He wants to own me now, here in this moment. He commands me with his eyes to lay there and watch him pleasure me like no other man has before.

I crumple beneath his touch. Every sordid lick and caress of my heated skin causes me to moan louder. Julian breathes my name, each syllable dragging against his lips with a raw growl that lingers as he kisses the sweet spot between my thighs.

Slowly, he pulls down my panties and runs his nose along my pubic bone, and my eyes flutter as a deep moan escapes my lips. Has it been this long? I can't trust myself to last much longer, deprived of a man's touch.

I wait with bated breath, anticipating his next move, his next touch. Julian lays down on the bed, rolling me to the side and positioning himself behind me, grazing his palms against my backside and tracing the contours like a map causing me to moan in delight.

Impatiently, I push back and grind myself against him. Julian is hard, so rock-hard that I'm scared he'll break me. I'm coming undone, desperate to have him inside me.

I turn around, so our bodies are facing, owning his lips and begging him to enter me. The clasp of my bra unravels, and his eyes widen as my breasts are exposed.

"Charlie, the first moment I saw you, I knew I had to have you. I was watching you in your cute tights and perky little ass trying to work the machine. These beautiful tits of yours were bouncing. I was ready to take you right there."

My heavy breathing becomes a laugh. "You noticed that? I wore the wrong bra that day."

He responds with a sly grin, then buries his head between my breasts before circling his tongue around my nipple.

My back arches, the sensation so unbearable I'm ready just to jump him myself.

"Of course, I noticed you." He breathes warmth against my skin. "You're so goddamn sexy. The guys in the locker room were having their own discussions on how to get you into bed."

"Really? And there I was thinking I looked all awkward trying to work a machine."

"Tell me..." he questions with a smirk, "... are you ready for me?"

I nod, in love with the way his eyes speak more than his words. He focuses his attention back on my lips, kissing my mouth with urgency and leaving me without a single breath to catch. My nails claw across his back, which I'm sure are leaving marks.

Propping himself up on his knees, he removes his belt entirely and lowers his pants, exposing himself. I'm in awe of the sight of his beautiful body and the realization of how much I want him. Neither one of us cares to wait, made clear as we both shift, so he can easily enter me.

I gently warn him to hold that thought, opening the drawer in my nightstand and fumbling amongst the random junk. The foil packet is squished in the corner. I pull it out, handing it to him, scolding myself for only remembering now to be safe.

Running my hands along his forearm, I relish the moment as he rolls it on. It doesn't take him long, his body commanding my full presence once again. Slowly, he enters me as I gasp at the unfamiliarity. I'm begging my body to hold on and last just a few minutes longer as he watches himself move in and out, biting his lip while spreading my legs enough to cause me to wince in delightful pain. This man wants only me at this moment, and I'll do every damn thing in my power to please him.

Just the thought of it has me on edge. I latch onto the pillow behind me. My blood is pumping hard, and every single part of me tingles in a mad delight as my body combusts beneath him. I call his name repeatedly, loudly, wishing this moment not to end.

Julian has a desperate need to control the moment, holding back his impending orgasm until it finally gets the better of him. The grip of his hands is tight against my waist as his body slams into me until his moans slow, and his hips follow suit.

He falls beside me, both of us out of breath and reeling from what's just happened. I turn to face him. I don't care anymore. In just forty-eight hours my life has changed in ways I never imagined.

Unable to hide my grin, I challenge him, "So, what now? You know I'm off to Hawaii this weekend, and I'll be gone for five days."

"Five days?" He climbs on top of me, burying his head into the crook of my neck. "Well, I guess we've got a lot of ground to make up, Miss Mason."

I squeal as he kisses a sensitive spot behind my ears, and squiggling beneath his body, I welcome round two with open arms.

FIVE

LEX

I slowly open my eyes and take in my surroundings.

It's dark outside with the moonlight peeking through the drawn curtains. The empty bottle of bourbon is lying on the nightstand as well as my wallet and phone. There's the stench of cheap perfume and sex in the air. Scattered across the floor are my clothes along with a red halter-top dress. I look at her sleeping peacefully beside me—a brunette—a rare slip-up. What's her name again? Brandy, Betty, Bindi? I carefully move off the bed, dressing quickly, and grab my belongings to leave the room.

The elevator takes forever, and upon entering, I swipe my hotel room key to the top floor. As seconds pass, my head isn't taking well to the copious amount of liquor I managed to drink last night.

Back inside my room, I start packing my suitcase and call my assistant, Kate. She answers almost immediately.

"Kate, what time is my flight to London?"

"Eleven, sir," she yawns as she answers.

"Book me a room next to the airport. I'll be there in twenty minutes."

This isn't the first time I have called Kate at five in the morning asking for a hotel change. I just don't want the aftermath of trying to cut loose the hussy from last night.

I arrive at the new hotel and shower before grabbing a quick bite to eat. I have plenty of time to spare, heading straight to the airport to wait in the business lounge until boarding.

The flight is quiet, thank God, which gives me a chance to catch up on work for the first few hours. When my eyes begin to grow weary, I shut the lid of my laptop and close them, remembering how last night began.

"Excuse me, sir, you left your credit card at the bar."

I looked up, and before me was a gorgeous woman wearing a red halter dress, black pumps, her long brown hair flowing down her back. Of course, she noticed when I eyed her from head to toe. Not bad, I thought to myself, it's been a while since I got some pussy.

"Thank you..." I searched her face, waiting for an answer.

"Brandy," she said, batting her eyelashes.

We sat at a table and started talking. She told me she was a flight attendant from Alaska and continued to talk, but all I could think about was the hair—the long, brown hair that flowed down her back. I ached to touch it, remembering how it felt running my fingers through it. Fuck no, don't reminisce. Brandy smelled fantastic like sex. Probably wasn't wearing anything underneath. Such a dirty little whore.

"So, tell me, Lex, what do you do?"

I broke out of my thoughts and quickly answered her question. This woman was really starting to bore me. I offered her another drink which she gladly accepted before inviting me to her room.

I don't remember much, only that she was loud and wanted me to pull her hair harder. She enjoyed being dominated, playing the innocent woman begging to be fucked. I don't do brunettes, but last night, I let my guard down. I fucked her twice before collapsing on the bed and passing out.

Lately, the tension has mounted. Many things are weighing on my mind, and blowing off steam usually does the trick, but as I sit here listening to the pilot announce our descent, I'm not any more relieved of the stress.

The plane arrives in London on time. As usual, my driver is waiting for me at the gate. I decide to go straight to the office, knowing I have a busy day ahead of me. It doesn't come as a surprise when we drive out of Heathrow to see that the skies are gray, the clouds forming in a cluster. It's summer, and you'd think that after five years of living in London, I'd be used to this, but I still miss the constant sunshine back home.

Our office is on the top floor and has a fantastic view of the River Thames. I'm proud of what I built from nothing. Years of pushing myself to build my empire, dedicating my life to my work, and goddamn, it's paid off. I know what my net worth is, and so does everyone else after *The Times* article was published.

When it comes to business, I regret nothing. I've made hard and fast decisions, took risks, and never let anyone influence me any other way. I know becoming a doctor was my father's dream, not mine. That's not to say I don't respect him. I've never met a man as driven as my father. His dedication and compassion astound me.

Yet our fallout years ago after I decided to quit the medical field and focus on building my empire was a kick in the guts I never expected from my own flesh and blood. Neither of us would back down. My mother was devastated, trying her best to repair our relationship. It took the passing of my grandfather for us to start talking to each other again, though our relationship still remains strained, something I choose to ignore.

I'm his son, and I failed him. Even Bill Gates would argue that in a heartbeat.

I enter the lobby to see the staff nervously shuffle around me. It fucking pisses me off every single time. They better not have been slacking off. I remind myself to contact human resources and have performance reviews done. These twenty-something girls think they have it all figured out, but gossiping during work on my time isn't acceptable. Fuck, I'm getting more annoyed by the minute. Slamming the door behind me, I walk to my desk and press the speed dial button to reception.

"Gretchen, get Kate in my office, now."

"Yes, sir," she rushes.

I sit at my desk and start checking my emails—same old bullshit. Honestly, some fuckers need me to hold their hand for everything. I may be the CEO, but fuck me, bend over, and I'll wipe your ass too! I didn't get to the top by playing on the safe side. The stress of this upcoming merger is really starting to aggravate me. I'm not a patient man, those around me know that. Years of planning and adhering to a strict project timeline has me itching to close the deal. I need to move forward, distract myself with another so-called impossible business venture which will pay off and add to the Edwards' fortune.

Trying to take my mind off this merger, I wait for Kate

to arrive, checking the share market and analyzing my stock.

"Good morning, Mr. Edwards." Kate walks into my office, taking a seat opposite me and opens up her laptop. She starts reading from her calendar, reminding me of what I have scheduled this week and when. "You have a three o'clock conference call with The Windsor Group regarding the merger, and your flight to New York leaves tomorrow morning at six. I'll accompany you on this flight, and your stay in New York will be till next Monday. During this time, you have meetings scheduled with the After Dark investors." She continues to scroll through her schedule, typing as she speaks. "I have made an appointment with a commercial realtor to look at potential office locations."

"Oh right, the Manhattan office." I sigh, bored by the prospect already.

It isn't my idea to have an office in Manhattan, but investors are pushing to dominate the U.S. market. They insist on a headquarters in North America, not just London, and Manhattan is the best place for this to happen according to the numerous market projections they made me sit through.

At first, I was reluctant. London is my home now, and the thought of being an hour away from my sister irritates me. I love her, as you would of family, but she's just, well, just *Adriana*. Personal bullshit aside, it makes complete sense and is the right move. Just a lot of work and not the type of work which stimulates me.

"Your sister called to remind you that since you'll be in the city next week, you have to attend that charity event."

Exactly why I loathe visiting.

Adriana is like an annoying five-year-old in a toy store when it comes to charity events. This will not be the last time I hear about it. I expect a call shortly telling me what to wear, who I should bring, and how much I need to donate. Fuck, this day is going downhill fast.

"Is that all?" I ask, annoyed with all this social bullshit.

"Yes, sir."

"It's going to be busy. Please book the Waldorf penthouse suite for me." I glance up from my screen. "That's all, you may leave now."

She scurries out the door, closing it behind her. I admire Kate for putting up with my arrogant persona. Originally, I hired her as an office junior, however, I was quick to notice she didn't run for the hills like every other pathetic little thing here.

For a twenty-six-year-old, she's by far the most mature of all the women working for me. Kate is originally from Manchester, having moved to London two years ago. At first, I really struggled with her accent and euphemisms, but after living in London for the past five years, I finally got the hang of it all. My mother often mentions my accent has changed, and my sister complains I call her a twat too often.

It only takes a few minutes before my phone starts ringing. I grab the phone, staring at the screen, debating whether or not I should answer. I place it against my forehead, willing it to stop.

"Adriana," I answer in a stiff tone.

"Oh my God, Lex, finally! I know you got my messages regarding the charity ball. Don't you dare hang up on me, Alexander Matthew Edwards! I've only got a few minutes to talk."

She doesn't stop to take a breath. Adriana is like an Energizer Bunny on Prozac. A few minutes to talk, bollocks! I expect this call to drag on for an hour at best.

"I've already RSVP'd your name on the guest list, and I have a date for you. Don't worry, she's blonde just like you like them. Her name is Brooke, and I know you'll love her." I can hear the trace of sarcasm in her tone. "So, I've ordered you a tux. I'll meet you wherever you're staying to drop it off. Oh, and the donation, we need to discuss that."

"I can find my own dates, you know."

"I know, dear brother, but Brooke is lovely, and it's been a while since you settled down," she says, lowering her voice.

"You know I don't do 'lovely.' She better be a fit bird."

"A fit bird? What the hell does that even mean? If by bird you mean because of the breasts, you're such a jerkoff, Lex. However, yes, she's a fit bird. I've gotta go, but I'll get Kate to give me the details of the hotel. Love you."

Our flight to New York is scheduled to leave at six. It's the standard seven-hour flight, and thank God for first-class. Never would I ever fly cattle class.

I meet Kate at the gate area. She's dressed casually compared to her normal corporate attire—tight jeans, tan-colored knee-high boots, and a white button-up shirt. With her blonde hair tied into a bun and bright blue eyes staring back at me, I'll admit she's very attractive. Not that I'd ever go there.

Golden rule number one—never shit on your own doorstep.

"Good morning, Mr. Edwards." She half-smiles.

"Good morning, Kate. Are you ready to board?"

She nods. We grab our bags, making our way to the priority line to board the plane first.

I adjust myself in my seat and grab the *New York Times* to read. Kate is busily typing on her phone, smiling while she answers a text—boyfriend, I bet. Women are so easy to read. Trying my best to ignore her, I busy myself by reading an article on tax evasion in the U.S.

The flight takes off at exactly six.

After we are at altitude, the seat belt signs go off, prompting the stewardess to start serving drinks.

"Good morning, sir. Would you like anything to drink?" She licks her lips as she waits for my response.

A redhead. Interesting.

"Bourbon and Coke, please. It's been a while since I'd joined the Mile-High Club. I might need directions to the restroom later, miss..." I searched for her name tag "... Miss Horne."

"And for your girlfriend?" she asks.

Kate bursts out laughing, rudely. I stare at her, waiting for her to stop.

Why is that so funny?

I'm a fucking catch.

I know I'm handsome. Call me conceited if you want, but I'm six-foot-two, work out at the gym every fucking day, plus I'm filthy rich. Women throw themselves at me daily.

"I'm sorry." She laughs, wiping a tear from her eye. "Just a gin and tonic, please."

Gritting my teeth, I pry, "Why is that so funny?"

"It's just that, well, Mr. Edwards, you aren't the relationship type. Far from it."

She stops laughing, her eyebrows drawing together with a worried look.

"I guess you're right, I don't do girlfriends or relationships," I admit, knowing exactly why I despise commitment.

Thank God, the bourbon is filled to the brim. Drinking it all in one go, my wandering mind, which has attempted to take a trip down memory lane, is immediately squashed. I press the call button, needing a top-off immediately.

"And you? I'm guessing you do. Hence, why your eyes light up every time your phone goes off?"

"Sorry, Mr. Edwards. That's my boyfriend, Jeff. He's in Australia visiting his parents, and the time difference is driving us crazy."

We speak more about how long they have been together and how they met. Kate is an interesting woman to speak to, always with an anecdote and holds your attention rather easily. Speaking to women, apart from my mother and sister, isn't something I do very often.

Kate knows what she wants in life, and I admire that.

We stop talking, but I'm left feeling somewhat bothered by the conversation about relationships. While Kate sleeps beside me, I stand up and stretch my arms, making my way to the restroom, passing Miss Horne on purpose.

After a quick glance, she follows me to the restroom at the back of the plane, closing the door behind her. Then I push her head down to my cock, finally releasing the tension building up inside.

We arrive at JFK at six o'clock Eastern time. The driver takes us straight to the hotel where I change into my sweats to go for a run. I love the city in the morning. The streets are getting busy, but there's still an eerie sense of calm. I run through Central Park alongside others trying to get in a quick morning run needing to burn off this energy. The past few days have been draining, and all I want to do is put them behind me. I run harder, pushing myself until my lungs burn. I debate heading back to my room but decide on hitting the gym first.

It's just before nine when I get back. Taking my time, I linger inside the steaming shower, allowing the water to ease my tense muscles. Crossing my arms with my eyes closed, I'm aware my cock is standing rock hard. What's fucking new. Ignoring its presence, I turn the faucet to cold, welcoming the brutally cold water.

My first meeting is with a commercial broker. After changing and eating the gourmet breakfast room service delivered, my driver drives me to the financial district, but not without the usual headache of the peak morning traffic.

The first office space is a small building with views mainly facing a brick wall with a neon sign for Chows Chinese Takeout. *Seriously, do I have to do the job myself?* Frustrated with my time being wasted, I glance at my watch to check the time.

"Mrs. Hampden, I'm not sure what my assistant has told you, but the Lexed Group does not have offices facing brick walls. Do I need to find another broker?"

Looking flustered and embarrassed, she pulls out her portfolio. What the fuck is this woman thinking? This is what happens when some geriatric has-been is still working when they should be retired and living in Boca. Pulling out my phone, I'm ready to blast the person who recommended her to me.

"Mr. Edwards, I apologize for the communication error. I do have one that I think will be more suited to your business."

The other building is two blocks over. The building is tall with modern architecture which stands out amongst the other generic buildings. Inside, my eyes scan the floor space. It's fully furnished, the reception area formal with black leather sofas and a large marble desk. I follow her around the floor before walking through the double doors to what would be my office. The view is amazing, the East River with the Brooklyn Bridge on the far left.

I call Kate right away, knowing office spaces like this in Manhattan are hard to come by.

"Kate, please have the lawyers draw up the contracts for this new office," I command, rushing through this conversation. "Human Resources can start recruiting for the jobs we discussed last week. I'll forward you a list of everything else I want taken care of by Monday morning."

I leave the building, finally relieved we have found a space that represents the Lexed brand.

It's lunchtime now, and the streets are busy. People around me are piling into restaurants, others darting in and out of boutiques. I find the restaurant where my sister and mother are meeting me for a quick lunch. At least that's what I anticipate but, of course, women can talk for days without taking a breath. Seriously, do they ever shut the fuck up?

My mother is the first to greet me, reaching up to place a kiss on my cheek, then rubbing her fingers across it to wipe off the lipstick she left behind. "Here's my boy. Why haven't you returned my calls, Lex? I know you're busy, but not hearing from you weeks on end worries me."

"C'mon, Mom. You know what it's like."

"No, I don't, Lex. I understand you're busy running an empire and all, but a quick call, text, or even an email wouldn't kill you. Better yet, send me a friend request..."

Thank God, for once my sister's timing is perfect. Practically running over to the table, she kisses my mother, then whacks the back of my head.

"What the fuck, Adriana?"

"Oh, hello, big brother of mine." She laughs while taking a seat.

Adriana is seven years younger. My parents would often tell me that when I was six, I begged Santa to bring me a brother or sister. Unfortunately, Santa delivered a year later.

Some say she looks like me. I can't see the resemblance apart from our eyes. She has light brown hair like mine, but today she's blonde. I can't keep up with her ever-changing hairstyles. Typical woman, of course.

"So, Elijah and I have set a date. It's February 14th, the day we officially started dating."

"Oh, honey, I'm so happy for you. Aren't you, Lex?"

I look over at my mother, her face willing me to say something pleasant. What possible thing can I say about a fucking Valentine's Day wedding? The holiday itself is a load of shit. Like we need a day to show someone we love them with candy hearts and giant bears which serve absolutely no purpose, and don't get me started on weddings.

"Sounds bloody ace."

"Bloody ace? Is that all you have to say?" Adriana asks, frustrated with my British slang.

"What would you like me to say? Tying yourself to someone will guarantee you a lifetime of happiness. Weddings are magical."

"You're such a jerk."

"So I've been told."

At this point, my mother places her hand over Adriana's, trying to calm her down. I order a drink while I wait for them to change the subject, then take my phone out of my pocket and scroll through my emails until my mother scolds me for my behavior. Again.

"Alexander, this isn't the man I raised you to be, nor the man I know and love. I know you have a tarnished view of marriage, but that doesn't excuse your rude behavior toward your sister."

Here we go again.

I grab some cash out of my pocket and throw it on the table. Standing, I walk away without a goodbye, knowing I haven't acted the way I should have, but I don't give a fuck anymore. People can get married as long as I'm not involved in any way, shape, or form. The word marriage itself hits a nerve with me. It ruins everything. It ruins people.

Back at my hotel, I bury myself in work until the night falls. This is what my life has become—working round the clock, not knowing when the day begins or the night sets in. I travel all over the world for business, not once taking a vacation. I isolate myself, losing contact with old friends. Relationships aren't for me. I fuck when I need to let off steam, and that's that. When a rare opportunity for peace presents itself, I sit with a bourbon in my hand. Those are the moments I dread the most—they bring my failures to the surface and allow me to think of the past.

I'm not that Alexander anymore.

He was buried the day I left Carmel.

I'm Lex Edwards, CEO of the Lexed Group. I control everything in my life and thrive on the power I hold.

No one tells me what to do.

I live my life exactly how I want.

Everything in my life makes sense now.

Everything is perfect.

Except for one minor thing—I'm fucking *miserable*.

SIX

"Charlotte Olivia Mason, are you daydreaming about your hot boyfriend again?"

Eric's voice interrupts my thoughts as he struts into my office, dressed head to toe in a new designer suit. I should've been daydreaming about Julian. Instead, I'm reminiscing about my trip to Hawaii. It seems like a life-time ago when, in fact, it was only two months ago.

"No, sorry," I mumble. "Just remembering the long walks on Waikiki Beach while watching the sunset, the nonstop cocktails, and spending time with my cousins.

"Right, 'your trip.'" Eric air quotes, still annoyed I didn't take him. "Why aren't you daydreaming about Julian? If I had a man like him in my bed every night, I'd never get to work on time."

My cousin's wedding at the top of Diamond Head was nothing short of magical. I couldn't have envisioned a more romantic backdrop of sweeping views of the Pacific Ocean with gorgeous blue skies above us. The wedding itself was intimate with about twenty people in total, of which ten of them were relatives.

It was nice to spend time with my family, especially my younger cousin, Noah, who I hadn't seen for a few years. We escaped the boring family sightseeing and opted to scuba dive instead. We swam with sea turtles, an amazing experience which I'd love to do again one day. We got drunk, and luckily he's of drinking age now, a total playboy at the clubs we opted to hit at night, but nevertheless, I enjoyed the entertainment.

Despite the holiday being exactly what I needed, I missed Julian. From the moment I landed, we have been inseparable. Making up for lost time, we spent a good portion of it in the bedroom, but of late, work has pulled both of us in different directions.

"Okay, you're doing it again. Charlie, snap out of it. Unless, of course, you're thinking about his wang. In that case, do share," he snickers, rubbing his hands.

"Eric, I'm not talking about Julian's wang with you, and I can't believe we're back to using that word. It's so crass."

"Wiener, johnson, pecker, bratwurst, one-eyed monster, baloney pony—"

"*Stop!* Your penis slang is unsettling. Baloney pony? Seriously, Eric, when have you ever said to someone, 'Hey, gorgeous, take off your pants and show me your baloney pony.' Who says that?"

"Um, no one. Err... do you ask a guy to take off his pants? Where's the dominatrix woman I had you pegged for?"

"Okay, enough pecker-wiener talk. I've got an appointment in fifteen minutes. Now what else is on the agenda today?"

The day flew by, and before I knew it, it was just after six. The office is deserted, and I'm buried under a mountain of paperwork. It's now or never. I start going through the papers until my phone rings, startling me.

As the name *Batman* flashes across my screen, I catch myself grinning before I answer. I came up with the nickname when I realized how strikingly similar Julian looked to Christian Bale.

"Hey, gorgeous," he greets me in what could only be described as his sex voice.

It does all kinds of crazy things to my lady parts. Why am I not at home so we can have phone sex or something? I miss him, terribly.

"Hello, yourself. Is this an early night booty call?" I tease, leaning back in my chair as I cross my legs to stop the throbbing pain between them.

"Mmm... don't let me think about your booty. I'm in a conference room waiting for the senator to arrive."

"Well, in that case, have you thought about my tits as well? They are very happy in that lacy black number you like."

"You're evil, you know that?"

"Batman calling me evil? How predictable."

"I think I need to take you down to the bat cave, show you what Batman's really into."

"Okay, but if any real bats fly at me, you can kiss your naughty rendezvous goodbye."

Julian laughs and continues to talk about how his day went. I enjoy listening to him. He's just as ambitious as I am. His love of journalism is evident every time he speaks. One thing I have learned since our time together—New York City is never short of a scandal.

After chatting for ten minutes, we agree to meet up after eight for a bite to eat.

I pack my bag and head out the door. It's dark, but the car lights brighten the streets. I wait on the sidewalk, hailing the next cab that drives past. It's my lucky day as one halts suddenly. Rushing over, I climb in and give the driver the address.

It's Monday night, and like always, I take the cab to Rocky and Nikki's apartment to spend time with my favorite person in the whole world.

"Cha Cha, it's you!" He throws himself at me as I walk through the door.

God, I love this kid. Hearing him call my name reminds me I was his first word. Not Mommy or Daddy, it was Cha Cha, and it stuck.

With his head nestled on my stomach, I pull him away so I can examine his face. His jet-black hair is a replica of Rocky's, same tendrils that hang just above his brows. But it's his cornflower blue eyes which make him the spitting image of Nikki. Tiny freckles cover his nose, his big smile contagious with his missing top teeth. I plant a kiss on his nose, embracing him again.

"Of course, it's me, silly."

Like his dad, Will talks a mile a minute, from everything about school and what happened to his best friend's dog, to the latest episode of *Star Wars*. It's an overload of information, especially from a seven-year-old. Monday night is our night. I come over after work, spend some time playing with him or doing homework, and then reading a book to him in bed. It only takes him ten minutes to complete his homework before he climbs into bed where I take my usual place beside him.

"What's this book about?" I ask when he hands me a book.

"A prince, but he's kinda a bad guy. He loses his princess and has to search everywhere to find her. But he fights all these monsters while hunting for her. He also has this superpower that he can read minds."

Great, one of those stories.

I put on a smile and open the book to Chapter One. By the time I get to Chapter Four, Will's eyes are drooping. I know the signs when he's close to falling asleep.

"Cha Cha, do you believe in fairy tales?"

"You're never too old to believe in fairy tales," I whisper back.

"Do you hope your prince will find you one day?"

I close my eyes for a moment, not wanting to explore the question. With a knot forming in my stomach, I quickly come up with an answer, hoping to veer off this topic.

"I don't know if I need a prince, maybe just someone who will love me."

With his eyes drooping further and a yawn escaping his mouth, he murmurs his last words of the day before falling asleep. "I love you, Cha Cha. I'll be your prince if you can't find one."

It's moments like this that completely melt my heart. The love from a child is unconditional and the most precious gift anyone can give you. I'm not one of those needy women wanting to find a man, get married, and get knocked-up, but there's a part of me that aches for that type of love—with the right man.

Placing a kiss on Will's forehead, I put the book on his nightstand, covering him with his blanket. I switch off the lamp, then tiptoe to the door and watch him. He looks so peaceful, his eyes fluttering every so often, and his tiny snore can barely be heard. My heart wants to burst with how much love I feel for this kid, a love tinged with longing.

As the knot begins to grow in the pit of my stomach, I close the door and leave to meet Julian.

"You smell good," he murmurs, leaning in to place a kiss on my cheek.

"Is that how we're greeting each other now? Because if we are, you smell good, too."

He leans in further, and whispers, "If I greeted you the way I want to, we would be kicked out and arrested for indecent behavior."

"Oh, c'mon, let's try that," I taunt him, playfully. "YOLO."

"Eric is warping your mind."

"I know. It was his word of the week last week, but let's get back to you taking me on the table—"

"Don't tempt me."

Pulling away, he grabs the menu. I do the same, covering my smile as his words linger. Damn, I'm all kinds of hot and bothered now. Why do we have to eat? Given that I haven't seen him in a week, we should've had dinner at my place followed by him taking me on all fours.

Enzo's is a small restaurant in Little Italy. It's a traditional Italian trattoria with checkered tablecloths adorning the small tables. Candles are lit, and soft piano music plays in the background. The waiter has a very authentic thick, curly mustache and plays the perfect part of the Italian host.

"I'll have a Budweiser and the lovely Charlie will have..."

"A Margarita, please. What can I say? I'm a sucker for punishment."

Julian smiles with a slack expression, stroking my hand with the tip of his finger so effortlessly. My insides are doing a happy dance, missing his simple touch and how he makes me feel with just one smile.

As for the Margarita, it's all fun and games now, but wait until I wake up in the morning with a splitting headache. It's all about pacing myself. I can do this.

We finish our first round of drinks before our meals arrive. Once again, our conversation steers toward the past. Julian grew up in a small town in North Carolina with his mother and sister. His dad left when Julian was three, and he never saw him again. He went to Harvard where he studied journalism, then met Serena, his girlfriend at the time. He thought she was the love of his life, but she changed colleges, and they couldn't do the long-distance thing.

"Have you thought about contacting her?" I ask him, curious, "Or should I say social media stalk her?"

"I did think about contacting her for a while, but I moved here, and well, life became hectic. I heard from a friend that she's in Boston, but I think the book's closed on that one. If it were meant to be, we'd have worked it out back then."

He lays his hand on mine, again, gently caressing while he seductively stares into my eyes. My body starts to tingle all over, sex goosebumps as I like to call them. It has definitely been a while since someone made me feel this way. My mind is going crazy wondering if it would be too slutty of me to say, "Hey, let's skip dinner and 'do it like they do on the Discovery Channel.'"

I've been spending way too much time around Eric.

"Enough about me," he says, thanking the waiter with a smile as the food is served. "What about you?"

"I believe I have one get-out-of-jail-free card?"

"Yes, and I believe you used it last weekend."

"Oh, that's right... when you fucked me in your bed. Oh no, wait, was that the time against the wall? No, my bad, it was when you did me on your kitchen counter," I tease in my sexiest voice as I run my foot up his leg.

"Nice segue, but you ain't getting out of this. I want to know more about you, Charlie."

With a small pout, I give in, noting to keep the information to the bare minimum. "Well, I told you I grew up in Carmel..."

"I honestly never figured you for a California girl. Why did I think you were from Phoenix?"

"I don't know. Why, don't I look like I'm from California? Because I'm not wearing Daisy Dukes with a bikini top?"

"Carry on, smart-ass."

"I went to Carmel High. My dad was a truck driver, so he was on the road a lot. It was just my mom, my older sister, and lil' old me until my sister left to go backpacking through Europe when I was fourteen. Mom and Dad split up when I was thirteen, then Mom moved back to Cuba to take care of my grandpa, who was really sick. The rest is just a drunken frat night Margarita haze before I landed here."

"Somehow, I can't imagine a drunken Charlie in college."

"Why is that?"

"You're just so... together. In complete control of your life and every aspect of it."

"I'll take that as a compliment."

"And back home? No serious boyfriends left behind?" he questions as I shuffle uncomfortably. "How were you not taken sooner?"

"How are you not taken?"

"Ugh, it's impossible to argue with a lawyer. Seriously, how did Charlie Mason not break any hearts in Carmel?"

Almost choking on my drink, I let out a cough. Julian waits patiently for an answer, raising his brows with a curious gaze.

It's the skeleton in the closet that's happy to remain in hibernation. Tonight isn't the night to bring up the past, but we're at that point in the relationship when past relationship conversations are inevitable. *Shrug it off, Charlie, it won't invite any more questions.*

I shift my eyes to the painting on the wall, unable to make eye contact.

"I dated a few guys in high school. There was this one guy my senior year, the typical high school crush type of thing," I say, followed by a casual laugh to lighten the topic.

Julian can sense my discomfort, moving onto another subject rather quickly. We chat about his career, the stories he has covered and, of course, we have a heated debate about *American Idol*. I enjoy his company, and for rest of the night, we don't stop laughing at the stories he tells of when he first moved to the city. I'm not sure if they are that funny or the Margaritas have gotten the better of me.

We take a cab back to my place where he makes me forget the world exists.

Twice.

When I wake up in the morning, Julian is long gone having to catch a red-eye to D.C.

My head is pounding, a string of loud thumps making it impossible to open my eyes. Damn that visit to Margaritaville! I never learn my lesson, assuming I'm mature enough to handle the hard liquor.

The alarm on my phone rings, and I somehow manage to hit snooze. I fall back asleep until the ringing starts again, and Coco decides my face is a good spot to get comfortable.

This time, I ignore snooze and make a mental note just to set my alarm later tomorrow. Why do I waste my time hitting snooze a thousand times when I could've slept in that extra twenty minutes uninterrupted?

I drag my tired self into the shower, get changed, and head to the office.

"Updates, please. Don't leave a single thing out," Eric exclaims the second I set foot in my office.

There isn't much to tell only mentioning how great Julian is and the fact that I drank an entire year's supply of Margaritas. My head is still pounding to a point I swear I can actually see my pulse throbbing out of the corner of my eye. Eric's high-pitched voice and thirst for information doesn't help calm the storm brewing in my head.

"You're my source of amusement, Charlie. I live vicariously through your sexcapades."

"I don't know why, E. You're twenty-one and look like an Asian version of Zac Efron. I should be living through you," I point out.

I sit back in my chair, glancing out the window. Life seems perfect. Julian is amazing, everything I'm looking for in a guy. He makes me laugh, his intelligence is a huge turn-on, and I can't deny how sexy he is.

Yes, Batman definitely ticks all my boxes, including the one below.

Life at work is busy and thriving on pressure is my thing. Everything I work hard for has paid off, yet I can't help but feel that all of this is too good to be true.

Just like my mom once told me—*perfection can never be reached.*

Shaking my head, I think to myself, screw that notion.

Life is perfect, and I'm sitting on top of the world while wearing my new Louboutins. Yet, somewhere in the dark passages within me, I'm trying to bury deeper the nagging feeling in the pit of my stomach that there's a dark storm gathering on the horizon.

A storm so brutal and ready to rock me to my very core.

SEVEN

CHARLIE

"I'm so jealous."

Eric is sitting in the chair opposite me, spinning himself around like a five-year-old boy. I have zero clue what he's talking about, crossing my arms as I wait for some sort of explanation to the inner workings of his mind.

"Of all the hot sex you're going to have tonight while I'm busy binge-watching *Grey's*."

"Tonight? What's tonight?"

"Uh, duh, your three-month anniversary with Batman... at that fancy restaurant in Brooklyn."

"Oh shit," I stumble out, checking my diary and instantly noticing the circle around the date. "I completely forgot. The Mackenzie case has been in the forefront of my mind all week. What the hell am I going to wear?"

"That little red number you bought last week, the one that accentuates your ass. And anyway, what's with you? You've been acting weird today."

I'm slightly taken aback by his comment. Sure, work has been over-the-top busy this week, but nothing I can't handle. "Weird as in how?"

"As in I need a good bang in my cooch, but even with that big dick inside me, my mind is elsewhere kind of weird."

"Wow, E, you really like to paint a picture, don't you?"

"When it involves Batman and his giant dick, I'm all about painting pictures, lots of mental pictures." He winks, flicking his perfectly styled hair to the side.

"Okay, when did I ever say he had a giant dick?"

"You never denied it..."

"I've never confirmed it, either!" I throw a pen at him, laughing, then I continue, "For the record, I'm not commenting on size, but I'm plenty satisfied. Now go, I need to get ready for this date I almost forgot about."

I sense his nervousness. The constant tap of his foot under the table is driving me to distraction, his hands clutching the napkin with a tight grip, turning his knuckles white. His smile is genuine, yet something's off.

Letting out a sigh, I suspect he's experiencing the 'itch.' The three-month itch. I read about it in an article in *Cosmo*. Men generally get more comfortable around this time in their relationships. Yet, others get the itch, the itch to change what has become familiar. It's common, and why should I expect anything different?

Except Julian is different. He's amazing.

He's the pin-up boy of the man your daddy wants you to marry. He treats me with respect and kindness, and I love spending time with him when our schedules permit it. I think we're going somewhere, especially after the exchange of *I love you* last week.

Placing his hands over mine, he curls his fingers into my

own, squeezing them gently, letting out a huge breath before he begins to speak.

"Charlie, you're the most amazing, beautiful, smart, talented woman I have ever met. The last three months have been nothing short of spectacular. I've been thinking a lot about us and where I want to be. I love you, Charlie, but this isn't enough for me..."

I can feel the bile rising in my throat.

Here it comes.

Opening my mouth, he politely raises his hand, prompting me to keep quiet.

"Charlie, I want you in my life every day. I want you to be the first thing I see when I wake up, the last thing I see when I go to sleep, and between those moments, I want you with me in my dreams."

Julian drags his chair out, standing before me. Confused, I wait on edge until he gets down on one knee, his eyes staring right into mine as a wave of panic hits my chest.

"Charlie Mason, will you marry me?"

Letting out a loose cough, I almost choke as I hear the words out loud. *Marriage?* I thought he wanted to break-up! This is in the complete opposite direction.

Struggling to breathe, my heart begins beating unevenly, but so loud I'm sure the whole restaurant can hear. In the space of a few seconds, he produces a small black box, opening it slowly to reveal a sparkling princess-cut diamond.

"But... but...we've only been together for three months," I stutter.

He removes the ring out of the box, delicately placing it between his fingers. "I love you, Charlie. I don't need any more time to figure that out. You're the one I've been waiting for."

This moment is beyond overwhelming. I glance around, watching the people who are sitting at the tables on either side of us waiting in anticipation for my reaction. My hands begin shaking as I raise them toward my chest, trying to still the loud thumping inside. The air around us becomes incredibly hot, sweat forming beneath my clothes as the pressure mounts.

My focus returns to Julian, his hand extends with a ring waiting to be placed on my finger. With a yearning look, I stare into the eyes of a man who has only shown me love and kindness since the moment we met. He protects me when I need it the most, yet allows me my freedom and respects my boundaries, often encouraging me to go beyond my normal levels of comfort.

He loves me and only me.

"You're kind of leaving me out on a limb here." He laughs, nervously.

I look around again, knowing every second which passes probably feels like an hour in Julian's mind.

What the hell am I supposed to do?

I catch myself by surprise, throwing all caution to the wind as I open my mouth and say, *"Yes."*

The moment the word escapes my lips, Julian's face brightens, his beautiful hazel eyes widen as his mouth follows suit. Unable to contain his joyous grin, he slowly slides the ring on my finger as the restaurant applauds around us.

Tilting his head, he places a kiss on my lips, almost like it seals the proposal. I sit back against the chair, raising my hand to admire the ring which perfectly fits on my finger.

"Charlie, you have just made me the happiest man alive."

Placing my hands on his cheeks, I pull him back into me, kissing him deeply, desperately trying to get lost in this moment. Gently pulling away, my mouth curves upward into a smile, staring at the handsome man before me who will soon be my husband. I glance at the ring again, still in shock this happened only a few moments ago.

"Shall we go back to my place to celebrate?" he asks with a cocky grin.

"By celebrate, I hope you mean fool around before having some extremely hot sex?"

Letting out a laugh, he nods. "You read my mind."

As we stand his phone rings, prompting him to answer. Annoyed, he talks for a few moments, his lips pressing together while grimacing. I only catch bits of the conversation, too busy staring at the rock, which feels like it weighs a ton on my hand and heart.

As his conversation finishes, I force a smile, flashing my ring enthusiastically.

"Charlie, I'm sorry."

"Did the bat signal go off?"

"Even if it did, I wouldn't leave, but a well-known politician has been caught in a rather compromising situation in Long Island. I need to be there in two hours."

"Wow, like cock wrapped around a twenty-one-year-old mistress situation?"

"Something like that."

"Two hours? That gives us plenty of time, Mr. Baker."

My head falls onto the pillow, my back arching as he buries himself deep inside me. His movements push me closer to that moment, the moment when I scream his name, but something feels different.

His pace picks up, his grunts deepening. In an act of desperation, he buries his head between my breasts, kissing the curves until his tongue finds its way to my erect nipples. I clench with pleasure as his teeth graze over them. I'm almost there.

"Imagine us, baby, every day for the rest of our lives buried in each other. You'll be my wife, forever mine."

His words *forever mine*.

I will be his.

I will belong to him like he'll belong to me—Julian and Charlie Baker.

The wave of panic sweeps over me again. I try to block it out, focusing on an orgasmic finish. I need it, more than I have ever needed a happy ending in my life.

"I need to feel you explode all over me. C'mon, gorgeous."

I buck my hips into him, allowing his body to go deeper. Argh. My frustration is consuming me.

Where the hell is this happy orgasmic ending?

Focus, Charlie.

I pull his head away from my breasts, forcefully kissing his mouth where the taste of my desire lingers on his lips. His tongue swirls around mine, my body shuddering as I moan loudly into the air around us. *I'm done.*

As the two of us lay side by side trying to catch our breaths, Julian turns to face me with a ridiculous grin, dragging my hand toward him to admire the ring.

"To the future Mrs. Baker. May we have a lifetime full of exploding finishes, until that is, of course, we're interrupted by a brood of kids, after which will result in late-night quickies."

"Kids?" I strain my voice choking slightly, any remaining desire sinking faster than the Titanic.

"Sure, you do want them, right?"

"I uh... yeah, I guess so, but not anytime soon."

"Don't worry, we've got some time. Practice makes perfect, right?"

Surely, he can feel my body tense up talking about this.

"How many do you want?"

"Mmm... I don't know... three, maybe four?"

"Four!"

"I want plenty of mini Charlies and Julians jumping in our bed every morning."

There it is, that wave of panic again.

This time, it's a tsunami.

Grand in its entrance.

A force to be reckoned with.

My stomach ties into all kinds of knots.

I hate that I'm this terrified, that I'm not basking in all this kids talk like every other female with a ticking biological clock.

"Hey, gorgeous, relax. It's going to be you and me for a while. Think you can handle that?"

I turn to face him, then reach out and run my hand along his jaw. The diamond shines back at me. I can handle this.

Cupid has served me the most perfect man on a silver platter, and I'm questioning myself? *You're an idiot, Charlie. Plain and simple.*

"I can handle that, future Mr. Mason."

I walk through the door, placing my keys on the hallway table. Kicking my heels off, I make my way to the sofa, sitting in the middle as I sink between the cushions. My chest tightens, my stomach churning as my breathing begins to accelerate. Coco purrs beside me, demanding attention after me being gone the whole day.

I said *yes*.

I really said *yes*.

Why am I not calling everyone I know?

The ring is taunting me, its weight now unbearable. It's beautiful, but this moment isn't what I imagined. I feel guilty as I sit here wearing this piece of jewelry with a symbolic meaning. This ring means the promise of committing myself to Julian for the rest of my life. I take the ring off my finger, sliding it across the table as far away from me as possible.

My phone begins to ring, startling me. I glance at the screen, smiling instantly as his name and goofball face flashes on the screen. Always perfect timing, he's just what I need right now.

"What are you wearing?" he asks in a low voice.

"A slutty black dress."

"Why do I believe that?"

"Because I'm a New Yorker, and that's what we wear on Tuesday nights..." I pause for a brief moment. "I miss you."

"I miss you, too," he responds at ease.

"When are you guys coming back to visit?"

"When are you gonna come home?"

Home—this is home, here in Manhattan.

"Finn, you know I can't go back."

"But one day, you will. You better come and stay with me, just like old times. I'll fight ya hard for the remote. We can eat cookie dough straight from the packet, and if you're good, and I mean real good, I may let you ride my Harley."

I laugh out loud just like old times. "Do I get to bunk with the kids?"

"I'm sure they would love that." He chuckles with his burly voice. "But, hey, your funeral, not mine."

"I miss them. I miss you, and I miss Jen. How is she? Please give her big hugs for me."

"She's right here."

The phone volume changes as I'm placed on speakerphone.

"Hi, honey. I miss you, too. It's been too long. Where's my weekly update on Batman?"

It's now or never.

"Actually, I have some news. Tonight... well... Julian kind of... I'm engaged."

There's a long silence followed by a child's cry in the background.

"Honey, congratulations..." Jen says, her voice unsure. "Listen, I have to put Milo down for the night. Call me tomorrow, let's talk more. I need details. I love you."

I heard the change in volume as I'm taken off speakerphone. "Finn?"

"Yeah, I'm here," he mumbles.

I nervously laugh. "So... me, engaged. Who would've thought?"

The silence only prolongs what's bound to be said. If anyone understands my hesitation in this moment, it's Finn. The boy who stole my heart kept it in his pocket for safekeeping, then became my best friend.

"Charlie, I can hear it in your voice. You're scared."

"Not scared, Finn, just a little apprehensive. I didn't think this day would ever come," I whisper.

"It's me. Your best friend since we were in our mother's wombs. The guy you so willingly lost your virginity to at the age of sixteen. I know you, Charlie, and this hesitation is because of him, and I hate that."

"Finn, I don't want to get into this. The past needs to remain exactly that, in the past. Otherwise, we will never move forward with our lives. Just don't say his name... please," I beg, hoping somehow Finn understands I'm so done and need this more than anything.

"Agreed, but when the past affects your future, then what? Julian is great, right? You said so yourself."

"He *is* great."

I'm not sure who I am trying to convince more.

"So, stop beating yourself up over it. He loves you, you love him. He treats you like you deserve to be treated, and according to my wife, he's sex on legs. Whatever the hell that means, but I can take a guess. Take the leap, Charlie. You'll see how great life can be, and as time moves on, so will your feelings. This is great."

He's right. I need to let go of any negative thoughts that ever crossed my mind.

"You put up a good argument. You sure you don't want to study law?"

"Miss Manhattan, big shot lawyer. Look, I gotta go. I love you. Please think about what I said."

"I will. Love you, too."

I hang up the phone, clutching it to my chest. Everything Finn said is right. I have this perfect man who loves me and wants to spend the rest of his life with me. I'd be stupid to say no. I know that, but I just can't let it go, this feeling of guilt like I'm doing something wrong.

I lean over, reaching for the ring, and place it back on my finger.

That night, I toss and turn.

The dreams.

The nightmares.

Please stop, I beg myself.

Somewhere around three o'clock, the exhaustion outweighs my racing mind, and just when I find the peace I had hoped for, it happens. Those emerald green eyes flash before me, and I crumble.

The memory becomes all too clear, taking me back to the moment it all began.

EIGHT

CHARLIE

Nine Years Ago

I woke up in the darkness, my throat dry like the Vegas desert.

Why did I let Adriana bring that second bag of Doritos to her room? Tossing and turning, I couldn't get comfortable as I lie there on her spare couch, desperate for anything to drink to cure the thirst.

Our sleepovers, a regular occurrence of late, had become nights filled with never-ending junk food and gossiping about who was blowing who at school.

I climbed off the couch careful not to wake her. Oh, who was I kidding, a hurricane wouldn't even wake her. She snored away as I tiptoed to the kitchen to grab a drink. It was dark, and I didn't want to wake anyone else, so I walked down the steps to the kitchen, shocked when I collided with another body.

"Holy shit!" a voice yelled.

The weight of his body forced me down. I was pinned

with my back against the stairs, unable to speak, my breath caught in my throat still not knowing who it was. With the moon hidden behind the stormy clouds, the room was darker than usual, masking his identity.

Oh my God, what if it's a burglar?

I've interrupted him.

What if he has a gang of thieves with him?

My stomach began to churn as my thirst increased, my chest tightening in fear.

He pulled himself up off me, accidentally grazing my breast as he stood. It was like a jolt of electricity shot through me causing me to whimper. I could've sworn he felt it too, his gasp following shortly after.

The flick of a switch interrupted my thoughts, the light blinding and making me go all cross-eyed. It was Alex, Adriana's older brother.

I hadn't seen him since he left Carmel after he graduated high school years ago, and Adriana never mentioned he was here. Alex was twenty-five and lived in San Francisco with his wife from what Adriana told me. Aside from that, she rarely mentioned him in conversations.

He stood in front of me, wearing only flannel pajama pants that hung low below his waist, showing off his perfectly muscular body and the 'V,' oooh, the 'V.'

I didn't know I was gazing at his body until he broke me from my trance.

"Charlotte?"

I looked at his face, his eyes drinking me in, the color emerald. I struggled to find the words, feeling utterly stupid for paying this much attention to him. He was Adriana's older brother, and I had spent most of my late childhood around him. After all, I was her best friend and practically lived in her room. But that was years ago, a distant memory from a troubled time in my life when my parents were at each other all the time, and this house became my escape.

"I'm so sorry, Alex."

I started to panic, my voice becoming squeaky. As the adrenaline started to wear off, I felt a sharp pain in the back of my head. It must have been from when he fell on top of me on the stairs. Without thinking, I rubbed my head, my face scrunching as I touched the lump that was starting to form.

"Are you okay? Come sit down."

Alex pulled one of the stools out as I walked over to the island countertop. Sitting myself down, I watched him grab a bag of peas from the freezer. He walked back over and stood in front of me, then held the peas against the lump now throbbing like one of those thumbs in the cartoons. His chest in front of me, gloriously exposed, the smell of his skin intoxicating. I closed my eyes for a brief moment, inhaling what smelled like aftershave and soap mixed with man sweat, but good man sweat, hot man sweat.

"Better?" he asked in a sweeter tone.

"Yes, thank you. I'm so sorry, I didn't realize you were here. Adriana didn't mention that you had returned from college." I spoke quickly, suddenly feeling self-conscious, and I had every reason to as I'd just caught him checking out my breasts. His eyes looked like they were on fire. I looked down, my nipples now prominent in my tank top. Oh fuck, I forgot to put my bra back on! I quickly folded my arms breaking him from his perverted stare.

"I... um, came back this morning." He laughed awkwardly, rubbing the back of his neck. "She probably didn't tell you because she was too busy sucking face with that scrawny geek she's seeing. I didn't mean to startle you back there. I'm sleeping on the couch tonight because our bed hasn't arrived at our new place yet."

"Are you back here for good?"

"Not one-hundred percent sure, but in the meantime, I wanted to get some practical experience alongside my dad at the hospital. Plus, Samantha got a job at the gallery not too far from here, so yeah, I guess it keeps everyone happy," he explained, sounding a little unsure of himself.

"I better head back to bed." I hopped off the stool, a little unsteady on my feet, careful not to knock into him again. "Adriana is making us go prom-dress shopping tomorrow morning. What are the chances of her battery being tampered with, so the car won't start?"

"That's right, I forgot you aren't related to Donatella Versace like my sister claims she is," he teased with a sly grin.

It was so true. Adriana lived and breathed fashion. I, on the other hand, didn't care at all. As long as I looked good, I couldn't have cared less what label I wore.

Walking back to the stairway, I turned around to look at him before I went back upstairs. "It was nice seeing you again, Alex." I took a few steps before stopping and turning around one more time. "And congratulations on your wedding. Adriana told me it was amazing."

This time, I headed back up the stairs realizing I hadn't gotten the drink I was so desperate for. Oh well, it was too late now. Sleep was all I needed because soon it would be morning.

I tossed and turned again trying to dissect what had happened downstairs. I felt awkward around him, yet comfortable at the same time. It didn't make sense, and why was I lying here obsessing about it?

After what felt like only minutes, I was rudely awakened by Adriana screaming through the hallway. Her voice, obnoxious and angered, was enough to wake me from what felt like the shortest sleep in the world.

"*Mom!*"

Pulling the blanket over my head, I had let out a long-winded groan, trying to ignore the family domestic that was going on outside. I was exhausted.

"Mom, how could you let him take it?"

This time her voice was even louder than before. I could hear more muffled voices followed by loud footsteps. The door to the bedroom slammed, her ballet distinction certificate frame falling off the wall.

"I mean seriously, out of all days, he comes up with shit like this?" she muttered to herself.

I pulled my head above the blanket, opening my eyes.

"Adriana, what the hell? It's like seven in the morning. What could you possibly be upset about this early?"

"My brother apparently took my car, claiming that it sounded like something was wrong with the battery. He left me a note saying he has taken it to Al's Mechanics to get it checked out," she seethed, crossing her arms as her nostrils flared in a heated rage. "I'm so annoyed, the car is fine. If something were wrong with it, the battery light would've come on. I asked Mom if I could borrow her car, but she has to help a friend of hers move today. I could strangle him right now!"

She continued, closing her eyes this time with a calmer voice, "Sorry, I don't mean to take it out on you. It's just I was really looking forward to prom-dress shopping, and now it looks like we're stuck here for the day."

Adriana plonks herself at her desk and opened a *Vogue*

magazine, roughly flicking the pages while cussing to herself.

"Oh, dang," I answered, sarcastically.

I pulled the blanket over my head, smiling as I fell back asleep.

NINE

ALEX

Nine Years Ago

I opened my textbook in an attempt to drown out her incessant nagging.

This is what it had been like lately, always wanting more. She had changed, no longer the carefree college girl I fell in love with. Samantha Benson was the girl on campus every guy wanted, and she chose me. Not that loser, Brad, who had been pining for her since middle school. Fucking jerk.

Our life together in college was an awesome experience. Samantha was incredibly beautiful, knew how to give extremely good head, and was studying art. She wasn't my usual type, but she was no airhead. My family loved her, her family loved me, and so it made sense to put a ring on that finger and one less worry in life.

I wasn't into the whole wedding fiasco, staying out of the way while Samantha planned the entire thing. It was a nice day as far as weddings go, but here we were six months later, and the cracks were starting to show. It wasn't enough that she wanted an expensive house with views of the Pacific Ocean and a Mercedes, both of which we couldn't afford on my intern's wage, and now she was nagging me to start a family. I wasn't ready for this shit at twenty-five. I still had friends who woke up naked next to strange chicks and kegs every night.

I told her I'd think about it if we moved back to Carmel. I missed my family, hoping they would convince her we were too young to have kids, especially Dad. He wanted me to follow in his footsteps, and there was no way I could do that with a baby around. Studying and practicing medicine required all my focus on just that. I didn't need any other distractions.

"Alex, are you listening to me?" she pleaded, irritation evident in her voice.

"Sammy, what do you want me to say? We just moved here. The house still has dust on it, our furniture hasn't arrived, and I technically don't have a paying job yet. Please explain how a baby will fit into this? We can barely support ourselves."

I was fucking annoyed. Yeah, babies were cute and stuff, but there was still so much more I wanted to do in life —start my internship, travel to Europe—the list went on and on. This all began when her sister had a baby, and now that's all she talked about. I'm so over her comparing our relationship to everyone else. Nothing I seemed to do pleased her.

"You said when we move to Carmel we could—"

Raising my hand, I cut her off. In typical Sam fashion, she'd twisted my words.

"I never said *when* we moved to Carmel, we could start trying. What I said, in case you ever want to listen to me properly, was let's settle back in Carmel and talk about this once we have found a house and have proper paying jobs."

"Well, Alex, we found a house, and I have a proper paying job. You, on the other hand, seem to be undecided on your career. It doesn't help that you're supposed to be the breadwinner, not me," she shot back.

"Fuck you for bringing this up again!" I yelled, banging my fists on the table. "You're so happy to tell everyone your husband is studying to become a doctor, yet behind closed doors, it's not good enough because I'm not paying for your expensive lifestyle."

I closed my textbook, grabbing my cell and keys off the countertop. I needed to cool down, so tired of the constant bickering, and the way she made me feel uncertain about decisions I made. I needed to relax and stop focusing on this negativity.

"I'm going to my parents' house."

I slammed the door and walked to the car. She quickly opened the door, standing there with her arms crossed beneath her chest, baring her teeth and angered because I was leaving mid-conversation. This wasn't the first time, nor would it be the last.

"We'll discuss this again when you decide where your home is, Alex."

And blinded by rage, she slammed the door without a goodbye.

"Adriana," I yelled, my voice echoing through the foyer.

My parents' house is eight-thousand square feet, large enough to lose yourself without having to live on top of each other. My grandfather, a wealthy man in his own right, had given this house to my parents as a wedding gift.

Inside the foyer, I listen for the direction of her voice.

"I'm here!"

Making my way toward the rumpus room, I stopped at the entrance, surprised to find Adriana not alone.

I didn't expect to see her again. Charlotte, that is. She was lying on the couch wearing a black tank top, jeans, and Converse. I could see her long brown hair was loose, falling down the side of the couch.

Charlotte was beautiful, nothing at all like I remembered her from years ago. She had outgrown the pre-teen stage and had become this stunning woman. It was impossible not to notice. I mean, come on, I was only human and twenty-five. Just because I was married didn't mean I couldn't admire beauty when I saw it. As long as I played by the rules—look, don't touch—I wasn't doing anything wrong.

Oddly, Charlotte is surrounded by M&Ms, a range of different colors scattered around her face and chest.

"Oh, hi Alex, come hang out with us. We were just playing who can catch the most M&Ms not using our hands." Adriana giggles, continuing with her game.

She aimed them at Charlotte's mouth, and surprisingly she missed. My sister doesn't have an athletic bone in her body.

My eyes met with Charlotte's. I don't know what it was, but something felt different about her. She wasn't like any other girl I'd met and definitely nothing like my sister. Thinking back to the other night when I ran into her in the kitchen, there was this feeling I wasn't accustomed to, a lot like a jolt of electricity when I accidentally touched her. I mean, fuck, accidentally grazing her tits had me hard for the rest of the night, but I had to remember I was married.

It didn't help that she wasn't wearing a bra that night, either. What made it even worse was that she caught me staring at her.

Charlotte scowls as she got whacked in the eye with an M&M. "Hi, Alex."

"Please don't let my sister assault you with the M&Ms. Geez, Adriana, you throw like a girl."

"I am a girl, duh."

She threw another one at Charlotte, this time landing right in her cleavage. I couldn't help but look. It sat there in the middle of her perfectly shaped tits. The lucky M&M jiggled as she struggled to control her laughter.

"Seriously, Adriana, are you looking to switch teams now? That's the third time you've gotten it in there!" Charlotte laughed. My sister was on the ground rolling around, her body shaking with laughter, screaming she needed to pee.

"Okay, girls, let me show you how it's done."

I grabbed the packet off my sister. "Charlotte, please stop laughing and just open your mouth."

I waited for her as she attempted to keep a straight face, something I was struggling to do as well. I focused on her mouth, her perfectly pink lips wide open. My mind wandered elsewhere. No, Edwards, 'focus' as Coach would say. I threw the M&M, landing it in her mouth. I roared as it went in, Adriana pouted as usual. She was so fucking competitive.

"No fair, Alex! You throw like a boy!" Adriana whined.

"Thanks, Alex. It's about time I get to eat one of them," Charlotte cheered, raising her hand to high-five me.

"Next time, come to me if you actually want to eat

them, since clearly Adriana here has no aim. I think she secretly just wanted to find them later when you were gone," I joked.

I was enjoying the company and finally managed to put the earlier argument and Sam's bullshit behind me.

The house phone started ringing.

Adriana jumped up like her life depended on it or more like the opening of Macy's' doors on Black Friday. I wasn't surprised when she announced who it was.

"Oh, it's Elijah! Back soon."

She ran out, taking the cordless phone up to her room.

"When she says soon, I can pretty much watch *Titanic* from start to finish, and she still won't be done," Charlotte complained, picking up the remote to surf through the channels.

"The joys of having a boyfriend I s'pose. So, do you um... have one?"

"Me? Please, have you seen the guys at our school?" Charlotte pursed her lips while she shook her head. "Apparently, wearing baggy pants and flashing your no-name underwear passes for style these days. Besides, I'm saving myself for Justin Timberlake."

"I think Britney thought the same thing and look where that got her," I pointed out.

"But can she catch M&Ms in her mouth like I can?"

"Hey, it has everything to do with the pitcher, not the catcher."

"I don't think you realize how difficult it is to have your mouth perfectly positioned and open for that long."

As soon as she said it, I laughed, and her face blushed slightly.

"Oh, man, that didn't come out right."

She joined me as I laughed, still flicking through the channels.

I watched as she went past the hockey. Leaning forward, I gestured for her to stop. "Hey, go back to the hockey."

"Err, no thanks, Alex. Yes, here it is."

She stopped on *Animal Planet*. Seriously, we're going to watch a documentary on Bonobo monkeys? I had to admit it was better than watching the fashion police, and well, I was watching the emperor penguins last night. It was mating season on *Animal Planet,* but I really wanted to see the hockey scores.

"Did you know the Bonobo monkey uses sex as a greeting, a method of conflict resolution and to celebrate when food has been found?"

Her eyes fixated on the screen, fascinated with the narrator's over-the-top narration of the monkeys.

"Wow! Imagine if we did that, no one would be able to get anything done," I teased.

Shit, I hadn't meant it to come out like that, but damn, imagine if it were true that we were fucking all the time? That thought alone made me hard. Really hard. I needed to get these thoughts out of my head. *Stupid mating monkeys.*

Charlotte broke her gaze from the television and turned to look at me while laughing.

"Keep dreaming, Edwards."

"So now that you have informed me of the intricate sex life of the Bonobos, can I please watch the hockey?"

She held the remote in the air, pushing my chest away as I made a feeble attempt to grab it from her. This girl loved to play hardball, and it was annoying at best.

"Alex, this is the last episode of the mating series," she complained while trying to hold the remote away from me.

I couldn't help but watch her. A part of me liked teasing her as I attempted to reach over for the remote. She swung it low, a move I anticipated. She held onto it as I fell on top of her, then began tickling her ribs.

"Alex... please stop." Her voice was shaking as she giggled, squirming her body underneath me.

"Mmm, I'll stop if you hand me the remote."

"No way. I was here first. Sorry, Alex, you snooze, you lose." She tried to tickle me back. Her touch felt like electric currents attached to a million needles running through my body, and I so desperately wanted her to move her hands onto my chest. I felt like a horny teenager all over again.

I slowed down, watching her deep chocolate-brown eyes taking me in, her chest was rising and falling. I was inches away from her face, I could almost taste her.

Oh fuck, what was I thinking?

No sooner had the thought entered my mind, my cock started twitching. She had to have felt it, I was fucking huge. Suddenly, her eyes changed. Was that lust I could see?

I heard my sister's voice. Quickly I pulled myself away from her, while Charlotte adjusted her tank top as she sat up. Her cheeks were flushed, and all I wanted to do was lean in and caress her face, satisfy the curiosity and need I was feeling.

"Okay, everything is set for next Saturday!" Adriana was excitedly chatting away as she entered the room.

"Next Saturday?" I repeated, my mind still foggy with what just happened.

"My eighteenth birthday, silly. It starts at seven. Sammy promised you guys would chaperone, so Mom and Dad didn't have to be here."

Now I remembered what I had been roped into, but for

some reason, I didn't mind going if it meant I got to see Charlotte again. *Fuck, what the hell was I thinking?* Okay, no, it'll be fine—Sammy will be there. I wasn't thinking clearly. It was time for me to leave despite wanting to stay longer.

"I better head off. See you tomorrow at lunch, sis. Bye, Charlotte."

I looked over, her eyes locked on mine. It felt like something passed between us, but what? What was it? The shiny band on my left hand suddenly felt like a lead weight, a reminder of everything in my life I had committed to.

"Just call me Charlie. Everybody else does." She smiled, batting her eyelashes.

I turned to face her one last time as I stared at the two pools of chocolate brown eyes. They were intoxicating. But why? I had no idea. This wasn't like me. When it came to women, I was controlled. She wasn't the first woman to catch my attention while married, though, I'd never done anything forbidden besides flirt. And even then, it lasted two minutes, and the novelty wore off real fast.

But she was different.

"Charlotte, I'm not everybody else," I told her with confidence.

Her lips pressed together in a slight grimace, and her eyes widened with a longing gaze.

"No, you're not, Alex," she stated, never breaking her stare. "You certainly are not."

TEN

Present

"M r. Edwards."

Everyone at the table rises, extending their hands. Shaking each one of them in turn, I take a seat and motion for the waiter to come over. This is one of my final meetings before I finally fly out on Monday morning, and I'm itching to get back home.

"Can I have a short black, please?"

The waiter scurries away as I turn to face Mr. Klein and the rest of his associates. The purpose of the meeting today is to discuss our chain of clubs in Manhattan, specifically After Dark, our newest and most profitable club.

Klein produces our latest figures, then delves into our budget. The club is profitable, thanks to reaching full capacity every Friday and Saturday night. The paparazzi swarm the outside as celebrities make it their new favorite spot. Overall, I'm content with the numbers along with the other clubs along the East Coast.

As I look over a paper forecasting this year's return, I'm

distracted by someone laughing at another table. The laugh, sounding almost angelic, if not a little familiar, is making it difficult for me to focus.

To drown out the incessant noise, I focus on Klein's recommendations for minor improvements we can make to the club to ensure long-term profit.

But then I hear it again.

I turn my head to the left to see where it's coming from.

A woman is sitting with a man at a table a few feet away. He must be telling her a funny story because her head and shoulders are shaking uncontrollably while her laughter barrels through the restaurant. This fucker is surely going to get laid tonight.

The woman is sitting with her legs crossed to the side. I eye her long, lean, tanned legs right down to her shoes. Oh, fuck me, *Louboutins*. If there's one thing I have a fetish over, it's Louboutin pumps. Something about the black and red screams dominatrix. I adjust my pants slightly under the table, knowing all too well meetings and hard-ons don't go hand in hand.

It's almost impossible not to check out the rest of her. She's wearing a high-waisted gray pencil skirt and a white silk blouse buttoned down low enough I can see the curves of her breasts. Her tits look fabulous, nice and full. What a lucky bastard. Her hair is pinned up, and yes, of course, she's a brunette. Fuck my life.

"Mr. Edwards?"

Klein breaks me from my daze by producing more spreadsheets, sliding them across to me. Analyzing the graphs on the sheets, my head is unable to shut out the noise.

"Sorry, Mr. Klein, you were talking about profit margins?"

The woman laughs again. I turn to look at the same time she lifts her head. She's wearing black-rimmed reading glasses, very librarian. Don't go there again, Edwards. I let out a small breath with the sudden realization at how unprofessional I am being.

Focus.

But something pulls me toward her, this force consuming me without any rhyme or reason. Quickly, I allow myself one last glance to squash this obscene curiosity I have about her.

She turns to look my way, and the most beautiful deep chocolate brown eyes meet with mine, and the second our gaze locks, my heart stops, the beats now at a complete standstill.

This can't be.

The ghost of my dreams, my fantasies, and most importantly, my memories. The past comes flooding back to me like a movie being replayed in my head.

I can't believe it's *her,* nine years later.

With a surge of panic, my mind is swirling with all the things I need to say to her. This is my chance, and I have to begin with apologizing for what I did. There are so many things I need to say because I never got a chance to. I'm so overcome with mixed emotions, unable to string together a coherent thought in my racing mind. My palms start to sweat, the voices around me droning in a low and incomprehensible murmur. My eyes feel like they are betraying me. This has to be my mind playing tricks, but as I focus once again, it's undeniable that everything I see before me is indeed the woman I once loved.

She does a double-take, panic-stricken, her eyes wide and cheeks flush. Leaning over to the man sitting across from her, she mouths something before rising from her chair.

Klein is still talking, and quick to cut him off, I excuse myself abruptly, desperate to follow her to what I assume to be the restroom. Her pace is fast, darting in and out of the waiters serving, making it difficult for me to catch up. I increase my steps until I'm only an arm's length away.

"Charlotte, wait."

I know she heard me, but she doesn't turn around. Stretching forward, I grab her arm, immediately hit with the familiar surge of electricity jolting through me as I touch her—how much I crave it, how much my body misses this feeling. Closing my eyes for a millisecond, I allow myself to get lost in this sensation.

Frozen on the spot, her body stiffens. Slowly, she turns around cautiously to face me. Her once-loving eyes turn to fire, her smile and laughter no longer apparent. Shaking her arm out of my tight grip, she manages to pull away, only to fold her arms under her breasts.

Oh fuck, no, no, no, now it's all I can see.

My eyes, unable to peel themselves away, admire the beautiful sight—round, full—and how I so desperately want to reach out and caress them.

Yet, despite being drawn to her body, the fire in her eyes bores into me, warning me of what's to come.

"Charlotte, please..." I beg again.

As soon as her name leaves my mouth, she clenches her jaw, a pained stare following as the color drains from her face. Her icy silence gives me a chance to examine what stands before me, connecting my memories to the present moment.

She's tall, of course, the pumps she wears giving her height.

My eyes drift toward her arms, noticing the sun-kissed tan enhanced by the white blouse she wears. Her hair is pinned up into a tight-knit bun. With a longing ache I want to take it out, have it flow down her back, just the way I remember her.

As my gaze wanders back toward her face, it's evident my memory stayed true to the past with nothing much changing besides her wearing a little mascara accentuating her long eyelashes, a trait from her Cuban heritage.

And because I'm a glutton for punishment, I allow myself to be drawn to her mouth. Unknowingly, my eyes soften over her full, luscious lips covered in a ruby red lipstick. My mouth becomes moist, remembering how she tasted when our tongues would battle feverishly lost in a deep kiss.

But nothing stands a chance against the deep chocolate-brown eyes staring back at me which completes the picture-perfect beauty in all its essence. Capturing me and making my heart beat so fast, I could've sworn it fell out of my chest the second I saw her. She has become this beautiful woman, even more so than the girl I left behind.

"I looked for you after you left," I tell her, desperate with my tone. Dropping my chin to my chest, the words seem frivolous when the pain runs so deep. I'm never at a loss for words, and this overwhelming feeling of shame is tearing me to shreds, overshadowing my normal confident persona.

"Obviously not hard enough," she angrily shoots back.

My eyes dart back up to meet hers, caught off-guard by the angered tone. I knew my leaving abruptly would hurt her, but we were young. You're supposed to get over these things. How ironic to be thinking that because one look at her and I know it's far from over.

"Can we please go somewhere and talk?" I plead.

I'm never one to beg for attention, let alone from a woman, but I want her to know how sorry I am. I need a chance to explain what happened, for her to understand my reasoning for leaving her behind.

"Alex, there's nothing left to say. It was years ago, a high school fling. It's all in the past. I really need to get back."

She called me Alex.

No one calls me that anymore.

I'm known as Lex in the business world because of my ruthless behavior. I have been compared to that of Lex Luthor. Overhearing a bunch of interns call me it once, instead of firing them, I enjoyed them being afraid of me. Not long after that, I demanded that my family stop calling me Alex because it was a shadow of who I used to be.

I'm no longer the Alex Edwards she knew. But this isn't the moment to correct her because her other words linger, *a high school fling*.

Charlotte tries to push her way past me, but I grab her arm again. She doesn't turn around. Instead, she stands completely still with her back to me.

"Is he your boyfriend?"

I don't know why I ask, maybe it's the sadist in me. I know it will infuriate her, but the fucker was all over her, and knowing it's her now, I want to go back and beat the living shit out of him. Drag him out of this place and demand he return what belongs to me.

"Excuse me?" She turns around abruptly, blazing eyes with her nostrils flaring like a bull ready to attack. "First of all, you have no right asking me that. It's none of your business who I'm fucking, Alex."

My blood boils as the words ricochet like bullets spraying against my bruised ego. So what, she's fucking him? Had she turned into a cold-hearted woman fucking men without attachment?

I'm losing control, ready to walk over and show him who the fuck she belongs to, but as I bow my head to calm the storm lashing within me, the shimmer of a large diamond catches my attention.

My eyes widen, my stomach twisting in a gut-wrenching knot as my heart pumps hard while my adrenaline spikes. Without hesitation, I yank her hand toward me to make sure what I'm seeing is indeed a ring on her finger.

"What's this? You're engaged?"

She allows her hand to linger for a moment, but then, with force, she pulls it back. Her face looks slightly guilty, then it quickly transforms into anger.

"Julian is my fiancé."

"Your fiancé? So, you're marrying that jerk?"

"Typical Alexander Edwards. It's all about you, right? Remember, you left me without a goodbye, without an explanation. I've moved on just like you did with her. Goodbye, Alex. Have a nice life."

I loosen my grip, stunned by her words as she storms off back to her table. Resting my back on the wall, I close my eyes for a brief moment to compress the rage consuming me. My pulse is elevated, and my vision is clouded as the pounding inside my head is dominating my normally rational thoughts. With my heart still beating erratically on the verge of combustion, my feet move on their own accord back to my table. I need to end this meeting *now*.

But like a force of nature, I'm drawn back to her again, unable to turn away. Charlotte sits back down before leaning in, whispering something in his ear. He places some bills on top of the black check holder, and they both stand. She grabs her purse and starts walking toward the main door. For a split second, her eyes meet mine, and undoubtedly something passes between us.

The same look which passed between us nine years ago.

The guy grabs her hand, holding it firmly.

My anger is on the brink again, losing control, my temper getting the better of me. I need to find a way to talk to her, to get her alone and to have that chance to explain everything. I'm certain if she knows my side of the story she will forgive me, understand my mistakes and regrets.

In a moment of clarity, it all starts to make sense.

I rule the business world, I am on top of my game. I have everything I want, at least everything I thought I wanted. Now, it stands before me, the one thing I never knew I desired more than life itself.

The one thing I would give up everything I own for.

It's no longer a figment of my imagination.

I touched her, felt that surge that no other woman in this lifetime will make me feel.

It's Charlotte who has been missing all along, and now, I'll stop at nothing until she's completely *mine*.

ELEVEN

CHARLIE

Eric yanks my hand toward him so fast my body jerks forward, crashing into his.

"Oh-em-gee," Eric screeches like a hyena on crack.

After I gain my composure, I allow him to examine the diamond ring adorning my finger, reminding me how surreal this all is.

"Charlie, this is a Harry Winston princess-cut diamond. I need a total replay. What were you wearing? What was he wearing? The speech... oh, did he get down on one knee?" Catching his breath he sits on the chair, crossing his legs in anticipation.

I replay the entire night to him and even re-enact the proposal part, getting down on one knee, which was interrupted when Nikki walks in. Her face falls slightly as if she thinks me accepting Julian's proposal is a bad idea.

She sways her head, motioning Eric out of the room. "Charlie, I think we should talk about this."

"Whatever it is, Nikki, it can be said in front of Eric." I laugh as Eric shrugs his shoulders, laughing with me.

"Okay fine, have it your way. Don't you think you should get to know him for a little bit longer rather than jump into marriage? I mean, what's the rush? You've only been dating, what... three months?"

I saw this coming, of course. Most people's reaction will be the same, but who are they to judge what the two of us have? I love him, that's what matters. I don't need to justify that, not to anyone. Funny, though, I have been putting off telling Mom and Dad, knowing their reaction will be exactly the same.

"C'mon, Nikki, you've met him. He's a great guy."

"Charlie, a great guy doesn't mean you have to walk down the aisle with him. Just enjoy him... *for now*."

"I love him," I shoot back, defensively.

"I know, but is it enough?"

Her question rattles me. Eric sits wide-eyed at both of us like he's watching some scene from *The Real Housewives of Beverly Hills*. Nikki stands there, arms folded, tapping her foot. Her usual glare, which normally has no effect on me whatsoever, intimidates me at this moment.

"What's that supposed to mean?"

"Look, Charlie, all I'm saying is that yes, Julian is a fantastic guy, but don't you think you're rushing into this? It's almost like it's just to move on..."

Stilling my movements, my expression doesn't waver as she trails off. I know her interrogation of my actions is fueled by my resistance to settle down with any man before Julian. My past is unknown to her and everyone else, apart from Finn. Every so often, during a drunken rant, I'd spill information about teenage years, but whenever I was pushed I'd shut down immediately.

It's my past, therefore, it should remain exactly that, in the past.

I'm not the same Charlotte Mason, that naïve high school girl so willing to give her heart only to be chewed up and spit out like a raw piece of meat. Things have changed, people change. Settling down at my age is quite common and not something to be shocked over.

"Eric, can I have a word with Nikki in private?"

With a mixture of disgust and hurt on his face, he walks out the door but stops at my desk to grab a handful of M&Ms I keep in a large glass jar. As the door closes, I focus my attention back on Nikki. "You're the first one to say how picky I am, that I never give any guy a chance. So here I am giving this wonderful guy a chance, and you have the nerve to tell me that I'm making a mistake?"

"No, I simply asked why the rush. Are you knocked-up or something?"

"No!" I blurt out.

"Then, I don't understand."

"You don't need to understand. All you need to do is be my friend. I love him, he loves me. Time means nothing when you know it's right."

"And is it?"

This back-and-forth arguing is no different than when we go to court. Nikki is playing lawyer, and I'm standing trial. I hesitate, trying to find the right words which will be good enough for her, so she will understand.

"You know what they say, 'hesitation is a product of fear,'" she quotes.

"Or maybe I'm just trying to find the right words, so you'll stop nagging me about this."

Nikki's arms fall limp as she sighs dejectedly, her shoulders slumping while she hangs her head and stares at the ground. After a moment of silence, she straightens her posture and meets my gaze. "Charlie, I'm not nagging.

You're my best friend. I only want the best for you. I'm sorry, I shouldn't be so judgmental. Now show me this damn ring. Oh, hang on a sec..." her lips curve upward into a sarcastic grin, "... do me a favor and open your door?"

I know without asking why she wants me to do that. Tiptoeing to my door, I open it quickly as a shocked Eric pummels to the floor with a paper cup.

As Nikki and I break into laughter, a somewhat disheveled Eric picks himself up, wiping his perfectly pressed outfit.

"Ladies, this is an Armani suit."

"You need a glass, Eric, not a paper cup. Such a rookie mistake."

I'm just about to leave my office to meet Julian for lunch when Eric barges in unnoticed, skipping to my table like a five-year-old girl. All he's missing are the pigtails.

"Guess what? You're *so* going to love me!" he squeals. "Thursday afternoon I have Carolina, a stylist, coming to your apartment."

"Shut the front door! But why?"

"The charity ball, silly."

"No way!" I stand, grabbing the tickets from his hand.

There are six tickets to the New York Annual Charity Ball to raise awareness for orphaned kids. These tickets are like gold dust. I'm speechless. All I can manage to mouth is the word *how*.

"Let's just say Daddy owes me big time after he accidentally dropped Mom's ten-carat Asscher-cut ring down the drain and made me go in head-down, ass-up to get it."

Eric comes from a wealthy background. His parents are

part of an elite family that goes back generations. Surprisingly, Eric wants to get a job and not work for his father. A few times we spoke about it, Eric mentioned his father's crowd isn't so welcoming of his homosexual lifestyle.

"Holy shit, E! Can Nikki get fitted as well?"

"Of course, but I want to be there when her boobs don't fit in the dresses, and she starts cursing at Carolina."

We both laugh at the thought. The girls are big, but there's no one complaining but her. Rocky even has names for them—Dolly and Pamela.

"Is she bringing the Dolce & Gabbana fall line?"

"You betcha." He winks.

"So, I'm going to ask Julian to be my plus one." I glance at Eric, hoping he will understand.

"Honey, I'm just glad your lady garden is getting watered," he utters, making circles with his fingers while pointing to my crotch. "Emma will be my date. We have it all planned out. We act like a couple, so we can walk around scouting out the potential. Then about halfway through, she splashes champagne on me and tells me that although I'm a fantastic lover with the biggest dick she's ever seen, she is sick of my workaholic ways. It's then we hope someone swoops in, patting me down, telling me I can do better than her. We start chatting, and before you know it, we're picking out china patterns at Williams-Sonoma."

"That's some plan. What does Emma get out of this?" I ask, trying hard to contain my laughter.

"She gets to walk around with me, the fantastic lover."

Poor Emma. I know all too well how Eric's power of persuasion can get you in trouble.

It's midday when I finally head down to that new Japanese restaurant around the corner. I enter through the revolving doors, spotting Julian immediately.

"Hey, gorgeous." His face brightens as he leans in, kissing me softly on the lips. He smells so masculine. I've been meaning to ask him what he wears, so I can go to Bloomingdales with Eric and spray it all over myself like some deranged stalker.

"What, no cape?"

With a knowing smirk, he tilts his head doing that sexy thing with his eyes. I mean seriously, I'm imagining wild things involving capes, masks, belts—all in the bat cave.

"It's at the dry cleaners," he playfully responds.

Julian grabs my hand, leading us to a table he has reserved. He slides my jacket off my shoulders, grazing his hand down my arm. I can feel goosebumps forming. This man is going to be my *husband*. Despite my earlier argument with Nikki, I relish the thought of being his wife.

We browse the menu discussing our options before settling for the chef's pick of the day. We chat about work, and I know I need to ask him to be my date for the charity ball on Saturday night, cutting it close.

The food finally arrives, and we devour each bite. Five-star rating from me. I don't know how Eric picks it every time. His gaydar is spot-on when it comes to food and fashion.

There's a moment of silence, my cue to get this over and done with. I'm so hesitant. Now, he'll be attending this important event as my fiancé. Almost like he can sense my hesitation, he lifts my hand to his lips and kisses my engagement ring. I feel my body ease from just his sheer touch.

"I love this ring on you," he murmurs.

"I love that you love this ring on me."

Placing my hand down, he flashes his perfect smile before taking a bite of his food.

"So, there's this thing on Saturday night. I'm wondering

if maybe you might be interested in going with me? I know you've said you hate mingling with the elite unless it's for a scoop—"

"The charity ball?" he asks, trying to keep a straight face.

"Um, yes, how did you know?"

"Eric already had me fitted for a suit. I was just waiting to see how long I'd have to wait before you asked." He chuckles.

I grab my napkin, swatting him across the arm. "I can't believe you! So, all this time I was nervous for nothing?" I laugh at my own stupidity.

"I'm sorry, it's just that you looked so cute all nervous and jittery. I thought it was because of the ring." He takes my hand, slowly kissing my knuckles. "Don't worry, I got my punishment. Do you know Eric made me try on twenty suits yesterday? I'm not exaggerating. And he made me walk up and down the store, posing in what can only be described as Zoolander's Blue Steel pose."

I burst out laughing again. That's so Eric. I have seen him do this to Rocky a thousand times. He channels his inner Tim Gunn. It's hands-down, the funniest thing ever.

"Oh, Julian, I know... oh... this is hilarious. I'm so sorry," I stumble out, unable to contain my laughter.

"Then he kept saying, 'Make it work, people!' By that point, I was like, 'What people? It's only me.'"

I'm on the verge of peeing my pants, and the funniest part is I remember how serious Eric is when he says it, standing there with his arms folded.

My head falls back, the ripple of laughter contagious between us. Julian is good at not taking himself too seriously, it's another thing I love about him.

"You're so beautiful when you laugh, Charlie. Make it five."

"Five what?"

"Kids."

This time, I relax. It doesn't terrify me. This man is perfect and I want his babies, all five of them. Who cares what other people think about us moving too fast? When it is right, it's right. Nothing will stand in our way, and I'm going to make damn sure it stays that way.

"Okay. Five," I agree, raising my glass to take a sip of wine. "But you realize our sex life will be spurts of random quickies in silence? At least that's what Nikki keeps telling me."

His smile widens. He pulls me in and kisses me as much as you can kiss a person in a crowded restaurant without being asked to leave.

"I love you, Charlie Mason, mother of my future five children."

A cold chill runs down my back—an odd feeling like when you know you're being watched, or when you are watching ghost hunters and you're trying not to shit your pants because you can feel a presence in the room. Calming myself down, I scan my surroundings. On my right is a couple arguing. I can tell it's about another woman, the words 'wandering cock' are said loud enough the people behind me turn and look. I divert my eyes straight past Julian where some Japanese tourists are holding up sushi in chopsticks against the light, examining the rolls. It's funny until an older lady looks at me, shaking her head in disappointment. Bored with them, I then gaze to my left.

With an incredulous stare, my posture suddenly stiffens, every muscle in my body turning rigid. My head begins to spin, cold sweats breaking out beneath my loose blouse. I blink my eyes, begging this hallucination to run its course.

But it doesn't, and staring directly at me are those eyes, those emerald eyes.

This can't be happening, not here, not now.

Suddenly, I begin to panic, my chest tightening as my breaths become quicker, suffocating my ability to come up for air. My stomach twists in knots, the urge to vomit lingering with everything else. This is a figment of my imagination. It has to be.

"Would you excuse me? I need to use the restroom."

I get up from my chair so fast it almost topples over and walk straight to the restroom, avoiding eye contact with anyone by keeping my head bowed. I hear him call my name, and trying to ignore him, the adrenaline runs through me with every step I take.

Hands grasp around my arm, and that surge shocks me causing me to whimper slightly. Only his touch has ever made me feel this way, and against my better judgment I turn around to face my demon.

"I looked for you after you left," he says, his voice haunting me as he speaks.

Is this him? His accent is virtually British, there's only a slight hint of American. This doesn't sound like him. Why would he have a British accent? I'm at a loss as to what to say. He looked for me? It's not impossible to find me.

The fury is bubbling up inside of me like a raging storm ready to strike lightning into the sky. My cheeks burn, no doubt flushed as I struggle to hold back my emotions. I had imagined what this moment would be like a thousand times over, each time the speech became longer and longer. I want him to feel pain, to scar him like he did to me. I want to break him, but my tongue is tied. The words won't form, and I blurt out the first thing which comes to mind. "Obviously, not hard enough!"

Alex narrows his eyes, confused, and almost speechless. I never thought in a million years our paths would cross again. Yet, here I am, angry and hurt, but most of all, trying to ignore how beautiful he still is.

He's towering over me in a black suit, crisp white shirt, and a dark blue tie. His hair is just as I remember it, a bronze-tinted color though cut slightly shorter and slicked to the side. My gaze wanders to his perfectly sculpted face with a strong jawline, cleanly shaven, showing off his tanned skin. The emerald in his eyes sparkles as he continues to stare at me like he's searching for something.

He wants to 'talk,' but there's nothing left to say.

Words can't erase what perhaps feels like lifetime filled with hurt and sorrow.

I deny what we were nine years ago because it's easier this time to push him away.

For a moment, I think he's changed as we speak, that maybe he has matured and grown past what we were. Maybe he just wants to say hello and be civil—that is until he mentions Julian.

Acting defensively, trying to protect my newfound relationship, I fire back at him with a barrage of hurtful comments.

I want him to feel the pain I have felt for years.

I want him to understand how much hurt he's caused me.

And more than anything, I want to scream at him for everything he has put me through.

But instead, I say a simple goodbye and walk away.

My heart sinks as a wave of guilt washes over me.

It's done, Charlie, I tell myself. *It's so done.*

Clenching my jaw unknowingly, I quickly muster up a smile, trying my best not to show Julian how angry I am, but I'm completely shaken. I can barely walk back, let alone think about finishing my meal. I need to get out of here right now.

"Are you okay, gorgeous? You look a bit flushed."

Julian pours some water into my glass, and suddenly my throat is very dry. I drink the entire glass of water, the feeling of nausea still churning in the pit of my stomach.

"I'm fine. I just nearly tripped over this lady's handbag she had lying on the ground, but I recovered without too much embarrassment." Inside my lie, I force a smile again. "Do you mind if we head out? I forgot I have a client meeting in an hour which I haven't prepared for."

"Of course not, gorgeous."

I offer to pay the bill, but he refuses, typical guy thing, of course. We begin to walk away from the table, and for a split second, my eyes meet his.

Those eyes that haunt me in my sleep.

Those eyes I can't escape no matter how hard I try.

Those eyes that stole my heart and never truly gave it back.

Those eyes which belong to the one and only *Alexander Edwards*.

Seeing him again takes me back to places I vowed never to return to, the pain I no longer allow myself to feel. Why does life want to throw a giant curveball when it's just starting to feel right? I'm the person standing in the middle of the crowd, and the only one to get crapped on by a bird flying past.

That sums my life up in one neat package.

Yet, I can't get out of my head the way he looks, the way he sounds, the way he smells. It's all surreal like I'm sitting in the DeLorean from *Back to the Future*, transporting back nine years ago, and there I am again. There he is again. How did this happen? And just a day after Julian proposed to me?

All afternoon I find myself in a daze, unable to rid my mind of what happened earlier. I try to busy myself with work, but it's futile. By four o'clock, Nikki barges into my office and knows straight away something is wrong.

"Okay, Spit it out. What's wrong with you?"

"Nikki, something happened today," I muffle out with my head buried in my hands. "I didn't really want to mention it, but it's eating me up inside."

"What is it?"

I raise my head, taking a deep breath. "I ran into an ex while I was at lunch with Julian."

"Sounds awkward."

"Yes, it was, but it's kind of more than that. I can't really explain it. There's a lot of history between us, and we ended on bad terms."

"Wait, is this Alex?" she questions, trepidation in her tone.

"Yes... but how do you know his name?"

"Honey, I've known you for eight years. In that time, I could give you a list of guys you've been with, none of them I believe were anyone special. Except in college, all you would talk about in your sleep was this Alex guy. I knew there was something there, but I never asked. I figured if you wanted to talk about it, you would."

"I didn't know I did that," I whisper, surprised. "It's weird, I never in a million years expected to run into him. Now that I have, I have so many questions I need answered. I hate that it took me forever to move on, and now this wound has opened up again.

"Sounds to me like you need closure. Did you get his number?"

"No. It took me by surprise. I said some things, not nice things. I need to forget about this, right? In a city with this many people, what are the chances of running into him again?"

"I don't know, a million to one. Charlie, you obviously have unresolved feelings. You can't have a future with Julian if you don't sort out your past."

I understand what she's trying to say, but I thought I had let go of the past. Nikki knows me too well.

Placing her arm around me, she reminds me of our fitting tomorrow night, taking my mind off today's events for like one minute.

It's so over between Alex and me.

Just like Nikki said—what are the chances of running into him again?

A million to one.

TWELVE

Nine Years Ago

amn this stupid car.

D I turned my key, the ignition stalling as I attempted to start it. Of all days, it had to happen today. It was pouring outside, and I didn't want to have to get out of the car in the rain, but it looked like I had no other choice.

It was now or never.

I opened the door as fast as I could, pulling the hood up to inspect the battery. My dad had taught me a bit about engines and cars. I knew enough to know the sound of the car meant the battery was dead. Fuck! And my phone had died because I was too busy texting all day at school. Serves me right for getting caught up in the gossip Adriana kept firing at me.

My car was parked around the back of the school, the parking lot now empty as students had left over an hour ago. I hung out at the library studying for my finals until the librarian had some sort of emergency and she'd asked me if she could close early. I ran back around and sat in the car, placing my head against the steering wheel.

This day totally blew.

There was a tap on the window.

Startled, I looked up and saw Alex. He was still wearing his scrubs and it left me tongue-tied. I never thought anyone could look so hot in medical attire, but then again, he could make a potato sack look good.

"Let me guess, dead battery?"

"I think so. Do you normally drive past the school looking for girls and broken-down cars?" I asked, cautiously, with the window slightly open.

"Geez, Charlotte, lay off *America's Most Wanted*. I'm guessing you watched that episode last week with that schoolgirl and the knife-wielding psychopath?"

Dropping his head under the hood, he tinkered with the battery then walked back over to the window. Stretching his arm in, he attempted to start the ignition. It made the same churning sound.

"Okay, dead battery it is. I have jumper cables at my place. We can go get them, so we can at least get your car started and get you home."

"It's okay, I can wait here."

He stared at me, confused by my cautious expression. "But didn't you watch the episode with that girl standing by the bus stop when a bus pulled over with the escaped prisoners?"

Yeah, I had. Damn him to point that out. It was still daylight, though it wouldn't be too long until the sun disappeared, so my nerves were getting the better of me.

"Okay, fine, let's go," I huffed, annoyed. "But you're following me home in case someone comes along and tampers with something else."

I locked my car and climbed into his black Jeep. I was drenched and my lips started to tremble as the cold took hold of me.

Alex turned the heat up in his car and took his scrub top off, wearing only a white wife-beater underneath. I couldn't help but look, obviously. He leaned over to the back seat and grabbed a Jersey with the name *Edwards* scrawled across the back and he tossed it over to me. "Here, put this on."

"No, it's okay. I'm fine, Alex," I replied, not very convincingly as my teeth chattered.

"I'm not taking no for an answer. Change into this, or you're going to catch a cold, let alone the flu. There's a bad case of this unknown virus making rounds. I'll turn around." He spun to face the driver's side window, allowing me some privacy.

I faced the opposite side of him, slowly pulling my top off. Even my bra was soaked. I undid the hooks and quickly pulled the jersey over me while I swiped off my bra. Not a bad effort in a small confinement. Suddenly, the atmosphere changed as I looked over at Alex, his face was in turmoil. Yeah, okay, I'd let this one go. I was half-naked for a second, and he was a hot-blooded guy despite the wedding band on his finger.

"Better?"

He leaned over and brushed away a wet lock of hair from my face. Suddenly, the car felt hot, the air was charged, my cheeks blushing from the rise in temperature. Whether it was from the heat or his touch, I couldn't tell.

We pulled up to his house. It was a small cottage in a secluded part of the town, very cute, reminded me a lot of Hansel and Gretel. He opened the front door, turning on the light. I followed him through the hallway as he continued to switch on some lights.

"Samantha isn't home. She's in San Francisco for the night babysitting her nephew." He looked over, watching my reaction. I was relieved. Not that I was doing anything wrong, but there was something about him that made me feel comfortable. I felt my body relax.

"Nice place. It's very cozy."

We entered the living room, my eyes drawn to the enormous fireplace nestled against the back wall.

"It'll do for now. Unfortunately, my wife doesn't seem to think it's good enough."

"I'd love a place like this. But then, again, I love fireplaces. Nothing beats curling up in front of one reading a good book."

"You don't sound like a normal teenager." He laughed.

"Define normal?"

"Well, definitely, not my sister," he chastised. "I'll be back in a sec. I'll try to find these jumper leads. Help yourself to anything in the kitchen if you're hungry."

Alone in the living room, I walked over to the mantelpiece to look at the picture frames that sat perfectly aligned. There was one of Alex on his graduation day standing proudly with his mom and dad, another of Alex and Adriana when they were kids. It was adorable. They were both wearing cowboy hats and holding up an ice cream cone with three scoops. It looked enormous compared to them. There were a few others which I assumed were of Samantha and her sisters. The one that caught my eye was the one of them on their wedding day. She looked stunning in her dress. Her face was radiant as she looked into his eyes. Alex was holding her, his eyes a different shade of emerald than what I normally saw. I had no idea how that was even possible.

Despite that, he looked happy, and I reminded myself again to ignore these feelings that were starting to build inside me. My focus needed to be on my grades if I wanted to attend an ivy league school next year.

"I found them," he murmured, standing close behind me.

We weren't touching, but the electricity was radiating off him. His slow breaths were blowing against my skin, whooping my body into a frenzy. I closed my eyes, just for a second, allowing myself to live in the moment. His face was inches away from mine. I started to panic because this struggle around him was uncharted territory. Until I understood what these feelings were, I needed to keep my distance.

Thankfully, his phone started ringing and broke us from the temptation. He took the call in the kitchen, talking briefly before hanging up and walking back to the living room, though, this time, stopping a few feet away.

"Sorry, that was Samantha, talking my ear off about her nephew." His tone is bitter, and I wasn't sure if it was because of the baby talk or the fact that she called and interrupted us.

"Are you guys thinking about having kids soon?"

I regretted asking almost immediately.

"She wants to, but I think we're way too young." He sighed. Clearly, it was a touchy subject.

Why, oh why, did I open my big mouth and bring this up? Now I had visuals of them having *sex*. I was getting annoyed with myself, and this strange possessive feeling was nagging at me. This jealousy was all kinds of wrong.

"I'm sorry, Alex. I didn't mean to pry."

"No, it's okay. It's just that I'm kind of sick of this topic being brought up. I don't understand why she can't see how young we are. That there are still so many things for us to do before settling down... like our careers, traveling. Are you sure you don't want anything to drink or eat?" he asked politely, changing the subject.

I was starting to feel awkward being here, not with him, just in this place—*her* house. The feeling tormented me, the voices in my head telling me to let it go, walk out, and not look back. "No, I'm fine. We probably should head back. It's getting darker outside."

He grabbed his keys and the jumpers, turning all the lights off before we headed back out to the car. I climbed in, this time the music was low, playing a Bon Jovi ballad. We were awkwardly quiet. Had I done something wrong? I wanted to look at him but was afraid he'd catch me in the act.

"I never got to thank you for helping me out with the whole prom-dress thing. It was quite funny watching Adriana's reaction. Unfortunately, she was a pain in my backside all day, but I'd take that over trying on dresses."

"So, it worked? I'm guessing you'll eventually have to go shopping for one, though, right?"

"Yes, unfortunately, I do. Stupidly, I agreed to go with some guy at school a few months back. I'm still kicking myself for saying yes, but hey, there's always online shopping."

"Who?" he asked, his voice changing tone.

"Who what?"

"Who are you going to prom with?"

"Oh... Carter. He's just a guy I've known pretty much most of high school."

"As in the Evans kid? Good luck with that. The jerk can't even pitch a ball right."

"Wait, are we talking about baseball or sex? Number one, I don't care for sports. Number two, I don't plan to have sex with him. Not every prom needs to end in a cheap rented hotel room, except for your sister."

Whoops, wrong person to bring that subject up with.

"Please don't go into my sister's sex life. In my eyes it doesn't exist nor will it ever."

"It's not that bad. You've got to get used to them being a couple. Sex is no big deal. At least she's with one person. Most girls our age change partners more regularly than underwear."

"Do you change sex partners more often than underwear?"

"Okay, this conversation has now hit an all-time high in awkwardness," I tell him, unable to stop my face from flushing in embarrassment. "No, I don't, but I'm not like all the other eighteen-year-olds. You said that yourself."

We finally arrived at my car, and I couldn't have been more grateful. He opened up the hood and connected the leads on the battery, attaching the other end to his car.

It finally started.

Hallelujah!

Alex removed the cables and shut the hood.

"All done. Sure you'll be okay?"

"I'll be fine." I smiled, relieved I didn't have to call Dad to come help since I knew he was on the road today and wouldn't be home until late. "Thanks for all your help."

Tilting my head upward, I kissed him on the cheek. I caught him by surprise, lingering more than I should have, lost in his scent and the feel of his skin. I pulled away, the loss of contact unbearable.

Alex sighed.

Had he felt it too?

Think of something else, Charlie, anything else. Why is the sky blue? What's the square root of pi? It's working. My inner self high-fived my brain.

"Don't forget, eight tonight. It's the continuation of the hitchhikers who went missing along Route 66."

"You're a twisted little one, Miss Mason," he replied, smirking as he shut my door.

The first thing I did when I got home was jump into a steaming hot shower. I stayed in there for like half an hour allowing the water to relax my muscles. I felt extremely tense, the kind of tense that would usually be eased with a massage. My thoughts drifted again, so I quickly turned off the water. How was I going to get through the night?

I was dressed in my pajamas when I plonked myself on the couch, armed with my bowl of popcorn and a rolling pin. It was my safety blanket, plus it would hurt anyone who came near me. I grabbed my cell, now fully charged, and decided to text Alex to say thank you.

It wasn't the rolling pin that accompanied me to bed that night. It was his hockey jersey. I held onto it tight, inhaling his scent.

Fact—he was married.

But was he happy?

The short conversations we had around this topic indicated that he wasn't, but he was bound to her, in sickness and in health, 'til death do they part and forsaking all others.

I was holding a match, lighting up the kerosene, playing with fire.

So what? We fuck once and that ruins his marriage? I wasn't that type of girl, and what about Adriana? She was my best friend and would never forgive me. These thoughts needed to leave my head. Immature, teenage dreams over someone I couldn't have.

I tossed and turned that night, replaying everything in my mind, falling asleep at the break of dawn.

THIRTEEN

LEX

Present

I sit at the table trying to concentrate on the business meeting.

It's impossible.

I need to take care of things, and my mind has questions that require answering. How the fuck did this happen? Out of all the places in the world, she's here, in New York City, eating Japanese with him, whatever the fuck he is. I have to wrap up the meeting. I need answers *now*.

"Mr. Klein, the numbers you have shown meet our profit expectations. Have your business plan ready for me before I leave on Monday."

"Of course, Mr. Edwards. It was a pleasure doing business with you again," Klein responds.

We all stand, shaking each other's hands. I sign the check and grab my phone, immediately dialing Kate's number, asking her to meet me at the hotel.

Outside the restaurant, I'm greeted by the warm breeze. *How long has she been in Manhattan?* She was all dressed up—fucking hot, actually. I wonder what her profession is? Fuck, I need answers. My mind is scattered, and I'm unable to process anything in my normally controlled fashion.

I hail a cab, not being bothered to call my driver to come pick me up. The cab pulls into the traffic, only to be met with red lights as soon as we turn the corner. Pulling out my phone, I scroll through my contacts until I find his number. Bryce Callahan was recommended by a close business associate and came at a high price. I never asked questions about his background, knowing that his line of work wasn't exactly legal.

"Bryce, it's Edwards. I need you to look into someone for me."

"Yes, Mr. Edwards."

"Charlotte Olivia Mason. She resides here in Manhattan, I assume," I tell him, only realizing this mission could be a needle in a haystack. She could reside in Brooklyn, Long Island, and the possibilities are endless with a state this large.

Bryce asks a few more questions, including her date of birth. I answer everything I can, desperate for anything on her.

"I need this information today. Anything you can get," I demand, not willing to waste any time.

"Yes, Mr. Edwards. I'll call you as soon as I find something."

I end the call, my mind still reeling from the events. Charlotte was angry, and I understand that I left without giving her an explanation, but then again it was nine years ago. I thought she'd be happy to see me, like two long-lost friends, except we weren't two long-lost friends. I promised her things. I promised her a future, and then I had no choice but to walk away, or at least I thought so at the time.

It's just after two when I arrive back at the Waldorf. The cab ride didn't take as long as I expected. Kate's already in the suite typing away on her laptop. As soon as I walk in, she stands to greet me. "Good afternoon, sir."

"Kate, nice of you to be early," I sarcastically respond, considering I'm the one who's actually late.

So, I sound like a prick, but I'm fucking going crazy.

This isn't like me.

I'm always in control.

What has she done to me?

And all this by just seeing and talking to her.

Removing my jacket, I throw it onto the couch and pour myself a bourbon. I don't normally drink during work, but today is different. I could easily down the whole bottle in one gulp if Kate wasn't standing there.

"What's the schedule for next week?" I ask, praying I can stay here.

"Tomorrow night is the charity ball. Your sister will be meeting you here at five o'clock sharp with your tux, and apparently your... um... date, Brooke." She clears her throat, continuing, "On Sunday morning you have another meeting with Mr. Klein to go over your expansion of After Dark. Two o'clock will be another inspection of the new office. Then on Monday morning we catch a red-eye back to London."

I'll have no time to find her or even spend time with her. I pour myself another glass, the first one obviously not doing the trick. The first thought floating through my head is to cancel going to the charity event.

Yes, I'll cancel that.

At least I'll have all Saturday night free to find her.

"Tuesday at eleven is the stakeholder meeting. That's

expected to run until five. The Hilton conference room has been booked for the event."

It has taken us months to organize this meeting. I know I can't get out of it. I grit my teeth as she continues on and based on the schedule she reads out, I won't be back in Manhattan for three weeks.

Pacing the room in short spans, I scrub my hand over my face willing the impending headache to stop. I'm starting to feel like a lovesick teenager except I'm thirty-fucking-four, a successful entrepreneur with money to do whatever the hell I want, which proves absolutely pointless at a time like this.

My phone starts to buzz—it's Bryce—so I make my way into the bedroom and close the door behind me.

"Bryce."

"Mr. Edwards, I have some information regarding Miss Mason."

"Go on..."

"Her current employment is at Mason & Romano where she's a partner in the firm."

"Firm?"

"Yes. She's a lawyer here in Manhattan. The boutique firm is located on Madison Avenue..." he advises, pausing while I listen quietly. "She graduated with honors from Yale."

So, she was in New Haven all that time? Her mother gave me no inkling of that when I went to look for her. I try not to focus on the regret starting to creep in at not finding her and telling her how sorry I was. *Why didn't I try harder? Why didn't I continue until she was in my arms again?*

"Her status is showing single. Never registered as being married."

For now. Anger is boiling inside of me at the thought. Images of the ring flashing before me, my grip on my phone tightens as I try to remain calm to process anything else he has on her.

"She currently owns an apartment in the Upper East Side as well as a home in Connecticut."

"What's the connection in Connecticut?"

"I haven't been able to get a connection yet."

"Thank you, Bryce. Please update me as soon as you find anything else."

I hang up the phone, a little more at ease now because I know more about her. *Yale, wow.* I always knew she was smart, but she never mentioned anything about wanting to be a lawyer. Our last conversations revolving around college was her trying to stay close to home, and after our relationship became more involved, a huge part of that was to stay close to me.

My curiosity piques—all of this is very unlike her.

She always walked away from drama, even at school. Being a lawyer and arguing for a living seems very left of field as her chosen profession. Financially, she appears to be well off, but this house in Connecticut keeps bugging me. It isn't the type of area you would invest in, so why would she own property there?

I walk over to the window, watching the city pass by. All I can think about is the fact that she has become this beautiful woman.

Her attire is another thing I wouldn't have expected—she always hated heels and dressing up. The glasses—oh, fuck me sideways. I stir at the thought, my cock hardening. I need a release, but Kate is outside, and even I have my boundaries. Adjusting my pants, I walk back into the living room.

We spend the afternoon on conference calls with Human Resources regarding the recruiting of the Manhattan office. If all goes according to plan, we'll have a fully functional office in less than two months. Now, more than ever, I want this office up and running, giving me an excuse to spend more time in the city.

By six, I'm done. Kate left to spend the night with a friend she had met in the city, so I decide to go down to the bar in the hotel lobby. It's busy for a Friday night, the usual business crowd letting their hair down after a stressful week. A few young girls are dancing. I sit at the bar and order a scotch. One of the brunettes from the dance floor walks up to the bar, stopping beside me.

"Bartender!" she yells, chuckling while intoxicated.

The bartender stands at the end of the bar, trying his best to chat up another girl. Young people, honestly. If he were under my watch, I'd have fired him on the spot.

"Oh, c'mon, excuse me!"

The bartender looks up, reluctantly walking over to serve the brunette.

"Can I please get another Cosmo?"

She's pretty hot, maybe early twenties. She has long brown hair tied up in a high ponytail while wearing a short, black skirt with a low-cut gold top. Tackily dressed, but she has a nice pair of tits. She waits at the bar before turning my way. Licking her lips, she looks me up and down, not at all ashamed she has made it so obvious.

"Alone tonight?" she asks, her body moving closer to mine as her hand rests on my thigh.

"That depends if you're going to walk back to your posse or stay and drink with me."

I know I sound like a cocky motherfucker but I have

this one in the bag, and I need a release after what happened today.

"You're not from around here? I love a man with an accent." She smirks.

Don't all American women? She looks at me, smiling, her lips covered in bright red lipstick. Jumping off the bar stool, she grabs my hand and drags me through the bar to the restroom at the back. Slowly looking around, she opens the door, pushing me inside. *What a little firecracker.* She grabs my pants, unbuttoning them quickly. Pulling them down, she releases my cock.

"Damn, you're one fine specimen. And this..." she says as she wraps her hand around my cock, "... needs to be in my mouth right now."

I look down, watching her take in all of me until I feel it tap the back of her throat. *Hmm, great gag reflex.* I close my eyes, remembering when Charlotte would do the same, her long brown hair covering me. I grab the chick's hair, lusting over the brown strands, watching her, but all I can see is Charlotte, all I can feel is Charlotte. It doesn't take me long before I need to blow, the girl pulling me out of her mouth as she jerks me off in her hand.

Quickly, she stands then washes her hands as I pull up my pants.

"Well, there's a first time for everything," she says, sounding pretty confident.

I'm amused these young girls think giving head makes them powerful. Quite the opposite. I didn't have to beg for it, darling. Fuck, I didn't have to do anything.

She smiles one more time then exits the bathroom. I walk over to the sink, washing my hands and splashing my face with cold water. *What was I thinking?* It isn't like this hasn't happened before, but I've never allowed myself to think of Charlotte when I was with someone else.

I exit the bar without saying goodbye as I walk past and head back to my suite. I'm so fucked, I need to forget. Why can't I forget? Making my way to the bathroom, I turn the shower onto scalding hot, desperate to wash away what happened downstairs.

I climb into bed, trying to shut down my mind, but I can't. I grab my phone off the nightstand and succumb to what I have put off doing for the last nine years—I type her name into a search engine.

There are random photographs of other girls, but no one who looks like her. I scroll through, desperate to find anything. It must be around the sixth page where I find a small picture. I click on the thumbnail linked to a Yale class website. There's a picture of Charlotte with a guy, Finn. I recognize him immediately. She's smiling, she looks happy.

Were they together after I left?

I can feel the anger brewing again, but I know I have no right to feel this way.

Knowing I have made the situation even worse for myself, I switch off my phone. Why the fuck can't I just let this go? There's too much history between us, and I need her to know how much I regret my actions. At the time I acted like a timid little coward, and I should've followed my instincts. I should have followed my heart.

For nine years, I've buried what we had and drowned myself in my work.

Yes, it paid off, but is it worth it in the end?

"Lex, hold still, or I can't get it in."

Inside my hotel suite, my sister, Adriana, is fussing all over me. The bow tie she bought isn't cooperating, and as usual, it's the biggest emergency ever. My attempt to cancel was foiled by Adriana giving me a list of clients who will be attending and therefore dubbed the event as a huge business opportunity.

I loathe these damn events.

They are just a parade of people showing off who has the biggest checkbook. Fair enough, it's for charity, but these leeches donate so their businesses will be all over the media. I'd have happily donated the money and not attend, but when you're related to Adriana Edwards there's no such luxury.

"Okay, done." She stands back, admiring her work. "You scrub up well, big brother. Thanks to me."

"If it weren't for the suit, I'd have no hope in hell with the ladies." I smirk, but quickly, my expression turns serious. "Listen, Adriana, there's something I need to talk to you about."

"Is it an apology for how you hurt my feelings and left the restaurant in a huff?"

"Uh, no... but I am sorry. Look... you know that wedding bullshit is too much for me."

"Not to anger the beast again, what is it you want to talk to me about?"

I have been putting it off ever since it happened, but now is the time to bring it up. My head is still a mess, and only Adriana knows the whole story. If anyone can make me understand what the hell is going on it's my sister, Charlotte's former best friend.

"What is it?" she repeats, distracted as she fixes herself in the mirror. It's a beautiful navy gown, Valentino, I remember her saying. Like I give a shit, but she still looks good in it.

"I saw Charlotte."

She stops adjusting her dress, her eyes meeting mine in the mirror before she abruptly turns around. "Where and when?" Her voice is anxious. I know what Charlotte meant to Adriana. Their friendship was a big part of her life that I screwed up for her. Another person caught up in the shit-storm I had created.

"I had a lunch meeting the other day. She was there at the restaurant with a guy." I clench on my words, desperately thinking of ways to get rid of him.

"Oh my God, Lex. Seriously? Out of all places, here? Did you speak to her?"

"Yes, I did," I croak, still feeling the sting from her words. "She was angry. I wasn't expecting her to be after all these years. I wanted a chance to explain, but she said not to bother, it was just a high school fling."

"But, Lex, it wasn't just a high school fling..." Adriana trails off, lowering her gaze. "So, you didn't get a chance to explain to her what happened with Samantha and the baby?"

"No, I didn't. She was quick to run off to her... *fiancé.*" I grit my teeth almost spitting out the words.

"Fiancé? How do you know?" I can hear the hope in her voice. Adriana, ever the optimist. "Maybe it was just a friend?"

"The huge ring on her finger was a dead giveaway. I asked, and she angrily answered that he was her fiancé."

"Lex, why did you do that?" Adriana raises her hands in frustration. "You know if she's anything like me, you probably pushed her closer to him."

"Oh gee, thanks, sis. What a wonderful thought to have in my head."

Pacing the area in front of us, I rub my hands over my face, regretting my actions once again. Did I really do that? Push her further toward him? They're engaged for Christ's sake! How much further can I push her? Fuck, this spiral of thoughts is making it all worse. I sit on the couch, bowing my head as I run my fingers through my hair.

"How did she look?"

Staring at the carpet, I try to calm down. My gaze moves upward until my eyes meet Adriana's. "Beautiful."

Our conversation is interrupted as Elijah, Adriana's fiancé, walks in the room followed by an attractive blonde woman.

"Brooke, please meet my brother-in-law, Lex," he introduces, forcing me to stand. "Lex, this is Brooke."

She's beautiful, short blonde hair, blue eyes—I'm not interested.

There's only one woman I want now, but I act like the gentleman my mother raised me to be.

Leaning in, I kiss Brooke's cheek with a welcoming smile. After a quick chat, it's time to head out. I linger behind her as my sister quickly pulls me aside.

"Lex, I know you're hurting. I promise we'll talk more about this later," Adriana whispers, patting my shoulder as we leave the room.

Hurt?

Is that what this is?

First, after I saw her, I wanted to apologize more than anything. Second, I wanted to fuck the living daylights out of her, feel myself inside her just like I had a million times in my head.

But now, I'm torn as my emotions wreak havoc within me.

I don't know what to do, but for tonight, I'll do what I do best—act like the arrogant CEO I'm known for. Better than a sad, pathetic loser pining for his ex.

FOURTEEN

CHARLIE

We arrive at the ball at six on the dot.

The street is crowded, lined with limousines and luxury vehicles worth more than my apartment. Flashes are going off right, left, and center. The paparazzi are scurrying around like rats up a drainpipe snapping away at those who pose on the red carpet.

As we walk through the large doors, we're blown away by the sight of it all. The grand ballroom is enormous. Its size big enough to hold all of the elite in New York City and then some.

The tall ceilings are covered in rows of draped sheer organza fabric, creating a medieval feel with a modern twist. A large chandelier hangs from the middle, its crystals reflecting the light which shimmers on the dance floor. Scattered across the room are artificial trees with the branches draped in fairy lights.

There's a band wearing black and white tuxedos, perfectly positioned on the stage playing soft swing music, their hums and beats drowning in the noise of the growing crowd.

More and more people enter the room, their gowns becoming more exquisite as they strut into the area. *I'm in heaven.* One after another, I can name the designer in my head. I know Eric is doing it as well, his mannerisms are mirroring mine.

I spot the head organizer of the charity ball, Mrs. Clyde, almost immediately. She reminds me of Meryl Streep in *The Devil Wears Prada.* Only in her appearance, mind you, as she's the sweetest lady you could possibly meet. Her generosity never ceases to amaze me, and all this is because of her.

"Oh-em-gee, you guys, this is amazeballs," Eric murmurs in awe.

With his phone in hand, he takes a few pictures then busily begins typing away.

"What are you doing?"

"Just taking a pic of the ballroom. There's a hash-tag charity ball trending."

I grab the phone off him, placing it in my purse. Eric needs to enjoy the night without being glued to his phone. I can see the withdrawals already, his left eye twitching with a pouty immature look.

"Oh, c'mon, Charlie," he whines.

"Uh-uh. I'm confiscating this from you tonight. You asked Emma out on a date, albeit fake, and you need to show her a good time."

Emma laughs, looking gorgeous in a red gown Eric chose for her. Her platinum blonde hair is styled in an up-tight bun, showcasing a stunning diamond necklace draped around her neck.

Eric will only last five minutes before hijacking my purse as Emma kindly points out, and I agree. His sulking is short-lived, immediately snapping out of his childish tantrum as a hot young waiter stands in front of us offering champagne.

We take in the amazing view before we're ushered to our table by a different waiter. We sit ourselves down as Julian places his arm around my chair, drawing me in closer. He smells fantastic.

"You look amazing tonight," he whispers in my ear.

"Not so bad yourself, Batman. Are you going to abandon me tonight with some emergency that needs to be taken care of on the roof?"

"Unless it's you up there naked, no chance in hell, gorgeous," he teases, leaving a kiss on the side of my neck.

My body is shivering in delight, my mind wondering how I can get on the roof. Is there some secret exit? Damn, he looks fine in his tux. *Tim Gunn knew his stuff.*

Mrs. Clyde takes to the podium to begin her speech as the room starts to go quiet. She speaks about the cause and what we, as a society, can do to help the kids live a better life. We applaud her, then everyone gets up to start mingling as the music continues playing.

People are lost in diverse conversations. Occasionally, I'll smile and nod, but my head feels like it's buried in a cloud of fog. Two days and it is just getting worse, now I am questioning my sanity. *Did that really happen? Did I run into Alexander Edwards after nine years? Or was it just a figment of my imagination?* I've barely slept, running on an empty fuel tank which doesn't mix well with champagne.

Taking a deep breath, I remember my promise to myself to have fun. Forget the past, enjoy the night with my fiancé.

This event is a once-in-a-lifetime opportunity and shouldn't be wasted on something I can't control.

I'm standing with Julian, talking to Mrs. Bennett, who's one of the committee members. Julian has his arm around my waist, talking passionately about a story he covered in a Hungarian orphanage. I can't stop watching him as he speaks, his face showing compassion, a truly amazing man. Batman has nothing on him. He's everything I want in a man, and I deserve someone like this.

Breaking me from my daydream, Eric and Emma come up behind me with champagne in hand.

"Charlie, have you seen the eye candy around here?" Emma says, scanning the area around us. "Lucky day to be single."

Rocky and Nikki join us, arguing as usual. They turned up late, and after a quick hello all round, I question why both of them look annoyed. Rocky probably left the toilet seat up or something stupid like that.

"Okay, Mr. and Mrs. Smith, what's wrong now?"

"You remember that girl I dated in college when Nikki and I broke up that first semester?" Rocky speaks cautiously as Nikki stands there, arms crossed, tapping her foot.

"What do you mean, dated? You screwed her once behind the bleachers after you won that game against Princeton," I point out, chuckling.

"Thank you," Nikki blurts out.

Sometimes my memory is too clear. This time it works for me but usually it's against me.

"Oh, well, gee, I thought we dated. Anyway, she's here, and Miss Drama Queen over here has a problem with it." He rolls his eyes, frustrated at his wife.

Nikki ignores him, jealousy looking extra special on her tonight as she wears a glamorous gold Versace gown.

"Aww, is Mrs. Romano jealous?" I mock, my expression changing from sympathy to utter annoyance. "Please, Nikki, you're one hot piece of ass. You can run circles around these chicks. Plus, you'll be the one tapping it tonight, not her."

"Thank you!" Rocky rejoices.

The corner of Nikki's mouth turns upward into a smile, prompting Rocky to lean in and whisper in her ear. She turns to face him, locking lips as his hands wander to her butt, grabbing it porno-style.

"Seriously, get a room. Or a bathroom cubicle. Or something."

The moment I say it, they quickly walk off toward the exit. I wonder how she'll get that dress off? *Mental note to ask her later*.

I can hear Emma and Eric whispering the words 'big hands' and 'I wouldn't kick him out of bed' but they are quite audible. I start to laugh. Eric always keeps things entertaining. I'm so grateful to be surrounded by amazing friends and a very handsome fiancé who I plan to tie up Cat-Woman-style later tonight at his apartment.

"Ten o'clock, Charlie. Oh damn, he's the shiz. Wow. Oh, crap, he saw me." Eric drops his eyes toward his shoes, pretending to be talking about something else.

"Ten oh what, Eric?" I ask, confused.

Eric nods his head toward the left.

I look, hoping to get a glimpse of this so-called ten o'clock candy. My head takes a moment to catch up with what my eyes see.

Green emerald candy which belongs to the one and only *Alexander Edwards*.

My mouth falls open, eyes widening, unable to turn away. Like a bad car crash, only it's the opposite, the most beautiful sight you could possibly imagine walking toward me.

Oh shit, he's walking toward me.

With a sudden urge to run, escape, and hide, the realization of his presence cripples my ability to do anything besides standing there, frozen in place. There's no way out of this.

"Charlotte, what a nice surprise to see you, again," he greets, politely.

My legs are threatening to cave. Alex is dressed in a black tuxedo with a bow tie, and I'm trying to ignore everything about him, but he looks so perfect. His accent is unfamiliar yet equally as mesmerizing, and it matches the handsome man standing before me.

But this man, in all his perfect glory, is nothing but a *stranger*.

His eyes are shining bright emerald, his face lighting up with a smile flashing his perfectly straight white teeth. I try to think of something witty to say, hoping someone will rescue me. Eric and Emma remain quiet, their mouths wide open like fly-catchers in shock. These two are pathetic.

Julian stops talking to Mrs. Bennett, switching his attention to me, then Alex.

Fuck, okay. Get your shit together. This can go really bad. Or, if you play nice, go away real fast.

"Alex, this is Eric, my assistant, Emma, one of my colleagues, and Julian, my fiancé," I rush, trying to push aside my nerves.

Why is he so calm and collected? I appear to be the only one panicked by this situation.

Julian extends his hand. "Lex Edwards, CEO of the Lexed Group?"

Lex? Why is he calling him Lex Edwards? How the

hell does Julian know him? Tilting my head to the side, curiosity overshadows my anxiety.

"Yes, the last time I checked," Alex answers, surprisingly shaking Julian's hand.

"How do you and Charlie know each other?" Julian questions, taking his hand off my waist to hold my hand.

I can hear Eric's voice in my head, hoping this is where they both slap their dicks out and start to measure them. Dirty bastard, and as the rascally grin forms on Eric's smug face, so I know I'm dead right.

Alex stares at Julian, his face showing no emotion. Maybe I'm wrong about him. Just maybe he has matured and moved past what happened. Moved past us. What if he's a happily married man with a family? Don't get ahead of yourself, and where on earth did that pang of jealousy come from?

"We've known each other for what... fifteen years? Since we were kids. We dated in high school," he answers with a cocky grin, knowing exactly what he's doing.

Alex is signing the contract for the pissing contest that's just about to start. Of course, he had to add that last bit. I'm not sure I'd call it dating, but more like fucking around behind his wife's back. So, I take back what I said about him maturing. Just like old times Alex, except this time I'm not going to be the sad girl on the side. I'm a woman now, and no man treats me any less than what I deserve.

Now the nerves are overtaken by anger. If we weren't in public, I'd have probably punched that beautiful face of his for talking to me like an arrogant bastard. Like the past was nothing. Like he didn't leave me in the worst pain imaginable.

"I've written a couple of pieces on Lexed. You may

have read the one published in the *Wall Street Journal* last year?" Julian speaks highly of his work, but what catches my attention is the fact that Alex is CEO of the Lexed Group.

Of course, I have heard of the company, I mean, who hasn't? But I had no idea Alex had anything to do with it. What didn't make sense is that he's no longer in the medical field. My curiosity is getting the better of me. I want to know more, but I don't want to have a conversation with him or even give him the satisfaction of thinking I'm interested.

"Ah, yes, quite an interesting article."

"So, Alex, are you from New York? Your accent is very Hugh Grant. God, I loved him in *Notting Hill*. Anyway, love your Armani suit," Eric rambles on.

For God's sake, Eric's obsession with older British men is borderline creepy. Hugh Grant? I know what Eric is trying to do, though. He has that mischievous look on his face, the one he has every time he's trying to get me laid. *But Batman's fucking me,* I want to yell at him.

"Actually, it's Lex. Not Alex," he corrects Eric, never breaking my gaze.

Pretentious bastard.

Fine, if he wants to play that game, I'll treat him like we have no past. Therefore, Alex no longer exists. It will be Lex, just like he wants it.

He continues, "I live in London. Our Manhattan office is currently being remodeled, so I'm planning to stay here for a while."

So, he lives in London, totally explains the hot accent. The distance is somewhat comforting, but then he said he'll be in Manhattan more often. The city isn't that big, not when your ex is suddenly lurking around every damn corner.

Again, the cogs are turning, and I think to myself, why London? I need to stop asking myself these questions. I don't need to know anything about him. He shouldn't be in my life in the first place. Period.

"And thank you, my sister chose the suit. She lives and breathes fashion. I'll introduce you later."

"Adriana is here?" I ask, nervously.

I haven't seen her since the day when she asked me to leave her family alone, in the middle of a busy street, and straight-out called me a *whore*. The past is quickly coming back to me like a freight train, and I don't know what to do.

Scanning the room, I don't see Adriana anywhere.

Surely, Alex has to know how uncomfortable all this is for me.

"Somewhere floating around with Elijah."

"Her and Elijah are still together?"

I don't know why I asked or why I'm surprised. Those two were destined to be together, but then again, I thought that about Alex, I mean Lex and me, once upon a time.

"Yes, they're still together. I don't think anyone else could put up with her. They live in Brooklyn. Adriana owns a boutique store downtown."

The music softens as the MC announces dinner is about to be served. People start walking back to their tables, and as I follow Julian, Eric, and Emma, Alex's hand wraps around my arm. Reluctantly, I turn around slowly.

Avoid his scent.

And avoid his eyes.

Taking a deep breath, I wait on edge for his words, knowing that whatever comes out of his beautiful mouth, will turn my world upside down. Leaning closer into me, I force my eyes to remain open.

"You look breathtaking, Charlotte," he whispers in my ear before walking away.

Somehow, I manage to walk toward the table without my legs giving way or gushing all over the floor. I'm annoyed at myself for even thinking of him that way.

Breathe, pull yourself together, and remember whose ring is weighing down your left hand.

"Are you okay, gorgeous?" Julian runs his finger down my cheek, staring at me lovingly.

"I will be soon." I smile, eyeing the waiters walking toward us. "Champagne and no food are a lethal combination."

We chat as we eat our meals, and thankfully, Julian doesn't bring up my history with Lex. Everyone is impatiently waiting for the guest singer to appear later in the evening. I look at my plate, a sudden loss of appetite as I close my eyes, his words echoing in my mind. *You look breathtaking, Charlotte.* I still can't believe he's here, not to mention Adriana. I'll bet all the money in my checking account, she's still angry with me. What will I say to her?

A cold gush of air sweeps across my skin, causing me to break out into goosebumps like I'm being watched. Alex, sorry Lex, can be sitting anywhere in this room, and wherever that may be, his stare will be boring into me and questioning me in a million and one ways of why I'm engaged to Julian without opening his mouth.

"So that's him?" Nikki whispers in my ear.

She's sitting on my right, Julian on my left. Thank God, Eric is telling some ridiculous and probably inappropriate story, which has Julian's full attention.

"Yes, it is."

"In a million years. What a coincidence. Okay, for the record, he acts like an arrogant prick. But damn, Charlie... hello, Momma. He must be huge. Is he?"

"Oh, geez." I laugh, welcoming her shallow question. "Eric is so rubbing off on you."

Nikki rubs my shoulder, knowing how tense I am and offers a sympathetic smile.

After the next course is served, and people finish their meals, the clusters of groups start forming again. The dance floor is filling up with the band playing 'The Way You Look Tonight.' Classic Frank, classic New York.

"Babe, let's show these rich folks how it's done." Rocky takes Nikki's hand as she follows him onto the dance floor.

Eric and Emma have already left the table. I can see them across the room hovering around Sarah Jessica Parker. *How predictable,* I think. If I know Eric, he will bombard her about *Sex and the City* questions like 'who was the biggest bitch on set' or 'why did she agree to wear those knee-high socks with heels.'

"Penny for your thoughts?" Julian asks, placing his hand on mine. "You're quiet."

I lean over and gaze into his warm hazel eyes. It isn't fair to him, this whole Lex thing, except there's nothing going on but in my crazy imagination.

"I'm just thinking how nice it would be to have you all to myself on the dance floor."

"Well, gorgeous, you'll be happy to know I'm thinking the same thing." He grins.

Julian stands, and like the true gentleman he is, he holds out his hand as I place mine in his.

"Gorgeous, do you know how happy you make me?"

"Mmm... the same as how happy you make me?" I smile, allowing his loving gaze to consume me.

His face relaxes like he's been waiting all night to hear those words. "I like hearing you call me your fiancé."

"I could've introduced you as my partner, but that sounds like we're lesbian lovers or something."

"I won't object to eating you out all the time," he teases.

"Neither would I."

I've always loved the banter between us, never taking our relationship too seriously. It's one of the best things about our relationship—the butterflies over such simple conversation, except tonight, my happy butterflies are battling, or more like knocking the living shit out of the nauseous ones. I'm not doing anything wrong, so why do I feel so guilty?

We laugh as we dance, his body against mine. I close my eyes, enjoying this moment of bliss. *Make this work, Charlie,* I keep chanting in my head. I deserve someone who will love me and only me.

"Mind if I cut in? For old time's sake?"

The blood drains from my body as *he* speaks the words. It's one thing to talk to him but another to be in close physical contact.

Julian narrows his eyes with a pinched expression, but being the gentleman he is, he quickly kisses my cheek and tells me he will be over by the bar. Lex grabs my hand without consideration for Julian leaving and places the other on my hip. The tightness in my chest causes my smile to waver. The sheer touch of him is causing a massive meltdown inside. He smells just like I remember—home.

Careful not to close my eyes, I refuse to go back to that place. What was once a meadow filled with love, promises, and sunshine has become a dungeon torturing me with pain. Nine years of trying to escape him, and now, he's holding onto me on the dance floor as if nothing ever happened between us.

I dance quietly, the band singing 'How Deep Is Your Love' by the Bee Gees. Trying to focus on anything besides him, the lyrics sound in my head, making the moment more intense than it should be. The band needs to switch it up, play some heavy metal rather than a song about belonging to each other.

"Charlotte, you really do look beautiful. Your favorite color, I see."

I still remember when I told him emerald was my favorite color on the dance floor at prom night. This is déjà vu, only this time without the happy ending in the class-room. The memories, all of which have been bottled up, begin to leak painfully slow.

Pulling away, slightly, to distance myself from him, I stare him right in the eye. "What do you want, Lex?"

"I see you at the restaurant, and you ran from me. I run into you again, and you avoid me. Can't two long-lost friends catch up after nine years?"

"Why do you keep saying we were friends? Because from memory, you upped and left. Friends don't do that."

"But we are, or should I say were? According to you, it was just a fling. It meant nothing," he deadpans.

He has me there. I was kidding myself by saying that, but I wanted more than anything for him to believe it. Why should he have the satisfaction of knowing how much pain he put me through? The jerk ruined my life. And I've spent a long time trying to fix what he so easily broke.

I quickly change the subject. Now isn't the time nor the place to dig up old memories, and I don't want Julian staring at us, wondering why my face looks ready to attack.

"Why are you here, anyway?"

"One reason... Adriana. She drags me to these things and makes me donate a shitload of money."

"So, you're no longer practicing medicine?"

"There's so much we need to talk about, Charlotte. I don't think the dance floor at this charity ball is the place. Meet me for a drink tonight and we can talk properly then."

He sounds so controlling. I mean, he always had that trait, but now I look at him differently. The weak man who chose his wife over me, instead of fighting for what he claimed he always wanted. I ignore his comment, avoiding being alone with him at all costs.

"How long have you and Julian been together?"

And there it is.

I've been waiting for him to bring up Julian.

The anger takes over again, ruining the moment. "Why, Lex? Does it matter? What about you? I'm guessing you're no longer with Samantha since you hooked up with another blonde."

I can feel the temperature in the room rise, or maybe it's just me.

"Calm down, Charlotte. Samantha and I are no longer married, and Adriana set me up with Brooke for tonight only."

This feeling of jealousy is an emotion I'm no longer accustomed to. I have no right questioning his personal relationships like he has no right questioning mine.

"Why do you ask?" A smirk widens across his face. "Are you jealous?"

Some nerve. Thankfully, the band stops playing, and the crowd ceases dancing to applaud them. Releasing my hand from his grip, I take the opportunity to say goodbye. "Thank you for the dance, Lex."

Walking away, I leave him alone on the dance floor,

spotting Rocky and Nikki standing by our table. I need my friends to drag me kicking and screaming into the present. These flashbacks are getting the better of me, and I know it's a vicious cycle to fall into.

"Some dance partner you got there, Charlie." Rocky snickers.

"Who Ale... I mean Lex?"

"Uh, yeah, Lex Edwards. Billionaire CEO. Mr. Playboy. You might be his first brunette."

"How do you know all this?"

"Charlie, he's always in the social section, you know... who he's dating, what he's wearing."

"Hold up. You read the social section?" I question, trying to hold in my laughter.

"Yes, but if it makes you feel any better, he's not seeing anyone now."

Surprisingly, it does make me feel better, but I quickly swallow the feeling. Why do I even care?

"Can I have my girl back?" Julian's arms wrap around my waist. He rests his head on my shoulder, holding onto me tight, kissing the side of my neck. I wrap my arm behind his head, welcoming his touch with a loving smile.

But inside, the wall I built up many years ago has begun to crack.

And across the room Lex's eyes find mine, his gaze stripping me bare. His lips are pulled back, baring his teeth with a vehement expression.

With every ounce of strength I have within me, I turn away, moving my body so I'm face to face with Julian.

This is the man I'm going to marry.

This is the man I am going to spend the rest of my life with.

I tilt my head, moving my lips toward Julian as I desperately kiss him whole. As we both pull away, I gaze into his caring eyes and remind myself of who I love.

But my heart falls silent, the silence screaming of my weakness.

And just like that, Lex's voice lingers in my ear, tearing down the wall of its last pillar of strength.

FIFTEEN

CHARLIE

"**G**orgeous, when do I get to make you my wife?"

Julian breaks my thoughts, and unknowingly, I need the reality check more than ever. We haven't spoken about the actual wedding planning, given he only proposed days ago, but deep down inside I question whether he senses my hesitation and is trying to steer me back in the right direction.

"That depends. Are you going to whisk me away to your bat cave now?"

He grins, pulling me closer toward his body. "For you, anything."

Lost in this moment, filled with promises of a new life together, I smile as I hold onto him. I need, more than anything, to feel wanted, to feel loved. My eyes meet with Lex's across the room. He's never broke from my gaze. The guilt is rushing through me, torn in ways I never imagined would happen again.

But this time, the tables have turned and I have someone to call my own. I'm not the person looking in from the outside, racking my brain as to what went on behind closed doors.

Finally, I'm happy, my world no longer broken. Looking at Lex, I know I can't go back there. Every happy memory I have of him is overshadowed by the tragic ending. I can't look at him without dragging up our past. What we had isn't some high school crush, no matter how much I tried to sell that story to myself.

"Charlie?"

I turn and see Adriana standing next to me. The one person who meant so much to me but again, she hurt me, leaving me to clean up my mess. Judging me when she only knew half the truth.

"It's y-you." Her voice quivers, the emotion building up as she attempts to get her words out. "Charlie... I'm so, so sorry." Tears trickle down her beautiful face, her eyes clouded with tears. She was young at the time and had done what most girls would do. Yet, I couldn't ignore the hurt of her betrayal for leaving me behind without allowing me even to explain myself.

But I was the one who had played with fire, or should I say her brother.

I let go of Julian, wrapping my arms around her into a tight embrace, willing to forgive her so we can resurrect our friendship. Everything about her feels familiar, and for a second, I wonder if this is what it would feel like to be inside Lex's arms.

"Adriana, please stop crying. You'll ruin your mascara and mine." I chuckle as a tear slides down my cheek.

Her smile radiates. Adriana has always had beautiful classic features with almond-shaped green eyes, not quite as bright as Lex's yet similar since they are related. The last time I'd seen her, the color of her hair had been natural mocha. True to her always-changing style, she had changed it to honey blonde with ombre running through it.

"I'd say wipe it on your dress, but wow, Charlie, what the hell has happened to you?" She beams through her tears. "You look stunning. Dolce & Gabbana? I'm in love with this dress."

Just like that, the old Adriana I knew and loved is back. It's easy to forgive her. She had been my best friend since I was eight, and some things were never meant to be broken.

"The moment I saw it, I knew we were soulmates."

As I speak about the dress, I notice Julian and the rest of the gang standing there, obviously waiting for an introduction.

"Oh, sorry. Adriana, please meet Rocky and Nikki. We've known each other since college. Nikki and I are partners in our own firm," I say proudly.

"Firm? As in lawyer?"

I nod, grinning. "This is Eric, my assistant, and Emma is Nikki's assistant. This handsome man here is my fiancé, Julian."

Adriana extends her hand toward Julian, shaking it in a very professional manner, but I can tell by the way she bit the corner of her lip this is anything but professional.

"Okay, so has anyone ever told you that you look like Christian Bale?" Adriana doesn't hold back, asking in her flirtatious tone as she fixates on him. *Oh, how I remember that voice.*

"Who, me? Never," he sarcastically responds.

I swat his arm as he laughs along with the rest of the group.

"So, from what I hear, you and Elijah are still together. Married, right?"

"Ah, yes and no." She lowers her voice. I knew something wasn't right, but I'm not going to pry in front of everyone. "It's kind of a long story we'll have plenty of time to catch up on later."

I nod my head, knowing we need to talk in private. "Do you guys mind if Adriana and I grab a drink from the bar?"

"Go ahead, I've got Eric here to keep me company," Julian says. Eric is beside him and he's already drunk on champagne.

As we walk toward the bar, Adriana links her arm in mine just like we had done a thousand times over inside the hallways of our school.

"He looked for you," she reveals, the second we get to the bar.

"Adriana, look... the past is the past."

"Charlie, Lex isn't the same. Not since you. You have to understand he was under a lot of pressure back then."

"I know he isn't the same. I've run into him twice now, and everything about him has changed," I tell her, not oblivious to the stranger who claims to be Alex, or Lex, or whatever. "He isn't the Alex I once loved."

"I know he comes across cold, but deep down he still has something for you, Charlie. You were the love of his life."

"But what about his kid, Adriana? Do you know what it was like for me to find out from the town skank that his wife was pregnant?" The resentment lingers in my rising tone, my expression hardening at this trip down memory lane. "He promised me they stopped having sex, and then to find out his wife was pregnant... Adriana, you just don't understand."

"It wasn't his baby, Charlie. They never had sex. Samantha lied about everything. When he found out, he went ballistic and took the next flight to Cuba to find you, thinking you left to live with your mom."

"But I wasn't there."

Bringing my shaky hand toward my forehead, the revelation shocks me. So, it wasn't his baby? I bow my head, questioning my decisions. Was I wrong? But no, I remember he still chose her first. He believed it was his baby, and he chose to honor his marriage over what we had.

I was second best. He had made sure of that.

"I know, but your mom told us you had moved elsewhere and were happy with someone else. She begged us to leave you alone, said you found a great guy and had moved in together. She said you were studying hard, and that if we found you, she thought your life would go backward." Adriana stops to take a breath, desperate to unleash what she must have been holding in for all this time. "It was my fault as well. I told Lex you deserved the best, and that he needed to let you be."

All of this is too much to process. My chest caves in, and holding onto the bar, I use it to keep my balance from my shaking legs collapsing beneath me. Beside me, there's a tray of champagne. I down a glass in one go, ignoring the bubbles tickling my throat. It doesn't erase the overwhelming feeling of this moment, and without hesitation, I take another repeating my actions.

"Adriana, I don't know what to say. I went to Connecticut to live with my grandmother. After she died, I just wanted to move on and do her proud, so I went to Yale. There wasn't another guy. How could there be after him?" I beg the question, but no answer will satisfy me or erase the past. "How could he doubt my love for him? Did he really think I'd move on straight away?"

"Your mom was very convincing. I'm sorry, you're right, but you really need to talk to Lex."

"It's just too much. There's more to this than—" I stop mid-sentence. Now isn't the time to get into the painful semantics of it all. I pull a business card out of my purse and hand it to her. "Let's catch up for lunch soon and talk about this, but for right now, I need time. It's a lot to take in."

She kisses me on the cheek, understanding I need my space.

Julian comes over, asking me if I want to dance some more. I gladly welcome the return to reality, reminding Adriana to call me.

As we dance away, Lex does the same a few feet away from me with his date. Every so often, his eyes wander my way, watching me watch him. He leans into the woman's neck, kissing her gently, closing his eyes as he does so.

My stare is fixated on them as the fury builds inside me. Why is he touching her like that? He slowly opens his eyes, directing them at me again. I can't bear to watch anymore, it's all too painful. I need a moment of clarity, so I excuse myself to use the restroom, blaming the champagne I drank earlier.

I exit the ballroom, clutching the bottom of my dress to avoid falling over in my rush. Inside the long corridor, I scan the surroundings looking for the restroom sign. Breathe, only a few more feet. My mind is scattered with thoughts, my stomach crashing with waves of nausea.

What if he had come after me?

Would everything have worked out for us?

My heart is sinking deeper as the thought crosses my mind with too many 'what if's in a world full of painful memories.

My arm is yanked into a different direction, and without a moment to think, Lex has pulled me through the double doors to an empty conference room. He lets go of my arm, pacing the area between us in frustration. "Do you love him?"

He doesn't deserve an answer. We are no longer together.

"I see the way you look at him. It is the way you used to look at me."

"Used to Al... Lex. Y-You walked away, not me," I stammer.

"I had no choice," he yells, wild eyes boring into me. "I looked for you. I didn't give up on us!"

"The moment you chose her, you gave up on us."

My heart is pumping so hard, remembering the ache which longed for him since the day he left. Once, a heart so full and content had experienced the ultimate break, torn apart, shredded into a million pieces with no remnants left and beyond repair.

His eyes are on fire, burning so bright and torturing me with its violent flames. With a pained stare, I'm unable to turn away until he grabs my face, pressing his lips against mine.

The force is so strong, crippling any emotion but the one which makes me focus on how perfect his lips taste. His tongue entangles with mine, the familiarity clouding any rational thought which wants to push him away.

My hands move toward his chest as I let out a small moan, dragging my lips away to break free as guilt consumes me whole. As if he knows the anguish he's putting me through, he locks me into an embrace, trapping me as he sucks hard on my lips.

The pain turns me on, traveling to forbidden places

which only existed when we were together. From the moment he left, I wondered what it would be like to taste his lips again, and no matter how much I thought about it, the reality is far off.

I missed how he tasted.

How he would kiss me passionately, every time, like it was our first kiss.

My head is screaming for him to let me go, but I can't stop. My body begins to tremble as he stiffens against my stomach. I can't let it go any further, terrified by how much I want him and how easily my heart has forgotten the pain he caused.

With his palm flat against my chest, I'm scared he can feel how rapidly my heart is beating, but I remind myself that it no longer beats for him.

Julian.

I pull away, out of breath.

"Lex, we can't. Please, you don't understand... I can't go down this path again—"

"I'm sorry I hurt you," he begs, placing his hands on my neck to try and drag me in, but I step back. "I'd give everything I own to erase it. It's something I'll always regret, but I'm standing here now, Charlotte. Please just let me explain everything."

"That's the thing, Lex. You just don't know—"

"What, Charlotte? Talk to me, please!"

I say the words I've been wanting to say since I ran into him—I have moved on.

It's time to accept that.

Walking toward the exit, I touch my lips before grabbing the handle of the door. Closure, it's time to live my life with a man who loves me.

Now, I have to walk back into the ballroom and face

Julian and my friends, pretending nothing's happened. I give myself a few minutes to calm down, taking deep breaths. A waiter scurries past, and I stop him, begging for a glass of champagne. Taking it kindly, I drink it in one go, discarding the empty glass on a table near the entrance.

"Gorgeous, there you are." Julian finds me as soon as I walk in. "Listen, something has come up, and I need to cover a story in Chicago first thing in the morning. My flight leaves in an hour. I'm sorry... I have to leave."

"What? But you can't leave," I plead, desperate to spend the night with him. "We had a whole night planned out. You, me... your bat cave." I need him here, so no other mistakes are made tonight, and more importantly, to protect me from the big bad wolf.

"Charlie... I, um... are you okay?" he questions, placing his hands on my shoulders.

I force a smile and wrap my arms around his waist clearing my throat. "Sorry, I just... call me the second you're back, okay?"

He pulls me in, kissing me deeply. As I kiss him back, I try to erase the guilt of the last twenty minutes. Trying not to show just how uncomfortable I am.

I can't help thinking it just isn't the same as Lex.

Don't do this, Charlie. The comparison game is nothing but a sick mind-fuck, destined to screw you up even more.

We walk back to our table so Julian can say goodbye to everyone, and moments later, he hurries out of the building.

Eric sits beside me, hugging me tightly. "I know you're upset he has to leave, but I know something that *will* cheer you up."

I don't tell Eric I'm not upset over Julian leaving. I'm still shell-shocked that I had actually kissed the ghost of my past, and how I let that happen—stupid move. I blame the champagne.

"Let's go to After Dark tonight. Dirty drinks, dirty men, and even dirtier dancing. We need to let loose after this stiff shindig, Charlie."

"Agreed. But only if we get to do shots," I tease, knowing Eric doesn't handle shots very well. Well, that's an understatement—three shots of tequila sees him dancing on a bar half-naked, five shots sees him head-down, ass-up over the toilet crying to God.

"Aw... shit, Charlie, you know what happens when I do shots. I get so loose," he whines.

"How is that any different from now?"

He laughs and does that snap-hand gesture he always does. Eric heads off to find Emma, leaving me to stand here by myself.

Why did I let it happen?

I touch my mouth, running my fingers against my swollen lips. This kiss was intense, but it was always like that between us.

Yet there are so many questions I want to ask, but even if he answers them, will it change things? I can't let go of the fact that he chose *her.*

Not me—*her.*

Samantha Benson.

"Okay, bitches, let's get a cab and get this party started."

Eric does his mini dance—the dance he always does before we go out to a club with music. He pulls on his jacket while I grab my purse. I don't know what compels me to do it, but I glance over at Lex one last time. He's staring directly at me with a smug look on his face. I can't say goodbye, not now. My emotions are all over the place, and nothing good comes within his presence.

I need tequila—STAT.

"First round of shots is on me," I cheer as we head out of the ballroom, ready to let loose and drown out tonight's sorrows.

SIXTEEN

LEX

I spent the short limousine ride chatting with Brooke. It turns out she's the daughter of one of the politicians from Long Island. Great, just what I need, more media scrutiny. Adriana sure knows how to pick them.

We arrive at the ball, red carpet swarming with paparazzi. We follow the crowd, hoping to avoid the craziness. Unfortunately, I'm not so lucky.

"Mr. Edwards, over here," one of the paparazzi yells.

I take my cue, posing, then the media frenzy follows. The bulbs keep flashing, blinding my normally perfect vision.

"Lex, who are you wearing?"

"Are you and Brooke Henley an item?"

"Is it true the Lexed Group is in a bidding war to buy—?"

Adriana shakes her head with annoyance and impatiently drags me into the building.

Thank God, the worst part is over.

We're seated toward the front, thanks to Adriana making me purchase the seats at twenty-five hundred a ticket. Sitting at the table beside us is Mr. Vandercamp and what looks like a new wife or possibly mistress. She's a clone of Barbie, a far cry from the Mrs. Vandercamp I remember.

Mr. Vandercamp is the owner of one of the largest importing companies in the States. Rumor has it he's in the middle of a messy divorce. With a Fortune 500 company, he is set to lose a lot of money. Too bad the old bugger didn't keep his dick in his pants.

We continue through the crowd, pausing to chat with acquaintances until finally stopping at Mr. and Mrs. Henley's table. Brooke introduces me to her parents. It's obvious her father isn't impressed she's attending the event with me. Who could blame him? I don't have the best reputation with women.

I scan the room, bored with the conversation between Brooke and her mother about dresses and designers. Across the ballroom, I notice a young guy checking me out, making it blatantly obvious. The girl on his right copies his move, and the one on his left slowly untangles herself from her partner's arm, revealing a stunning dress.

Emerald green, if that doesn't take me back to prom.

She turns to glance my way, and our eyes fixate on each other.

It's *her*.

My heart races uncontrollably, a dry throat starting to become uncomfortable as I stare, allowing my insecurity to get the better of me. Again. I despise myself for being so weak in her presence. *Man the fuck up, Edwards.*

Straightening my shoulders with my chest out, I adjust my cufflinks and take easy breaths, willing my confidence to return. This time, I'm not going to let the opportunity get away. Leaning into Brooke's ear, I tell her I'm going to mingle.

With every step I take toward *her*, the expression on her face is of disbelief. And attached to that is the most beautiful woman in the entire room.

Her long dress flows down her perfectly toned body, each curve making me harden beneath my pants. What I wouldn't do to have my face between those full breasts right now. Her hair is styled to one side, wavy in a 1950s style. It's much longer than in high school, but then again, that feels like a lifetime ago.

"Charlotte, what a nice surprise to see you again."

I take the initiative to introduce myself since she stands still, completely speechless. She stammers as she begins to speak, affected by my presence. After she introduces her colleagues, the moment comes that I've been dreading. She finally introduces her fiancé—Julian Baker.

He extends his hand, repeating my name. With a controlled stare, I don't let him see how much I loathe him for taking what belongs to me, not even when he wraps his fingers around her beautifully manicured fingers. With every fiber of my being, I try to contain my jealousy, rambling on about us dating in high school.

There's history between us, and no matter what the future holds, nothing or no one can erase that.

The conversation bounces between my accent, the office in Manhattan, to Adriana. Although I welcome anything which comes from Charlotte, her Asian friend is intrusive with his questions. Thankfully, we're interrupted by the MC announcing dinner is to be served.

I continue to stare at Charlotte, her eyes never leaving mine. If only I could get her alone, to explain. I am certain I can convince her my mistakes were justified by the unfortunate situation I found myself in. But as her friends begin to walk off, I seize the opportunity with desperation, grabbing her arm as I whisper how breathtaking she looks tonight.

For the split second she lingers next to me, I inhale her heavenly scent. It's like a drug, and just like that, I find my addiction again. She walks away from me, leaving me standing like a lost puppy.

Fucking pull yourself together, Edwards.

Stakes are high, and you can't afford to lose.

"She's here," I tell Adriana, back at our table.

Adriana searches the room in anticipation, and after going back and forth with Elijah as to what she will say when she sees her, she throws her napkin on her table and begins to walk off amongst the crowd. Adriana hasn't even bothered to touch her food, and neither have I, desperate for the hard stuff to calm down my anxious nerves.

I excuse myself, heading straight for the bar since the champagne served to us at the table is awful.

"What can I get you, sir?"

"Scotch, neat."

"Hi, Lex." Charlotte's assistant, Eric, is standing beside me, maybe a little too close. Or is that my paranoia? "So, I'm guessing Charlie and you were more than just friends back in high school, hence why you can cut the sexual tension with a dil... um, I mean, chainsaw?"

"It's a little complicated," I retort, hesitating.

Where's he going with this? And was he about to say dildo?

"I'm surprised she never mentioned you, considering I'm her BFF. You would think a gorgeous man like yourself would've been brought up during at least one drunken escapade." He motions for the bartender to serve him, ordering two Martinis, then quickly turns back to me.

"Well, since you're so-called BFFs, Eric, tell me, how long has she and Julian been together?"

"Three months," he responds, grabbing his Martini and swirling the stick.

I don't know what I wanted to hear. It's great they haven't been together for long, but the engaged part, I can't comprehend. They were only together for three fucking months, and she's already engaged to him? Why would you rush that? Unless she was... no, fuck, it can't be that. She's drinking champagne. Calm down, Edwards. I need to play my cards right, desperate for information, anything about her I can get my hands on.

"I own a club, After Dark. Not sure if you've heard of it?"

Of course, he has heard of it. Aren't gays known for their fashion sense and club life? The second his eyes light up, I know I'm on the ball.

"Oh-em-gee, like hello! It's the hottest spot in town right now," he squeals, clapping his hands in delight.

Bingo. I need to get Charlotte into a more relaxed environment. I do what any other determined man trying to get his hands on his ex-girlfriend would do—I take one for the team and flirt a little with her gay BFF.

"So how about I put you guys on the VIP list for tonight?"

Eric clutches his chest, eyes wide and glowing with an elated smile. I'm slightly worried he's going to grab my face and kiss me. I have no problem with gays, but I like pussy, sweet beautiful pussy. Oh, fuck, if that doesn't stir things up again. I'm like a goddamn fifteen-year-old with this walking hard-on. I don't want Eric thinking he's had a hand in that.

"That would be awesome."

Eric leans over, hugging me tightly. It's weird, like oh-em-gee, weird. Jesus Christ, this kid is rubbing off on me already.

I straighten my posture, finishing the remnants of my scotch and order another.

"Oh, I love you! I better get back to my table." He grabs the second Martini, and begins to walk off, then turns around with a grin. "And, Lex, don't worry, I'll make sure she comes alone."

I scan the room, hoping to find her alone. Amongst the other dancers, she's there with him. My blood begins to boil watching his hands all over her. With a slight growl, my teeth begin to clench as I take long steps toward her, zigzagging through the crowd, excusing myself as I bump into couples holding each other tightly while they dance to Frank Sinatra.

"Mind if I cut in?" I interrupt, flashing a friendly smile. "For old time's sake?"

Charlotte's tanned skin turns almost pale. Julian, on the other hand, is annoyed. He whispers something in her ear making her smile, then he walks away like a good little boy should. I place a hand over hers, and the other on her waist. I ache to hold her closer, the familiarity is just too much. *I have to get through this.*

She questions what I want. Accusing me of calling us friends, and I'm quick to tell her that, according to her, our relationship meant nothing. Just a high school fling.

And there, I pointed out the one thing she said to me which hurt me more than anything.

That we were nothing.

That everything I said meant nothing to her.

She's quick to change the subject, avoiding the topic completely. Then comes the thousand questions. Her curiosity is piquing as to why I changed careers. There's so much she doesn't know about me, but I don't want to have this conversation on the dance floor. I ask her to meet me afterward for a drink, and knowing she heard me but chose to ignore me, I decide to do what I do best—I rile a reaction from her.

"How long have you and Julian been together?"

"Why, Lex? Does it matter? What about you? I'm guessing you're no longer with Samantha since you hooked up with another blonde," she snaps.

I calmly explain the scenario, a small part of me hoping it makes her jealous which can only mean she still cares. Her face scrunches up when she gets angry, and I smirk, hoping she will lighten up, but boy, am I wrong.

The crowd stops dancing to applaud the band, and she takes the opportunity to end the dance, thanking me before walking away.

Defeated, and unsure of my next move, I walk back toward my table, forgetting about my date, Brooke. She glances at me with a blank expression on her face.

"Who is she, Lex?" Her tone is flat, she's not at all jealous.

This is strange. I'm not used to calm women around me.

"Who? The brunette?" I look over and see Julian with his arms around her. Fuck! One minute away from me, and she's running into his arms.

Exerting my anger, I crack my knuckles, penetrating Charlotte with a cold stare. Each time his lips touch her, my pulse quickens, causing my body to tense followed by an outbreak of sweat.

"Just someone from high school. No one special."

The words hurt even to say them.

"Listen, Lex, there's something you should know."

Brooke twists her napkin, nervously looking around. "I only agreed to this date to please my parents."

I laugh at the irony of it all, welcoming the distraction. "Your parents? Brooke, I don't think your dad likes me one bit."

"See, the thing is that, um..." she downs the rest of her champagne, placing the empty glass on the table, "... I'm not interested in you. Sorry, I mean, not just you... in men."

Rubbing my chin, I watch her with confusion, trying to understand before it clicks. "You prefer your own kind?"

She laughs, immediately relaxing her shoulders and letting out a sigh. "Yes, I do, Lex. I'm sorry, I haven't gone public, and my father's in the middle of an important campaign."

"Secret's safe with me." I grin. "But only if you do one thing... pretend you're at least interested in me for the night. It might come in handy later."

Yes, I have a plan. It just needs to be executed.

Charlotte can control herself as much as she wants, but little does she know that I know of her weakness. Jealousy runs deep within her veins, and somehow, I need to ignite the flame beneath that jealousy and make it burn wild.

"Deal. I'm sure I can play a straight lady for one night."

We both laugh this time, knowing how fucked-up this all is. I'm glad there's no longer this awkward tension between us.

"I'll be back," I tell her. "I need to use the restroom."

Inside the restroom, I shut the door behind me, unzipping my pants to pull my cock out. *It's throbbing.* With every stroke comes pleasure. I close my eyes, remembering her standing in front of me, her chest exposed slightly in her dress, her tanned skin itching to be kissed, the trail leading to her full breasts. I try to remember what her nipples look like, how they felt in my mouth. The squeal she'd make when I tugged on them with my teeth.

Instantly, I blow all over my hand.

It isn't taking me long these days.

Grabbing a wad of paper, I wipe my hand, then throw it down the toilet and flush. I give myself a moment to calm down before I zip my pants and head out of the stall to wash my hands. Just as I stand there at the basin, Julian walks in.

"So, did you enjoy your dance with Charlie? Just like old times, hey?"

His tone wreaks of jealousy but I fucking thrive on it.

"Just like old times. But, hey, you heard her, we were just high school kids back then," I answer, playing dumb.

"But you weren't in high school. If I remember correctly from my research, you graduated seven years before her. So, when you and Charlie dated, you were like, what, twenty-five? And she was eighteen?"

"What's your point?"

"And you were married at the time. See, Lex, this is the thing... we always want what we can't have."

"I had her. What the fuck are you trying to say?"

He wants to play dirty, but he's messing with the wrong guy.

"Exactly. You *had* her, but you couldn't keep her." He checks his face in the mirror, adjusting his bow tie at the same time. "Just remember who she's with now and whose bed she'll be in tonight." With a cocky grin, he pushes the door open and leaves the restroom.

Leaning on the countertop for support, my knuckles turn white from the pressure. Gritting my teeth, I silence the profanities begging to be shouted inside the confinement of this room. The animosity toward him is like acid burning every single inch of me.

I stare into the mirror, nostrils flaring with a tight expression. If Charlotte is anything like she was back in high school, jealousy is the curse she was never able to break, and my desperation is willing to prey on her weakness.

Back inside the ballroom, I make my way to our table and lean into Brooke's ear. "Time to call in a favor?"

She nods with a devilish smile, following me to the dance floor where I find us a spot in Charlotte's view.

Charlotte is staring at me with a ray of mixed emotions. I lean in to kiss Brooke on the neck, closing my eyes, pretending to inhale her scent. My eyes slowly move up searching for Charlotte's reaction.

Tormented, Charlotte lets go of Julian, walking swiftly toward the exit. I quickly excuse myself, assuming she's running out of the ballroom. I spot her walking down the hall, flustered. Moving in at a faster pace, my grip tightens on her arm while I drag her into a small conference room.

Unable to control my emotions around her, I pace the floor between us, and we both yell at each other in frustration. Words carelessly leave our mouths, hurting each other to erase the guilt of the past. In the heat of the moment, her expression turns pained, and defensively she brings up Samantha again.

Watching her, my mind is out of control. I'm unable to fight the urge anymore, crushing my lips against hers.

The taste of her soft lips melts onto mine. Our tongues feverishly battle each other as I press her body into mine, keeping my tight grip, never wanting to let her go. She doesn't push me away, so I take advantage by cupping her face, desperately releasing the built-up tension which has grown over our years apart.

Suddenly, she begins to resist. Refusing to allow her to give up on us, I trap her arms forcefully, willing we continue. Pressing my cock against her thigh, I ache to be inside her. I groan into her mouth, wanting her to know how much I need her.

My hand trails her cheekbone and slides down her neck, finding itself flat against the middle of her exposed chest. Just one move to the left or right, and I'll have her in my hands. Her perfect tits are calling out to me, but it's almost like she can read my mind. Finding her strength, she moans, then pushes me away.

As we struggle to catch our breath, she pleads with her eyes, shaking her head on the verge of tears.

"Lex, we can't. Please, you don't understand... I can't go down this path again."

No matter how many times I say it, it can never erase what happened. I apologize, telling her how much I regret my actions. She has to see that none of it was supposed to happen.

Charlotte Mason was meant to be my girl, my wife, all along.

"Lex, I've moved on. It took me a long time to finally accept what happened between us. If you care for me at all, even as a friend, please just leave me alone."

Her eyes never leave mine as she says those words. Turning around, she places her hand on the door, stopping to touch her lips before leaving me alone in the room.

I run my fingers through my hair, reeling from what just happened, unable to calm my racing heart. What the fuck is happening? Maybe I just need to get her out of my system. Just one last time, one fuck. Maybe it isn't about love anymore, maybe it's primal curiosity.

But her last words hang around me, a dire warning to leave her alone.

I walk out of the ballroom, running into my sister. "Lex, there you are. We need to talk."

"Not now, Adriana." I continue to walk away, unable to think clearly.

"It's about Charlie."

Stopping mid-step, Adriana catches my attention.

"What's wrong?"

"All that stuff Charlie's mom said was a lie. There was nobody else. Maria just said that so you wouldn't look for her," Adriana rushes, her expression full of regret.

She accompanied me on that fateful trip to Cuba and knew what I had gone through and the reason behind my decision at the time. All of this, the whole mess of what we once were, is becoming this tangled web of lies.

"I thought I was doing the right thing. I thought she deserved to be happy, even if it was with someone else."

Staring down at my feet, my emotions are exposed as the regret begins to seep in. In just one night, Charlotte has brought out everything I've been burying since the moment I left her on that cliff. I promised her things, things I knew I shouldn't, all because I was terrified of losing her.

And in the end, I lost her completely with my careless actions.

"I know, Lex. But it's done, and now she's here. What are you going to do about it?"

"I don't know. She asked me to leave her alone..." I scrub a hand over my hair, "... said she's finally happy."

"You did that last time and look where it got you."

I don't answer her, walking back to the ballroom in a

dull state. The fight within me is compromised, not knowing which way to turn.

The night starts to wind down, and I watch as the crowd slowly disperses. Charlotte is with Eric and Emma, grabbing their things. She glances at me before quickly turning away.

So what? I don't even get a goodbye? This isn't like Charlotte at all. The old Charlotte wouldn't ignore me. She'd be in my face cursing until the sun set if she had a problem.

If you care for me at all, even as a friend, please just leave me alone. Her words replay in my mind over and over again like a broken record.

I don't want to make more mistakes.

The past is the past, and to move forward, I have to forgive myself for all the wrong decisions I made. But it isn't just about me forgiving myself, it's about her forgiving me too. And more than anything, I need it like the air I breathe.

Outside, the concierge opens the door to the car. "Mr. Edwards, your driver is here."

"Thank you."

I tip the young guy, then press the security screen down to speak to Kyle.

"Where to, sir?"

I have to make this right. I owe it to us—no more indecisiveness. You need to follow your gut and act accordingly.

"After Dark, please."

SEVENTEEN

CHARLIE

The ten-minute cab ride to After Dark drags on for what feels like a lifetime.

The guilt, betrayal, and the momentary indiscretion all weigh heavily on my shoulders like a lead weight. *It was just a kiss.* It means nothing, and he initiated it. I pulled away. Therefore, I shouldn't feel guilty. *Really, Charlie?*

I studied law at Yale. How stupid can I be? The problem isn't my brain. The problem is my heart pulling it along, guiding it in the wrong direction. I can practically hear the GPS in my head telling me to make a U-turn as soon as possible.

It doesn't take Eric long to break the uncomfortable silence. He keeps his voice low while Emma sits in the front speaking loudly on her phone.

"Okay, Charlie, are you going to tell me about Lex? The suspense is killing me."

I can hear the anticipation in his voice, but I just want to forget tonight ever happened. This emotional rollercoaster is becoming tiresome, and I'm drained from the twists and turns, wanting desperately to get off the ride.

Every time I see Alex, the surge of anger consumes me whole. Anger for leaving me behind, for choosing her, but mostly because my heart craves him, forgetting about the giant scar it left in the middle.

The kiss replays in my mind, his desperation through his forceful nature. Then the guilt washes over me, and now I'm back to square one, again.

"There's nothing to tell. We dated in high school."

"So, when you say 'dated,' were you in love with him? Why did you break up?"

This is the type of conversation that needs to take place over a bottle of tequila, never-ending packets of Hershey's, and a box of tissues and not in the back of a cab. Eric won't give up, always stubborn and impatient, so I give him the best answer I can, but knowing Eric, he'll keep pursuing his line of questioning.

Facing the window, I swallow the hard lump inside my throat, my shoulders drooping as I fumble with my clutch.

"I thought I was in love with him, but I was just a kid. I didn't know what love was. We parted ways, and I went to college."

"Okay, but, honey cakes, he's drop-dead gorgeous. Don't you want to tap that ass again?"

Here we go. Eric tends to get all dramatic when he's had too much champagne. This is just the beginning.

"E, he might be gorgeous, but look, he's just another big-shot CEO. His ego is so big it has its own air supply and should come with a government warning, and quite frankly, any woman is just a notch on his belt, anyway. These types of guys don't stick around. Oh, and aren't you forgetting a very important factor... hello!" I remind him, flashing my ring in front of his face.

"Oh yeah... but are you sure about it?"

"What's that supposed to mean?"

"All I'm saying is that every time you are near him, your tatas jump for joy, and your beaver is singing 'Celebration,' and I swear I can almost hear a gospel choir singing 'Hallelujah.'"

"Honestly, Eric, how on earth do you come up with these things?" I laugh, trying to lighten the mood.

Eric distracts himself by taking selfies with his phone. Thankfully, the subject is officially dropped.

After Dark is a new club to hit the nightlife scene in the Meat Packing District. Several people are waiting in line, and according to Eric, it's the new '*It*' place. High-profile celebrities are dubbing it their new place to unwind, something Eric's all over.

Worried we won't get in, I suggest we find another place to have a drink.

"Eric Kennedy, party of three."

The large security guard opens the rope, letting us in. How did Eric pull that off? I know people have been trying to get in for weeks as the list is long and distinguished.

We walk past the rope and into the club.

Eric is on a power trip as he raises his chin, walking into the club with a strut.

The club is huge compared to others I've been to. The bottom level is the dance floor, lit up in an aqua color. The mezzanine level where we're standing, circles the dance floor. There are black leather booths that follow the flow of the circle, each one occupied with patrons. Facing directly opposite from the entrance is a long and crowded bar, but nevertheless, we need drinks to help me forget about my tangled love life.

We follow Eric to the bar. I motion for the bartender, which isn't hard as he's already eyeing me up, or should I say he's eyeing my chest. This dress is seriously the biggest man-magnet, making me slightly self-conscious amongst these younger guys.

The image of Lex's hand resting on my chest, inches away from the curve of my breast, flashes before me. *Argh, I need to get drunk.* The tequila can't come fast enough, the bartender lining up shot glasses and pouring the liquor into them accordingly.

After we knock back our first round, I order a second, ignoring the burn lingering inside my throat. They need to keep coming if I want to erase this entire night and every image of Lex touching my body.

By the third round, Eric abandons us. As predicted, some hot guy steals him away, and for all I know, he's probably tied up in the back room. Not complaining, of course, Eric is kinky when he's drunk, and he is never afraid to share the details the morning after.

"Look, Charlie, I don't want to upset you, but if you ever need to talk you know I'm here, right?"

Emma's offer is genuine. I know I can confide in her without the biased judgment. Plus, she's a great listener.

"Thanks, Emma, but all I want to do is forget tonight ever happened. How did I go from no men in my life to a fiancé and ex-boyfriend?"

"Maybe it's fate. Have you thought about that?"

Emma is a believer in fate, love, and destiny. It wouldn't surprise me if she attends those finding-love seminars and writes affirmations on her bathroom mirror. Great for some, definitely not for me. Love has always screwed me sideways, and we didn't have a great relationship until Julian came along.

"Or maybe it's just the universe wanting to fuck me up big time," I holler, throwing back another shot.

We laugh so hard, and for the first time tonight, my tense muscles begin to relax, and the world feels like a chilled place. The tequila is just what the doctor ordered.

A young, good-looking guy comes up to Emma and starts chatting with her. *There goes my drinking buddy.* I order another shot, but this time there's no counting down. I down the shot, the burning no longer apparent.

"Hi, baby, can I buy you a drink?"

My skin crawls as the words linger. *Oh God, what a loser.* The man beside me looks like he stepped out of one of those muscle magazines, wearing a shirt that reads, 'I Love Ass.' Seriously, do guys think that will get them laid? I'm just about to tell him where to shove his drink and T-shirt when another voice stops me.

"She's with me."

I don't have to turn and look, that familiar pull, the familiar scent forever engrained in my memory like a permanent fixture unable to move.

Sliding to my left, Lex is standing beside me, still in his suit but sans his tie. His chest is slightly exposed, revealing his tanned skin. He looks just like Eric had described him—drop-dead gorgeous. My walls are breaking, unable to deny how much I crave him, but the rational Charlie is now controlled by alcohol and is trying her best to wave her flag—the one with the poison symbol on the front also marked *danger*.

Mr. Muscles appears amused. "I wouldn't leave her wandering the bar alone. A sexy little thing like her can really do some damage."

Lex's lips pull back, baring his teeth with an icy glare. The guy, a coward, backs off with his hands raised in the air calling defeat. I want to laugh, given the size of the guy, but I'm distracted by Lex's presence. Suddenly, I'm aware that once again, Lex thinks he can control me. Inside my chest, my heart pounds loudly as I clench my fists into a tight ball.

"You didn't have to do that. I can take care of myself!"

Just as he opens his mouth, Eric practically throws himself between us.

"Lex, thank you so much for sorting the door for us."

What? How can Lex get us in, and when did Eric become best buds with him? I remind myself to grill him later, unable to think straight right now. I need to escape this torture, and scanning the room in panic, my thoughts to exit via the back door are foiled when Eric grips onto my arm, predicting my escape.

"Charlie, did you know Lex owns this place? I mean, seriously, how hot is this club."

A wide smirk appears on Lex's face as Eric continues, rambling on about every detail like the suck-up he is. I'm ready to kill Eric with my bare hands. Didn't his parents teach him not to play with fire?

"Good evening, Mr. Edwards." The bartender is quick to attend to Lex. "What'll it be?"

"A round of tequila shots, Dylan. Can you send them to the VIP area?"

"Coming right up, sir."

The bartender grabs the bottle and starts pouring the shots, aligning them on a tray.

Lex grabs my hand, much to my disapproval, and weaves me in and out of the crowd. Perhaps the earlier shots worked to my detriment, the room is spinning as we walk past people dancing. Eric, Emma, and her new boy-toy follow close behind us as we take the stairs up to another level.

The hostess greets Lex, practically throwing herself on him with her tits out on show. Stupid whore. He still holds onto my hand, burning through my skin like fire, yet I'm unable to pull away.

He's just a friend, and friends can hold hands.

But you're not even friends.

Okay, shut up now.

The VIP area has a quiet ambiance to it, not like downstairs. There's another bar, less crowded with gold leather bar stools in a row. Lex directs us to a secluded circle-shaped booth like the one downstairs but with sheer golden curtains surrounding it and a full view of the entire club.

I sit down in the booth, willing the dizziness to stop. Lex slides in beside me, sitting as close as possible—the heat of his body pressing against mine. I try desperately to distract myself, but the butterflies are working overtime, fluttering inside my stomach working back-to-back double shifts.

"You own this club?" I blurt out, willing my mind to focus on anything else.

"Yes, this and another one. Perhaps if you took the time to talk to me, you would know what I do with my spare time," he answers sarcastically.

Asshole.

Eric asks more questions about the club while my thoughts remain silent. Throughout the conversation, Lex manages to drape his arm over my shoulder, twirling his fingers around a lock of my hair like he had done so many times before.

I pretend not to notice, though every twirl is like fireworks exploding inside of me. It's the tequila—hard liquor makes you desire forbidden things. This isn't you, Charlie. It's the tequila.

"Let's dance, Em," Eric says, eyeing me with a mischievous smirk.

Eric and Emma, along with her male friend, disappear, leaving me alone with the hungry wolf. I want to scream at them to come back, traitors for telling me they had my back when, in fact, they have left me to be chewed up and eaten to pieces.

The bartender, Dylan, arrives and begins lining up the shots in front of us. Without even thinking, despite my earlier blame of the bottle, I down the shot, letting out a rasp as my tongue burns once again. Within seconds, a calm wave washes over me, the anxiety fading away as I relax into the booth.

Lex hasn't touched his yet. Instead, he grabs my arm and twists it, so my wrist is facing him. He pours the salt on it, slowly sliding his tongue up my arm, his eyes never leaving mine.

My body begins to tremble, my legs parting slightly as he drinks the tequila then sucks the piece of lemon, slowly swirling his tongue around it. There's a delayed reaction as my head is trying to push the desire away, but the force is so strong it causes my skin to flush. Just for a moment, I imagine his tongue between my legs, my nipples hardening under the silk fabric I'm wearing. I desperately want to reach out and assault his beautiful mouth. Like a moth to a flame, I'm drawn but scared, and I fly away.

"Another shot?"

He knows what I'm like when I get drunk. Hell, I know what I'm like when I get drunk, but for some reason, it doesn't stop me. I've lost all sense of reason, allowing my desire to guide me rather than my morals.

"Are you trying to get me drunk, Mr. Edwards?"

Oh fuck, my tone sounds too flirty.

The tequila is in full-on assault mode, and Lex is so close, my body is in overdrive. It doesn't help that I'm barely wearing anything under my dress. I squirm beneath the table, his expression amused. Yes, I want to tell him I'm fucking soaked, and I'm sure your mouth on my pussy will scratch the itch, but instead, my face remains poker-straight.

"The last time I recall you drinking this much, it ended up being a very interesting night, indeed," he teases.

Breathe, Charlie.

Know your boundaries, you're a strong, independent woman who knows a player when you see one. He just wants to get laid, nothing more.

I make the mistake of lowering my gaze toward the crotch of his pants, undoubtedly the hard fixture is impossible to ignore. My eyes widen, watching him squirm just like I did. Two can play at this game. I'm just about to say something when my clutch begins to vibrate. Welcoming the distraction, I pull out my phone, the caller ID—Batman.

Lex leans over and sees the phone lighting up. His face is furious, and with his jaw clenched tight, he yanks the phone off me and hits the reject button on the screen.

"Why would you do that?" I berate him.

Fuming, I grab the phone from his hands. Not once have I said to Lex we are back on. Just because I kissed him, it doesn't give him the right to go all caveman on me. In fact, I told him to leave me alone, something he's chosen to ignore.

The phone vibrates again, but this time a message appears on the screen.

Julian: *Hey, gorgeous, just wanted to make sure you got home ok. Sorry I had to leave. Can I make it up to you tomorrow night? Dinner at my place. I'll make sure Alfred has the night off.*

Lex snatches the phone back from me and reads the message. The steam is practically pouring from his ears, his knuckles white as his grip tightens around my phone. He bows his head, refusing to look at me. How dare he read my private messages? I'm ready to blast him, give him a reality check his arrogant ass needs, but a tall, lean man comes up behind him and starts whispering in his ear.

Lex's demeanor changes, a concerned expression that doesn't bother me the slightest as I'm grateful he's distracted.

"I have to take care of something. Don't even think about responding to that message," he warns before quickly following the man down the stairs.

Arrogant prick! He has no right telling me what to do. I'm no longer at the mercy of Alexander Edwards. Julian is the man I'm going to marry, he's who I choose to build my new life with.

So why am I sitting here in Lex's club flirting like a fucking sixteen-year-old?

Another mistake.

Take a shot and have fun without Lex, you don't need him.

With my purse in hand, I abandon our table and scurry down the steps until Eric meets me halfway.

"Why didn't you tell me Lex was going to be here?"

"Because you basically said you were over him and that Julian was the love of your life... yada, yada, yada."

Is that what he got from our earlier conversation?

"I'm over h-him," I stammer. "It's just awkward because there's a lot of history, and I'm not perfect, you know. Seeing him is very... uncomfortable."

"Well, Charlie, you would have to be blind not to see how much he wants you. Julian's a great guy, but why not play the field a little?" Eric raises his perfectly shaped eyebrows up and down in a suggestive manner.

The laughter is echoing in my head. Lex is not the field-playing type, and that was evident two minutes ago. Back in high school, someone had spread a rumor that Carter, another senior at school, and I had sex in the janitor's closet during our study break. It took weeks to calm Lex down, and I had Carter openly admit to the biggest school gossip, Stacey, that it was another girl, not me.

"C'mon, Eric, let's dance."

I yank his arm, pulling him toward the dance floor. As I make my way to the middle, sweaty bodies press and rub against me. It's even more crowded than I thought. I move my body in rhythm with the music, closing my eyes, intoxicated by the beats and the sway of bodies around me. As I open my eyes, Eric has turned around to dance with some guy. I don't want to watch Eric play who's-the-bigger-tease, so I spin back around falling straight into Lex's arms.

His emerald eyes burn into mine, the touch of his hand sliding down my arm and settling on my hip. Unwillingly, I close my eyes again, this time inhaling his scent, forgetting what happened upstairs, and surrendering myself to the moment.

It's only one moment, Charlie, and then it's over.

Lex moves in rhythm with me, our hips swaying to a remix of 'Red Red Wine.' He continues to slowly grind himself against me, spinning me around, so my back is against his chest. With his arms wrapped around my waist, my vision is compromised with all the movement making me slightly dizzy. To drown out the nauseating feeling, I close my eyes, welcoming the darkness.

With his lips brushing my ear, he sings the lyrics, every word sending my body into a complete frenzy. His hands slowly move upward from my stomach, grazing my breasts.

The urge to resist him is a battle I can no longer fight as a warm sensation floods every inch of me, leaving me breathless. I reach my arm behind me to grab his head, burying him into my neck. The pain he'd left behind is buried and caught in revenge. I want him to feel what it's like to want me and be unable to have me.

Desire is driving me to tease him with my touch, but my passion stems from a very bitter place. I need him to feel what it's like to taste what he can't have. Our tables have turned, and this time, I hold the cards in this sick and twisted game my mind is playing.

But then, I lose control of the moment. I don't have a single minute to think, caught in the speed of which he drags me off the dance floor and through a door marked 'Staff Only.' The doorway opens into a dark hallway leading to a kitchen.

The kitchen is dark, but I can see the large stovetops backing against the wall, the rows of stainless-steel counters creating an island in the middle, and the refrigerators lined up, side by side.

Confused, I turn to question him only to be pushed against the fridge as his lips crush against mine. The glass door is cold, making me shiver, yet my skin is on fire, melting away the moisture.

His tongue battles desperately with mine, wanting more. Letting out a moan, his hands grip my face, pinning me down before he releases and runs his palm down the middle of my chest. There's no wasting time as he slides his hand beneath my dress, my body convulsing at the graze of my hardened nipples.

I moan into his mouth, my legs threatening to give way while he forces them to spread even further.

"Charlotte, can't you feel how right this is?"

I want to give him all of me and take everything he has to give me—nine years' worth of suppressed sexual desire. And foolishly, I want him to taste the forbidden fruit. Poison him with just one bite.

He greedily sucks my lips while tugging on my hair, then continues kissing down my neck until his mouth is on my breasts. A groan escapes his beautiful lips as he sucks the left one hard while pinching the right nipple, then quickly alternating.

I'm lost, drowning in a pool of pleasure. My hands are running through his hair, guiding his head as he tastes me. As I open my eyes to watch him, the sparkle in my ring nearly blinds me. Like a splash of cold water, reality is staring at me, judging me for my poor decisions.

I push him away, creating distance.

"Fuck you, Lex. You don't own me," I shout with uneven breaths.

"I'm taking back what's mine."

He latches onto my waist, pulling me back to him. I moan loudly, the fabric of my dress sliding above my thighs in a mad rush. Lex clasps his hand around my panties, a tight grip as he growls into my ear. Pushing them aside, he plunges his fingers inside me, my scream echoing in the room. Biting into his shoulder, he pushes his fingers deeper, relishing in the pool of wetness surrounding me.

Every thrust is bringing me closer, my moans expelling

at a fast pace. I'm almost there, begging him to finish to the end, but all of a sudden, the thrusting stops.

My chest, still heaving, begins to slow down. Opening my eyes, I demand to ask him why he stopped. Staring into my eyes with forbidden lust, he raises his fingers to my mouth, smothering my lips with my own desire.

What a dirty bastard.

Running his tongue along my bottom lip, he tastes all of me that's left, leaving me wanting more of him. My hands drop to his waist, fumbling with his belt. I need his cock to ease the fire that's ravaging through me.

Just one time, that's all I need.

One time.

There's a commotion near the door, and in sheer panic, we pull away from each other as I straighten my dress, double-checking my breasts are positioned back behind the fabric.

A janitor opens the door to the kitchen, pushing his mop and bucket.

"Apologies, sir. I was sent to clean the floor."

"That's fine, you can continue," Lex orders, barely able to speak.

I quickly head out the door without a goodbye.

You can do it, Charlie, just walk away and pretend it never happened. But Lex is quick, pulling me back to him and pinning me against the wall.

"We're not finished, not until my cock has been inside every part of you, and only I'll be the one to touch you. You understand that, Charlotte? You belong to me. You are mine and always were." I close my eyes as he trails kisses down my neck. "This dress, Charlotte, what are you doing to me?"

"Nothing you haven't wanted since the moment we saw

each other at the restaurant," I tell him, unable to catch my breath.

He stops kissing me and lowers his eyes to meet mine.

"That's where you're wrong, Charlotte." His intense stare rattles me, the anger driving his eyes to shades of black. "It's not since the moment I saw you in the restaurant, but since the last time I saw you on the cliff top."

The memory comes barreling like a cyclone ready to destroy.

How easily you forget.

How easily the pain subsides by the touch of his lips on your own.

He broke you, Charlie.

Broke what you had even though he promised never to hurt you.

He chose someone else.

I need to hurt him the same way he did to me.

"Don't fucking do this, Lex. What happened back there meant nothing. It was just the curiosity of what it would feel like again. Don't go reading more into this." I pull away from him, suddenly finding my strength. "Yes, Lex, I'd have fucked you because I was turned on... plain and simple. I've fucked you before, so I know what I'm in for, but it would've been a mistake if we did. You're nothing to me. My fiancé will be back tomorrow, and I plan to marry him. I'm not yours, and the quicker you realize that, the better."

I storm out of the kitchen, searching for the nearest bathroom. As soon as I see it, I push past the women waiting and rush inside, closing the door behind me. My heart is beating fast as I touch my swollen lips.

He does it to me every time.

But I asked for it.

I allowed it.

I craved it.

What have I done?

I spent nine years trying to forget him. And in just one moment, time stood still, and every part of me that had let him go is crying out for him.

I calm myself as best as I can, knowing I can't face him again. Walking out of the stall, I stand in front of the sink and splash cold water on my face, willing the guilt to disappear down the drain along with my sins. Adjusting my dress and fixing my hair, I walk back into the main area to find a very disheveled Eric.

"Charlie, where have you been? I've been looking all over for you."

"Well, for starters, I wasn't in Chris Pratt look-a-like pants, and that appears to be the only place you were looking."

"Time to go?"

"Yes, please," I beg.

It's three in the morning, and I'm beyond ready to leave. Physically, I'm exhausted, and everything's becoming a giant blur. Emma left with boy-toy, so Eric and I walk hand in hand as we head out of the club.

The cool night air is refreshing against my skin and stops the nausea that has threatened me all night long. The streets are quiet with an occasional cab driving past. There's a commotion at the front of the club, prompting Eric and me to stop in our tracks to see what's happening.

"Why won't you let me in? For old time's sake?"

The voice sounds familiar, but I've had several shots and am possibly hallucinating. I have no energy to turn around, telling Eric to continue walking.

"Look what the cat dragged back. Is she the reason why, Alex?"

I stop dead in my tracks, my posture stiffening at the sound of that voice again. Squeezing my eyes shut, I listen to the sound of my beating heart before they burst open, forcing me to turn around.

Lex is standing at the entrance with that same tall man and the familiar voice.

I can't believe my eyes.

Samantha.

EIGHTEEN

LEX

"C'mon, Alex. Let me in."

Samantha pleads with me to let her enter the club, grabbing the lapels of my shirt in a drunken haze.

"Like fuck I will. What are you doing here, anyway?"

"Oh, Alex, you know, I needed an escape. I need you."

The careless smiles fade away, her lips beginning to tremble as her eyes glass over. I'm no fucking therapist, but Samantha is all shades of fucked-up. One of the many reasons why I ended our marriage.

"First of all, my name is Lex," I growl, my temper sparking while I remove her hands off me. "Second of all, this isn't the time nor the place to fucking cry. Go back to your hotel or wherever you came from and get some rest. I'm not allowing you in the club."

Straightening my shoulders, I warn David and his team not to let her in. My resentment runs deep, so deep because she cost me my entire *life*.

As I walk away, her cries become louder, but I choose to ignore her, praying to God Charlotte stays inside the club, or she will assume the worst when, in fact, I no longer have any sort of relationship with Samantha Benson.

Back inside, I scan the VIP area to find our table empty.

"She's on the dance floor with Eric."

I turn to look at the person beside me, it's Charlotte's friend, Emma, the young, sexy, innocent-looking blonde.

"Thanks. Emma, right?"

"Yes, and you're welcome."

She walks back toward the bar, accompanied by the guy who sat next to her at the table.

The club is at full capacity, on the brink of violating the fire code. I've warned Reginald, the club manager, repeatedly, to make sure security is doing the job or everyone's ass is on the line.

Weaving my way through the crowd, my eyes are drawn to where she's dancing with Eric. Her back is facing me and unable to resist any longer, I join her without any warning and press her body against mine.

I'm not prepared for how amazing it feels to have her in my arms, almost as if I never let her go, and she has always belonged to me, and only me. Like the missing piece to my broken puzzle, she fits perfectly in my embrace, my body thirsty for her like a drug.

With every sway of her hips, she pushes against my cock, teasing me with her perfect ass. I'm no longer imagining things, certain she wants me just as much as I want her.

She let me dance with her at the charity ball and allowed me to kiss her privately inside the conference room. Upstairs, she allowed me to lick the salt off her skin, and despite her intoxicated state working in my favor, I'm not going to play nice.

I want her drunk or not drunk. Call me selfish, but I

need her more than anything.

My desire to fuck her nice and hard overshadows any rational thinking that I might lose Charlotte if I push her. Knowing the kitchen out back isn't in use tonight, I grab her hand, pulling her away from the dance floor.

I lead her into the kitchen, taking her immediately against the refrigerator. I lose all sense of control with her, kissing every part of her body, finally taking her nipples in my mouth. I tug on them with my teeth, hearing her moan just like she used to every time I fucked her.

My cock is throbbing with every moan escaping her beautiful lips. I know she wants me, desperate to have me enter her.

But I'm not going to play nice.

She thinks she can taunt me with a ring on her finger? She doesn't know who she's messing with. I didn't become a billionaire by playing nice.

I play dirty to get what I want.

And I want her.

The obsession with making her mine again is my only focus.

I thrust my fingers into her, groaning as they slide so effortlessly. Careless in my actions, I keep finger-fucking her roughly, relishing in how soaked her pussy becomes around my fingers.

Inside my pants, I'm ready to fucking blow. All this control I had, perhaps I am fucking wrong. I'm tormenting myself just as much.

With her chest heaving, and her body wriggling from the intensity, I sense her impending orgasm but pull my fingers out just in time. Raising it to her lips, I watch her taste her own juices before running my tongue along her mouth and tasting her arousal.

I need her to *beg* for it.

The sadistic side of me wants to see her suffer. I need the power trip, desperate for her to beg me to fuck her nice and hard like it's always been only *me*. I must be the only thing on her mind, the only person who invades her dreams and visualizes when she opens her eyes. The only voice in her head, the only scent she can smell.

She has to understand a world will not exist without *me*.

We both stop, uneven breaths between us as our stares fixate on one another. She lies completely petrified under my command, her lips quivering while her hands fumble with the buckle of my pants. I'm in control, the narcissist emerging is savoring this moment of gratification.

A creaking noise startles us both, forcing us to pull away from each other.

It's only the janitor. He apologizes for the interruption, and I allow him to continue, immediately regretting the words escaping my mouth.

Why the fuck did you let her go?

Charlotte is quick to escape, but I catch up, warning her that she belongs to me. And in true style, she shouts hurtful words in an attempt to protect herself.

I tell her she's wrong, that I've wanted her since the last time I saw her on the clifftop back home, that my life has been full of nothing but regret. Every decision I thought was right led me to a lonely dead end.

Only after I left Samantha, did I start picking up the pieces. I decided Charlotte was better off without me after being told she had moved on. I buried myself in my work, building my empire, never taking a moment to feel the regret that constantly lingered, and here she stands in front of me telling me that what just happened was nothing but lust and curiosity—don't read more into this.

How dare she assume I'm just like everyone else.

I might have been young and foolish, but I loved her like no other man could. I've fucked-up so many times that I'll admit now, I just need a final chance to make things right.

Until she tells me tonight's all one big mistake.

You're nothing to me. I'm marrying him.

I lean against the wall, willing her hurtful words to stop. The lack of her presence is leaving a huge ache inside me, rubbing the self-inflicted wound inside my chest. I need to let her go, just for tonight. Maybe I'm pushing her, but I don't know what else to do. She isn't a business deal, and I should stop treating her like one. And perhaps my earlier desire to control her has caused more damage for me than it has to her. She will go home to *him,* and I'll spend the night alone. Our worlds have reversed, and there isn't a damn thing I can do about it now.

Inside the corridor, I stand there trying to regroup my thoughts, but all I see is her running back home to him.

A door opens, and Reese is standing at the entrance.

"Sir, the lady outside is refusing to leave. How would you like me to proceed with this?"

"I'll take care of it," I grit, willing this night to end. "The last thing we need is to be in the tabloids. Are the paparazzi still there?"

"No, sir, I believe David took care of them earlier."

I pat him on the shoulder, following him to the main entrance of the club.

"Alex, baby, please. It's been an hour. Let me in," Samantha whines, looking like a train wreck with her mascara rather questionably sliding down her cheeks.

I grab her arm, forcefully, and pull her aside. "You need to stop causing a scene outside my club. I don't know what has gotten into you, but I'm putting you in the next cab that drives past."

"Why won't you let me in? Please, just for old time's sake? C'mon, angel."

Her arms wrap around my waist, latching on like a leech. I'm disgusted by her overbearing affection and the use of the word *angel*. It triggers an unwelcome memory.

As I try to peel her away from me, she laughs. "Look what the cat dragged back. Is she the reason why, Alex?"

I swiftly turn around and see Charlotte standing at the entrance. Her eyes stare back at us, dull and lifeless. With her hands clutching her stomach, Eric holds onto her arm, pulling her away in the opposite direction.

Removing Samantha's arms off me, I push her away and run to the cab Charlotte is hopping into. Eric has placed her inside before I can reach the cab, shutting the door on my face. Charlotte is facing straight forward without a single blink, obviously in a catatonic state.

I bang on the window. "Charlotte, please, it's not what you think."

Eric opens the window the same time he asks the driver to wait.

"Look, Lex, I don't know what to think, but Charlie is pretty wasted right now, so I doubt she'll remember what she saw."

"I need to talk to her. I need to explain," I tell him in desperation.

"She's my best friend, and I don't want to see her hurt. Just give her time. At least let her sleep this off." He waves goodbye, closing the window as the cab drives off.

Back at the hotel, I sit on the balcony running my hands along the rim of my glass filled with scotch. My phone sits beside me, tormenting me as I so desperately want to call her. I need to make sure she's okay, to explain what happened, fearing I may lose her again.

As the sun begins to rise, I realize calling her so early in the morning would only parade my desperation. Despite the lack of sleep, my mind refuses to shut down, my eyes betraying me when I attempt to close them. The images of last night teasing me—the look on her face as she moaned at my touch, the pure ecstasy that her body so obviously craved.

In frustration, I press my phone against my forehead, trying to control this obsession with her. *Put the fucking phone down.* Placing it on the table, I replace it with a scotch in my hand, drinking the last remnants of the bottle.

It no longer burns, unable to mask the pain of my careless actions last night.

No matter what I do or say, Charlotte isn't willing to forgive me. I have to find a way to make her talk and listen. Still uncertain if she knows why I had no choice but to choose Samantha nine years ago, forgiveness will be forthcoming.

But if I've learned anything over the last forty-eight hours, Charlotte is headstrong with a vengeance.

This battle should've been a straight win, but I'm no longer dealing with the girl I left behind in high school.

Charlotte is all woman, and her shield is her most powerful weapon. It's held so close to her heart it's almost impossible to get back into a place where I once belonged.

NINETEEN

ALEX

Nine Years Ago

I t had been the day from hell.

I had just finished a fourteen-hour shift with Dad at the hospital where we lost a teenager to a drunk driving accident. It was the first time I had dealt with death, and no matter how much they prepared us for this during our studying, the reality was far more grueling.

My dad stood there calling the time of death as I ran to the toilet heaving, barely making it as I violently vomited—my body shuddering while collapsing to the floor.

How on earth would this get easier over time?

I started questioning myself if this was the right vocation for me. I'm not like my father—he's strong, always in control. Six fucking years of my life dedicated to medical school. What the hell was I going to do? I couldn't talk to Samantha about it. She just saw the status attached with calling me *Doctor*. Mom and Dad would never understand, and Adriana, well, she was too preoccupied with Elijah and immature at the best of times.

I peeled myself off the floor and washed my face before I headed outside.

"Son, are you okay?"

"Yeah. Sorry I ran out, Dad. It was just a lot to deal with."

He placed his arm around my shoulder before walking me to the reception area. The nurse at the front desk looked at me sympathetically.

"It's part of the job, Alex. It doesn't always end in saving a life."

"I know, but she was so young. Only seventeen, it's not fair." My voice began choking, and I knew I needed to get out of this miserable place.

"Life isn't always fair, Alex. Remember that."

With his last words, I walked through the sliding doors and into the cool night. It was a little after six when I arrived home. Samantha was in the living room reading some trashy magazine.

"Hey, honey, you look beat."

"Yeah, pretty much the day from hell."

Putting down the magazine, she motioned for me to sit next to her. I threw my bag on the ground and sat, ready to talk about today's events.

"I went to see Dr. Housman today."

"What the hell for?" I knew I sounded annoyed, but what the fuck was wrong with her? Dear God, she better not be knocked up. We used condoms, plus she was on the pill. "You're still taking the pill, aren't you?"

"Yes, I am, and no, I'm not pregnant. But nice to know you haven't moved forward with that decision," she barks, with her arms crossed. "Dr. Housman did some preliminarily tests, and she found that I wasn't ovulating. I'll need fertility pills should we decide to have kids."

"Okay." I breathed a sigh of relief, exhausted and not one bit interested in talking about starting a family. "So, we'll deal with that when the time comes."

"She said the younger I am, the better."

"No, Samantha." I raised my voice, fucking irritated that this was what she focused on. After the day I had, I thought she'd want to know what happened. Instead, she put the baby bullshit right on me. "We aren't having children any time soon. End. Of. Discussion."

I grabbed my bag and headed to our bedroom, sat on the bed and untied my shoelaces. Sliding my shoes off, I stood and undressed, desperate to get rid of my clothes.

Inside the bathroom, I turned on the shower waiting a few seconds for the hot water to come through, but slowly the mirror started fogging up as the steam floated across the room. As soon as the water fell on my skin, I felt myself relax. I wanted to forget today ever happened, but every time I tried, I saw the lifeless body lying on the operating table as my father tried to revive her. I didn't realize I was crying until I tasted my tears on my lips. Vigorously, I rubbed my face before turning the water off and climbing out.

With a towel wrapped around my waist and another to dry my hair, I walked back into the bedroom.

"I'm sorry, baby, I just got paranoid that I could be the reason why we never have kids." Samantha sat on the bed, grabbing a tissue off the nightstand.

"Seriously, Sammy, you need to stop listening to your sister. When the time is right, the time is right. I don't want to talk about this. I'm exhausted and just want to go to sleep."

My phone started to ring. I walked over to the desk, leaning over to see Adriana's name flashing on the screen. I answered the phone abruptly which didn't deter her as she rambled on about some issue with her Mac.

The girl never shuts up. I told her I was busy. Fuck! Why couldn't she get Elijah to help her out? Then she said she was at Charlotte's.

I don't know what came over me because in a heartbeat I agreed to go over.

Like a rainbow after a storm, it was exactly what I needed. Trying to disguise my enthusiasm, I told her I'd be over in fifteen minutes, then hung up the phone. Sammy watched as I changed into my jeans.

"What's going on?"

"Adriana's Mac died, and she needs it for tomorrow night."

I left out the part about going to Charlotte's. I don't know why—I had no reason to feel guilty.

"Oh, I thought we could climb into bed together. It's been a while, Alex." She curled her arms around my waist and started kissing my chest.

"What do you want me to do? She needs help, and you were the one who agreed for us to chaperone this stupid party."

"Fuck, Alex, it's always an excuse with you." Sammy pulled away, storming off with the bathroom door slamming behind her.

I quickly got changed, not wanting to deal with the drama that is my wife. We weren't fucking anymore because I was either exhausted when I got home from the hospital, my shifts were on rotation, and well, I didn't trust her. The whole baby thing was warping my mind.

I needed to get out of here, so I grabbed my keys and closed the door behind me, ready to chase my rainbow.

My finger pressed against the doorbell, patiently waiting for Adriana or Charlotte to answer. With my hands in my pockets, I stood there rocking back and forth, willing the nervous energy to disappear before someone answered.

I hadn't done anything to be ashamed of, though I knew it was only a matter of time, unable to rid my mind of impure thoughts despite my commitment to Sammy, but they were just thoughts.

So what if I enjoyed Charlotte's company? She made me laugh, made me forget the world existed for a few moments. She's uncomplicated. My vows were still intact. No, there was nothing to feel guilty about.

Then she stood in front of me like I was in some dream. She captivated me, her beauty leaving me speechless.

"Oh hey, Alex. You okay? You look like you've seen a ghost."

"Hi, Charlotte... I uh..."

Fuck, I had nothing to say. Now wasn't the time to be giddy. Man up. Okay, so I want to see her naked, every inch of her spread out in front of me. Okay, shit, no more manning up.

She grabbed my hand and pulled me to the living room where her parents sat. She introduced me to her father who simply said, "Hello." Her mother stood and walked over to me, then she placed her hand on my cheek. *How odd,* I thought to myself.

"Un ángel camina entre nosotros," she chanted as she touched my face.

An angel walks amongst us? What an odd thing to say.

I replied in Spanish, saying 'thank you.' Thank God, I understood and didn't look like a complete moron in front of her. Though, I am surprised to see her mother here considering her parents are divorced.

"You understand Spanish?" Charlotte asked with a wide grin on her face.

"Yes, it's what happens when you'd rather study than play dolls with your sister."

She laughed and led me to her room where we found Adriana on her phone with some sort of party emergency.

"Hey, Alex." Adriana waved, then turned to Charlotte. "Sorry I have to love you and leave you. The caterer needs me to pick the final menu."

"Adriana, you can't just leave your brother here," Charlotte rushed, panicked.

"Sure, I can. He's the computer geek. My Mac is doing some weird cross-eyed guy warning thingamajig. All my songs are on there, and I need them for the party."

Without any time for either of us to respond, Adriana vanished through the door like Superman on crack.

"I'm not a computer geek, just FYI."

"You don't look like a geek," she pointed out, moving toward her desk where she sat down. "Far from it."

I stood near the door, unsure of how far I should come in. I'd never been inside Charlotte's room, and with curiosity, I scanned my surroundings. The color of the walls was olive green, bare and without any picture frames aside from photographs taped on her ceiling. From where I was standing, I couldn't see the photographs and whose face were in them aside from the fact they look liked they had been taken at school.

Her double bed was sitting in the middle of the room with pristine white sheets, several pillows and a cushion in the middle which said *Sleep with Me*.

"Nice room," I mentioned, noticing the books on her

nightstand. I'd read the same books in senior high. "What do I look like?"

"Alex... please, you know. You'd be blind not to see it."

"Well, call me blind."

"You know you're hot," she spoke with poise. "You're smart. I mean, you're a doctor! You're the whole package."

"The whole package? Obviously, you don't know me well. I'm not perfect, Charlotte."

How could I even begin to explain how imperfect I was?

"Maybe not, but you're pretty damn close..."

It dawned on me that her words were sincere, and I had never heard anyone use the words 'perfect' and 'Alex' in the same sentence, except for my mother. But the thing which resonated was how confident she was when she said them, leaning back into her chair with her arms stretched above her head, not a single moment of hesitation as the words flew out of her mouth.

As the minutes passed, I found myself unable to look away, caught in the dilemma of wanting her innocence, her purity, but my words came out unexpected.

"What did your mom mean back there?"

"That angel stuff? Long story. Just this legend she believes in. Don't worry, she's always trying to bestow her wisdom upon me. I'm eighteen. Isn't this the time of my life to go wild? You know, get drunk and tattoo some random guy's name on my ass?" She laughed, biting on a pen while she watched me. "She shouldn't even be here. My parents are trying to be amicable. Something about trying to settle property they inherited. I kinda zoned out."

"You're not like that," I answered at ease. "Wild and irresponsible."

"No, I'm not." She hesitated, distracted by a loud yell

that echoed throughout the house. The voices were muffled, but soon I realized it was her parents arguing.

"Alex, you should probably go. This isn't something you want to hear." She sighed, her voice saddened by the excessive yelling.

Charlotte threw herself on her bed, staring at the ceiling, her hair a tangled mess around her as a lonesome tear fell down her cheek. Without thinking, I sat beside her, removing a loose strand of hair away from her face.

"Do you want to talk about it?"

"You wouldn't understand. Hell, even I don't understand."

"No, but I'll listen. That's the least I can offer."

She wiped her sleeve across her cheek. "You think I'd be used to it by now, you know, my parents being separated. Mom's here, and I should be grateful they can sit in the same room together..." She paused as if she was trying to find the right words. "I just don't understand how you promise that 'in sickness and in health,' 'till death us do part' that you'll be with one person. How do you hurt someone you're supposed to love? Dad's hurting, I know he is, but he's too proud to show it. My mom doesn't understand. He still loves her, though he has a crappy way of showing it. She doesn't look at him the way she used to, or maybe she never did. All she talks about is the past, the big bad wolf, or she refers to them as the dark angels. How they come into your life and steal what's yours, your heart and soul. I figured out a long time ago it wasn't my dad. He didn't steal her heart... someone else did. She never let it go, and now, my poor dad..." she trails off.

"Charlotte, if it's not meant to be, then maybe your dad is better off. Give him the chance to find someone who'll love him the way he deserves to be loved."

She sits up in a rush, leaning on her elbows for support with overly bright eyes staring back at me. "So, you're telling me it's okay to make these promises, place rings on each other's fingers, make vows before God, your family, and friends, only to walk away when something better comes along?"

Sitting so close to her, I couldn't help but feel this overwhelming need to touch her, to hold her in my arms. Her honesty and compassion astounded me. She wore her heart on her sleeve, and I wanted nothing more than to place it in my hands and promise to cherish it for the rest of my life. With her big brown eyes staring back at me, my heart began racing, not because I was afraid but because it felt right, and that alone was the most terrifying part. She instilled honesty in me, and I had no choice but to express how I felt —how she made me feel.

"Not something better, Charlotte. Something right," I whispered, my gaze fixated on her. "And yes, I'd walk away if that's what you're asking."

TWENTY

CHARLIE

Nine Years Ago

"Charlie, do you want to talk about it?"

What was there to talk about? I hadn't slept. My mom decided to take off again in the middle of the night, leaving my dad to worry relentlessly about her. No note, no nothing. Just her belongings gone. How could I understand? I hadn't been in love before nor had I been married. My opinion didn't matter even though my life had been turned upside down once again by the two people who were supposed to protect me.

"Not tonight, Adriana."

I examined my eyes in the mirror. The dark circles were impossible to hide.

"So, listen, since you look like sex on legs, we need to discuss some sort of signal in case you want to get some nookie-nookie."

"Adriana, did you just say nookie-nookie? Okay, grandma..."

"You know Finn will be here," she teased.

Here we go again.

If I had a dollar for every time this topic was brought up, I could buy, well, a new pair of Converse. Finn and I had a fling last year after being friends forever. It resulted in us losing our virginity down at the beach. It wasn't the best place to lose it, mainly because there was sand everywhere. So, I was in no rush to try that again after what could only go down as the worst first time in history. We tried again a month after in his bed, and unfortunately, it was no better than before. There was no sand but also no spark, plus it was damn awkward. He was huge, and I was small, so it just kind of hurt.

I wasn't sure what the big deal was, especially when I was fully capable of helping myself. Adriana would tell me how wonderful it was to be in love, but she had Elijah, and he's all she could think about.

"Honestly, he is a great guy, he's my best friend," I told her, pulling my skin beneath my eyes to make it look more presentable. It didn't work, the bags were there to stay. "Stop trying to play matchmaker. If anyone needs the signal, it will be you."

"I thought I was your best friend?"

"Jealousy looks striking on you," I mocked, with a sardonic grin. "You know what I mean."

The doorbell rang, and I had never seen Adriana run so fast. She could've qualified for the Olympics at the rate she was going. I opened the bedroom door to hear muffled voices. It was Elijah.

I had learned my lesson—give them five minutes before entering the room.

I checked my phone and saw a message from Finn. I quickly responded knowing Adriana would be ecstatic. In her eyes, the more, the merrier. I thought of the aftermath, the cleaning tomorrow morning. Her parents only agreed to this if the house was back to its original condition by ten o'clock the next morning. I didn't know how Adriana expected to pull it off, but I had no doubt, she'd make me haul some serious cleaning ass.

After ten minutes, I decided to head downstairs. They must've finished their make-out session by now.

"Adriana!" I yelled as I raced down the stairs. "Finn said the guys are coming, too."

Landing in the kitchen, I was surprised to be greeted by Alex and Samantha. My eyes locked into his. Samantha was sitting on his lap.

Everything I felt in the past week had slapped me right in the face. They were here as a married couple. That's right, *married,* I had to keep reminding myself. Suddenly, our flirtatious texts seemed foolish and adolescent. *What was I thinking?* I had no right lusting after a married guy.

But something felt different like it was more than just a crush. He acted different. I couldn't explain it, but I knew I had no choice but to snap out of it.

"Charlotte, nice to see you again. This is my wife, Samantha," he introduced her as I awkwardly stood there not knowing what to say.

Samantha was stunning with long, silky, golden blonde hair stopping just beneath her breasts. Her eyes, azul colored, gleaming as she holds onto her husband, caressing his chin with a loving gaze. Adriana's description didn't do her justice, neither did the photographs at their house. I reached out my hand to shake hers, but instead, she jumped off his lap and pulled me into a hug.

"Finally, I get to meet you. Adriana talks nonstop about you. It'll be good to have another friend in this boring, miserable place," she squealed, holding me too tightly.

I looked at Alex, unsure of what to say. His face was just as confused as mine.

"Oh, wow. Nice meeting you, too, Samantha."

"Call me Sam, please," she said, adjusting the hem of her dress. "Samantha is what my parents call me, and this guy when he wants to act formal."

I forced a smile. "Okay... Sam."

Thankfully, the doorbell rang, so I excused myself to mingle with some of the guests. As soon as I was out of the kitchen, I took a moment to gather my thoughts, letting out the huge breath I had been holding.

I hated that she was a beautiful woman, and together, they would make beautiful babies. Although I had turned eighteen already, I had never felt so young. I needed to hang out with my own kind and shake myself of these impure thoughts.

The house was filling up, and I started recognizing a lot of people from school. I did my best-friend duty and greeted the guests. Most were already into the punch I assumed had been spiked, and the speakers were blaring the latest pop song. I had been humming along to the beat when I felt a pair of bulky arms wrap themselves around my waist.

"Finn!"

I turned around as he hugged me tight, lifting me. I missed him. He was one of my best friends despite our awkward history. I wrapped my arms around his neck, and behind him, I noticed Alex standing with Elijah. Alex looked at me strangely, almost angry.

Finn put me down, the grin on his face contagious. "Charlie, I've missed you. You never visit me anymore," he complained.

"I know, I know. I've missed you, too, Finn. Come on, let's get a drink."

We walked over to the drinks table. Finn grabbed a cup of punch, and his facial expression said it all. Yep, it had been spiked, but thankfully, Finn could hold his booze. I, on the other hand, didn't want a repeat of the last eighteenth birthday party I went to. I grabbed a bottle of Coke, knowing I'd probably be the only sober one here.

Finn put our drinks down and pulled me onto the makeshift dance floor. He had the moves and I'd always enjoyed dancing with him. He grabbed my waist and pulled me into him, then I rubbed myself against his thigh. This is what we did. We didn't care that people thought we were a couple. We were just having fun.

Once the song had finished, and I pulled away from Finn, out of breath I said, "I'm going to check on Adriana. Behave, Finn."

I found her standing in the kitchen with Sam, pouring Grey Goose into a new batch of punch.

Alex was standing at the corner doing something with his phone. I made a conscious effort to avoid contact with him at all costs. He was acting weird, and I had no idea why.

"Hey, Char," she greeted a bit too cheerfully.

"Adriana, why are you spiking the punch? Did we not learn from the last party?"

"Oh, lighten up, Char. I'm eighteen now. *Woo!*"

This was like a bad scene straight out of *Girls Gone Wild*.

"So, Charlie, Adriana tells me you and Finn..." Sam teased. Alex instantly looked up from his phone, his face enraged as he gazed at me. "You looked pretty cozy on the dance floor."

It was so awkward to have this conversation in front of Alex. I felt the need to defend myself.

"It's not like that. We're great friends. Have been since we were born."

Adriana laughed loudly, the punch in full effect. I sensed that what she was about to say would not paint the best picture of me. "Please, Char, good friends don't just lose their virginity to each other."

Alex shot me a fierce glare before leaving the room, almost stomping out.

What was his problem?

"Adriana, I can't believe you said that out loud," I berated her. "My personal life isn't up for discussion with everyone."

I left the room to look for Alex. I wanted to know what his problem was. I continued searching the house but couldn't find him. Searching the gardens—still no sign of him. Then I walked onto the street where, under the pale moonlight, I saw his shadow leaning against his Jeep.

"Alex?"

He turned around, his face softening as he saw me. I leaned against the car as well, knowing it was best that I didn't make eye contact with him.

"Alex, did I do something to make you angry? I'm sorry about that conversation in the kitchen. I didn't particularly want my sex life announced to the whole world. Adriana will get an earful from me tomorrow," I joked, trying to lighten this tension between us.

Pressing his lips together with a slight grimace, he asked, "So, it's true?"

"What's true?"

"You and Finn are an item?"

"No, we aren't. I told you, I don't have a boyfriend."

"So what? You're fuck buddies, then? It sure looked like it when you were dancing."

His hands caught my attention. His fists were clenched, knuckles stark white even in the darkness. I didn't get why he was so fucking angry, and it was now making me angry. I was shocked at his response. What did he care, anyway? He was married, he had a wife to go home to. Why would my sex life bother him in the slightest?

"First of all, we aren't fuck buddies. We did it twice over a year ago. It wasn't good, so we never did it again. Second of all, he's a good friend, and yes, we like to have fun. It's harmless. Besides, both of us agree we're better as friends. And lastly, why would you care? Are you worried I'm going to have unprotected sex like the rest of the teenagers here and get knocked up before graduation?"

"Charlotte, it's just... you—"

"What about me?"

Without warning, he leaned over, his lips crashing against my own. I could taste his desperation as it was mirroring mine. My head was screaming at me to stop, but my body was aching for it. His hands were now cupping my face, but I wanted more. I needed him to touch every part of me. I grabbed his jacket, pulling him closer to me, the kiss becoming more intense, his tongue searching for more. I wanted to give him everything right then and there. I didn't want to stop. My heart was beating fast, and my body felt like it was on fire.

He quickly pulled back, a look of shock on his face.

No, no! Please don't regret it.

His pupils were dilated like an animal ready to attack, but slowly, his eyes stared down at the ground, his posture crumpling. Laying his hand flat on his thigh, the gold band blinded me—a symbol of love and devotion.

What we just did was very wrong.

"Charlotte, I'm so sorry. I shouldn't have done that... I'm m-married," he stammered.

Biting down on my lip, my body turned numb. How could something so wrong feel so right? I needed to get away quickly, erase the mistake we had just made. I ran back inside, leaving him alone under the watchful eyes of the stars.

When I got back inside the crowded house, my heart was still beating fast, adrenaline running through my veins. I found the drink table again and knocked back a cup of punch. There, that felt better, but shit that vodka was strong. I felt the warmth spreading through my body, instantly calming my anxious nerves.

"Charlie, where have you been? I scored with the hot chick from your school, but I don't know her name." Finn motioned for me to look at his left. There were a few girls dancing on the dance floor, the girl with the short red hair making eyes with Finn.

"That's Jennifer. She's in my English class," I told him, trying my best to block out the kiss for just a second to no avail.

"Well, damn, she can really put out. No offense, Charlie."

I shook my head, patting his arm. "Absolutely none taken."

The lights dimmed even further as Elijah brought out the birthday cake. The crowd started singing 'Happy Birthday.' I stood there, suddenly feeling very self-conscious. Sam stood beside Adriana, singing loudly. On her right stood Alex, his eyes locked on mine. I could feel his gaze penetrating me, those beautiful emerald eyes that took me in under the stars.

I yearned to tell him that I had been thinking about him nonstop since the night I ran into him in the kitchen. That every night I'd lie awake imagining his kisses, his touch, and that I have made myself climax imagining him inside me, pushing me over the edge.

And now that I'd had a taste of him, I was scared I couldn't stop.

It had consumed me.

He had me, heart and soul, all in that one *kiss*.

TWENTY-ONE

ALEX

Nine Years Ago

I had been dreading this party since last night.

I knew I'd see her again, but every time it just got worse. The yearn to kiss her beautiful lips became hard to ignore, and despite my feelings toward her being all sorts of wrong, I could've sworn she felt everything too.

Already the night started off bad when Sammy decided to sit on my lap as Charlotte walked down the stairs. I wanted to push Sammy off but knew I couldn't without raising suspicion.

As usual, Sammy did her over-the-top greeting with Charlotte. It was obvious Adriana was rubbing off on her. I couldn't stand superficial girls. Charlotte was different, though, or at least I thought she was before I saw that Danes kid all over her on the dance floor. What the fuck was that? I was standing with Elijah while he rambled on about Apple's latest stock price. I couldn't give a damn, I just wanted to know why that guy's hands were all over her, and why she was rubbing her pussy against his leg.

My anger rose with every sway of her body against his. The need to punch him straight in that face of his becoming more tempting by the second. And this music, lyrics about fucking pussies and whores? My sister was a goddamn idiot.

I'd had enough, escaping to the kitchen to find Sammy spiking the punch.

"Very mature of you, Samantha," I sarcastically pointed out as she poured the whole bottle of vodka into the punch. My sister taking a cup and downing it in one go.

"Oh, lighten up. Who crowned you king?" she retorted.

"Funny, Samantha, 'cause the shit is on me if anything happens. Adriana, lay off the fucking punch."

"I'm eighteen, Alex. Geez, Sam, I don't know how you put up with him."

I was just about to tell her where to shove her eighteenth birthday party when Charlotte walked in. She avoided making eye contact with me, probably for the best. I was still fuming about what I witnessed on the dance floor.

"So, Charlie, Adriana tells me you and Finn..." Sam teased.

I wasn't leaving the room now. I wanted to hear her response. She defensively responded to Sam until Adriana dropped the bombshell.

"Please, Char, good friends don't just lose their virginity to each other."

What the fuck?

So she lost her virginity to him?

Was she still fucking him?

She said she didn't have a boyfriend.

I was furious, storming out of the kitchen. I needed to get out of the chaos, finding refuge under the stars, the fresh air clearing my mind. It wasn't long before she found me. I could feel her near me before she even spoke.

"Alex?"

There was trepidation in her voice, and immediately, I felt myself weaken. It was unfair to be angry with her. It wasn't her fault I was married, or that I felt like a miserable failure studying for a career I no longer wanted.

And it wasn't her fault she was so unbelievably gorgeous. Those fuck-me boots didn't help the hard-on that became present anytime she was near me.

She continued speaking, apologizing for what went on in the kitchen. The next part caught my attention—her sex life. If I was angry before, it was nothing like what I was feeling now. I wanted to take her over to my car, spread her legs, and make her mine. Tell her I'd be the only one fucking that pretty little pussy of hers.

I didn't know what had come over me—I was fucking married.

The turmoil inside me was taking its toll.

I asked her if she and this Danes kid were an item.

"No, we aren't. I told you, I don't have a boyfriend."

"So what? You're fuck buddies, then? It sure looked like it when you were dancing."

The instant it left my mouth, I regretted it, but I didn't know what else to say. I wanted her. Couldn't she see that? Clenching my hands, I tried to control my anger.

She rambled on about their history, something I had no interest in hearing, but it did explain a lot. Then she asked me why I cared.

Why did I care? Because I hadn't stopped thinking about her since the moment we ran into each other at my parents' house. Something about her drew me in, especially when I looked at her beautiful chocolate-brown eyes. Her beauty was so natural from her soft skin to her long brown hair. Every night I pushed my wife away and instead lay in bed wishing Charlotte were next to me. I avoided sexual contact with Sammy because I'd rather jerk off in the shower thinking about this other girl I couldn't have.

"Charlotte, it's just... you—" I stopped.

Could I say those words out loud?

"What about me?"

I don't know what came over me. I leaned in, my lips crashing against hers. She tasted like fucking heaven. I cupped her face, keeping my hands from wandering to her ass. Our tongues battled, wanting more, and she never pulled back arousing me even more. I could feel her tongue swirling in my mouth. Imagining the exact thing being done to my cock was pushing me over the edge. I felt like a horny teenager ready to blow his load because of one kiss. But it wasn't just any kiss, it was Charlotte. She pulled me in closer. I knew I could've had her then with only the stars watching, but reality was kicking in. My wife was just inside. No, this wasn't fair to Charlotte. She deserved better, not some married guy lusting after her.

I pulled away and apologized for the kiss, and she quickly ran back inside. What did I expect her to do? Beg me to be hers? I took a deep breath, closing my eyes and remembering the moment that was only a few seconds ago. I could still taste her on my lips, smell her scent on my jacket, and, oh shit, her scent on my jacket.

I opened my eyes and unlocked my car, grabbing some gum from the glove box. I looked for something I could spray. Nothing. *Shit.* I locked my car and walked back through the front garden. Standing in groups outside were those typical rebellious teenagers smoking. I walked over and stood next to a guy who was blowing rings into the air.

"You wanna puff, bro?" he asked.

"Nah, I'm sweet. Thanks, man."

I patted him on the shoulder, walking back in the house, the guys probably thinking I was a fuckwit for standing around them for two seconds.

"Alex, there you are! Shit, why do you stink like weed?" Sammy scrunched her nose as she attempted to hug me.

Mission accomplished.

"I was just outside for a second talking to some dude. Sorry about the smell."

She grinned, and I wondered how much vodka she'd had.

"Don't worry, baby, that's why showers were invented, and tonight, don't expect to have one alone." She winked at me while trying to grab my cock in the middle of the hallway. Thankfully, Elijah interrupted, "Birthday cake time," he cheered.

He brought out the cake, and the crowd started singing 'Happy Birthday.' I saw her standing across the room next to that jerk. I couldn't take my eyes off her. She stared at me, her face now unreadable. It was times like this I wished I could read minds.

It wasn't a mistake, Charlotte. I played the words over in my head, hoping she had some telepathic gift and could hear me.

As the singing stopped and Adriana blew out the candles, the crowd cheered before dispersing back to their little groups.

I needed to find her again. I didn't know what I'd say, but I was hoping the words would come to me once I stood in front of her. Searching the dance floor, she was nowhere to be found.

In the hallway, all I saw were cliques of girls standing

around. I walked into the kitchen. There were a few girls there, but no one I recognized. I was about to walk upstairs when I heard her voice from the den, and she wasn't alone.

"Look, Carter, I only agreed to go to prom because you nagged me like a two-dollar whore."

"Oh, come on, Charlie. You know we're meant to be. Why are you wasting your time on that jerk?"

"His name is Finn, and he's one of my best friends. Don't you dare talk shit about him."

"Whatever. You can do better than him."

"And what... you think you're better than him?" She laughed.

As much as I hated this Finn guy, it seemed I'd found a new frontrunner.

"C'mon, Charlie, no one will know. Just once, let me prove it." His voice softened.

"Don't fucking touch me, Carter."

I pushed the door open, both of them shocked to see me. "You heard her. Don't you dare fucking touch her if you value your balls."

"Oh, look who's back, big-shot Edwards. How's medical life treating you? I heard Daddy pulled some nice strings so you could intern at the hospital?" he mocked.

I was ready to punch his fucking face when she stood in front of me with her hands on my chest. "Let it go, Alex."

Carter laughed, then I looked up and saw Charlotte turn around and punch him directly in the nose. He shrieked like a fucking schoolgirl. "What the fuck did you do that for?"

Charlie bent over, her fist clenched, the pain visible on her face. "Don't ever talk shit about any of my friends. You understand?"

I examined her swollen hand, her knuckles red raw.

Damn, what a punch. We left Carter standing in the den, wiping the blood from his nose.

Back in the kitchen, I made her sit down as I searched the freezer for that bag of peas. Placing it on her hand, I let the bag reduce the swelling, so I could examine it further.

"Sorry, this will hurt but just for a second. I need to make sure it isn't broken."

I opened her palm and laid it flat in mine. She could move her fingers slowly, so I knew it wasn't broken. It didn't stop her from moaning as the pain increased.

"Not broken, but it will bruise. Do you normally punch people who talk shit about your friends?"

"He had it coming, that jerk," she growled, followed by a sharp cry as she moved her hand.

"Oh Charlotte, poor baby," I whispered, running my fingers along hers.

I wanted to kiss her, take her home, and remove the pain she was feeling. She looked into my eyes, and her cheeks turned pink.

"Oh my God, Char, what happened?" Adriana stumbled into the room, almost tripping.

Jesus Christ, she's wasted. Mom was going to hang me out by my balls for this. I didn't even want to think about what Dad would say.

I backed away from Charlotte. Adriana was too drunk to notice, anyway. She explained what happened which was pointless because Adriana would remember nothing in the morning. I decided to find Sammy. It was time to go home. I was physically and mentally exhausted.

"Oh, here he is, my hot-as-fuck husband, Dr. Edwards. Well, not yet, but soon I can say Dr. Edwards to anyone I want," she slurred.

"Sammy, I think it's time to go."

It was well after midnight, and the party had dwindled. The guy she was chatting with decided to leave as well as the remaining partygoers. The music finally stopped, and the DJ packed up his equipment.

"I've got it from here, Alex. Why don't you take Sammy home?" Elijah suggested.

"Where are Adriana and Charlotte? I should probably say goodbye."

"Charlie took Adriana upstairs where she's passed out on her bed."

"Thanks, Elijah. I'll be back around seven to help clean up." I shook his hand before turning around to find Sammy passed out on the couch. She remained asleep the entire way home and still hadn't woken up when I put her in our bed. She snored so loud I knew I had no chance in hell of sleeping, but at least I avoided that shower she was planning.

I grabbed a spare blanket and settled on the couch. My phone lay beside me. Should I? It was two o'clock. She was probably asleep, but I texted her anyway.

Me: *I'm guessing you're asleep. I'm sorry I lied that I was sorry.*

Only a moment later, my phone buzzed. I smiled, taking a deep breath praying she wasn't agreeing with me.

Charlotte: *I'm awake. I obviously didn't drink enough vodka. You can be sorry, it's ok. I understand, Alex.*

I typed a message back quickly, not holding back my thoughts.

Me: *But I'm not, that's the thing. I didn't mean to say it. I wanted that to happen. I've wanted it for a while.*

Within seconds, she'd responded.
I paused, thinking about the obvious—my marriage.

Charlotte: *I'd be lying if I said I didn't feel the same way. But this can't happen again. It's so complicated. For starters, you're married.*

I didn't know what came over me, but I was sick and tired of hiding my feelings. And it hurt me to admit that this wasn't an easy situation. It wasn't high school anymore. Well, at least for me it wasn't.

Me: *I know, Charlotte. I'm just saying I'm not sorry. It won't happen again as much as I want it to. You're right, it's too complicated, and of course there's Adriana to think about.*

I waited for her response, but it never came. I figured that she either didn't want to talk about it or she'd fallen asleep. Every part of me wishing she fell asleep. Tomorrow, I'd see her again.

I fell asleep rather quickly, reminiscing how we kissed so passionately under the stars.

We kissed.

I had broken a vow.

So what difference did it matter if I broke it again?

TWENTY-TWO

CHARLIE

Nine Years Ago

There were a million and one jackhammers going off inside my head. Why on earth did I drink that spiked punch? Oh, that's right, because I had kissed my best friend's brother.

My best friend's married brother.

I was so fucking screwed.

I had no time to lay there and think about what I'd done. The house was trashed, and we had three hours to have it back to its original condition or Adriana was toast.

"Morning, Charlie. Would you like a cup of coffee before you start?" Elijah offered.

I looked around, surprised and secretly pleased that he'd done a lot already. God, he was such a good boyfriend. "Wow, you've already done so much."

"Yeah, well, I can't have Adriana grounded on her eighteenth birthday. What kind of boyfriend would I be?"

I patted him on the back. He was such a great guy.

"Okay, so the kitchen is done. I'll tackle the rest of the

house if you attempt the pool house and pool." He laughed, knowing he'd left the worst part for me.

I pouted as I walked to the door, opening it to welcome the cool, fresh air. Fuck, the backyard was trashed. I grabbed a garbage bag, walking around placing all the garbage inside. I cleaned up the grassed area, which took me ages, then headed to the pool house. As I walked in, my mouth dropped. The bed was unmade, and sheets were strewn all over the floor. Empty cups lie around the room.

Urgh, and condom wrappers were on the floor.

I seriously didn't want to think about what I could catch in there right now.

"Looks like someone had a good time in here last night... twice." Alex laughed. "*Wow*, four times."

I'd have no choice but to turn around and face him. Act mature, be a nice friend. That's all you were.

As I slowly turned, he stood there leaning against the doorframe. He was in his sweats looking like a fucking god. It did nothing to make me regret what happened last night. I felt stupid standing there in my boxers and Ugg boots.

"Well, someone isn't going to have a good time right now, and that would be me. This is rancid."

Alex helped me clean up the room, stripping the bed and replacing the sheets. We worked in silence. It was better that way. I didn't want to talk about last night. We said it wouldn't happen again, and I was sticking to my word, but damn, he looked amazing.

Alex grabbed a tissue to pick up the used condom under the bed. He held it up in front of me, and I was mortified.

"Eww!" I squirmed, but he continued to dangle it there, laughing as he did. I ran to the bathroom as he followed me, but sense prevailed, and he placed it in the trash. Then he scrubbed his hands vigorously.

"Wash them real good," I told him. "Oh God, that was nasty."

He smirked, still washing his hands. "I bet you would be thinking differently if it belonged to Justin Timberlake."

"Well, dang, he wouldn't be wearing one if he were with me."

Alex laughed and splashed me with the water and I screamed at the coldness.

"Now I'm wet!"

He turned the tap off, drying his hands on the towel hanging on the rack. "Weren't you before?"

"Oh, wouldn't you like to know?" I teased as I walked back into the room.

Suddenly, I felt his arms around my waist, my body stiffening in his embrace. He leaned into my neck and whispered in my ear, "Yes, I would, Charlotte. You don't know how much." His lips brushed against my skin, and succumbing to my desires, I allowed him to do it. Reaching my arm up behind, I pulled him into me. His hands were still around my waist, then I felt them slowly move up to my breasts. I waited in anticipation before I heard a commotion outside. Like a splash of cold water, we pulled away from each other.

I grabbed the garbage bag and pretended to pick up trash as Alex looked at me with a satisfied smirk before walking out of the pool house.

I heard the voices—it was Sam and Adriana.

"Adriana, seriously, we need to get cracking. Andrew and Emily will blow up, and you'll be grounded for a year if they see the house like this."

"I know, I know. The house is done. It's just the pool now."

"What about the pool house?"

"Charlotte did it," Alex lied. "I just showed her where to find the spare sheets."

"Eww, like people fucked in there?" Sam complained.

"I know," Adriana wailed. "I'm never drinking again. Or throwing a party."

"Wait till you get to college," Sam snickered. "The parties there are wicked."

"That's what I've heard. I better go find Elijah."

I heard Adriana walk away as I pretended to clean, hoping they would leave.

"Nice influence, Samantha," I heard Alex say. "Is that really how you want to tell an eighteen-year-old to spend her time in college?"

"It's more fun than staying in Carmel," she bit back sarcastically.

"You want to bring that up again?"

"Fuck, Alex. How can I not bring that up again?" she argued back. "I'm tired of this boring place. Being married doesn't mean you have to stay at home every day. I miss the city. I miss the crazy parties and the drinking."

"I don't want to talk about this anymore. I'm going to finish cleaning."

"No, I'm sick of you not wanting to talk or do anything for that matter." Her voice was loud, carrying through the eerily quiet backyard. "God, I even miss the fucking around. It's like you came here and became a celibate doctor. Do you realize we haven't fucked in like a month? Even then, it was a pity fuck. I had to beg you for it."

"Don't do this now," he warned.

"I'm so sick of our marriage, Alex. It's turned stale." I heard her storm off.

I stood there awkwardly, trying to take it all in. The door opened, and I shuffled to the bedside, pretending to clean. He came up behind me again, turning me around quickly and he crashed his lips onto mine. I dropped the garbage bag and wrapped my arms around his neck. He tasted so good. I kissed him faster, the urgency and thrill of wanting more. As we slowly stopped to catch our breath, he looked me in the eyes.

"It's you, Charlotte. You're the reason behind what she said outside. All I think about is you. I don't want to stop this. Do you trust me?" he pleaded.

I didn't know what I was thinking. I didn't know why I believed him, but I couldn't help but tell the truth, lay my feelings out in front of him.

"I trust you, Alex," I whispered, my lips brushing against his. "More than anyone else in my life."

TWENTY-THREE

CHARLIE

Present

My head is pounding like a woodpecker constantly banging one spot.

Unable to open my eyes, they feel like they are sewn together, impossible to open the lead weight —ramifications from last night's events. Vigorously, I rub my eyes before opening them again, slowly, to be met with daylight. The sun is shining through the windows, something I'd normally enjoy but not this morning. I sit up, trying to make sense of everything.

I know the pounding head is because of the alcohol I consumed last night, but I don't recall how I got home or who I came home with.

Panicking, I run out of my bedroom, stumbling on my shoes and clutch lying on the floor. The pain in my big toe ricochets as I knock it against the wooden floor. Hopping on one spot, I ignore the throb and rush to the living room, immediately noticing the couch is empty.

Thank fucking God. I don't want to deal with anyone right now.

I take my time limping to the kitchen. Pouring myself a tall glass of orange juice while leaning into the cupboard, I grab the much-needed Advil.

The events of last night replay in my mind as I hobble back to my room. I remember the charity ball and the kiss I shamelessly had with Lex in the ballroom while Julian waited for me. I remember going to the club to have a good time, but that was ruined when Lex showed up.

Eric mentioned it was Lex's club. That was it.

How did I even get home?

I swallow the juice and Advil, climbing back into my bed to fall asleep again.

My eyes spring open, the sun still shining directly into my face. Turning to my side, I lift my phone to check the time. Nine o'clock.

The screen is full of notifications—four text messages and a slew of emails. The first two are from Eric.

Eric: *Lunch at Noodle House at noon. We need to talk.*

Crap, what have I done? I suddenly feel an urge to vomit, thinking I can't remember things for a very good reason. Racing toward the bathroom, I topple over the toilet, dry retching as nothing comes out. Peeling myself off the cold tiles, I drag myself back to bed and check my phone again.

Eric: *Adriana will be there, but she is meeting us at 12:30. Don't be late! Check the photos I tagged you in. I look hot AF.*

I laugh, regretting it almost immediately as my head spins violently. It'd been a long time since I drank that much, and I vow never to touch tequila ever again.

The next message is from an unknown number.

Unknown number: *Hey Charlie. Hope you don't mind Eric inviting me to lunch. If it's too much I totally understand.*

As much as I don't want to revisit my past, Adriana holds a special place in my heart. I don't know why she feels it will be too much for me as long as she steers off the topic of her brother. I let her know I'm looking forward to catching up, moving onto my next message.

Batman: *Gorgeous, I'll be back around 4. Any chance we can have that raincheck dinner tonight? My place around 7? If you're good, I've got a surprise for you. Batman has lots of tricks up his sleeve.*

My mood brightens until the dark cloud begins to hover over me. I hesitate to respond. The guilt incinerating me from last night's actions, and it just isn't all the guilt of our sordid kiss. Lex has this power I hate admitting and it starts to weigh heavily on my mind.

I'm not cheating on Lex, we aren't together.

So why do I feel guilty for having dinner with Julian and quite possibly some good sex in his bat cave? I shake my head, attempting to clear my thoughts, responding right away.

After a few flirty texts back and forth, going back to sleep is impossible. No matter how much I try to distract myself, I can't be trusted with my thoughts right now. The tension is too much, and the only way to release it, apart from raiding the goody drawer is to go for a run.

The mornings are full of dedicated runners. I run as if my life depends on it, trying to forget the past twenty-four hours. My body aches as I push myself as hard as humanly possible. I stop by a bench, stretching my muscles, then pull on my hoodie to escape the morning chill. People run past me, some fast, some slow, and some run in groups, some by themselves.

A group is coming my way, running fast, but there's one guy who runs alone, faster than anyone else. His body tenses as he picks up speed. He wears his hoodie, and I can see his phone strapped to his arm. An illusion, I tell myself, it's not him. I've been down that road before thinking I saw him everywhere I went. He quickly runs past me. Tailing him are the rest of the runners in the group.

I continue to stretch my muscles when a woman slows down, stopping at the bench as well. She bends over, resting her hands on her thighs, trying to catch her breath.

"Sorry, I didn't mean to intrude, but blimey, I can't keep up with you lot."

"Don't worry, I'm the same." I smile, noticing her thick British accent. "I think I spend more time as a bench-warmer than actually running."

She laughs but slows down as she holds onto her rib

cage, still trying to recover. Sitting down on the bench, I decide to join her.

"Do you run here a lot?" she asks

"Most mornings. Today I really need it."

"Tell me about it. I haven't had a moment to relax since I got here."

"You're not from here?"

"Manchester," she answers proudly. "A long way from here."

"Sometimes, the distance can be welcoming."

It isn't a coincidence I chose to reside in New York City, wanting to be as far away as possible from the West Coast. Not that it matters now, my past has finally caught up with me.

"Yeah, I do miss home." She gazes wistfully into the sky. "But then again, home is where my man is."

The feeling of being in love, there's nothing like it in the world. If you're lucky enough to have it, then hold onto it. How ironic, I think, the part about holding on. I did until the end, until there was nothing left to hold onto.

"Well, I best head off," she announces. "I've got back-to-back meetings today. Can you believe that? It's a Sunday for goodness sakes. It was really nice to meet you."

"Nice meeting you, too." I smile as she takes off, her long blonde hair shimmering in the morning sun.

Eric is already sitting inside at a table. As usual, his hand is glued to his phone. He glances up and stands as I walk toward him. With a kiss on both cheeks, he sits back down and motions for me to do the same.

"How's the hangover?"

"How much did I drink?" I moan, sinking into the chair. "Everything is such a blur."

"Let's see, probably a bottle at the charity event, then maybe..." He starts counting his fingers. Oh God. I hang my head in shame, waiting to hear his response. "Maybe five shots at the club? I don't know. I lost count after you disappeared on the dance floor."

He sips his latte, grinning.

"Eric, I need you to be honest. What happened last night? I don't remember anything after the shots I had at the bar?" I beg of him. I don't tell him about the quick flashes running through my head, which are possibly my imagination running wild. "I mean, what happened with Lex and me?"

"That gorgeous man was all over you in the VIP area. We left to go dance, then when we came back, he'd disappeared, so you and I decided to dance, but before I knew it you and Lex were all over each other on the dance floor. Then you guys disappeared."

I freeze, unable to say a single word. Covering my face with my hands, I let out a heavy sigh. Holy shit, did I fuck him in the club? With my eyes shut tight and drowning out the noise of the people around me, I try to remember what happened, but everything is so hazy. We were in a dark room, and I remember something felt cold on my back. My stomach begins to tie into knots, a loss of appetite knowing I'll never get the answer without confronting Lex.

"Okay, so I take it from the silence you're worried you fucked him?" Eric is straight to the point. "To be honest, Charlie, when I saw you coming out of the ladies' room, you didn't look like you had been fucked."

"And how in hell would you know what I look like if I had been fucked?"

"I don't know, legs wobbly, more disheveled?" He scowls, pursing his lips. "Your hair was pretty much intact as was your dress. Maybe he just felt you up. I wouldn't worry about it too much."

Maybe he thinks I shouldn't worry about it too much, but this is Lex we are talking about here. This isn't any new guy I can simply ignore. Every touch means something, and I crossed the line into dangerous waters without a life jacket.

Suddenly, I think of Julian, and the guilt is accompanied with nausea. I can blame the alcohol, right? *You're not eighteen anymore.*

My thoughts are interrupted as Adriana strolls toward us. Eric and I stand, hugging her before we sit down again to order our lunch. My appetite has dwindled to nothing, so I order a salad, but even when it arrives I barely touch it.

We chat about the charity ball and what gossip was splashed on page six this morning. Adriana proudly talks about her boutique, how she started it, and the designs she will stock as well as her own creations. I'm so proud of her and what she's achieving. She has wanted this for as long as I can remember, and to be successful in New York City is a big achievement in the fashion world.

Eric excuses himself when his phone rings with a potential booty call. Welcoming his absence, I turn to face Adriana when he's out of sight.

"Adriana, I need to ask you something..." I hesitate, wondering if I should involve her in the mess I've created for myself. "Have you spoken to Lex since last night?"

She places her fork down, wiping her mouth with her napkin while grinning. "Yes, I have."

"Why are you smiling?"

"Were you so wasted you don't recall last night? So now

you're trying to find out what happened between you and Lex?"

I wring the napkin on my lap, anxiously trying to string a sentence without sounding like a whore. "Yes, kind of. Look, I'm not that kind of girl," I rush, trying to defend my actions. "I don't usually go out and get wasted on a Saturday night. Most of the time, I'm at Nikki's house spending time with her son."

"Hey, listen, Char..." The nickname brings back the nostalgia of our friendship. "You don't have to explain anything to me. One look at you, and I know you aren't that type of girl. You never were. That's why Lex loved you so much."

Her words are like tiny knives, stabbing me one by one in the heart.

Loved. That's why he loved me so much.

Past tense, I keep telling myself.

He isn't my future anymore.

"Look, he didn't tell me much, to be honest, only that you didn't have sex. He was clear on that when I asked him. Oh, and that stupid bitch, Samantha, was there," she huffs.

"What? Samantha was there?"

My memory begins to clear. We were exiting the club, and I heard laughter, familiar laughter. The feeling of wanting to be violently ill on the sidewalk engulfed me when I saw her face, and Lex trying to restrain her from entering the club.

"Yes, she was. She wasn't allowed to enter the club, so she made a big scene, and Lex, of course, had to calm her down. It's not the best publicity for the club since the paparazzi swarm that place."

Adriana continues to explain what happened. How Samantha was already drunk, and how she's having massive custody issues with Chris, her ex, regarding their daughter. Adriana had only heard about her through the grapevine after ceasing contact with her after she and Lex split up. A part of me feels sorry for Samantha after hearing what she's going through, but it isn't my place to get involved. I'd played a part in ruining her life many years ago and regret still weighs heavily on my shoulders for my careless actions.

Eric comes back to the table, excitedly talking about a date he's going to have with this guy tomorrow night and what he should wear. I point out since the date involves a movie that he might want to leave his Versace suit hanging in the closet. He pouts, as usual, any excuse to wear that suit.

We say goodbye to each other. Adriana and I make plans to have dinner on Tuesday night, just the two of us to catch up on old times.

Back at my apartment, I plonk myself on the couch and try to piece the puzzle together. I didn't fuck Lex last night, but who knows, maybe I gave him head or something.

Shit. I'm mad as hell at Lex.

No good can come of being around him.

I need to focus on the positive, my fiancé, my future husband.

It's seven on the dot when I knock on Julian's door dressed in my off-the-shoulder black dress. The moment his door opens, his loving smile onsets my guilt.

"Geez, Alfred is slacking off. Batman has to answer the door himself?"

He grabs my hand, pulling my body into his, and kisses me deeply. His tongue softly teases mine, desperation in his moans until I pull away momentarily, a reaction of guilt, and play it off as a joke.

"If that's how you'll greet me every time, you might as well fire Alfred."

"Come inside, gorgeous."

As I walk into his apartment, it still takes me by surprise at how much it actually looks like the bat cave in the movies. The walls are dark but still have a warm ambiance.

We stand in his living room, which is very much like mine, not too large. A brown leather sofa sits in front of a massive flat-screen television. What's it with men and their obsession with size? Opposite to that are rows and rows of bookshelves. They are crammed with so many books, which is expected considering he writes for a living.

He takes my hand, leading me to the kitchen, where I'm surprised to see the dining table set up with the plates and cutlery perfectly positioned, and two candelabras sitting in the middle of the table, the flames burning brightly.

"Oh wow, Julian, this is beautiful," I say in awe.

A romantic gesture, but that's Julian, he's such a romantic guy.

He motions for me to take a seat, then he pours some wine into a glass. I'm not sure if I can handle any more alcohol, but I don't want to offend him so I take tiny sips as he serves the first course.

We chat about the charity ball which led to a conversation about his work with Hungarian orphans. I watch him as he passionately tells the story about his journey and how much work he has done to help the children. The emotions are getting the better of him when he chokes up slightly. I lean and place my hand on top of his.

Here, before me, is a man who has a huge heart. He has so much compassion, more than anyone I've ever met.

Julian will never leave me without an explanation, nor will he ever hurt me so deeply.

And it always comes back to this.

Why am I constantly comparing him to Lex?

When we finish our meal, he clears the table while I wander back to the living room.

"Are you ready for your surprise now?"

His eyes dance as if a piece of forbidden fruit is being dangled before him.

I eagerly wait in anticipation as he walks out of the kitchen with a small plate of—wait! Is that? Yes, red velvet cupcakes with buttercream frosting.

"How did you know these are my favorite?"

My curiosity piques with drool almost trickling down the sides of my mouth

"A little birdie told me... Bakers in Brooklyn."

That's my favorite place in the whole world. They make the most scrumptious desserts, and these red velvet cupcakes are my weakness—next to Louboutins, of course.

"That's funny, Bakers like your surname," I point out.

"Yes, like my surname and my auntie's."

It takes a moment for the penny to drop. "Your aunty owns Bakers in Brooklyn? Julian, I could marry you right now."

I lean over, positioning my body, so I'm straddling him. Grabbing the cupcake, I take a bite, closing my eyes and immersing myself in the different flavors. As I lick my lips, Julian's hands sit nicely on my hips as he slowly grinds himself against me. I don't know what feels better, the taste of him or the cupcake.

Then, he slowly pulls my dress above my thighs. His kisses move to my neck as he cups my ass making me moan, my eyes closing in delight.

The image of Lex plunging his fingers inside me flashes

before me, breaking me from this moment. Letting out a whimper, my eyes open wide and in shock.

Oh fuck, I couldn't have let him do that to me.

The sound of my phone vibrating in my purse interrupts us, a distraction that can't be any more welcome. Julian pulls away like a gentleman, asking me if I need to answer it. I come up with an excuse about waiting for an important text from a client.

I just need to dissect the image—how every part of me begged for Lex to fuck me hard against the cold refrigerator door—but now isn't the time. My ring almost jumps off my finger and punches me in the face, reminding me where I am, who I'm with, and most importantly—that I said *yes*.

Climbing off Julian, I take a deep breath while fumbling in my purse. The guilt is a chain around my neck, and worried he can sense it, I side-eye him only to see him fiddling with his watch.

You're being paranoid. I obviously don't have 'I got fingered by my ex last night' tattooed on my forehead.

Finally finding my phone, I pull it out with an unknown number on the screen.

Unknown number: *Good evening, Charlotte, I want a chance to explain to you what happened last night. Please, it's not what you think. Just let me explain. Lex.*

How on earth did he get my number? *Eric, the little snake.*

Julian takes a call that comes through on his phone, excusing himself to the kitchen. I sit there, numb for ten minutes, wondering what I should reply with. I can't come up with anything, so I send him a text asking him to explain.

> **Unknown number:** *I haven't seen Samantha in eight years, not since I left her. Adriana told me she is going through a nasty divorce, and her ex is fighting for custody. She was drunk last night and wanted entry into the club, but I refused, and so she made a scene.*

I don't know what to believe. He told me he wouldn't lie to me, yet this whole situation is one big fuck-up. Part of me wants to believe it's true, but it still hurts like hell. Typing back, I ask him to check in the mirror to see if his nose is getting bigger. He responds quickly, turning my words around as usual.

> **Unknown number:** *My nose looks fine to me, can't say that about other parts though.*

Unable to hide the smile playing on my lips, it's obvious some things never change. I'm not sure how to respond without encouraging his naughty behavior, but of course, my sadistic inner self is telling my fingers to type.

I quickly respond, Julian stepping back into the room, apologizing.

There's a last-minute press conference tonight at town hall for a political scandal that has exploded, and I see it coming—he has to leave.

"I'm sorry, gorgeous." He takes my hand, kissing my knuckles. "I promise when we live together and we're married, it won't be this bad."

Marriage—the word strikes a chord best not played in my head right now.

This is the life of a journalist—chasing the lead.

I assure him I'm fine. We'll have plenty of other nights to enjoy each other's company. He kisses me deeply, thanking me for being so understanding.

On the cab ride back home, I play with my phone, desperately wanting to ask Lex about the kitchen, but I don't want him to know I have no clue what happened. Using my tactics when in court, I try to hold the upper hand, not showing any weakness.

But Lex is a game-player, and his method is downright dirty.

Inside the cab, I squirm on the leather seat. When my apartment is in view, I can't pay the driver any faster, exiting the cab and running upstairs in a mad rush.

Shutting the door behind me, I head straight for my room and change into my nightie. Quickly washing my face and brushing my teeth, I climb into bed despite the early hour.

I need to release this sexual tension and now.

Turning on my lamp, I reach into my bedside drawer and pull out my good friend, Mr. Rabbit. Relaxing, I place it in between my legs, slow swirls making the ache unbearable.

Dropping Mr. Rabbit on the bed, I slide my hand further, rubbing, delightfully surprised by how incredibly wet I am. I move faster, imagining Lex fucking me hard and fast against the wall. I remember how his cock would throb inside me, and how intense his thrusts were.

It's enough to push me over the edge, an orgasm barreling through me as I arch my back and moan loudly.

Trying to catch my breath, poor Mr. Rabbit is lying helpless beside me. What a waste bringing him out.

With a satisfied smile, my eyelids become heavy, and I drift into a peaceful sleep.

And in my dreams, I only see *his* face, I only feel *his* touch.

The man who promised me a life together nine years ago.

TWENTY-FOUR

LEX

The day is overcast, mirroring my mood.

I've no idea how to approach the Charlotte and Samantha situation, and so to clear my head I run through Central Park.

My legs run faster than ever, pushing through the burn as sweat builds against my shirt and drips from my forehead. The time I run is my personal best, and the only positive thing I have control over.

I stop at a playground to catch my breath. Around me, children are playing, so happy with not a care in the world. An attractive redhead sits on the park bench, and a small boy runs into her arms. Her face becomes familiar, and moments later, I realize it is Charlotte's friend, Nikki.

I'm not one to strike up conversations with strangers, but this has a purpose close to my heart.

"Hi." I wave, taking small steps towards her. "Nikki, is it?"

Raising her eyes to meet mine, she crosses her arms with a forced smile on her face. "Yes, it is, Mr. Edwards."

I sense the sarcastic tone, and with my guard slightly

up, I have to play this woman differently if I want to extract any information regarding Charlotte.

"Please call me Lex."

"Whatever," she mumbles.

The young boy beside her moves his attention to me. "Are you a friend of Mom's?"

"Actually, I'm a friend of her friend."

"He's Charlie's friend," Nikki tells him, gritting her teeth.

"Oh, how cool." The boy jumps off the bench, his face animated as he speaks, "Do you know Cha Cha takes me to baseball every Saturday morning? It's totally awesome. She can play some mean baseball, and the coaches love her."

Charlotte plays baseball? I laugh at the irony. She always hated sports.

"Honey, can you go play with Bailey while I speak to Lex?"

The boy nods, kissing Nikki goodbye before running off.

Nikki swings her head my way, a darting gaze bouncing off her angered face. "Stay away from Charlie, Lex. You're no good for her."

"You don't even know me," I respond as politely as I can without telling her to fuck off and mind her own business. "It's a bit presumptuous of you to say I have bad intentions."

"No, I don't, Lex," she states, matter-of-factly. "I don't know the history you have, though I'm pretty sure it was more than just a high school crush. I do know that while I shared a room with Charlie in college, she'd cry herself to sleep every night and wake up asking for you."

I'm rendered speechless, forgetting how much I hurt her. My arms become heavy as my shoulders slump, the weight of my past actions rearing their ugly head once again. I didn't stop to think about what happened after I left, and I didn't bring it up with Charlotte because I don't want to drudge up the memories or reminisce about my stupidity.

"She's better off with Julian," Nikki continues, relaxing her stern gaze. "He treats her how she deserves to be treated. I know enough about your type to know you will only hurt her again."

Déjà-fucking-vu.

Someone is telling me Charlotte is better off without me.

This time I'm not backing down, refusing to make the same mistake again.

"You might want to let Charlotte decide that for herself." I straighten my back, chest out, and give her a polite smile. "Goodbye, Nikki."

I start jogging away thinking about what Nikki's just said. I don't care what she thinks. Charlotte and I have history. After what happened last night, I know she will go to Julian's place. I just need a plan. Running back to the hotel, frustrated of getting nowhere, I hit the gym. My body thrives off the pain.

Back in my room, I climb into a steaming hot shower. The water is amazing, soothing my muscles and relaxing the tension almost instantly. My mind begins drifting to last night, caressing her on the dance floor, feeling her body tighten as I sang to her.

Wrapping my hand around my cock, I begin to slowly stroke it, remembering how I pushed her against the cold fridge, watching the condensation run down the door as her skin burned, sucking on her beautiful tits, and feeling her wet pussy all over my fingers. Her body has changed. She has become a woman. Her hips are curvaceous, her ass nice and tight. I start stroking faster, imagining her lips on my cock. The way she used to take me in deep, the way she screamed my name as I fucked her.

As the pressure mounts and fire rises in my belly, I explode all over my hand, wishing it had been in her mouth.

First thing I need more than anything is stamina. I order room service which doesn't take long. A hot breakfast will give me the energy since I've barely eaten anything the past few days. After I finish my meal, I grab my phone, scrolling through until I locate Eric's number. He gave me his number at the charity ball in case I need anything. To be honest, I'm not sure if he wants dick or he's trying to set up Charlotte, so I text him, asking for her number which he has no problem giving me.

I wasted most of the day in meetings, bounded by contracts and meetings scheduled from months back. As the early evening sets in, I officially go crazy playing this waiting game. I need to tell her last night with Samantha wasn't what it looked like, so I decide to text her.

As I wait, my anxiety grows as the clock ticks by. What the fuck is she doing that she can't respond straight away? My mind wanders. *Don't go there.*

Charlotte: *Explain*

One word is all she gives me. No 'hello, how are you today.' She's brief, and I don't blame her. Charlotte needs to know the truth, and so I finally explain the situation, hoping she'll understand. She's quick to question me as to whether I'm lying, telling me to check in the mirror to see if my nose has grown.

I can't resist, it's just too easy.

Typing quickly, I tell her my nose may not have grown, but I can't say the same for down below. Anxious I may have pushed our boundaries, the bubble hovers on the bottom of our text for what feels like forever.

Charlotte: *I didn't know you and the mirror had a thing for each other. Get a room.*

This is the Charlotte I remember, feisty and witty with a comeback for everything. I smile, thinking of a comeback to keep our conversation rolling.

Me: *I tried but turns out it prefers it in a dark kitchen against the cold fridge.*

I don't know what she remembers about Saturday night since she drank so much. Beneath my pants, my cock hardens again. Jesus fucking Christ, I need to rub another off if I plan to get any sleep tonight. This tension is killing me and waiting for her text feels like hours on end.

Charlotte: *Ha! Funny! I could've sworn it was an elevator.*

Well, fuck me. She remembers.

I had told her once about a reoccurring fantasy in which she was wearing fuck-me boots, a short, pleated skirt, and nothing underneath as we rode an elevator. Everyone would exit, and I'd push the stop button, fucking her into oblivion. If the universe has any favoritism toward me, in the city that never sleeps, with thousands of elevators all around us, maybe my fantasy will come true.

Me: *It still is, baby.*

She never responds to my text, and my self-control debates whether or not I should push her for more. I finally sleep on it for only four hours, and as soon as dawn kicks in and the sun rises, I send another text.

Me: *Are you free today for a coffee? I promise I'll be on my best behavior.*

I have back-to-back meetings this morning with stakeholders and agents. I email Kate asking her to send me today's schedule all while I wait. Considering it's only six-thirty in the morning, I don't expect a response until my phone lights up.

Charlotte: *That depends. Do I get a chocolate brownie as well?*

My lips curve upward into a smile, and resting back into my chair, I read her text again. I had forgotten what it felt like to smile, to look forward to something, or should I say someone, to feel those damn butterflies that women always ramble on about. Fuck, when did I become such a pussy?

Me: *Depends on what you're wearing.*

I can't help myself. Maybe they are horny butterflies

since they've been kept in captivity for so long. She texts me the address and warns me to behave.

Fuck, here we go again. My cock throbs as she calls me *Mr. Edwards*. The image of whips, kinky shit, and a librarian come to my mind. It does nothing to ease the tension.

And so I force myself to ignore it, attempting to concentrate on work. I fail miserably. I can't focus during my first meeting. I have stakeholders talking my ear off about profits, revenue, and budgets. Thankfully, I have Kate there to take notes.

"I have a quick catch-up with an old friend," I advise Kate at the end of our meeting.

"That's fine, Mr. Edwards. Your next meeting is a lunch meeting at midday." She tells me she'll email me the details, then we part ways.

I take a cab to Café York, a small coffee shop, very cozy and intimate. It's just before eleven when I arrive, and Charlotte hasn't arrived yet. I check my phone to see if she has texted me until a surge of warm air floats past me.

"Sorry, it's been one of those crazy mornings."

Charlotte hovers at the table, out of breath. My eyes wander toward her shoes—Louboutins—my fantasy right there. Controlling myself, I lift my gaze slowly up her legs to the high-waisted skirt, thick black belt, and finally, the black pin-stripe shirt, slightly unbuttoned revealing the top curves of her beautiful tits.

Today, she's wearing reading glasses.

Kill me now.

I stand, leaning in to kiss her cheek, the gesture making her body stiffen. I'm not immune to her scent, its purity and seductiveness all rolled into one, but I need to control myself if I want to keep her around me.

We both sit, ordering coffees and, of course, her brownie, the waiter quick to serve us.

"Charlotte, about Saturday night—"

"Can we just drop the subject?" she interjects. "Adriana explained the whole Samantha thing to me."

"You spoke to Adriana about the other night?"

"Well, no, I mean, yes. I had lunch with her yesterday. She mentioned Samantha and explained what happened which I can only assume she heard from you since she wasn't at the club. I was pretty wasted. I don't recall much of the night."

"Would you like me to refresh your memory?" I tease.

She smiles, only slightly. "How about we keep that a secret?"

I change the subject, not wanting to push her any further. "So, you're a lawyer?"

"Yes. Nikki and I opened our practice about a year ago."

The waiter returns with our coffees and the brownie. I welcome the caffeine hit, exhausted from the lack of sleep and change in time zone.

"That's quite an achievement," I tell her, prying into her past with a desperate need to learn more. "Where did you study?"

"Yale. I pretty much worked my ass off to get where I am."

Her ass. Don't. Fucking. Go. There.

"So, you came here after..." I don't want to say the words, cautious of her wary expression.

"No, I went to live with my grandmother in Connecticut. She passed away about five months after I arrived." Charlotte lowers her gaze toward the table, running her fingers along the rim of the cup. "She was an amazing woman. She taught me a lot during that time. After she passed, I wanted to make her proud. So, I got into Yale, studied hard, then moved here with Nikki and started my career."

I reach out to touch her hand. "I'm sorry about your grandmother."

Her phone starts vibrating on the table, breaking our conversation.

"Sorry, I need to take this..." She answers abruptly with, "Tate." Listening to the voice on the other end, I watch her eyes roll in frustration. "Fine. I'll be there, but I'm telling you, we won't settle for that amount."

This isn't the Charlotte I know. This woman is a hard-ass. Fuck, it's turning me on.

"I'm so sorry," she says, hanging up the phone.

"It's fine. I get it, the whole work thing."

"So, what is it you do, Mr. Edwards?"

Oh no, there she goes again.

"Too much, I can't keep track anymore. I'm a workaholic."

Call me Mr. Edwards again. Pretty please.

She takes a bite of her brownie, licking her lips with enjoyment. Is there a restroom in here? My pants feel like they are two sizes too small. My brain tries to remember the closest hotel, desperate to take her anywhere and shove my cock inside that beautiful mouth of hers.

"Delicious?"

She licks her lips again. "I've had better."

I take the fork off her plate, tasting a piece. "Tastes perfect to me."

We sit there, quiet with tension mounting between us. Her chest is heaving, and my focus is all on her lips. Biting down, she doesn't realize how tempting she is with a simple, innocent stare.

Despite my reluctance to do so, I need to inform her of my intentions, rather than her assuming I'm leaving her without a goodbye. "I'm heading back to London tonight."

Her demeanor changes instantly as the words leave my mouth, eyes widening as her brows furrow. The change catches me by surprise, so quickly, I reassure her, "I expect to be back in New York next Friday."

"As in, two weeks away?" she asks, quietly.

Averting my eyes, my chest tightens at the realization I'm about to leave her again. Good ole Lex, you just can't get your shit together. I want to stay with her, but the meetings scheduled in London are crucial to the Lexed Group. They have taken months to plan, one of them a business conference with shareholders in attendance.

"Yes," I say, watching her grab her purse.

"I've really got to go." She stands, avoiding eye contact. "My next meeting is in twenty minutes."

"Can I call or text you?" I beg, standing up.

"I'm really booked up with appointments this week and a few events I need to attend."

"With Julian?" I ask, regretting it immediately.

"Lex, don't."

"Charlotte, c'mon..." I reach out my hand, but she recoils. "Why do you have to go? Please stay a little while longer."

"Goodbye, Lex." She storms out of the coffee shop, and once again, my whole world is crashing down around me.

Leaving me here alone, I try to figure out what I've done so wrong. I told her my intentions of going back to London and of my return date. Surely, as a business owner herself, she knows the kind of responsibilities I have to uphold.

But something changed in her, and I don't know why.

This isn't goodbye—far from it.

I'm going to go to London to sort out all the shit there, then get set up here. All I have to do is get through the next two weeks without seeing her.

If I can last nine years without her, I can last two damn weeks. At least that's what I tell myself.

Yes, I can do that.

I'm used to being in control.

Then why does it fucking hurt like hell to leave?

TWENTY-FIVE

CHARLIE

Meeting Lex for coffee is a bad idea.

I thought I could act mature, ignore his flirtatious ways, but I am weak. And then he mentions flying back to London. My reaction takes me by surprise.

I am *livid*.

At him.

At me.

He's sitting in front of me, and every part of me hates the fact that I miss him, even though I no longer know him. He isn't the man I fell in love with many years ago. Lex Edwards has changed into this controlling, heartless creature who only thinks about his needs.

When I ask him how long he will be away I have officially let my guard down, regretting the words immediately. I can't understand my actions. I've spent years building up a thick skin given my line of work, and in just a few short days, everything I've spent years achieving is now an afterthought.

Around him, I crumble, and I *hate* that.

I no longer belong to him, but then again, did I ever?

I tell him I have something important to do at work, then I quickly grab my things. He asks if he can call or text, but I ramble on about being busy during the week. Then he mentions Julian. I am way too exhausted to get into it, so I tell him to just stop. It's a battle neither one of us will win.

Walking out of the café as fast as I can, I hail the first cab in sight. As I sit in the back of the cab, I try to calm myself down. *Why did I let all this happen?* I should've been firmer from the beginning. But no. I let him dance with me, I let him kiss me, and I even let him finger me. This back-and-forth turmoil is wearing me down, and things must change. I have to muster the strength, align it with my values, and say goodbye to someone who's no longer a part of my life, romantically.

Back at the office, I sit across from my client, Mrs. Vandercamp.

"You look on edge, sweetie."

"Mrs. Vandercamp, thank you for your concern, but let's get down to business."

"Man troubles?"

I purse my lips, shaking my head. "Honestly, it's not worth talking about."

"I heard you attended the charity ball." She forces a smile. "Unfortunately, with Mr. Vandercamp and his bimbo there, I wasn't able to attend."

"Right, Barbie with an overkill of fake tanning lotion," I snort.

"Sounds like her. I can't thank you enough for helping me fight this."

"It's my job. Plus, you deserve it after all the humiliation Mr. Vandercamp has put you through."

"I didn't think things would turn out this way. George

was the love of my life, and now we can barely be in the same room together, even for the sake of the kids..." She pauses, playing with the canary yellow diamond ring nestled on her finger. "When I first met George, it was love at first sight. I was dating another man, a man who had asked my father's permission to marry me. He was great, but he wasn't George. I thought I could tame him, thinking I was the woman who would be his wife, have his babies and that he wouldn't need anyone else. I was so naïve..."

When Mrs. Vandercamp enlisted our services through a recommendation, both Nikki and I were hesitant given the legal battle between her and Mr. Vandercamp. From a monetary perspective, the divorce is messy. However, Mrs. Vandercamp only wants her house in Martha's Vineyard and the businesses she's built while they were married. Everything else, he can keep.

Nikki has her opinion on the matter, yet Mrs. Vandercamp has made it clear she wants to move on, not wanting the negative attention of a legal battle for possessions she doesn't care for. Mr. Vandercamp, on the other hand, has other plans, almost like he hates seeing her not care, and he's making her life miserable. Thankfully, Tate is a shark in the courtroom and eagerly took on this matter. Today, she just wants to chat while passing the time waiting for him to end his other meeting.

"A leopard can't change its spots. Perhaps it's time to move on. The ship has sailed, and you need to focus on the future," I tell her.

As I say the words and it dawns on me how hypocritical I sound. Everything I just said is the opposite of what I'm doing or have done with Lex. We have history, plenty of it, and no matter what happened it can't be erased.

Evolving as a person means never looking back.

Move forward, work toward the future—that has always been my mantra.

But how can I see the future when the past keeps biting me in the ass?

"I've been seeing someone," she admits, her eyes sparkling at the mention of this so-called lover. "He treats me like a queen, but I don't want to get hurt again. I don't want to screw this up."

"If he feels the way you do, you won't screw it up. Some things have a way of working out. Relationships are hard. It's trying to find that right balance. Enjoy each other's company, be considerate of each other's feelings, and most importantly is trust and honesty. Without it, you've got nothing."

Sheesh, talk about channeling my inner Dr. Phil.

"Perhaps I should hire you as my shrink?" She laughs, clutching her chest. "I don't remember the last time I have smiled so much, not since George and I first started dating. Maybe I do deserve this. If George wants a different girl on his arm every week, then so be it. I want more, Charlie. I want a real man."

I think about her words and Lex's and my relationship. There's no longer a blank canvas ready to paint a future. Instead, there is this painting of a man and woman, and the history behind it is too much to paint over. It can never be the same. Yet, I allow myself to remember the pieces of the past. These pieces bring me so much happiness, the moments that are stuck in my head.

First loves, they always stick with you.

Maybe that's what this is—this unwarranted pining for him—that first love feeling.

But the truth behind it is I don't trust Lex, and I'm not honest with him therefore, we have nothing.

Why is that the most gut-wrenching feeling in the world right now?

TWENTY-SIX

CHARLIE

Nine Years Ago

I sat in the waiting room, a nervous wreck.

I had heard enough horror stories to know that unprotected sex led to teen pregnancy, and I couldn't have thought of anything worse at eighteen. After a sleepless night, I decided to bite the bullet and drive to a clinic the next town over so the doctor could prescribe me the pill. Maybe I was jumping the gun. We hadn't had sex yet, but it was inevitable. He was twenty-five, and anytime I was near him, his cock practically waved hello and invited me over for a nightcap.

"So, Charlotte, how can I help you today?" Dr. Hanson asked.

"I... uh... want to go on the Pill."

"Charlotte, before we continue, do you have any concerns with my intern sitting in?"

"Uh... no. If it helps the medical community then it's fine with me."

He left the room, and I sat there for a few minutes

playing with a model of the human body that sat on his desk. As the door opened, I fumbled with the heart which fell to the floor. Surely, I wasn't the only one who touched this? I reached down to pick it up thinking this couldn't be any more embarrassing until a hand reached it before mine.

I recognized the hand immediately.

Fuck. Me. *Sideways.*

I looked up into eyes that belonged to Alex. This wasn't happening. It had to be a dream.

Wake up, Charlie! For fuck's sake, wake up!

"Charlotte, this is my intern, Dr. Alex Edwards. Now let's continue our discussion. Charlotte, are you sexually active?"

I couldn't have thought of anything worse right now, the temperature rising in the room as sweat broke out beneath my top. There was simply no way out of this. Just answer his questions and get the hell out of there.

"Um, yes... I mean, no... maybe."

"Perhaps I need to rephrase my question. Have you had sexual intercourse?"

"Yes."

"More than once?"

"Yes."

"How many sexual partners have you had?"

I couldn't look his way. My body had already crawled into a dark hole, my brain just waiting for an opening to follow. "Only one."

"Will you be continuing to have sexual intercourse with this person?"

"Definitely not."

"Did you use protection such as condoms?"

The hole was getting darker and darker, and I wanted to climb up and curl into the fetal position. How on earth could I be this unlucky? My eyes shifted toward where he was sitting, and the second I saw the smirk across that smug face, I instantly avert back to the wall.

"Yes, Dr. Hanson."

"That's a very responsible attitude, Charlotte. I understand these questions seem personal. However, it's my responsibility to make sure you're educated on everything associated with being sexually active."

Oh, dear God, what the hell was he going to ask me now?

My feet shuffled nervously, and my knees pulled together while I rode this embarrassing moment out. If he asked anything to do with my vagina, I'd be out of there in a flash.

"I'm guessing your intention is to be intimate with a specific person at this stage. Charlotte, how much do you know of their sexual history?" Dr. Hanson questioned, his brow raised.

Oh, how the tables had turned.

Now, I was going to be discussing the questions I had so desperately wanted answers to but had no balls to ask.

"To be honest, I think he's slept around... a lot," I answered, staring right at Alex.

His smirk disappeared, and now he looked like he could crawl into that hole with me and die. Although we wouldn't die in there, we'd be using all our time to procreate and populate the dark hole.

"Is he still behaving this way?" Dr. Hanson asked with concern in his eyes.

"No, he's with someone long-term."

"Is he still sexually active with her?"

"I'm not sure, Dr. Hanson. He is a man, after all." I searched his face, looking for the answer that would reassure me and ease the ache in my gut that appeared anytime I thought of them having sex.

"I strongly suggest you use both condoms and the Pill. Sexually transmitted diseases are easier to catch than you may think." He scribbled some notes and handed the chart to Alex. "Everything looks fine to me. I'll leave you with Dr. Edwards to check your blood pressure and write up your prescription. It was nice to meet you, Charlotte."

He closed the door. I had no choice but to deal with the most embarrassing situation in my entire life, worse than the time my dress accidentally flew up in first grade, and everyone saw my Strawberry Shortcake underwear.

Alex grinned as he placed the blood pressure machine around my arm. "So, I'm a player, am I?"

"More like a manwhore. I hate you right now... you know that, right?"

"Aww, no you don't. You love me right now. Otherwise, why would you be here getting a prescription for the Pill in case your sexual activity picks up?"

I shook my head, covering my face with my hands. "You're a jerk."

He removed the blood pressure machine and wrote something on his chart. Placing it down on the table, he wheeled his chair over, so he was right in front of me.

"Since when do you work here? I thought you just interned at the hospital?"

"They were short-staffed..." He paused before grabbing a lock of my hair and pushing it behind my ear. "So, tell me, Charlotte, are we doing this?"

"This?"

I could see he was trying to find the right words until he finally responded, "You came here today to make sure you were protected. That *we* are protected."

"I just wanted to make sure, you know... just in case."

Alex leaned over my shoulder and turned the lock on the door. He pulled himself back and placed his lips on my mine, hungry for the very reason I was there.

Surely, this was fate, right?

Following my instincts and ending up here of all places?

"I've never wanted anything more, Charlotte. You have to believe me."

I looked into his eyes, those pools of emerald green pleading with me to understand that his desire drove him to this insanity that was becoming us. I placed my arms around his neck and pulled him into me, hoping this gave him the reassurance he needed. "I believe you. And anyway, if it wasn't your words that told me, it's the general saluting me right now."

He placed his forehead against mine. "You're crazy."

"Insane is the word you are looking for," I corrected.

Laughing, he stood and unlocked the door. I followed his lead before he turned around and ripped the paper off the pad.

"Here you go, Miss Mason. The reason you came. Hope you have fun," he teased.

"Thank you, Dr. Edwards. I'm sure the pleasure won't be all mine."

And with that, I walked out, accompanied by the swarm of butterflies which formed in my stomach, making it impossible to hide the huge grin on my face.

TWENTY-SEVEN

LEX

Present

I'm trying to make sense of what had happened with Charlotte.

As soon as I mentioned heading back to London, our lighthearted conversation had suddenly turned sour. Her demeanor changed, her lie about being busy barely believable. She no longer wanted to speak to me, and I don't know why. She rushed out so fast I had no time to ask her what the hell I did wrong.

The flight back to London feels like the longest five hours of my life. The last few days have been a whirlwind, and everything I've become suddenly means nothing. People used to tell me that time heals all wounds, but what the fuck do they know about me? I can't sleep, I can't eat, I can barely breathe. I left her, again. It's only for two weeks, but time doesn't matter.

I run my fingers through my hair trying to get a grip on things. Fuck, someone tell me how to make everything right with her.

After a quick trip by taxi from the airport, it's six in the morning when I arrive at the office intending to prepare for an important meeting we have scheduled today. Seeing as it's so early here in London I second guess myself, but I decide I'll text her anyway, apologizing for my sudden departure, anxious to stay in her good graces and not let what happened at the café create this unwarranted distance between us.

> **Me:** *I'm sorry I had to leave for London. Can I make it up to you with more brownies? I think next time you'll remember how much you like them.*

Knowing the time difference, I don't expect a response straight away, and willing my overanxious mind to calm down, I check our share prices trying to distract myself.

Just before nine, I walk to the boardroom and set myself up at the head of the table. People file in, and knowing how anal I am about punctuality, we start on time and dive straight into acquisition mode with the head of our operations team taking the wheel.

Somewhere during a graph on projections of the Asian market, my phone lights up on the table.

> **Charlotte:** *The brownies were great, fantastic just as I remembered them. My problem is that I hadn't had them for a while and suddenly they were on my plate. While not eating said brownies, I found that there are other desserts I enjoy as well.*

My lips pull back, baring my teeth as my pulse elevates. My fingers wrap around my phone with a tight grip to control my need to throw it across the room. What fucking game is she playing? With a tight expression, I stare blankly at the screen unable to process the numbers.

This is not at all like me. For all I know, I could've signed away the rights to Lexed. My attention isn't where it needs to be, and barely able to control myself, I terminate the meeting, commanding my executive team to report back to me later.

Kate rises from her chair, watching me with a concerned expression. "Mr. Edwards, is everything okay?"

I know Kate is sincere with her concerns for me, but what the fuck am I supposed to say? My ex-girlfriend who I still have feelings for thinks her current beau is better than me, and it makes my blood boil to think they are fucking? I can't imagine anything more juvenile.

"Just a few things I need to take care of."

Back inside my office, Kate knows better than to follow me and push for anything. My office is my sanctuary, off-limits to anyone unless I permit them to enter.

Sitting at my desk, I run my hands along the woodgrain, admiring the neatly organized space. The control freak within me uses the quiet time to calm the fuck down. With my computer screen on, emails flood my inbox, but I couldn't care less. I scroll through, different day, same old bullshit. I turn away, swiveling my chair to face the window.

I know nothing about her.

Well, not nothing exactly.

She's a lawyer, and then there's the information that Bryce has given me, but I still know nothing about her personal life. I tap my pen on my desk, frustrated I'm getting nowhere. Maybe I'm going about this the wrong way. Maybe I need to scour social media.

Opening up a Facebook page, I manage to guide myself

through the platform. I don't have an account because I don't have time to talk to people from ten fucking years ago, despite my mother and Adriana begging for me to activate one.

There are ten Charlotte Masons, none matching her. I try Charlie Mason, same result. Fuck. Okay, what if I look for Eric? I type Eric Kennedy, and twenty-five results come up. I scroll through the profiles immediately spotting his face. The profile picture is of him on some beach doing that annoying duck-face thing while holding the phone up in the air, obviously taking a self-portrait. I click on his friends' list, which thankfully isn't private. I figure, if Charlotte is on here, she'd have to be friends with Eric.

Scrolling through the names, I stop at a Charlie Brown. I click on the photograph of a bird, a phoenix, I think, but the page is private. I scroll further in case there's anyone else. Nothing.

Back to Eric's profile page, I stumble across his latest status update, saying he's going to watch a movie and tags Charlie Brown. As I open up the comments, the muscles on my neck begin to tighten, veins straining against my skin as the heat begins to rise from my accelerated breathing.

It's her all right.

She commented about going to see the movie with a companion and about sitting in the back, and all I read are lewd comments from Eric and someone named Rocky about blow jobs.

I clench my fists, ready to punch the fucking screen. I leave her alone for one minute, and she's giving that fucker head in the movie theater? Who the fuck is she now? This isn't the Charlotte who's the love of my life. The Charlotte I'll fucking move heaven and earth for if she asks. I bury my face in my hands, trying to get a grip on my anger.

On impulse, blinded by rage, I type profusely in a text.

Me: *Why are you still seeing him?*

I sit there for exactly thirty-four minutes and twenty-one seconds with no response. I'm losing my sanity, and to make it worse, I have an important meeting at the Hilton in less than an hour. What the fuck am I going to do? Every second I'm gone, the closer she's getting to him. For all I know, she could be at the courthouse saying 'I do' right this minute.

Charlotte has always been mine.

And now isn't the time to be complacent.

I need to go *now*.

I have to fucking see her.

Pressing the intercom, I call Kate into my office.

"Kate, please book the next flight to New York City," I command, neatly organizing my papers while shutting down my computer.

"Um... sir, sorry, I d-don't understand," she stutters, narrowing her eyes. "The meeting at the Hilton starts in forty-five minutes. We actually need to leave now."

"I have to go back to New York. Something urgent has come up, and I need to be there now," I tell her, irritated by her lack of direction to follow orders.

"Sir, this meeting has taken months to organize, and we have a lot riding on this merger."

Fuck, does she think I'm an idiot? Of course, I know that, but this can't go on any longer.

Every second that passes, Charlotte will slip further away from me, and I refuse to allow that to happen.

"Have Brooks replace me. He's done the groundwork.

I'm heading to the airport now. Please book the Waldorf indefinitely. I expect you to fly in tomorrow."

"But, sir, I can't stress enough the importance of your presence at this meeting."

With a pained and watery gaze, I think she's going to cry on me. For fuck's sake, she just needs to do the job she's paid to do.

"Kate, do as I say, or you can find yourself another job," I warn, placing my laptop into its case.

She races out of my office, probably ready to burst out crying for all I know. Following her, I lock my office door behind me and head out to Reception. I don't say goodbye to anyone, bowing my head and walking straight for the elevator. When it arrives, I embrace the quiet solitude. Exiting the elevator, I rush toward the street and hail a cab while sending a quick text to my sister asking her to arrange some clothes for me as I have no time to pack.

By the time I arrive at Heathrow, Kate has booked my business-class seats with the flight leaving in one hour. The flight isn't as crowded, and by the time we board, I get comfortable in my seat and wait for the plane to depart.

Charlotte: *He is my fiancé. He treats me the way I deserve to be treated. I don't have to fight with him every time I see him.*

I don't respond to her straight away, making her suffer in silence like she did me. Placing my phone in my pocket, I close my eyes, desperate for some sleep to shut down my racing mind. I barely slept last night on the plane to London, not to mention I was hitting the gym twice a day to get rid of this tension that constantly hangs on my shoulders.

The announcement comes on that we're about to land shortly at JFK. I rub my face, trying to wake myself up. I can't believe I slept the whole flight—that's very out of character. Fastening my seat belt again, I stare out the window.

I'm accustomed to flying, rarely spending enough time in one spot. London is home, but even then, I rarely spend much time there. Mom and Dad are still living in Carmel but spend most of their time traveling abroad, and Adriana has moved to Brooklyn with Elijah.

As we deplane, I make a quick detour to the men's room to wash my face. Contemplating a quick session in the stall, I decide against it, my hand needing recovery time.

Making my way through the airport quickly, I hail the first cab on the rank, giving Charlotte's work address praying she's still there.

> **Me:** *I don't share. You must know that by now. I will be back in Manhattan next Friday when we can discuss this face to face.*

I force the lie with a plan in mind. In just twenty minutes, she will find out the truth.

As the cab drives through the streets, I gaze out the window unable to count the number of times I've been to Manhattan in the past nine years. To think, all along, she was here. After Bryce told me about her house in Connecticut, it didn't make sense. But then she said she stayed with her grandmother, so I'm assuming she inherited it.

Life has changed for both of us. Who would've thought nine years ago we'd both wind up here? I'm still coming to terms with her graduating from Yale and opening her own law practice. I'm proud of everything she has accomplished but, of course, I can't tell her that—she never wants to talk about anything, always shutting me down if I get too close. The rare moments when she will open up, I soak up everything she gives me, but then she realizes what she has done and puts up that wall again.

I pay the driver, climb out, staring at the building in front of me. My email keeps pinging, knowing the aftermath of not attending today's meeting will be an absolute nightmare.

As I walk into the lobby, I head straight to the elevators. Pulling my phone out of my shirt pocket, I open the text sent two minutes ago. I read her words, my blood boiling as they sink in, dragging their sharp edges along my skin.

Jealousy and rage are what got me here in the first place, but I want nothing more than to rip him into pieces and purge him from her mind and heart. *She's my fucking girl!* And I'm the idiot who listens to everyone else instead of following my instincts.

I ride the elevator up to her floor, my stare fixated on the doors. The elevator pings open, and the glass doors with Mason & Romano written on them are in front of me. As I walk toward them, Eric is shutting the door behind him.

"Lex! What are you doing here?"

"Is Charlotte here?" My tone is stiff, warning Eric of my intentions.

"She's still in her office." He lets me in, but before closing the door entirely, he says, "And she's alone."

There's a faint light coming from the double doors where Eric has pointed. With every step I take, the anger swirls inside me, my hands automatically curl into fists itching to swing out and punch the wall after what she said in her text message.

Beside the window, she's standing quietly, lost in thought. Is she thinking about me? Her expression is pained, my anger suddenly turning to compassion. I'm tired of living without her, and she needs to know that.

Seconds pass, yet I stand still watching her, the expressions she makes, the breaths she takes.

It's now or never.

"Are we done, Charlotte?"

TWENTY-EIGHT

CHARLIE

I finally give in, expressing my emotions in an explosive text.

Me: *Stop treating me like I am yours! Do you think it was fair that I had to share you with Samantha? Do you think it was fair that I had to find out through the town whore that the one person who had my heart and soul knocked up his wife when he promised me he was no longer fucking her? You have no idea what it feels like to be abandoned by the only person who you trusted your life with, the only person who was your entire world, then not to even be given the chance to say goodbye. Yes, I love Julian, and yes, I'll continue to see him. Maybe now you'll understand what it's like. What happened the other night was a mistake. Huge mistake. It's over, Lex. We're so over.*

I sent the text, my heart beating furiously in my chest. Although I'm angry at him, I am angrier at myself for allowing this to happen in the first place. Did I really think having a make-out session would erase the past or give me closure? The scars are still ingrained in me, and no matter how hard I try to erase them, they'll forever remain a part of me.

Staring out the window, the darkness is setting in. The streets are still lined with people, the city never shuts down despite the time of day.

So, I made a mistake, a big one.

I sigh out loud, this feeling of hurt, there's no point denying it. I know I made the right decision by telling him to leave me alone, but I need closure, right? Fuck, Charlie, honestly, what the hell is wrong with you?

"Are we done, Charlotte?"

The voice behind me is just an illusion. Don't do this again, Charlie, ache for someone who'll never be who you need them to be.

"Tell me we're done."

I dare not move nor release a single breath. My limbs become completely frozen on the spot. Inside my chest, my heart is pounding louder and louder, the noise becoming increasingly unbearable.

Deep, heavy breathing sounds behind me, as the hairs on my arms stand at attention while chills run down my spine. Slowly, I turn my head, my eyes meeting his across the room.

With every step he takes closer to me, the temperature in the room becomes stifling hot causing my breathing to pick up at an uneven pace.

He stops just shy of where I stand, close enough for me to smell him.

Don't Charlie.

Reaching out, he runs his finger along my collarbone, my body tensing at his touch.

"Lex, what are you doing here?"

"Well, you said you weren't mine. I don't take these things lying down, or maybe I should. It's obvious you're forgetting who you belong to. Who you've always belonged to." His eyes are blazing, the tone of his voice dominant yet calm. That kind of calm terrifies me because I know it only means one thing—I have no chance of escaping.

He pushes my hair behind my shoulder, and leaning forward, he grazes his lips against my neck, inhaling my skin. The walls start to cave, the touch of his lips on my skin breaking them down piece by piece.

"I had to come back to remind you," he murmurs.

His kisses become ravenous.

My self-control non-existent since the moment he walked in.

Why resist, Charlie? You're fighting an uphill battle.

I yank his hair, pulling his mouth onto mine. His lips taste like heaven, his tongue meeting mine. Unable to stop, my tongue refuses to break from his, barely able to let go as he pulls away.

His eyes blaze with desire as he wraps his hand around my waist, laying me on my desk while forcing my legs open. Letting out a moan, his eyes widen while admiring my garters, running his hands up my thigh before he forcefully pulls me toward him then I wrap my legs around his waist.

Out of breath, with my heart running a marathon, his fingers clasp the buttons of my blouse, unbuttoning them at a slow and agonizing pace, exposing my breasts. There's no delayed gratification, no admiring my naked form. His mouth ravages my breasts, sucking hard while I arch my neck, groaning beneath his touch.

"What are you doing to me?" I pant, desperate for answers.

"Well, Miss Mason, it's time to make you remember who you belong to."

He unzips his pants, his cock throbbing hard as it springs free and slaps against his ripped stomach. I watch him, wanting to taste it so bad, remembering how good he tasted inside my mouth.

Painfully slow, he grips my panties in his hand, sliding them to the side as his cock glides against my swollen clit. I brace for him, my body pleading to be at his mercy and feel him whole. The torment in his expression drives my desire beyond their limits, begging to take all of me right now. He guides himself inside me, my back arching in delightful pain.

I'm losing this battle. There's no chance of coming out a winner. I desperately want more, his lips and hands to touch every part of me.

My phone begins to vibrate on the desk beside where I lay. Unable to answer, given my position, I allow it to ring out. It finally stops vibrating, only to start up again a few minutes later. Lex stops mid-thrust, trying to catch his breath. Grabbing my phone, he brings it to his sight, and without a shadow of doubt, his flared pupils and guttural roar are because *Batman* is calling.

"Answer it," he demands.

What? He's still inside me. This is insane.

"Let it go, Lex."

"Answer it or I will," he threatens, holding the phone in the air above me.

Should I call his bluff?

Can I even take the risk?

Lex lowers the phone to me as I struggle to untangle myself from him, but he forcefully holds me down.

Clearing my throat, I hit accept. "Hello?"

"Hey, gorgeous. I miss you. Come to my place tonight?" Julian asks, oblivious to my predicament.

Lex continues fucking me, slower, while he buries his head in my neck. His hand trails my breast, pinching my nipples as I try to respond without screaming my lungs out.

Is this happening?

"I'm still at work," I respond, trying to keep my tone even. "Rain check?"

Lex quickly pulls his head away from my neck, his eyes turning a darker shade of green as jealousy rears its ugly head. With a vengeance, he pushes his cock deeper, my teeth biting down to refrain from moaning, the taste of blood lingering on my lips.

"Are you okay?" Julian questions, worried. "You sound out of breath."

"I'm fine, just had to run for my phone. I'll call you tomorrow. There's something here I need to sort out."

"No worries. Till tomorrow, gorgeous. I love you."

What the fuck do I say?

"Me, too."

I end the call as fast as humanly possible before letting out the loudest moan, relief washing over me from holding it in. Lex withdraws himself out of me, leaving me to whimper.

We aren't done.

No one came.

"Did you just tell him you loved him?" he spits, nostrils flaring with rage consuming him.

"How dare you make me answer that call, Lex!" I lift

my hand to slap him across the face, but he quickly grabs it, his grip overpowering mine.

"Tomorrow night you'll be busy fucking me. You belong to me, Charlotte. Don't mess with me anymore. You won't like the punishment."

"Fuck. You!"

"Since you had no problem keeping quiet over the phone, you'll have no problem keeping quiet now."

He flips me around, pushing my chest onto my desk. Forcefully, he uses his legs to spread mine as far apart as they'll go. His cock slides back inside, and leaning over, he covers my mouth with his hand while pounding into me.

My desk is shaking, the papers flying everywhere. The screams are muffled in his hand, my body ready to combust from the intensity of his animalistic demand to own every part of me.

Quickly, he turns me back around, my hands gripping the edge of the desk.

Tilting his face, inches in front of mine, he commands me with his eyes. "You're such a little bitch trying to make me jealous. No one else will fuck you like this. Come for me. *Now*."

I bite into his hand, exploding all over him, the rush consuming every inch of my body and finishing with a blissful warmth. His thrusts are desperate as he lets go of my mouth, pounding me hard one more time before his body shakes, exploding inside of me.

Our breaths, shallow and uneven, command the room with its noise. Slowly, he pulls himself out of me, collapsing on my body.

What the hell am I doing?

I continue to lay still, trying to catch my breath.

Realization of our indiscretion comes crashing like a

tsunami, the guilt following its footsteps afraid of not being felt. My chest begins to tighten, and consciously, I begin to button my blouse while he rests beside me breaking the silence between us.

"Lex, I meant what I said."

He drags his body back on top of mine removing my hands from my blouse, undoing what I had done up, and finishes undressing me. His eyes immediately wander to the tattoo of the phoenix just above my pubic bone. Searching my eyes, he looks for an explanation, but it's one I'm not ready to give.

"And I meant what I said, Charlotte."

Trailing kisses down my body, he orders me to sit up on the desk, my legs spread. He lowers himself onto my pussy, tasting it slowly, circling his tongue around my clit. I'm caught by surprise, my body craving to convulse again as he sucks harder. Taking two fingers, he slides them inside of me, fucking me carelessly. My arousal, mixed with his own, is dripping around his fingers, only adding to the pure lust of this moment.

I need to taste him again, pushing his head away I demand he sit on my desk.

Taking a moment to admire how sexy he looks chained to my desk by the power I hold over him, I wrap my hand around his shaft, sliding my mouth up and down, tasting him whole.

"I am not finished with you," he sputters, momentarily beyond words.

"I'm not finished with you." I stand, climbing on top of him. Instead of fucking him, I turn around, positioning myself to sixty-nine. His body tenses, his groans intensifying.

"Oh fuck, baby, bring that pussy here."

My moans intensify, his face buried between my legs while my mouth wraps around his cock. With every sordid lick, I take him in deeper, both of us competing against each other in this sick and twisted game we are playing.

"Lex, I can't... take it anymore, I'm going to..." My body begins shaking. Frantically, I grab his cock, sucking it hard while I ride the orgasmic wave to another climatic finish.

Catching my breath with him buried in my mouth, the familiar taste hits the back of my throat, and succumbing to my own fantasies, I savor every last drop.

Once again, we lay silently trying to come up for much-needed air. My arms are like jelly, but I manage to climb off of him, collapsing on the desk beside him as I stare at the ceiling trying to calm the adrenaline running through me.

"When did you get the tattoo?" he questions with a low voice.

"Back in college."

"What is it?"

"A phoenix."

He pulls my body up, handing me my clothes. I'm feeling self-conscious, quick to bring my blouse to my chest. Beside me, he begins removing his shirt.

"Why are you taking your shirt off now?"

Watching him expose his chest, my jaw unwillingly drops at the sight of his tattoo, inked above his perfectly sculpted abs. Without thinking, I reach out, running my fingertips along it. The design is some sort of tribal tattoo, but when I look closely, the shadow is of a lion. It runs down the side of his torso and along his ribcage.

"Lions are a sign of power," I mumble to myself, mesmerized by the amount of detail.

"Yes, they are, and the phoenix?"

I don't want to discuss it, not now, not here when I'm so vulnerable.

"It's late," I tell him. "We need to go."

He doesn't push me for answers, instead helping me tidy my desk as I shut down the computer. With my purse in hand, I pick up my phone and see the text message on the screen.

Batman: *Remember Batman has all these fancy tricks up his sleeve if you need a pick me up.*

Lex glances my way, watching me read the message, though this time, ignoring it. My phone begins to buzz in my hand.

Adriana. Shit, I forgot!

I place her on speakerphone, so Lex doesn't question me. "Adriana."

"Charlie, I'm in your lobby! The doorman said he could let me up, but I thought I'd call you first."

"I'm sorry, Adriana, I got caught up in something. Tell Jean he can let you in my apartment. I'll be there in fifteen minutes."

"Okay, sweet, see ya soon."

Lex grins, bowing his head.

"Why are you smiling like that?" I ask, unable to hide my smile.

Seeing him smile makes my heart flutter stupidly. That arrogant prick is so fucking beautiful.

"You know Adriana is going to ask you a million questions, right? She'll want nine years' worth of information in the space of an hour."

"I know. I wouldn't expect anything less from her."

We enter the elevator. I lean over, attempting to push

the ground floor button. My hand is rudely pushed away. Lex slams his finger on the stop button.

"Time to make this a reality," he growls, pushing my skirt up, taking me from behind.

Round three, here we go.

"I'm here, I'm here..."

I bolt through my front door, praying I don't have anything running down my leg. This is all kinds of awkward, and Lex coming inside me was an afterthought. The bastard didn't even have the nerve to ask me if I was on the Pill. *Asshole.*

"Hiya!" she beams, throwing her arms around me tightly.

I excuse myself, quickly, changing in my room to my sweats and a tank top. When I come back out, Adriana is reading a book from my coffee table.

"Anyways." She puts the book down, facing me as I sit on the couch beside her. "Your place is amazeballs. What's the name of your interior decorator?"

"Um, me... and have you been talking to Eric because I swear, Adriana, the two of you were separated at birth."

"Oh-em-gee, he's totally awesome, right? I can't believe you did this yourself. You never liked designing or fashion before."

"Things change, people grow. The designing part I started to enjoy when I lived with my grandmother. She had a taste for random knick-knacks, but somehow, she made it work." I smile at the memory, welcoming the conversation. "On the weekends we'd go to flea markets looking for one-of-a-kind pieces. As for fashion, part of it was because of Nikki. We shared a room in college, and every time I'd have a date, she'd lend me her outfits. I kind of got a taste for it."

"Will you please tell me more about your grandmother?"

"She was an amazing woman—" I hesitate, unsure how long I can go on without breaking down. "I only met her a few times when I was young because she and my mom didn't really get along. When things in Carmel got too diffi-cult, my dad spoke to her, and she welcomed me with open arms. I wouldn't be the person I am today without spending those last five months with her. She was such a compas-sionate woman, so much wisdom. She held onto me when I needed hope and gave me the strength to see the future."

I stop abruptly, knowing I can't go on. Can I pour my heart out to Adriana and tell her my grandmother was there, holding my hand on the darkest day of my life? My heart tightens as I close my eyes, reliving the memory.

"She was sick, but she never told anyone. The day she passed away was when I found out." The room falls quiet, my vision clouding as the emotions come to the surface. "Adriana, will you tell me what happened when you found out?"

Adriana shuffles on my couch, tucking her legs beneath her knees.

"I noticed Lex acting weird, but I had no idea about the baby. Samantha called us over one night, and she announced the pregnancy. Lex was furious. He didn't want this to happen. My parents, of course, saw it as a blessing." She clears her throat, but I sense she's trying to be cautious with her words. "The next day we went over to see if Lex had calmed down. Samantha was home by herself, and she was visibly upset. She'd been crying, and as my mom consoled her, she told her that Lex was having an affair. When she said your name we were all in shock. My father was livid. He was ready to kill Lex. I was numb. You were my best friend and I felt betrayed by you."

"Adriana, it was never my intention. I loved him so much…"

She raises her eyes to meet mine. "I thought about that. I thought maybe what you and Lex had was like Elijah and me, but Samantha kept telling me that you used me to get closer to Lex, and that all along you had your eye on him. I don't know why I believed her. The biggest regret I have isn't following my instincts. Instead, I gave up on our friendship."

I let out a huge sigh, my shoulders wearing down. "You know what? It's done, and now we move on."

"Yes, I know. It's like fate played a part." Moving close to me, she rests her head on my shoulder just like old times. "Now, will you be my maid of honor?"

I turn to face her, the excitement hard to contain. "Of course, Adriana."

We hug tightly again, and I think to ask the most important question. "Who's designing the dress?"

She rambles on about the designers involved, and my heart fills with joy. I can't believe Elijah has waited so long to propose, but I guess, like many of us, life just gets in the way.

"We planned our wedding three years ago, but right before the big day, Elijah became sick. We found out he had cancer. Thankfully, with plenty of chemo, he was able to walk away cancer-free and has had a clean bill of health for three years."

"I'm so sorry. I can't begin to imagine how difficult that must've been for you."

"It was, but luckily, I had my family to support us. Lex exhausted himself finding the best cancer centers in the world. I don't know what I would've done without him," she tells me, falling silent for a few moments. "You know, he will be the best man at the wedding?"

I expected that to be the case. It isn't about us, it's Adriana and Elijah's special day.

"It's cool, Adriana. I'm sure we can both be in the same room as each other."

My mind flashes to my office. Yes, we can be in the same room as each other but maybe not with our clothes on.

"Charlie, look, you don't need to answer... but were you with him tonight? I won't ask anything else because he's my brother, and that would be TMI."

I laugh, how awkward. I thought our sharing days were long gone. My phone vibrates, distracting me from responding to her.

Lex: *My sister left you alone yet?*

I think of a response but, instead, laugh to myself. My body is utterly exhausted, and even stringing together a sentence is difficult.

"Something funny?"

I show her the text, her eyes rolling until she joins me, laughing. "Charlie, have you thought about this? Aren't you still engaged to Julian?"

Well, if that isn't a slap in the face.

With Lex around, I've suddenly taken leave of my senses.

The guilt begins to seep in, all from the mention of his name.

"Adriana, it's... I mean, Julian is a great guy. He worships the ground I walk on. But—"

"But he's not Lex."

No, he isn't Lex. He's a sweet, humble, compassionate, caring man. He treats me with respect, always sincere with his intentions. He makes me smile, never argues with me. Meanwhile, Lex has become this cold, arrogant son of a bitch who treats me like I'm his possession. Instead of making me smile, he angers me to the core.

"It's been a long day." I yawn, then continuing, "And Lex is, well, he's complicated."

"You're telling me?" Adriana hoots. With her purse draped over her shoulder, she leans in to hug me one more time. "I better head off, but you and me... we're back on."

"I wouldn't have it any other way." I smile.

As I climb into bed, my muscles tighten after the intensity of what had happened earlier. You'd think I was done, yet here I am, drenched between my legs, the images playing in my mind vividly. His cock eagerly waiting near my mouth.

Me: *Yes, I am all alone now.*

I want to write more. Tell him to get over here now and fuck my brains into next week right here in my bed.

Lex: *Me too.*

A quick but meaningful response. Bastard. Letting out a long-winded sigh, I text back quickly.

Me: *You're not alone, you have your hand. Pink wrote a whole song about it.*

Lex: *As much as that song brings pleasure to people,* I'd *rather you bring pleasure to me, right now.*

Fuck, I'm screwed. I read the message a dozen times, and every time I read it, my hands automatically make their way down to my pants, rubbing slightly to ease the pain. I quickly type a message, then continue to explore.

Me: *Greedy, always wanting more.*

Lex: *Charlotte, with you... never enough.*

His last text sends me over the edge, and I come on the spot. Granted, it's nowhere near as good as when I'm with him, but I've already been fucked twice today.

Exhausted, I drift off to sleep within minutes.

"Well, hello, there, Miss Mason. You look awfully happy this morning," Eric comments with one of his eyebrows raised.

"It's going to be a busy day. You know I thrive on a full schedule."

"Uh-huh, full schedule." He turns to Emma, whispering, "More like a full load of man juice in her waterhole."

"Hey, I heard that," I yell, walking toward my office.

As I open the door, like a crime scene before me, the memories of last night come flooding back. I try to settle in, strapped for time since today has back-to-back client meetings.

"Charlie... earth to Charlie!" Eric is sitting across from me, planner out with his pen in his mouth, watching me with a curious gaze.

"Sorry, Eric, let's start."

"Should we start by discussing why it smells like raw, animalistic sex in your office?"

"You watch too much porn."

"No... although I do believe I now have an unhealthy obsession with Andrew McCarthy."

"Um, what? How is that even possible? You were born in like, what..." I count my fingers trying to figure out what year he was born.

"A true gentleman does not reveal his age. Anyway, they played the movie *Pretty in Pink* last night, and let me tell you, I don't know at what point they ever thought that dress was prom-worthy. I have dish towels that look better than that."

"The fact that you're a *Pretty in Pink* virgin should've been raised a long time ago. It's like *the* movie of all movies. Not seeing it is like not knowing Madonna sings 'Material Girl,' and I'd like to also point out your dish towels are purchased from the same place the Queen buys them from, thanks to your mother."

"Fine, so shoot me. Less about tea towels and back to your bang-bang on the desk."

"Sorry, E, subject closed. We have a brief to work on."

"You're such a party pooper, Charlie."

"Yeah, preach it to the world with your hundred-dollar royal dish towels."

We briefed for an hour before Eric left my office. The first few appointments were nothing out of the ordinary until I heard a knock on my door. "Come in."

"Charlie, there's someone here for you." Eric glances at me nervously.

Oh fuck, please don't tell me it's Lex. There's no way I can resist him, and I'm not comfortable fucking him in broad daylight with the whole office present.

"Who is it?"

"Mrs. Benson."

"I don't know who that is, but fine, let her in."

He leaves the room, returning with her a few moments later.

"Hello, Charlie."

"Samantha?"

In my head, all I hear is the imperial march from *Star Wars*, and she's Darth Vader. The realization of her inside my office is surreal. A week ago, I hadn't seen Lex for nine years. Not only have I fucked him, now I'm standing here in my office with his ex-wife, the woman whose life I broke by my immature indiscretion.

"I'm sorry I didn't arrange a meeting. Can we talk?" she asks.

I motion for her to sit. "Is there something I can help you with?"

"I want to apologize. Charlie, I'm sorry. The whole thing with Alex..."

I'm stunned by her need to apologize. She'd never done anything wrong. She married the man of her dreams, hardly a mistake.

She fumbles with her hands as she speaks. "I knew well before the pregnancy that he loved you. I could see the way he looked at you. I made mistakes, so many, but the one thing I don't regret is my baby girl."

A tear falls down her cheek, catching me by surprise. I hand her a box of tissues, unsure of what to say.

"I'm sorry, too, Samantha. He was yours. I was young and stupid and shouldn't have let it get that far."

Like words trapped inside a vault, the release is more satisfying than I had ever anticipated. I wasn't a victim in the games we played, I held an equal part in creating the tangled web.

"I know life would've been different for you if I had just let you be together," she stumbles, sniffing.

"You made vows to each other. I had no right—"

She holds out her arms, interrupting me. "I hope you can forgive me."

Accepting her embrace, we both hold onto each other tightly.

"Charlie, his heart never belonged to me, it always belonged to you, and it still does. Don't let your stubbornness get in the way of true love."

She pulls away with a smile on her face and glassy eyes, walking out of my office with a gracious wave.

I'm left dumbfounded.

For years, I envisioned what it would be like if we ran into each other. The nasty names she would call me, the way she'd pull my hair and kick me to the ground like a wrestler gone wild. Caught in my own emotions, I never once stopped and thought about her feelings or how I destroyed her marriage. And now, we've both forgiven each other for the mistakes we made, and the feeling of remorse is lifting from my shoulders like a cloud disappearing over the horizon.

Acting on impulse, I grab my phone and dial Adriana.

"Hey, girl. What's up?"

"I need a favor from you. A really big favor."

I can't believe what I'm asking of Adriana, but I want him to know he doesn't hold all the cards. Lex Edwards has turned into an egotistical, selfish bastard. He thrives on power, that much I know.

But underneath his powerful exterior, lies a weakness.

And I know exactly what that is.

We are both pawns in the wicked game we're playing, but I know we are beyond being able to stop.

So now, Mr. Edwards, hold on.

I'm going to get you where it hurts the most.

TWENTY-NINE

LEX

It has been the day from *hell*.

I know the consequences of not attending the shareholder meeting at the Hilton but being here with Charlotte has definitely been worth it.

It's three in the afternoon the following day, and I have just gotten off my final conference call, the fourth in a row to be exact.

Kate's sitting with me, letting out a breath when the call ends. "Mr. Edwards, I know it's none of my business, but may I ask what called you to Manhattan so urgently?"

I stand, walking toward the window. Placing my arm against the glass, I lean on it for support. "There was someone I needed to see, someone who meant a lot to me once upon a time."

Kate glances at me, bewildered.

Yes, that's right, Lex Edwards actually has a heart.

He wasn't born a cold-hearted prick.

"Um, sure, okay... I... uh... how long do you expect to stay here with her?"

"I don't know. It's complicated."

"I understand. I'll organize for you to be set up here indefinitely. Would you like me to assist you here or fly back to London and be your point of contact there?" She quickly jots down some notes on her pad, that I have no idea what, but I seriously need to give her a pay rise.

"Let's play it by ear. Can you get the office here fast-tracked? Regarding any designing aspects, please liaise with my sister."

She finishes writing more notes and packs up her laptop, advising me she will work on everything immediately. As she begins to walk out of the suite, I call out to her, "Kate?"

"Yes, sir?"

"I apologize for leaving you to deal with the aftermath of me not attending the meeting."

I can't believe I apologized, especially to an employee. Lex Edwards doesn't apologize for anything or to anyone. I continue to gaze out the window at the city below.

"Is she worth it, sir?"

Unable to deal with all the emotions that come with having Charlotte back in my life, I let out the breath I've been holding in a long drawn out sigh. I control everything I do and usually everyone around me.

I just can't comprehend that everything I've grown accustomed to is slowly slipping away. I'm scared of losing control, terrified she's holding on to every piece of me, and with just one flick of her finger she will break me.

"She always was."

"What do you want?" I answer, flatly.

"Nice way to greet your only sister. Listen, I had some

pieces sent to your office here, and I need you to approve them ASAP."

"Adriana, I'm exhausted, and have so much work to do. I'm sure it's fine. I trust your judgment."

I don't have any fight left in me. My emails are piling up, and I have to haul some serious ass if I want to get through this mess I have created. Many employees and associates are angry at my reckless behavior, and I don't blame them either.

"It sounds to me like you need a breather. Look, the office is a ten-minute cab ride from the Waldorf. Please... go have a look. Anything you don't want has to be returned first thing in the morning."

I haven't left the suite all day. As much as I nagged Charlotte to take a break via texts, I can't find the time either. Thankfully, she's too busy, but it disappoints me that I don't get to taste her today. I agree to go but tell Adriana to stop bothering me for the rest of the night.

As I take the cab to the office, my mind drifts off to last night, specifically the elevator.

How could I not stop the elevator? As she bowed her head with a smirk on her face, I pressed the button. She knew why, and she was more than ready. I lifted her against the wall and pushed her panties aside. Within seconds, I slid my cock inside her. She roughly tugged on my hair while smashing her lips on mine.

"Make me come again, Lex. Fuck me hard," she screamed.

I spread her ass cheeks, gripping onto them tightly as I slammed into her. She was so fucking wet. She had already come twice tonight, plus I had already blown inside her. The sound of my cock pounding her pussy was sending me over the edge quickly.

"Lex," she murmured.

With my head buried in her neck, the sound of her calling my name was like heaven on earth. The smell of her skin was intoxicating. I constantly found myself inhaling the air around her. It was like a sweet floral smell mixed with sweat. Sweat that she was covered in because I was fucking her so hard.

"Lex, look at me," she demanded.

As I looked into her eyes, the depths of chocolate brown were full of lust, desire, and something else I couldn't quite decipher.

"Always look at me when you're fucking me," she commanded.

Well, fuck me, that sent me hurling into a fucking orgasmic finish. I don't know how long I came for, but it felt like minutes. Then, I slowly pulled myself out and grabbed her body as she stood there, legs shaking. We fixed our clothing, then I pressed the stop button again to activate the lift.

"I thought you had to be in London?"

Adjusting my tie, the grin on my face was obvious. "My plans changed."

I didn't let on to the fact that I was in deep shit for the spontaneous decision I'd made, or that I was this close to losing a fifty-million-dollar deal.

"For how long?"

I could almost see a hint of hope in her eyes as she waited on my response.

"Indefinitely."

. . .

I break out of the trip down memory lane, annoyed the cab is at a standstill due to the peak- hour traffic. Irritated, I text Adriana one after the other with messages full of profanity, and cursing her for making me take this trip. The sound of my email keeps pinging, and I reluctantly open my inbox to find an email from Victoria Preston, Executive Director of Preston Enterprises, informing me they declined our tender due to my absence at that meeting. She's also quick to mention that she is staying at the same hotel and would like to discuss our proposal in further detail.

Victoria Preston is one hell of a manipulative ball-breaking bitch. Of course, we want the contract, it's worth fifty million dollars. I avoid dealing with her after her attempt to seduce me at the last governor's ball in London. She's a spoiled brat who was born with a silver spoon in her mouth.

I pinch the bridge of my nose knowing there's no way I can get out of meeting with her. It infuriates me that she's staying in the same hotel because I know it's no coincidence. Responding to her email, I mentally prepare myself for a long night ahead. We have a lot riding on this, the reality of which is settling in and enveloping me whole.

As I quickly ride the elevator up to the floor that is to be our new office, my phone buzzes. No fucking shit, it's Adriana. I clench the handset ready to have it out with her.

"Fucking hell, Adriana, I'm here!"

"And what do you think?" she calmly asks.

I walk through the doors with my phone still glued to my ear. I abruptly stop at the entrance to my office. "Adriana, I need to go." I end the call, not even waiting for a response.

Sitting in my enormous leather chair is Charlotte, dressed in a trench coat, pantyhose, and those famous

Louboutins. My cock stirs at the sight of the trench coat. I'm hoping it's just like in the movies—nothing underneath. Her legs are crossed, and I can just barely get a glimpse of the garters around her thigh.

She stands, slowly walking over to me. I'm speechless, and hard as fucking hell, quite possibly ready to blow in my pants like some horny fifteen-year-old boy at any moment. Grabbing my hand, she pulls me over to the desk, then sits me down in the chair, standing tall in front of me. I ache to reach out and run my hands along her smooth skin, but I wait.

"This is the thing, Mr. Edwards... I don't appreciate unexpected visitors in my office. Gestures like that will lead to serious punishment."

I can't resist, raising my hand and placing it on her thigh. Slowly sliding it down, I make my way under the coat and cup her perfect ass. "I'm all for following rules."

She undoes the knot in her belt, opening the coat. Underneath it, she's wearing a strapless black corset with the garters attached to her pantyhose. The fabric of her French-cut panties so sheer, I can see the moisture building against the fabric. My woman is fucking wet as hell waiting for me. As I pull the coat off her shoulders, she straddles me in the chair.

"Let me think of the ways you need to be punished... hmmm." She slowly grinds against my cock. With both my hands on her ass I struggle to compose myself, caressing them, hard. "My problem is that every time I sit at my desk at work, I'm reminded of what you did to me. As you can imagine, being the workaholic I am, it seems to have interfered with my day. So, I think it's only fair that if I have to deal with that, then so should you."

Charlotte slowly stands then sits on my desk. She slides

back, opening her legs wide in front of me, then slides her fingers down, slowly rubbing her clit in circles.

This is gonna kill me.

Watching me watch her, she pushes the fabric aside making contact with her bare flesh. She whimpers as she speeds up, arching her back when she slides her fingers inside her.

Fuck. Me. Dead.

I quickly unzip my pants, releasing my cock. I stroke it slowly as I watch her, savoring every moment. Her eyes hungrily watch my cock as I increase my strokes, spreading the pre-cum all over my hands. She takes her fingers out of her pussy, inserting them in her mouth, tasting them one by one.

My chest is pounding, and pulling her roughly toward me, my lips crush against hers. The wait is killing me, my patience growing thin by the sheer desire running through my veins. I flip her over, unable to wait anymore. With her ass in my full view, I spread her legs as far as I can, slamming my cock into her.

The ache causes me to groan. Shutting my eyes tight, I hold back from finishing too early. *Fucking control yourself.* Taking small breaths, I manage to stop the climactic finish and slam my hips against hers. She begs for me to fuck her harder, moaning as my cock goes in deeper.

"I want you, baby. All of you," I whisper in her ear.

She knows what I want, and goddammit, she's more than willing. Dirty words escape my mouth, brushing against her ear as she moans softly through the intensity, pushing her ass further into me. Her beautiful sounds push me, warning me to control my movements and slow down.

I lean over with my cock still inside her. Pushing her hair aside, my teeth graze her ear. I remain still for a moment, listening to her heartbeat, admiring the glow of sweat lingering on her skin. Her breathing slows, but I know she's anxious. Her tight pussy is wrapped around my cock, and I know she's almost there, holding back just like me wanting to take this further.

"You want me, Charlotte. You want my cock to touch every part of your body. You want to scream my name in your dreams, wake up achingly sore, remember how hard I make you come so that no one will ever fuck your little pussy or ass again but me."

Her body shudders as I say the words. Pulling my cock out, she rubs it against her ass.

A breath escapes my lips, my jaw clenching tight at the thought of entering her ass right now. We did this, only once, so I tell myself to be gentle.

Spreading her cheeks wide, I admire the beautiful sight before me. I slowly slide myself in as she rubs her clit, listening to her moans and attentive to her movements. Her ass is so fucking tight with no chance of me holding back any longer.

Her back arches, the grind slow but gaining speed, sending me into a frenzy. I'm doing everything in my power to hold back, take it slow and not hurt her, but the more I clench the harder she slams into me.

Wrapping her hair around my hand, I tug on it forcefully until her body begins to tense.

She's close.

"Lex please... fuck me... harder."

Charlotte's pleas are cut short, the familiar warmth contracting around my cock causing me to push deeper. Shouting a string of profanities, the heat rises until I'm seeing stars, incoherent as I ride out the orgasm.

Both of us remain silent, catching our breath from the

intense fuck. I slide my cock out slowly, rubbing the small of her back as I do so. She collapses on my desk which causes me to chuckle.

"What's so funny?" she asks, reaching for her coat.

"Can't handle the intense workout?"

"I'll have you know that I do Yoga and Zumba, and I run most days."

Her face is flushed a beautiful shade of pink as I pull her into me. I kiss her softly, a far cry from the usual intensity that passes between us. Her lips are soft, and her tongue caresses mine slowly before she abruptly pulls away.

"Lex, we're just fucking. Friends with benefits. Fuck buddies. Whatever you want to call it."

I don't have the strength right now to argue. If that's what she wants, then I'll let her believe that's all it is, but I know better than that. Charlotte doesn't do fuck buddies. She isn't the type. And she's always worn her heart on her sleeve being unable to hide her feelings.

However, the questions still remain.

Why is she still with him?

Why is she still marrying him?

So, what? The fucker took her to movies and dinner and shit.

But she's mine.

She just needs to realize it.

"If that's what you want, Miss Mason."

We move in silence, exiting the building and standing on the sidewalk. I ask her what plans she has for the rest of the night.

"Just chill out and read," she replies casually. "I need to be up at the ass crack of dawn tomorrow. You?"

"Work, of course. Pulling an all-nighter. Feel free to join me if you get lonely."

"I'll keep that in mind," she says, amused.

As she attempts to say goodbye, I grab her one more time, kissing her deeply. I want to let her know exactly how much I need her.

But once again, I feel the resistance.

I let it go.

For now.

The morning flies by as I sit with Kate discussing our meeting with Victoria Preston. My phone buzzes, and not recognizing the number, I pick it up. "Lex Edwards."

"Please don't hang up, Lex." I recognize Samantha's voice immediately.

Fucking hell, I don't need this complication now.

How did she get my fucking number?

"What do you want, Samantha?"

"Please just listen to me, then I'll leave you alone. I'm sorry for my behavior at the club. I had no right being that drunk and forcing myself on you and causing a scene."

I listen, but I am fucking angry as hell. Kate sits silently overhearing every word I say. Why this bitch thought she has the right to come back into my life when Charlotte has is beyond me.

"Things haven't been good between Chris and I, and... wait before you say anything, I just wanted to let you know that I saw Charlie. I wanted to apologize for what I did to her."

"Excuse me?"

I. Am. Fucking. Livid!

She had no right contacting me, and she especially had no right speaking to Charlotte.

"Lex, she forgave me for my mistakes. Why can't you? We were all young and stupid at the time."

"Don't give me young and stupid, Samantha. You fucked up my damn life!"

I slam my finger on the end call button and throw the phone on the couch. Pacing the room, I try to calm down, wondering why Charlotte never said anything.

Is she lying to me?

What else is she not telling me?

Kate prompts me of the time and my meeting downstairs. We grab our briefcases and head down to the restaurant until Kate informs me she's forgotten something, so she heads back to the room leaving me alone with the wench.

"Mr. Edwards... a pleasure to see you again," Victoria greets, purposely exposing her chest like the whore she is.

"Ms. Preston."

"Please, sit. Would you like a drink?"

The waiter stops at our table, takes our order, then scurries off. Victoria gazes at me, taking a sip of her wine. She purposely licks her lips, parting them slightly while holding my attention. She has really large lips, the kind that would chase you in your nightmares wanting to drown you in saliva. I guess they would be good for head, though.

Argh, I'm only thinking this way because I am furious at Charlotte for holding back important information like Samantha visiting her.

Kate arrives armed with the proposal documents, so I introduce her to Victoria. Of course, Victoria being the stuck-up bitch she is, puts on her fake greeting followed closely by a condescending look at Kate.

"So, Mr. Edwards, the main proposal was highly praised, however, during the initial startup, we'll require you to be very hands-on. As you can imagine, your absence did question your dedication to us as your client, which is why we originally declined the offer."

Bitch. One fucking time, seriously.

She makes it sound like I am at home scratching my balls all day watching MTV.

"Ms. Preston, I assure you that our dedication to this project is above and beyond what you expect. I apologize for my absence, but it was due to an emergency situation that needed to be taken care of here in Manhattan."

"Look, Mr. Edwards, my team will only sign this proposal if you can commit to your side of the contract. We also now request that the majority of the work be done in London."

Fuck! My gut had me thinking it would boil down to this, with long fucking hours at their main headquarters. How am I ever going to see Charlotte if I'm in London?

Maybe Charlotte doesn't actually give a fuck about me?

Maybe she just needed a retribution fuck?

Maybe she was me two weeks ago? The Lex Edwards who would sweet-talk ladies when he needed a quick fuck. The type who would disappear in the middle of the night without even a quick goodbye or "thanks, I had a lovely time sticking my dick in your pussy."

But then I think of the times when she's let her guard down.

When she asked me to look her in the eyes. How emerald green is still her favorite color. And when she told me there would be a next time.

There's hope that she still feels something.

"This is a one-year contract, Mr. Edwards. Do we have your commitment that this will be carried out in that speci-fied timeframe?"

A fifty-million-fucking-dollar business deal, and I question it because I don't want to leave the States. She hands me the papers with a pen, eyeing me, waiting for a reaction. I hesitate, looking at Kate who's watching me puzzled by my delayed reaction. I grab the pen and begin signing the documents, the weight of the world now resting on my shoulders.

Kate announces that she'll make copies and return in ten minutes. Leaving me alone with Victoria, I dread where this conversation will lead.

"It will be nice to have you back in London," she beams, playfully. "We should have dinner when you're back to discuss any other ideas you might have."

"Look, Victoria, this is strictly business. You know I don't mix business with pleasure."

"Oh, please, Lex, like you haven't fucked your little assistant, Kat, Kathy, or whatever her name is," she sneers.

"Her name is Kate, and no, she's a valuable employee. I meant what I said. Don't play games with me."

Kate returns with the copied documents. We wrap up the meeting with Victoria advising she'll email me a confirmation of when the project will begin.

Walking up to my suite in small steps, I hang my head with an empty feeling inside of me. The last twenty-four hours have been heaven and hell in equal measures. I want Charlotte so fucking much, yet I can't overcome the rage over Samantha, Julian, and the fact I'm still second best.

"Mr. Edwards, you look exhausted. Let me take care of things for the rest of the day. I suggest you have a good sleep," Kate offers.

She has a point. Even though it's close to lunchtime, I have no problem getting some sleep. I'm never this worn out, but right now, I'm no nearer to answers to the questions that are remaining. And working until three this morning has only made matters worse.

I have to refocus with a plan of attack.

Jesus Christ, I'm treating this whole Charlotte thing like a goddamn business proposal. But maybe I need to tackle it that way? The only thing I'm sure about is that she's mine, and no one is going to take her away from me.

Not now. Not ever.

Still, I can't shake my hostility toward her for forgiving Samantha.

Why did she do it?

What about me?

Why won't she forgive me?

THIRTY
CHARLIE

The rain doesn't deter me from my usual morning run. Instead, it cools me down, allowing me to run even harder.

I stop off at my usual bench trying to catch my breath. The last forty-eight hours have been draining, to say the least. Apart from a heavy workload I was struggling with due to my unstable personal life, I have Lex to deal with.

"Hi again!" The familiar blonde girl stops by the bench.

"Hi. Haven't seen you for a few days. Did you leave Manhattan?"

"Yes, briefly, but here I am again." She laughs, then reaches out her hand to introduce herself. "I'm Kate, by the way."

I shake her hand. "Charlie."

"I'm sorry, I don't know why I'm laughing." She clutches her stomach, letting out a sigh. "I'm so stressed out with work right now I think I'm losing my marbles."

"I know how you feel. I'm in the same boat. I have so much going on, and it doesn't help that my love life is like a rollercoaster ride right now."

"Man troubles?"

"Man troubles, plural," I confess.

"Oh, wow. I wouldn't want to be in your shoes. I'm glad I've got myself a good man, just happens he's on the other side of the world," she says while catching her breath.

We both take a seat at the bench, resting while we watch other runners woosh by.

"A long-distance relationship requires patience. I don't know how you do it."

"It's not easy. Love is great, but at the end of the day, every couple has needs. Hard to fulfill when you're across the other side of the world," Kate complains.

"How did we end up with complicated relationships?"

"I know, right?" Kate laughs. "So, I'm thinking..." she scrunches her eyebrows together, "... you pick who you like best and roll with it. Maybe start with who's most attractive?"

We laugh in unison. There's something comforting about confiding in a stranger.

"Well, man number one is gorgeous... like Christian Bale gorgeous."

"Oh, holy hell! And number two?"

"There are no words... *he's beautiful.*"

"Sounds to me like number two is a lady door knocker."

I burst out laughing, again. *Lady door knocker! British slang has me in hysterics.* As I wipe away a tiny tear from my eye, I compose myself enough to respond to Kate.

"I guess you could say that, but it's so complicated."

"I'm no love expert, but I swear there must be a full moon or something because weird shit is happening everywhere."

"That would explain a lot."

"Take my boss for example... he's the most arrogant

bastard you could ever meet. I mean the number of times I've had to clean up his mess is, well... *it's a lot.*" She sighs heavily with exaggeration. "After every girl he fucked and left hanging, who do you think was the one dealing with all the clingy-girl bullshit? You got it! Me! Seriously, I deserve a pay rise because that's not in my job description."

How unprofessional of a boss. In our office the only males we employed are Tate and Eric. Eric is interested in men, so no clingy-girl bullshit, and Tate, thankfully, is as professional as you can get. The real deal which is why we hired him.

"So anyway, something weird is going on. I only know that a woman has come into his life, and I think he has feelings for her. I nearly fell off my chair when I found out. I'm telling you the man has no heart. But gosh, something has changed," she finishes.

"Sometimes, that one person can change everything you believe in. Maybe she captured his heart. Is he at least nice to look at?"

"He's a drop-dead BILF."

I raise my brow. "Uh, what's a BILF?"

"Boss I'd like to fuck... although I never would. I love my job and get great perks. I've just learned to tolerate him and always be one step ahead."

"Nice body?"

"Oh, hell yeah." She chuckles, shaking her head with a knowing grin. "He works out so much he looks like a Greek god. I've never seen him shirtless, though."

"Sounds to me like you got yourself a great job."

"Yes, I do, but right now I need to focus." Kate looks at her watch, instantly dropping her shoulders. "Oh shit, it's seven. I had better head back. I'll see you tomorrow?"

I smile. "I'll be here."

"Cheerio, then!"

I run back home thinking about how the last few days have unfolded. I know I was taking a risk by asking Adriana to get involved with planning for me to be in Lex's office, but I wanted him to know it isn't just him who gets to call the shots. Looking back, I can't believe I allowed myself to be so bold and carefree. Yeah, I'd fantasized about that shit all the time, but to make it a reality is surreal. He was barely able to control himself, and that's what I wanted— Mr. Control Freak to lose himself.

Every touch, every sound was sending me over the edge, but then he said he wanted all of me. I knew what he meant, and not one part of me hesitated. As he filled me, I groaned with pleasure. He's the only one who has ever been inside there. The pressure was intense, and it didn't take me long to come. He followed quickly, gripping me tight as the waves of pleasure died down slowly. It felt amazing, but then he kissed me softly and I pulled away. I wasn't prepared for emotions to be involved. This was strictly hardcore, nothing-off-the-table kind of sex. Just fucking. I reminded him of that, and he was quick to acknowledge it, which hurt slightly, but I had to convince myself that's all this was. *Who am I kidding?*

As I sit in my office daydreaming about the night before, Eric and Nikki walk in, both of them taking a seat. Eric grabs a handful of M&Ms as Nikki scolds him for putting the brown ones back in the jar. What the hell is his problem with eating the brown ones?

"So, the lady who walked into my office yesterday was Samantha Benson."

"Wasn't she that chick at the club that Lex was trying to offload?" Eric asks, raising his perfectly sculpted brows.

"Yes, she was."

"How do you know her?" Nikki questions.

Answering this question is inevitable. I've been dreading it, but I knew it would come out sooner or later, so it might as well be now. "She was Lex's wife."

"So, they got married after you guys split up?" Eric's eyes widen with curiosity. "When did she remarry and have the kid?"

"Eric, I don't think they got married after Charlie and Lex split up," Nikki says, turning back to face me. "Am I correct in assuming you were together while he was married?"

"Something like that." I lower my tone, feeling ashamed at the situation. I know it had been more than me just being a homewrecker, but how can I explain what our love was to them?

Eric clasps his hand on his mouth. "Oh..." and then it dawns on him, "*Oh!*"

"Guys, look, it wasn't like that. We were in love, like earth-shattering love. At least, I thought it was."

Nikki leans over the table, placing her hand on mine. She knows me well enough to know that it had meant something. After all, she was the one who would hold me tight when I screamed Alex's name in my sleep.

"Charlie, what happened?" Eric narrows his eyes, still confused. "And what's going on between you two now?"

"He left, didn't say goodbye. I found out from the town slut that Samantha was pregnant."

"Hold up, the kid is his?" Nikki exclaims.

"No. She was screwing around as well, but she did tell him it was his. His family put pressure on him to stay with her after Samantha told them about me. Apparently, months later, she confessed to him that the baby wasn't his, and he left her. He told me he looked for me but not in the right place, and my mother had told him I moved on."

"But you hadn't, Charlie. I was there..." Nikki trails off.

"No, I hadn't. He believed what she said and decided that I deserved more."

"I'm sorry, Charlie. I knew he meant a lot to you. I mean, you didn't start to date till the end of college, no matter how much Rocky and I tried to set you up."

"Oh, gee, Nikki, the blind dates Rocky set me up with were so hideous." I shake my head, smiling at their pathetic attempt to set me up with so many losers.

We laugh, reminiscing until Eric breaks us from our trip down memory lane. "So, what did she want to see you about?"

"She needed to tell me how sorry she was and asked for forgiveness. We all make mistakes, Eric. Sometimes we need to forgive to move on."

"And Lex?" he asks, reluctantly.

Letting out a sigh, I lean back into my chair. These two people are my best friends, and yet I always held this part of me close to my heart, tightly closed up in a sealed box. Is now the time to spill my heart and soul and reveal all the scars?

"Lex is... it's complicated."

"It can't be that complicated, Charlie. I mean, you're fucking him all over Manhattan," Nikki points out.

"I am not fucking him all over Manhattan!"

"Woman has a point, Charlie. You've had a certain glow all week. You know... that I've-been-done-in-every-orifice look."

Nikki and Eric both laugh. My face turns crimson. Is it that obvious?

"We'll take your silence as a yes. Nikki, you notice how

she's been walking funny as well, almost with a limp?" Eric jokes.

I throw a pen at Eric.

So, at least they know that part. The rest will remain my secret, for now.

***

"Hey, Charlie." Eric peeks his head through my door. "There's someone here to see you."

Who now, I wonder? As I stand up, flattening the crease in my skirt, Julian walks into the room. *Oh, fuck.* I haven't seen him since movie-night, and in that time, I have screwed Lex more times than I care to admit.

"Hey, gorgeous. I was starting to think you had disappeared."

Julian strolls over to me, grabbing my waist and pulling my body against his. Tilting his head, he plants a kiss on my lips, an uneasy feeling consuming me as I force a smile.

"Sorry, Julian. Work has literally kicked my butt all week."

"I see. I know there's something I'd like to do to that butt," he teases, placing his hands on my ass, caressing it slowly.

I pull his hands off. "Mr. Baker, this is a professional environment. Plus, Eric is known for barging in."

The guilt deepens at the mention of a lie.

"Fine, but later, you're mine." He winks, cupping my chin before kissing my nose. "I brought something for you."

He places a white shirt box with a red bow in front of me. I look up at him, curious as to what's inside. He motions for me to open it, and I do, stunned by what's there.

"We haven't spoken about the actual wedding plans," he mentions, eyes watching for my reaction.

I force another smile, afraid that with one look, he'll know what I've done. Pulling the bridal magazines out of the box, I pretend to be interested while flicking through them. Yet my stomach becomes queasy, the reality hitting me hard as I watch my hands shake slightly as I hold the magazines.

"So much to organize…" I trail off, the enormity of the situation overwhelming.

"We can always hire a wedding coordinator. However, that would be a disappointment to my mother."

"Your mother?" I ask nervously.

"Yes, she's dying to meet you. She'll be traveling through New York in three weeks on her way to some sort of book convention."

"As in, erotic romances?"

I'm trying my best to push away how awkward this conversation has become. I've never met his mother, so this is a big deal in a relationship.

"Thanks for the visual." He laughs, running his hand through his hair. "So, a little birdie reminded me it's your birthday on Saturday."

"Little birdie has a big mouth. Yes, it is."

"Any plans?"

"Big-mouth birdie said he's taking me out to dinner. You're welcome to join us," I offer, taking note to scold Eric for even mentioning it.

"I'm sorry, I have an important function to attend. However, I'll join you after dinner, plus I'm free for breakfast on Sunday morning. Preferably in bed."

"Oh, Batman, you sure know how to use those cheesy lines."

"Hey, Batman resents that." He kisses me goodbye, promising me he will call me tonight when I'm done with work.

As he leaves the room, I breathe a sigh of relief. *What the hell am I doing?* These are not the actions of a sane person, so far from it. I sit in my chair opening a magazine, casually flicking through the pages. Not an ounce of excitement stirs within me. Surely, my bridezilla gene is supposed to have kicked in by now. I sit here almost numb—*almost.* The Valentino gown is to die for.

I'm reading an article on the dos-and-don'ts of wedding planning when a loud sound startles me. The commotion comes from my doorway where Lex is standing tall, and an extremely panic-stricken Eric and Emma stand behind him trying to catch their breaths.

"I'm sorry..." Eric gasps for air.

"It's okay, Eric."

Lex catches sight of the magazines, forcing Eric and Emma to scurry away like two timid dogs.

"You have no right barging into my office like this," I tell him, trying my best to speak in a flat monotone, but the anger is rearing to go, ready to bite his head off and give him an earful about workplace protocol.

"What do you expect? You won't talk to me, but you talk to everyone else. In fact, you forgive everyone else but not me. Why?" he asks, exasperated.

What the hell is he talking about?

"Excuse me?"

"You easily play make-up with Adriana and Samantha, but with me, you shut me down every time I try to apologize."

"Please leave," I warn him. "This is my place of business. I don't bring my personal life to work."

He stands before me with flared eyes and unruly hair, his body language is enough for me to realize he's deadly serious. His eyes dart to the magazines on my desk.

"Answer me!"

"I've nothing to say to you."

His lethal stare is painful and piercing with a purpose to tear me apart. Lex may be angry, striking at me fueled by the pain he's feeling, but nothing and I mean nothing, can erase the pain that seeps into every part of me like poison.

I crave his words, hurtful as they may be, they are his soul coming out in pieces for me to hear. But the deadliest sound of all—is silence.

Turning his back, he leaves my office without a goodbye.

I can't cry, the tears long gone and dried up. Instead, I sit here dazed, unable to cope with the burst of anger I bestowed upon him. *He deserved it.* That was nothing compared to what I went through.

He hasn't won.

I'm still standing here.

This time, I am the one wearing the ring.

And soon, I'll become *Mrs. Baker.*

THIRTY-ONE

ALEX

Nine Years Ago

L ast night I had a dream, the kind of dream that when you woke up, you closed your eyes and tried to fall back into that blissful sleep praying that somehow the dream would continue.

Charlotte was beside me wearing nothing but a sheet around her naked body. Her head rested on my shoulders as we sat for what felt like hours. My hands were positioned above the piano keys, but they were still. Faintly, I could hear a piano playing in the background. It was beautiful, and as much as I tried to move my hands to mirror the playing, they remained frozen.

I realized when I woke up the next morning that it was my subconscious telling me to play again. Between work and studying, I never had time to sit and play anymore, so here I was in my parents' living room attempting to play the piano. As a child, I had also learned to play the guitar, but playing the piano had come naturally.

As I found the right keys, my fingers moved to the rhythm in my head. Sensing I was being watched, I stopped, surprised to see Charlotte standing at the door.

"Please don't stop, Alex." She smiled.

I motioned for her to sit next to me on the piano stool. She reluctantly did so but with a space between us. I ached for her to lean her head on my shoulder just like in my dream, but with Adriana home, I forced myself to ignore every voice which screamed in my head to reach out and touch her.

"I didn't know you played. Actually, I wasn't sure why your parents had a piano at all because Adriana doesn't have a musical bone in her body."

"I used to play," I told her. "It's been a while."

"Will you play that song for me again? I love that song."

"You knew what song it was?" I asked with a raised eyebrow.

"Of course, I do. It's 'Right Here Waiting for You.' Eighties music is my jam."

I started to play the notes again. Closing my eyes, I couldn't help but sing along, remembering each line of the song, and because she was right beside me, I wanted to sing the words to her that I couldn't say out loud.

As the chorus began, Charlotte started to sing along with me. Her voice was amazing, so angelic and perfectly fitting for the song. I continued on, both of us in harmony and singing the entire song to each other.

When the song ended, I tried my best not to look her way, but it was impossible. Almost shyly, she continued to stare at the keys. Her cheeks were flushed, and I wanted to place the palm of my hand on her face and feel the heat of her skin, knowing she was feeling it because of me. But the risk was too high with everyone inside the house.

"Alex, your voice is amazing, and you play the piano..." she trailed off and paused for a few seconds then continued, "Why did you choose to study medicine?"

"I play guitar, too." I smirked, knocking her shoulder.

"Anything else, Mr. Musical Prodigy?"

"Does the triangle count?" I joked. "No, but I always wanted a drum kit. Mom and Dad refused, saying drums lead to rock 'n' roll which leads to drug addiction. Besides, Charlotte, look who's talking. Your voice is just... wow."

"Maybe we should run off together and become a dynamic singing duo like Sonny and Cher." She bowed her head, laughing

"*'They say we're young and we don't know,'*" I started to sing, trying not to laugh.

She placed her hand on my shoulder as we laughed together until we heard a noise behind us. Both of us turned around. Samantha was standing under the arch. *Fuck.* I didn't know how long she was standing there for, but I wasn't doing anything wrong aside from loving the girl who sat beside me.

"Hi, Charlie. It's good to see you've managed to get Alex playing the piano again," she said, with a slow, steady gait.

"Not me, Sam. I just heard him. You've got yourself one talented man here," Charlotte responded while sliding off the piano stool.

Raising her chin, she crossed her arms with a knowing grin. "I do, don't I?"

"Well, I'm off. Nice jamming with you, Alex. Adriana

is dragging me to a party across town. Apparently, she has someone she wants me to meet."

What the fuck?

Was that supposed to make me feel better?

Calm the fuck down, Alex.

Charlotte just said that so Samantha wouldn't be suspicious. She wouldn't do anything to hurt me on purpose, especially with another guy.

"Oh, that's right. That friend of Elijah's with the tattoo of a skull on his neck." Samantha chuckles.

"That's the one. Sounds just like the man my daddy wants to kill. Anyway, have fun, guys." She waved, avoiding my eyes and leaving us alone.

Samantha sat beside me on the piano. She reached out for my hand and toyed with my wedding band. I pretended not to notice and attempted to play a tune with just my right hand.

"A pretty girl, that one. Don't you think?"

Back the fuck up.

Samantha is asking me if I think Charlotte is pretty?

I was one-hundred percent sure this was woman code for testing the waters.

Tread very carefully.

"She's okay, I guess. She's Adriana's best friend. Have you met my sister?"

She moved closer to me on the piano, wrapping her arms around my torso. "Alex, take me home and fuck me the way you used to fuck me every night before we moved here."

"I didn't fuck you every night, Sammy. You confusing me with someone else?"

"Should I be asking the same thing?"

There was a pause and pauses reflected guilt.

"Samantha, I work fourteen-hour shifts and still have to study. I'm not only mentally but physically exhausted at the end of a long day."

"Well, how about now?"

Confused, I looked at her as she climbed onto my lap.

"Sammy, this is my parents' house—"

"Everyone's left for the night, Alex. It's just you and me. I'm your wife. Fuck me, please," she begged.

I didn't know what to do at that point. If I gave in to her, would that shut her up? I closed my eyes as she unbuckled my belt. Maybe I could do this? Surely, Charlotte would understand that I'd have to do this to keep up the charade. If Samantha had no reason for concern, then Charlotte and I could continue seeing each other. Yes, this was exactly what I needed to do.

I felt my hands moving involuntarily to her tits, squeezing them while trying my best to ignore the enormous amount of guilt I felt right now. She began grinding herself against my cock, moaning into my ear a high-pitched moan she made when she was aroused. My hands found their way to her ass until I moved them into her panties. She was fucking soaked.

"That's it, baby. I know you miss me," she whispered in my ear.

She pulled her skirt up, ready to sit on my cock when we heard a commotion at the door.

"Oh my God!" Adriana shrieked.

Fuck! Fuck! Fuck!

I pushed Samantha off me like I was caught red-handed doing something wrong.

"Sorry, guys, I didn't think... oh my eyes! Where's the fucking bleach?" she complained, shaking her head.

"Sorry, Adriana, we thought everyone had left."

"I left my phone inside. This is hilarious! Charlie would've pissed herself laughing at this. Okay, guess I'll leave you to it. Bye."

She waved as she walked out of the room. *Fuck*, she was going to tell Charlotte. Poor Charlotte, hearing this and then having to meet that tattoo guy. I needed to do something and fast, ignoring the bile rising in my throat.

"I forgot to ask Adriana something." I rushed out, desperate to find them.

Samantha wrapped her arms around my neck. "So just call her, Alex. Let's get back to where we left off."

I yanked her off me, without another word, and ran outside as fast as I could.

The car was already reversing down the driveway, and all I saw was Adriana laughing.

And beside her, a very heartbroken Charlotte staring right back at me.

THIRTY-TWO

CHARLIE

Present

Eric clutches my hand tight, rushing me along the busy streets attempting to reach the restaurant in record speed. Easy for him since he's wearing flats. My new Jimmy Choo shoes are getting scuffed which doesn't impress me one bit.

"Eric, seriously, can you slow down," I cry, struggling to keep up.

"I just don't want to be late. Tango will bump you off if you aren't on time."

Tango is a very upbeat Spanish restaurant in Chelsea. As a treat for my birthday, Eric is taking me to dinner. I'm more than happy to stay at home and drown myself in my sorrows, but Eric suggests a day full of 'us' time—shopping, massages, pedis, and of course, dinner at the best restaurant to show off our newly dressed and pampered bodies.

"Here we are!"

We walk into the restaurant where crowds of people are standing in the bar area waiting to be served. All the tables are taken from what I can see, and guilty of slowing us down, I'm praying our reservation still stands.

"Sir, madam, please let me escort you to your table."

The waiter leads us through the crowd, passing the tables which are all occupied. I nudge Eric, shrugging my shoulders with a confused expression. I bet the table is somewhere at the back, next to the kitchen and restroom. Oh, well, at least they have karaoke after ten. The waiter pulls a large velvet maroon curtain aside, followed by a loud, "Surprise!"

My hand clutches my chest as my mouth falls open in shock. Standing around a huge table is Nikki and Rocky, Adriana and Elijah, Emma, Becky, a new assistant in our office, Julian, and of course, Lex. My eyes dart back and forth, panic rising in my chest.

Julian and Lex in the same room?

I'm going to strangle the person who planned this.

Eric.

He's dead to me.

Forcing a smile and ignoring the knots forming inside my stomach, I push aside these thoughts for a moment. Aside from the confrontational aspect of Julian and Lex in the same room again, the way Lex and I left things off is unfinished. We haven't spoken to each other since the fight in my office. He hasn't tried to contact me, and I'm too damn stubborn to contact him.

"Wow, you guys, this is... unbelievable." I sigh, taking it all in. "You really shouldn't have."

Time of death, Eric—after this party is over.

My eyes scan the room, admiring the emerald green balloons covering the ceiling. It almost looks like St. Patrick's Day if you didn't know it's my favorite color.

"Isn't it? Nikki came up with the idea and invited

everyone," Eric rushes, quick to point the finger at the child who deserves to be in the naughty corner.

I glance at Nikki with dagger eyes. Her face contorts into a devious grin, knowing the game she's playing with my so-called love life. I could strangle her with my bare hands. How on earth will I get through this night in one piece? I eye the bottles of sangria sitting on the table, calculating how many will it take before it all becomes one big blur. My momentary plan to escape is interrupted as one by one each of them comes up to wish me a happy birthday.

"Happy birthday, hot stuff!" Rocky squeezes me tight, lifting me high. His hugs are suffocating only because of his large frame. He lets me go, allowing me to catch my breath.

Adriana hugs me next. "Char, happy birthday! Seriously, you're rocking this Dior dress."

"I know, right?" I beam, running my hands along the fabric. "I also bought it in blue."

"Don't even think about borrowing it, Adriana. I called it first." Nikki pulls up beside her. She leans in, hugs me tightly, whispering in my ear, "Surprise. Betcha didn't see this coming."

"I'm so ready to kill you right now." I grit my teeth. "Payback will be sweet, my friend."

"Let the games begin," she continues with a smirk.

It's going to be one hell of a long night.

I start getting fidgety knowing I'll have to say hello to Lex sooner or later. It has only been three days, eighteen hours, and ten minutes since the last time he touched me. Shit, I need to put things in perspective. Since when does my *vagina* rule my life? Don't answer that question.

Julian is standing before me, breaking me from my sadistic thoughts about Lex. He looks so dashing in his dark jeans and black sweater.

Can he see the guilt in my eyes?

Can he feel the touch of another man lingering on my skin?

Smile and just act normal.

"Happy birthday, gorgeous." He wraps his arms around me holding me close before slowly letting go to kiss my lips. All around us, eyes are watching, some with adoration, and others with contempt.

"Thank you. You forgot the cape again?"

"I'm saving that for the end of the night," he whispers in my ear.

My body flushes at the sound of his voice. I don't know how this night will end, or who it will end with. I avoid eye contact with Lex because no doubt he's pissed right now. To quote him, 'he doesn't share.' Not that I am his, but try telling him that.

I continue to receive hugs from the others, of course, the last being Lex. He stands in front of me wearing black jeans, a blazer, and a charcoal gray shirt. His mop of messy hair is gloriously styled, his chiseled jaw grinning at me, his eyes lighting up the whole room. He's sex on legs, I can't deny that. I try my best to keep my cool, worried Julian is watching us interact.

Yet all I want to do is lay him on the table, pour sangria all over his cock while I suck him off nice and slow.

You only want what you can't have, Charlie.

"I guess I better hug the birthday girl," he says, leaning in to hug me.

I wrap my arms around his neck, inhaling his scent, careful not to close my eyes. The eyes are always the giveaway.

"That dress isn't helping the fact that I want to fuck you right now," he whispers.

"Is that a challenge, Mr. Edwards?"

I pull away from his embrace, trying not to linger while I leave him standing with a perplexed expression. I shouldn't have said it, still angry at him for what he did, but my brain is all up in that sex cloud trying to climb its way out, and unfortunately, not in time for me to respond with something more appropriate.

We all sit at the round table. Julian is seated on my left and Nikki on my right. Lex sits directly opposite me next to Adriana and Becky. Becky already looks like she's hyper-ventilating. Why Nikki hired her is beyond me, or for that matter, even invited her. Yeah, she's hot for a twenty-two-year-old. Damn, I feel old now. I try not to watch her interact with Lex, but I can't stop myself. I pretend to be looking around at the restaurant and people, but when I make my way back to concentrating on the guests at my table, I glance at them again.

The waiters rush to our table filling our glasses with sangria which prompts Nikki to tap her fork against her glass gaining everyone's attention.

"I'd like to propose a toast to the birthday girl, my best friend," she announces. "You have given me eight wonderful years of friendship, and there's no one else in the world who can put up with my shit like you do. Oh, except for you, babe." Rocky raises his glass, proud of his pussy-whipped status. "For something fun, I want everyone around the table to tell their story of how they met Charlie. I'll start with Rocky and me."

Oh God. Clumsy, awkward, Charlie stories aren't on my list of things to reminisce about.

"We met Charlie during our first year of college. She was to be my roommate. It was Friday afternoon, and she wasn't supposed to arrive till Saturday morning." She laughs, shaking her head. I join her, knowing exactly how this story will go. "Well, Rocky and I decided to take advantage of our last day alone together. It was also the first time we decided to, um, experiment with a few things."

I start laughing harder, the embarrassment still fresh in my mind.

"Anyway, Charlie had arrived early and walked in on us, Rocky tied up to the bed with a blindfold and chocolate sauce dripped all over him. I was shocked but not as much as she was. She freaked out and ran from the room, straight into the door. Her nose was bleeding and I didn't know what to do. I wanted to help her, but Rocky was tied up, and I had to untie him. I stood there naked, rushing between the two of them, covered in chocolate as well."

The whole table is laughing hard, Rocky's in tears from the hilarity.

"I gave Charlie a hard time after that but soon learned it was impossible to hate her. She became my best friend, supported me through the birth of Will, gave us the honor of being his godmother, and helped me follow my dream professionally. I couldn't have done it without you, Charlie." She raises her glass again before leaning over to hug me tightly.

"For the record, I'd like to point out that Rocky was tied to what was supposed to be my bed. I couldn't sleep without nightmares for weeks." I chuckle.

"Better than the time you walked in on us in the kitchen," he roars.

"Oh gee, Rocky, it took me years and hundreds of dollars in therapy to forget that. The moral of this story is always close your eyes and knock on a door when you visit Rocky and Nikki."

The whole table is laughing hysterically. Rocky

continues to ramble on about his sexual conquests until Nikki punches his arm, reminding him she's sitting right beside him.

"Me next!" Adriana raises her hand like an overeager first grader. She stands, holding her glass like it's a wedding toast or something. The image alone already makes me want to burst out laughing.

"I met Charlie at school. We were both in middle school. It was my first day having moved from Chicago. I was eight and going through this stage of wanting to look like Blossom."

"Oh-em-gee, I loved her!" Eric bursts out. *Of course, he did.*

"Anyway, I was a little upset that day because no one would talk to me. It came around to lunchtime, and I sat at the table alone. She came over to say hello. I knew her name was Charlotte because I thought it was such a beautiful name. She had long brown hair and these big brown eyes. I was envious given that I had a short bob cut, not at all like Blossom. She asked me if she could sit down and introduced herself before reaching into her bag to grab her lunchbox at the same time I did. We pulled out our lunchboxes which both had Joey Lawrence on them. It was a match made in heaven." She smiles, her eyes glassy. "From that moment, I knew I had a best friend in her."

A hint of sadness enters her story, but quickly trying to change the tone, I ramble on about Blossom. "Our friendship didn't help kill the Blossom obsession, that's for sure."

Lex shakes his head, grinning. "If I had to watch another episode or hear Adriana talk any more about it, I was going to go insane. I remember she had a shirtless Joey Lawrence poster stuck on the ceiling above her bed. Dad made her remove it, and she cried for like a week."

"I totally forgot about that," Adriana gasps. "When Dad made me take it down, we put it up in Charlie's room above her bed. That lasted one night before Charlie's dad made her take it off."

I nearly spit out my wine remembering what happened next.

"The next afternoon, my dad and Dr. Edwards gave us the birds-and-bees talk. That it was inappropriate for young girls our age to be looking at older boys shirtless. It was so funny. Two grown men trying to explain to us in simple terms, and Adriana, of course, kept asking technical questions."

I broke out into laughter, the whole table following. Adriana was such a big part of my childhood, and I missed her so much. She gets up from her chair and walks over, embracing me tightly. I don't want to let go, and when I feel a tear fall down on my shoulder, I do what any best friend would do, I tell her not to ruin her makeup.

"I hate to break it to you guys but she still has a crush on him. Although no poster over our bed." Elijah laughs.

"Hello, he's a DILF!" Adriana blurts out.

Emma raises her brows, curious. "DILF?"

"Dad I'd like to fuck," Eric answers instead of Adriana.

"Okay, okay. Enough about me." Adriana raises her hands in the air, then turns to face Julian. "How about you, Julian? How did you meet Charlie?"

I'm surprised she asks given that Lex will give her an earful later, but if there's anyone who'll put up with his shit, it's Adriana.

Lex's shoulders stiffen, obviously not wanting to hear the story. I watch him gaze at me intently like he's trying to read my mind or something. Julian drapes his arm around me causing Lex to adopt a sullen look. He clenches his napkin into a ball, shifting his gaze to the table.

This is the calm before the storm.

I'm waiting for him to lose it.

It's only a matter of time.

"Nothing like you guys, considering it was only three months ago. We met at our local gym. I had seen her working out. I mean, she's gorgeous, it's impossible not to spot her. That day, I decided to go talk to her. I walked over, and the first thing she said if I recall correctly was, "Um... yeah, go for it. I've wiped it down and everything, so like you don't have to worry about sweat or rashes. Wait, is a sweat rash why we're supposed to wipe it down, or can you catch like herpes? Look, I don't know anything about herpes, so can we forget I ever mentioned that?"

"Oh my God, Charlie, you didn't say that." Rocky claps his hands, chuckling loudly. "And for the record, sweaty chicks are *hot.*"

The table erupts into laughter again, everyone except Lex. The embarrassment is overwhelming. To this day I can't believe I said that. I'm usually fine around guys, but the moment he walked up to me, I acted like a fifteen-year-old girl meeting One Direction.

"Um, yes, actually I did. Much to my embarrassment." I blush.

"Aw, Charlie, it sounds like love at first sight," Nikki pouts, obviously trying to provoke Lex. I kick her under the table which is followed by an ouch and a what-did-you-do-that-for look.

"That's why I wanted to make her my wife. You'd be stupid to let a woman like this go," Julian gushes, leaning in to kiss me on the cheek.

With every fiber in my being, I try desperately not to

make eye contact with Lex, but I slip and meet his eyes. There's no denying he's furious, but Lex is an expert at the classic poker face. Willing, he will make sure his feelings aren't shown through his facial expressions. He may be staring with a blank face, but his eyes reveal his true feelings. They are dark, reflecting his mood. I know him better than anyone else. And truthfully, he can say the same for me.

I don't know what to do, so I drink because drunk Charlie is better than anxious Charlie. There's no way I can pull him aside for a moment without Julian questioning what I'm doing. And besides, this isn't the place to talk. Too many eyes, too many ears, and way too much of a chance of getting caught.

"Okay, me next, please," Eric chimes in.

How many glasses of sangria has he had? Judging by the loudness of his voice, I'd say at least four, and by five, he will be up on the table dancing. I swear he's such a cheap drunk.

"We met about eighteen months ago. She rear-ended me."

Rocky burst out laughing, spitting out his drink. "Dude, is that even possible?"

"Her cab, Rocky." Eric sighs, trying to hold in his laughter. "So, as the cab driver got out and argued whose fault it was, Charlie started ranting on about being late for work. I argued, of course, saying it wasn't as bad as me as I was going to be late for an interview. Another cab pulled up behind us, and we both rushed at the same time to get in. I beat her to it, shutting the door quickly as the cab pulled away. I leaned out the window, and I recall my exact words... 'Sorry, honey, you can stomp your pretty little Louboutins all you want, but you ain't making me late.'"

"Oh, Eric, please don't tell me this was your interview to work for Charlie?" Adriana squirms.

"Spot on. I sat there in her office pleased with myself for being on time. As she rushed in all huffed, I was shocked and the look on her face? Priceless."

"But I hired you, anyway," I remind him. "Like my left arm, I can't live without you."

He stands, rushing to my side. There's no one in the world like Eric, and my life has never been the same since. "My yin to your yang."

The fun continues with the rest of the guests taking turns telling everyone how they met me. The sangria keeps flowing, and my glass keeps emptying. I have officially lost count, but at least my nerves are calming and now I'm starting to get giggly.

"Oh-em-gee, Lex, we can't skip you," Eric exclaims.

"I don't think I can remember when you first met Charlie..." Adriana says quietly.

Lex takes a sip of the sangria. My mind is hazy, trying to even remember when we first met. I sit still, focusing intently on him.

"I was fifteen. I had pretty much spent the summer working my ass off for this collectors Batman comic I had seen in a store in Sacramento." His eyes are fixated on the table again, with his fingers skimming the rim of the glass in front of him. "I finally saved up and bought it and went to our living room to read it. Adriana was in there watching TV and eating the last of a baked cookie. She and I got into a fight as siblings tend to do, so I decided since it was a nice day out, I'd go up to our treehouse and read it. I climbed up and found a little girl crying in the corner. I hadn't met Charlotte yet, but Adriana raved on about her all the time, so I assumed it was her."

My heart stops, knowing exactly the moment he's referring to, and the pain I had felt at the time when I thought my world was collapsing. I was a kid, but it didn't mean it didn't hurt. It was the first huge fight my parents had after which my mom stormed out and left for three days.

"I sat down beside her to ask if she wanted to talk. She was upset about her parents having a big fight. I remember her asking me if she should go look for her mom. I was only fifteen, so giving a kid advice was hard. I remember telling her that it would somehow work out. She saw me carrying the comic and said Batman was her favorite superhero of all time, so I did what anyone would do when they see her smile."

"You gave her the comic?" Nikki asks, her eyes widening.

"Yes, I gave her the comic. She looked so happy."

"I can't believe you did that," Adriana and Nikki say in unison.

For once, he appears shy. Alexander Edwards is never shy. His eyes meet mine, a corner of his mouth lifting up into a half-smile. I can't believe he did that. I remember the comic book. I'd read it every night. Batman was my favorite. How ironic with the whole Julian thing going on. At the time, I didn't know how hard he worked for it, and maybe if I had known, I wouldn't have allowed him to give it to me. But I was only young, and he was my best friend's brother, no one special, just someone who annoyed us and hogged the remote when we wanted to watch television. The gesture was so kind-hearted, but that was Lex.

Was, I have to remind myself.

Julian interrupts the moment, raising his glass and wishing me a happy birthday. My friends cheer, but no matter how hard I try, I can't get that story out of my head.

It's almost like a scene out of a movie. I was staring at it, watching people around me, but no matter how hard I try I can't focus. All I think about is that comic book and what it represented.

Everyone is laughing, enjoying each other's company. The salsa band is playing a soft Spanish beat. The food arrives and looks fantastic. We each pile the food onto our plates, getting lost in random conversations. The weight of Julian's arm on my shoulder weighs like a ton, with his need to constantly touch me greater than other times we have been together.

I take a sip of my sangria and slowly glance at Lex, careful not to be caught by Julian. My heart plunges as I watch him chatting with Becky. She loves the attention, and he looks happy speaking about something I can't hear.

My blood begins to boil.

What's this feeling called again?

Oh right, jealousy.

Lex glances up and catches me looking at him, his lips pressed firmly together. So, he wants to play games. I lean over to Julian, snuggling myself in his side. His lips brush against my ear as he whispers sweet words followed by dirty ones.

Unable to control my cheeks from flushing, my eyes carelessly wander to Lex. His now dark eyes are piercing through a vicious stare, his face tightening as he tries to intimidate me from across the table.

We battle for how long I don't know, until he leans over to Becky, whispering something in her ear before standing and walking away from the table.

I can't leave, not now, not without raising suspicion with Julian. As my fingers tap the table repeatedly, Julian places his hand on mine to calm me down.

"You seem anxious?"

"Me?" I say, over the music. "I'm fine. Just a lot of sangria and the need to burn it off."

Julian plays with my engagement ring, his expression fixed. I'm waiting with bated breath for him to ask me about Lex. Inside my head, I'm trying to come up with answers to satisfy him, but nothing is worthy.

"We haven't seen each other much..." he trails off, unable to make eye contact. "Not since the charity ball."

"We've both been busy. I promise it'll get better. Even you said we needed to find our groove."

"Yes," he lifts his gaze to meet mine, lips pressed firmly with a penetrating stare. "When we get married."

I swallow repeatedly, hyperaware of my reaction to the word 'marriage.' Just as I'm about to say something, Adriana walks over to me, almost as if she can sense my discomfort.

"Char, come to the bathroom with me?"

Julian forces a smile, gesturing for me to go. Elijah is sitting on the other side of him and he uses the opportunity to discuss an article Julian wrote about the Haiti government.

Adriana grabs my hand, guiding me through the tables as we walk to the opposite side of the restaurant where the bathrooms are located. She stops before we get there, pulling her phone out of her Louis Vuitton purse. Excusing herself, she walks toward the exit to answer the call.

The restaurant is noisy, and as I stand here by myself, I decide to find Lex and ask him what his problem is. As I walk into the hallway where the bathrooms are lined, he exits the men's room, surprised to see me.

I push his chest, angry for so many reasons. "What the hell is your problem, Lex?"

"Charlotte, don't do this here, or you'll regret it."

"Regret what?"

He pulls me into another bathroom marked for private staff only. Within seconds, he locks the door and pins me against it. "I warned you," he breathes, inches away from my lips.

With fire burning in his eyes, I know no matter how angry or hurt I am over our past and present, the control Lex has over me is far greater.

We're fire and gasoline, a deadly combination ready to explode without a moment's notice.

And the terrifying part is, I have no control around him.

I'm holding the match, watching him pour the gasoline, ready to watch us burst into flames. *Again.*

THIRTY-THREE

CHARLIE

L ex slams his lips to mine.

With my back forced against the wall, he nearly knocks the wind out of my lungs, desperate with his need to take me inside this small private bathroom.

I hardly have a moment to react, the weight of his body pressing against mine. I'm aware of his cock pressing against my stomach, my desperation exerted in a deep moan as he presses his tongue to the seam of my lips before delving inside my mouth.

My arms reach and tangle around his neck, pulling him closer to me. We both lose ourselves in this heated exchange, and despite how very wrong this is, I'm unable to stop, my body possessed by the need to have him inside of me.

Time is of the essence, and without any further delay, I drag my hand down to his belt, unbuckling to drop his pants to his ankles. Pulling myself back, creating a small distance, I gasp for air, glancing down to see his beautiful cock throbbing between us.

With my hand, I wrap it around him, stroking him as he

whimpers. He aches just like me. With every stroke, he groans, the pleasure overwhelming. I slide down and take all of him in my mouth. He arches back, pleading with me to stop or he'll blow in my mouth.

I'm a fucking tease.

I slide his cock as far as I can in my mouth until I feel it slightly entering the back of my throat. He doesn't push further. The more I hear him writhing in pleasure, the more I take him in.

"Charlotte..." he purrs, struggling to put a sentence together.

I'm taking him deeper into my mouth, but I want all of him, and it surprises us both how easy it is, given his size. He grabs my hair, guiding me in and out, until I can't take it anymore, the throbbing is unbearable.

"Fuck me now, Lex."

He rams me against the door, pushing my panties aside to slide himself in me. I gasp as he enters, struggling to keep my voice down, but my moans are uncontrollable.

I'm lost, succumbing to his power over me, over us. Pushing the top of my dress down, his mouth alternates between kissing my lips and tugging on my erect nipples. It has only been three days, yet it feels like an eternity since he made me feel this way. His breaths against my ear and his words, which are barely a whisper, only add to the plea-sure of it all.

I mouth a string of profanities, incoherent with my choice of words as his grunts become more intense, and the warm feeling rushes to every inch of my body. Closing my eyes, I'm barely able to breathe while he silently holds onto me. It takes me a moment to compose myself before the reality of what I said begins to set in.

"Charlotte, I... we need to talk."

"No. Look, I'm sorry. You're right about the whole regret thing." Shit, what am I saying? I can't stop myself. Stupid fucking sangria. The damn Mexicans know how to get us white folk drunk, that's for sure. "We shouldn't have... I shouldn't have said—"

He cuts me off, pulling back, his temper flaring once again. "Why do you keep fucking doing this? I want you. Why is it so hard for you to admit your feelings? Why the fuck can't you even talk to me?"

"Because we're done. I told you that," I tell him, bowing my head.

"You keep saying that, but you only want us to fuck? I've got feelings, too, and this is bullshit. You never had a problem being open with how you felt before."

"That was different," I mumble, not wanting to elaborate.

"Why?" He fixes his pants, then runs his hands through his hair, frustrated. "Why the hell are you such a cold-hearted bitch now?"

His words run deep to a place I had buried until the moment I saw him at the restaurant. Every moment we spent together many years ago has turned into painful memories. And this pain, it's sharp, cutting like a razor blade against my delicate skin. Perhaps, I'm the cold-hearted bitch, but what he doesn't know is he controlled the knife that tore me to pieces.

He turned me into a broken mess, a mess that I was forced to clean by myself.

I grieved for him, for what we had, but I no longer grieve. Now I'm angry. How dare he make me feel like I had any control over how it ended between us. And how dare he think I could so easily forget the permanent scars he left behind.

"*You...*" I scream back, my body shuddering. "*You* did this to me. *You* made me afraid to feel anything."

I step away from him as he stands there, his mouth wide open. Adjusting my dress, I fiddle with the stupid lock, on the verge of tears, but no, Charlie does not cry over boy troubles, not anymore.

His face changes, he's suddenly composed. "Tonight will be the last night you see Julian. I told you, I don't share."

"Don't tell me who I can or can't see. This is my life, Lex. You decided to leave it, so you deal with the consequences," I shoot back.

"I won't make that mistake again. You tell him tonight that it's over. You're mine. I don't share, and I will not back down. The sooner you realize that, the better."

It isn't the yelling or screaming that frightens me, it's the calmness in his voice.

The lock finally comes undone after a lot of fumbling. Rushing out of the private bathroom I quickly enter the ladies' room, running into Nikki. "Whoa... you okay, Charlie?"

I motion for her to move as I run into a stall. Slamming the door shut, I close my eyes, willing the tears to stop. As my legs become sticky, I'm distracted by the need to clean myself up.

Taking a deep breath, I discard the toilet paper and flush, exiting to see Nikki waiting.

"You do have it bad... just for the wrong person."

"Nikki..." I stumble on my words not knowing what to say.

Placing my hands on the vanity, I stare into the mirror. I look a mess, and my lips are red-raw, though my lipstick has faded. My hair is unruly and out of place.

Removing my makeup from my purse, I touch my face up as much as possible and fix my hair, then re-apply my lipstick.

"Listen, Charlie, you can't always be in control of everything, including your thoughts. Sometimes we just need someone to confide in."

"I don't want to talk about it... not now."

I've grown accustomed to bottling up my feelings, and I'll not spend my birthday opening the can of worms known as my past. We need to have some fun now, and if that means I have to ignore all the drama I've managed to create for myself by drinking copious amounts of sangria, then so be it.

As I walk back to the table, my short-lived confidence turns into panic as Lex is nowhere to be seen. A few minutes later, I catch sight of him walking back to our table with Adriana.

She's chatting away, but he appears dazed. She can do that to you sometimes, but I know it isn't because of what she's saying. As they sit down, he looks at me momentarily before Rocky starts talking to him about baseball.

I'm glad he came back, despite my earlier need to push him as far away as possible. But now what? What do I do? He carries on, pretending I'm not here which is good because Julian is still here, and I have to decide tonight.

This is stupid.

Such a big decision can't be made in one night while drunk on your birthday.

"An incredibly good associate of mine works for ESPN here in Manhattan. It's the only reason I get great seats all the time. Tomorrow night I've got box seats to the Yankees' game if you're interested. I'd like to introduce you to him," Lex says to Rocky as he finishes the last of his meal. He looks famished. Of course he'd be, after that fuck in the bathroom.

"Dude, are you fucking serious? Are you talking about Bradley Sanders?"

"Yes, that's him. We own part shares in a country club in The Hamptons," Lex tells him.

It's all I hear of the conversation before Eric announces it is gift time. I leave the seat beside Emma and walk back to my own, adjusting myself as I sit in soaked panties which are extremely uncomfortable. Can everyone at the table see that I've just been fucked by Lex against the bathroom door?

Julian doesn't act any different, thank God. He places his arm around me again, Lex watching this time with an amused look on his face.

Eric and Adriana speak in unison, holding a box wrapped in silver paper with a huge green bow. "This is from Elijah and us, of course. Happy Birthday!"

As I unwrap the gift paper, the box alone makes me want to cream my pants. The tan-colored box marked with the signature *Christian Louboutin* is placed before me. I open it slowly, savoring every moment but excited as hell. Before my eyes appear a pair of emerald-studded pumps. The studs shine like diamonds as I hold them up to the light. They are breathtaking.

"Oh my God, you guys... I can't even... *wow!* This is unbelievable, but I haven't seen these in the fall line?"

"It's not what you know, it is who you know, Char." Adriana winks at the same time Eric happy claps.

I walk over to give the three of them a hug. As I sit back like Cinderella, I place the shoes on my feet. They fit perfectly. The gifts keep coming, and each time I feel more and more grateful to be surrounded by such a great group of friends.

Julian announces that my gift is to be given later. "For you to open in private."

I turn to kiss him on the cheek, but he moves so our lips meet.

"Aww, aren't they so cute," Nikki gushes, staring directly at Lex.

Smiling, I pull myself away, wiping Julian's bottom lip with my thumb.

Note to self—kill Nikki with bare hands.

"Our turn!" Nikki and Rocky hand me a box.

If birthdays from the past have taught me anything, it's to open gifts with caution. I undo the bow of the first box, slowly sliding the lid off to reveal a hardcopy of one of my favorite books.

"Open the book," Rocky persuades.

I open the book, the inside signed by none other than the author herself.

"Are you kidding me? How on earth did you get this signed?"

"It's who you know," Rocky repeats.

Stunned to receive such a gift, I run my fingers over the front cover. Oh, book boyfriend, we meet again.

"Don't forget the next box, Charlie."

I open the lid of the next one, and low and behold, my instincts are correct. I lift what appears to be a crystal vibrator. "In keeping with the theme of the book and the fact that you broke your rabbit," Nikki points out.

"I never said I broke it."

"Oh my God, that's just like mine. Right, Elijah?"

Lex cringes, shaking his head with disapproval. "You didn't just say that."

"Go on, there's more," Nikki coerces.

It's like a Mary Poppin's bag of sex toys. I pull out hand-cuffs, a butt plug, and a flogger. After a table discussion on how each should be used, I thank Nikki and Rocky, avoiding at all costs looking at Lex, who seems to be amused with all the toys. My purse vibrates, and beneath the table, I read the text.

Lex: *I've already planned on when and where all those items will be used on you.*

The phone slips from my hand, falling onto the floor. As I excuse myself to find it, I can't help but look over at Lex's legs. I nearly have a coronary as I watch his hand rub the front of his pants. *Son of a bitch!* I sit back up and try to compose myself as best as I can. He isn't looking my way, but the smirk on his face says it all.

"Time to open your gift from Lex." Adriana pushes Lex's hand toward me.

Instead, he stands and walks over to me, handing me a small box. "Happy Birthday, Charlotte."

Lex is known for giving extravagant gifts. I fumble with the bow that sits on top of the brown box. I'm nervous, and having the entire table watch me, anticipating my every move, makes it even worse. As the bow comes undone, I lift the lid. Inside sits a Tiffany's box. Already, my heart is fluttering at the iconic blue box in my hand, terrified of the contents that lie under-neath. I lift the lid of the box, and my heart stops when my eyes catch sight of the contents. It's a necklace, but it isn't the neck-lace that makes me want to cry, it's the pendant attached—a white-gold phoenix bird encrusted with diamonds.

"Lex... I... thank you," I choke.

If only he knew what it truly means to me. How this tiny little bird represents so much more than I can ever tell him at this moment. I stand, legs shaking, and hug him really tight.

"How did you know?"

"Your tattoo. I know it means a lot, I just wish you would tell me why," he whispers.

I completely forgot about the tattoo and the night he asked me. He pulls away from me, taking the necklace out of the box and motions for me to turn around. Placing the pendant on my chest, he fastens the clip at the back. Like placing the missing piece from a puzzle in its spot, everything at the moment feels right.

The night goes on, and we relax, drinking away, telling stories. An announcement comes on advising us that the karaoke stage is now open. The restaurant cheers. I notice that the cheering comes from the busload of Japanese tourists who sit toward the front of the stage. Unusual, since it's a Spanish restaurant.

"Oh-em-gee, Charlie! Duo time!" Eric races to the stage, grabbing the karaoke books. Five of them to be exact. My friends scour through the books, discussing songs they want to sing. I drink another glass of sangria. I fucking need it if I'm gonna sing karaoke with Eric. I hear Julian rustle his belongings beside me, only noticing now he has remained quiet since Lex gave me the necklace.

"Is something wrong?"

"Look, Charlie, I'm going to go." He gets up from the table, unaware he will actually just get up and leave and not say goodbye to anyone. As he walks out, I throw my napkin on the table and follow him outside. We're met by the cool breeze, and instantly, he turns around to face me with a pinched expression. "Is something going on between you and Lex?"

I'm caught off guard, my mind catching up, thinking of how to answer this question correctly.

"Julian, he's just a friend."

"I'm not a fool, Charlie. I know what type of guy Edwards is. Is that what you want?"

"Julian. Lex is the past. I don't want anything with him." The words hurt as they leave my mouth. Here I am trying to save this relationship, but why? I'd ruined what Julian and I have with my indiscretions. From this moment on, our relationship is nothing but a lie. The guilt, unless I come forward with the truth, will never ever be built on honesty and love. I've ruined it and all because of someone else sitting inside that restaurant.

There's a visible flush in his cheeks, his arms are crossed tightly in front of his chest. The truth desperately wants to be told, but I hold back, terrified of losing Julian all of a sudden.

"I'm going crazy, okay? This is—"

"Nothing," I reassure him. "Lex is nothing."

"Well, it doesn't feel like nothing to me," he raises his voice, the jealousy seething in his tone. "I love you, I asked you to marry me. Then he walks back into your life, and I'm what? Your plan B in case he fucks you over again?"

"Julian..." I reach for his arm, but he retracts.

"Listen, Charlie..." He hesitates, then reaches in his pocket and produces a small box. "Happy birthday. You decide who it is you really want. But for now, I need time... I can't do this right now."

I stand alone on the sidewalk as he walks away, turning the corner. My hand clutches the tiny box, not knowing what to do. I walk back into the restaurant and stand by the doorway. Opening the box, inside sits a key, the top part shaped like the Batman symbol. I read the note attached to the key.

The key to my bat cave... our new home.

I place the key back in the box as a tear slips down my cheek. What the hell am I doing, and most importantly, what the hell do I want?

Well, I know what I want but I'm afraid that if I say it out loud, there will be no way back. Chances are that the road is a dead-end leading me back to where I started.

I return to our table, a little unsteady as the sangria has finally managed to make its way through my veins. When I finally spot everyone, they are cheering on Rocky, who's singing 'Call Me Maybe.'

Nikki looks mortified, bowing her head and shaking it repeatedly. As the song finishes, the crowd roars, and the Japanese tourists pull out their pens and autograph books, begging him for an autograph. Rocky grins as he signs away and takes photographs with the tourists. Our table is in hysterics. Finally, Nikki cracks a laugh.

Eric is still trying to decide what to sing. He sits there belting out lines to each song, trying to get pitch-perfect like he's auditioning for *The Voice*.

My attention moves to Adriana, who is persuading Lex to sing. Lex has a beautiful voice—smooth and soothing. He isn't the type to get up and sing in front of a crowd, however, his sudden burst of courage intrigues me.

He walks over to the stage as they call his name, speaking briefly to the man in charge of the music. Stepping up to the stage, he settles behind the piano. The lights dim, and the crowd roars as he begins playing the notes. My heart is beating so loud in competition with the volume of the music played. As the crowd sits silently in adoration, the tune becomes increasingly familiar. Bruno Mars, 'When I Was Your Man.'

I close my eyes, taking in every word of the song. This means more to me than anything.

Is it time to finally forgive?

He's hurting.

My Alex is hurting.

He is right. He does have feelings too, and I can't have become so cold that I cannot acknowledge that. We need to talk, but not tonight. Not on my birthday. Not on the same night my fiancé walked out on me and told me he was hurting too.

I'm the wrecking ball, destroying everything in my sight. People are hurting because of me, because of my careless actions.

I don't know who I have become, but as I gaze at him on the stage, admiring his courage to bare his soul to me in front of everyone, the light inside my head turns on.

"I know the song we'll sing," I say, my voice barely a whisper.

"What is it, Charlie?" Eric asks.

I lean over and tell him. If I can't talk to Lex, I'll follow his lead, express my feelings through this one song, and hope he understands what I need from him.

What I need to fix us.

THIRTY-FOUR

LEX

The little blue box sits on my nightstand, a constant reminder of her, tormenting me as I sit in my hotel room just staring at it.

It has taken me most of yesterday morning to pull strings at Tiffany's to get the diamonds encrusted into the pendant. Thank my fucking lucky stars the manager knows who I am, so after a ton of money was sent their way, it was hand-delivered to my suite. I know this means a lot to her. When I asked her about the tattoo, she brushed it off in typical Charlotte fashion.

When the fuck will she open up to me?

We are huddled in a private area of the restaurant. The room is decorated with emerald balloons—Adriana's idea, of course. I stand next to Elijah as he's telling me about a new job he's starting in Brooklyn.

"So, I'll be teaching art classes for the youth down at the YMCA. It'll be a nice change."

"Sounds good. How are you feeling, though? Are you sure you're up for it?"

Elijah is the closest person I have to a brother, so my

worry is with reason. His cancer scared our family, and there was no way we could lose him. Thankfully, a well-known cancer rehabilitation clinic in Geneva had an opening for him, and even more grateful that one of my clients know the owner, so all I had to do was wave my AMEX, and they suddenly had an opening. I didn't give a shit about the money, we just needed him to live. He recovered well, but I know he still has to take it easy.

"Much better. You know I owe you my life, right?"

"How about you just take care of my sister and make sure she annoys me less, and we'll call it even?"

"Deal! But, hey, you know Adriana. I can only promise to try." Elijah laughs.

We chat amongst ourselves until Julian walks in. Nikki is all over him, grabbing his arm and acting like a love-struck teen. What the fuck? So, she plays nice with him and treats me like the scum of the earth. He walks around greeting everyone, leaving me until last.

"Edwards. Didn't think I'd see you here." He shakes my hand. Stupid prick.

"Well, she is my friend, and I was invited."

Adriana hushes us as she announces Charlotte has arrived. We close the curtain and dim the lights. When we yell surprise, her face is priceless. She sees me then looks at Julian. I know she's panicking. *Good,* I think. Maybe now she'll get rid of him. She looks so fucking hot in her tight black dress with those sexy heels. I want her legs wrapped around me, and I want to taste her sweet pussy on my lips.

But instead, I get a very uninviting embrace.

I wish her a happy birthday, followed by a comment about her dress. I know the effect I have on her. It's so fucking obvious. It doesn't stop her from sitting next to that fucker, though. What the fuck can I do? It irritates me to the core that he has his fucking arm draped over her like she's his property. Not for much longer, buddy. Enjoy your moment of glory because soon you'll be back on the dating scene wishing you were me.

The group tells stories about how they met Charlotte. It seems everyone at this table means something to Charlotte, even that fucker. I try to be mature. Okay, that's a fucking lie. I'm ready to get all UFC on him, so I do the only thing I can—I flirt with the little blonde chick beside me. I laugh, pretending to be engrossed in her story about her trip to Cancun. It's so obvious she's flattered with my attention, constantly pushing her tits together to show me her non-existent cleavage.

Charlotte is becoming more jealous, and when she decides revenge is the way to go and leans into *him*, I fucking leave. I may have damaged the toilet stall in the bathroom by kicking it, but fuck, she knows exactly how to press my buttons. Surely, she realizes I have an anger-management problem. After calming myself down as much as I can, I run outside the bathroom and into Charlotte.

She asks me what my problem is. I warn her, but she doesn't want to listen. I have no choice. I need her. It has been too long. The taste of her lips feels like heaven on earth. Her skin entices me, the smell driving me insane. It drives my addiction further, and I can't hold back.

I know we're fucking in a restaurant bathroom, but I have never wanted her so badly, partially blaming the dress. Charlotte makes me feel things no other woman has, and fuck, the way she takes my cock deep in her mouth—I'm ready to blow right then and there. Goddamn, the girl has skills.

She looks up at me through her lashes, her eyes are pure lust. The sight leaves me speechless, but I need more. So, I grab Charlotte and fuck her hard against the door. I hold back as long as I can, that is, until she said I was hers.

She belongs to me.

She said it from her own mouth.

The first thing that registers is that I need to blow in her pussy right now. As the waves of intensity subside, her words echo in my mind, and I like what I heard. No, I love what I heard until she does a complete one-eighty on me and takes it all back.

We fight over everything. Every time we fuck, we argue afterward, making me want her even more. I try to clear my head. There's no way I'm walking out with another hard-on.

I head back to the table and avoid eye contact with her. Willing our fight to blow over, a vicious cycle we constantly find ourselves in, I sit there chatting with Rocky about sports. He actually turns out to be a pretty neat guy, but too bad his wife is a stuck-up bitch. Adriana interrupts us by shoving the karaoke book in front of me.

"C'mon, Lex, just one song," she pleads.

"You know I don't sing in front of crowds."

"Stop being a fool. You know you have a fucking awesome voice. Just do it."

"I never said I didn't. I just don't want to sing in front of a crowd. You know it's not my thing."

Eric announces it is gift time, thank God, so Adriana is momentarily distracted. I have to admit, Charlotte got some amazing gifts. The heels again didn't help my obsession with her legs. When Nikki gave her all this kinky shit, I couldn't help but send her a text. I know she's avoiding me, I mean Christ, she just had me in her mouth, then I fucked her until she came. She probably still has my cum dripping out of her pussy. Fuck, if that doesn't stir things up again. I take the opportunity to rub my cock as she bends down to pick up her phone. I know she saw, she couldn't have come back up any more flushed. I turn away, unable to hide the smirk on my face.

"Time to open your gift from Lex," Adriana says eagerly.

Charlotte looks apprehensive. I walk over to her and wish her a happy birthday. As I hand her the box, she slowly takes it from me. I want her to know how much she means to me, and that I want to find a way to heal us. I watch closely as she pulls out the phoenix pendant and necklace from the box.

She holds it in her hands, and if you look close enough, you can see her hands trembling. Charlotte thanks me, then stands up to hug me, real tight. I'm taken aback by how long she holds on for. I know this bird represents something significant in her life. I have googled the meaning. To be reborn, new beginnings. Did she get the tattoo after I left her? I want to ask, but if I push again, chances are I'll lose her, or she will go running into the arms of pretty-boy beside her.

I take the pendant from her hand and motion for her to turn around as I fasten the clip. The phoenix sits perfectly on her chest. Her heart is beating fast, I can see her chest rising and falling.

The party continues, and several times I catch Charlotte in a daze touching the phoenix. It isn't until a short time later that Julian stands up and walks out. She follows him, but I'm not angry like last time. He looks pissed, and maybe a little defeated. He has ever since the comic-book story. He'd have to be the stupidest moron not to see something is going on between us. I mean, I fucked her in the bathroom. She smells like my cock. What more evidence does he need?

In the meantime, I have an idea. She won't talk, and therefore will not listen, but music means more. I'll find the courage to sing, despite the nerves of doing it in front of a crowd.

"Great, Lex," Adriana squeals when I tell her. "What song?"

I don't answer her. Instead, I get up and walk over to the stage and speak to the head of the band. I ask him if I can borrow their piano. Charlotte is seated at the table, her expression confused. I don't know what happened outside, but it's time.

I sit at the piano, taking in a deep breath. I position my fingers over the keys, the lights dim, and my heart is going a thousand miles a minute. The crowd cheers loudly, and somehow, somewhere, I find my voice.

The words flow freely as do my fingers along the keys. I know she has to have known this song, my eyes focus on her as I sing, and she sits there, still. I want her to know how I feel, how much pain I'm in, how much regret I have about leaving her, and that it's always been and will always be her.

The crowd erupts into a roar followed by whistles. I stand and then walk down the stairs. I'm stopped by a few cougars on the way back to our table, something that Rocky can't help but comment on.

"Excellent job, man," he says, leaning in closer. "Did you see the MILF in the red dress? Holy mother of—"

Nikki slaps the back of his head, and I can't help but laugh.

Charlotte is sitting quietly, her eyes never leaving mine like she's about to say something. I wish I could read her mind. Fuck, am I finally getting through to her? She leans over and whispers something to Eric. He quickly gets up and walks over to the man organizing the music.

I watch her knock back a whole glass of sangria, and almost instantly, she looks calmer. Eric and Charlotte's names are called, and they make their way to the stage. I can't help but admire her stunning figure as she walks past me. Those emerald green pumps look amazing against her tanned legs. I grab her wrist as she walks past. "Good luck, Charlotte," I offer.

Her gaze meets mine again like she's searching for something, but I have no clue because she will not tell me. Eric ushers her along, and they walk onto the stage. Her body appearing more relaxed.

Yes, she's fucking *drunk.*

I recognize the song almost immediately. Her voice is angelic, and she closes her eyes as she sings her part. I sit and stare, taking in every word as she begins to sing 'Just Give Me A Reason.'

Eric sings the male part, but I begin to tune out, lost in a stream of emotions.

Is this how she feels?

That we are broken.

I push the thought away.

Of course, we can be fixed, it's us, after all. This isn't some high school fling. If I were the one who broke us by leaving, then what exactly does she need from me to fix us?

The crowd cheers and whistles as the song finishes. The words were plain and simple. We can learn to love again, and we aren't broken.

At least I acknowledge the mistakes I made and keep making. At least I'm trying. She has to see that or else she wouldn't have so openly sung this song.

Charlotte comes back to the table and plonks herself on her chair. Eric pours her some sangria, why the fuck for I have no idea. She needs to stop drinking.

As she continues to gaze at me, I watch her, not knowing who will break eye contact first, it's like we're both trying to read each other's mind. I'm the first one to look away only because a lady beside me asks for a light to which I politely indicate that I don't smoke.

Music plays, and the crowd gets up to dance. The atmosphere is relaxed. Sangria is deadly—it creeps up on you when you least expect it. Adriana and Elijah are on the dance floor. Eric is teaching the tourists how to do the Macarena which, I have to admit, is worth watching. Nikki and Rocky disappear, but their belongings are still here. A quickie in the bathroom, no doubt.

"Leexxx," Charlotte slurs her words as she comes and sits on my lap.

"Charlotte, you're drunk."

"No, I'm not. I'm just really, really, really, happy, you know?" She smiles as she takes another drink.

"Enough sangria for you."

I pull the glass away, but she whines.

"Nooo, Leexxx... look, I'm fineee. See, I even like you right now."

"So, you didn't like me before?"

"Nooo, I hated you... hated you for leaving me alone... leaving us."

"You hated me, Charlotte?" I ask cautiously.

She wraps her hands around my neck and pulls me in close, smelling my skin.

"Of course, I hated you... but now I like you again." She kisses my forehead, then smiles. My arms wrap around her waist, holding onto her as she struggles to compose herself.

"What do you mean by us, Charlotte?"

"You and me, *us*." Her tone changes. "Let's dance... please, Lex."

She jumps off my lap and drags me onto the dance floor. We dance, and she holds onto me tight. She sings to me, and I sing back to her. It's our only way of speaking to each other. I can't even remember what the song is because I'm so lost in this moment with her. The band announces it's the last song of the night, so what do they play? Whitney Houston. I let Charlotte have her fun with the girls as they dance all '80s like to the music.

I walk back to the table and find Eric, Rocky, and Elijah laughing while looking at me.

"What?"

"Why can't you guys just kiss and make up already?" Eric laughs.

"Or kiss and fuck already," Rocky chimes in.

"Oh wait, too late, you guys have already done that," Elijah chides.

"Funny, you guys. Since the three of you are so interested, why don't you ask Charlotte the same questions?"

"Dude, she'll have my balls if I ask her that."

"I thought Nikki already wore those as earrings," I sarcastically answer.

"Ohhh, snap!" Eric cheers.

"Sorry, man, but he has a point. Why the fuck are you so whipped, anyway?" Elijah jokes.

"Dude, my wife's hot. She's my baby-momma, plus she's as kinky as shit in the bedroom. There was this one time—" Nikki comes up behind him and pinches his ear like a naughty first- grader.

"What were you saying about me?"

"Uh, nothing... that you're beautiful... a great mother and a gentle person."

Eric almost spits out his sangria. I hide my laughter behind the wine glass in my hand. Elijah tries his best to keep a straight face but is failing miserably.

"I'll deal with you later," she responds in a commanding tone.

Rocky's eyes light up, his hands rubbing together with delight.

"Okay, I'm outty, you guys," Eric chirps. "My friend texted me and turns out a really hot model was seen at a club. I'm just waiting to find out where." He continues texting on his phone, faster than the speed of light. Charlotte and Adriana come back to the table, both of them looking relaxed and chilled.

"You ready to go, babe?" Adriana askes Elijah.

"Ready when you are, princess," Elijah murmurs.

"Dude, I ain't the only one without balls." Rocky chuckles.

"What can I say? I'm the luckiest guy alive..." he pauses then continues, "... with no balls."

Adriana snuggles by his side and says goodbye to everyone. Then she quickly pulls me aside. "Are you okay, Lex?"

"Yes, I am. Please take Elijah home and do whatever it is you young kids do these days."

"Well, actually we were thinking—"

"Adriana, it's an expression. I don't want to know."

She hugs me tight. "I love you, big brother."

"Love you, too, lil' sis."

She may be a royal pain in my ass, but I can't have asked for a better sister. I don't know how I'd function without her sometimes. She also comes to the rescue whenever I need her, and she's the only one who will put up with all my shit. I've been an asshole to her, something I now regret.

"Charlie, you wanna come home with us?" Nikki asks.

"Uh, no thanks. You kinky fuckers will kill my buzz."

"I'll take you home," I offer.

"I think she's safer with us," Nikki argues.

"Since she's my *friend*, I'm sure I can get her home safely." I stress the 'friend' part since Nikki is such a fucking bitch.

"Babe, he can take her. So, tomorrow night, yeah? Yankee Stadium?"

"I'll send a car to your place, and we can go together."

"Sweet, bro."

They say goodbye, and I take Charlotte's hand as she struggles to walk. Her eyes are glassy, but she still looks so beautiful. I just pray she won't puke all over me.

"I can take myself home, you know. This isn't the first time I've partied *like it's 1999*."

I don't say anything. There's no point. We walk outside, and I hail a cab. I manage to get her inside after an incoherent argument about being an independent woman, giving the driver her address, and we are on our way.

It's only a fifteen-minute cab ride, and part of me feels curious. I'll finally see the place she lives in. I know that no matter what I see it will represent her. It may have been only fifteen minutes, but she's passed out by the time we arrive. I carry her out of the cab and to the entrance of her building. Her doorman is a pleasant old man who greets me as I step out.

"Ahh, Miss Mason... what trouble has she gotten herself into?"

"I'm sorry, sir. Would you mind letting us in? I don't feel comfortable rummaging through Charlotte's purse. You know women these days with all the junk they carry. Plus, I don't want to wake her."

"Here's the spare. Would you kindly bring it back down on your way out?" He hands me the key. *He must know her well,* I think.

"Thank you. Of course, I will."

We arrive at her floor. I manage to open her front door and switch on a light. Before I can stop and take it all in, I find my way through the hallway until I reach what I assume is her bedroom. Opening the door, my assumption is correct.

Her perfectly made bed sits in the middle of the room as I gently lay her down, sliding her shoes off and covering her with the blanket. She lays peacefully, curled in a ball. Her gentle breathing is the only sound inside the room. She looks peaceful, breathtaking, and I dare not wake her for my own selfish reasons.

There's a faint sound of a cat, and in the shadows, it appears from behind the curtain and climbs onto the bed beside her. I decide not to pet it, just in case it attacks me for being a stranger in her home.

My eyes move around the room. It feels warm, decoratively speaking. She has a large vanity with all these perfumes and girly shit perfectly positioned and neatly organized. Shit, she's just as fucking anal as me. On her nightstand is a lamp, dock, and a book. The room is slightly lit, so I open the page that's bookmarked.

Fuck, it's like porn. I chuckle slightly, placing the book down before it causes a problem I'm unable to satisfy.

I place her purse on her nightstand and take out her phone in case she needs it, noticing a text on the screen.

Batman: *You know we've got something good,*

Charlie. You even said it yourself in your office on Thursday. You know where to find me. I love you, Charlie Mason. I want you to be my wife, don't ever doubt that.

What the fuck? So, the day after I fought with her, she runs to him. Again. I can't stop myself, I go into her messages, reading the trail of their conversation.

Batman: *Happy birthday, gorgeous. Sorry, I can't make dinner tonight, but I'll be free afterward The bat cave is ready... and so am I, baby. I just want to taste you again, feel myself inside you. Stay over and just maybe you'll get breakfast in bed, just the way you like it.*

I sit on the edge of the bed, bowing my head while clutching the phone. My heart is racing, rage pulsing through my veins.

Is she still fucking him?

I want to shake her, wake her up, and demand she answer.

It isn't only the anger taking over me, it's the jealousy that he touched her, he'd been inside her, and he gets to wake up with her. Something we have never experienced.

Even back in the day, we were always trying to be discreet. Not once did I have the honor to hold her in my arms all night and wake up beside her. This becomes too much for me to handle. I'm not thinking rationally, raw emotions controlling me, and I need to leave before the damage becomes irreversible.

I stand up to walk away as she slurs her words.

"Lex, I love you... please don't leave us."

Us, there's that word again. *I love you.* How I've longed to hear those words come out of her mouth.

I want it to be real, desperately needing her eyes to connect with mine when she says the words my heart needs to hear again.

With my shoulders fallen, defeated by the long night, I decide to leave the room but stop inside the living area. It's a cozy room with a ton of books on the shelves and a wall filled with frames. I walk over and look at each picture. She looks happy in every one of them, not like the miserable girl I supposedly left behind.

There's one black and white photograph capturing my interest. She's laying her head on the lap of an older lady, sitting on a porch swing. Charlotte is covered with one of those homemade crocheted blankets. She appears gaunt, her eyes almost black, but there's a hint of a smile. The older lady rests her hand on her cheek. It must be her grandmother she spoke about.

And just one look at this picture cements the damage I caused. I failed *us* as she put it.

I'm an idiot to think we could've so easily gone back to the way things were.

I'll never stop wanting Charlotte, but I don't know how to fix *us*. For now, I need a break to clear my head and think about the right way to make *us* one again.

There's no doubt that being around her causes a massive problem—we either argue, or I fuck her. And neither one of those things gets us any closer to a resolution.

I close the door behind me, leaving her apartment, my head riddled with guilt.

Back at the hotel, I finish the bottle of Jack Daniels, unsteadily opening another bottle, knowing the addiction of the drink will land me in serious trouble.

The guilt now turns into resentment, and anger rises within me like a tide.

With my phone in hand I call Bryce, excusing my call in the middle of the night, willing he'll dig up some dirt for me.

"Are you sure, Mr. Edwards?"

With my chest tight and vision compromised from the hard liquor seeping through my veins, I stare at the blank wall, my lips curving upward into a satisfied smirk.

I want Julian *gone*.

And now, there's no stopping me.

THIRTY-FIVE

CHARLIE

Nine Years Ago

"Okay, sorry, I promise I'm listening now. So, who's going to the concert tonight?"

I hadn't spoken to him despite his numerous attempts to contact me. His desperation to explain what Adriana saw was evident in every text message he sent.

What was there to explain?

He was caught fucking his wife on the piano two minutes after I walked away.

That night, skull-tattoo guy and I made out for like an hour on the beach while I was completely drunk on some concoction. He wanted more, but I pulled out the period card at the last minute. It was enough to turn him off, but not before he begged for a blow job, another thing I so willingly declined.

"Me, Elijah, Finn, Jennifer, that chick from English class with the huge rack."

"You mean Lily?"

"Yeah, that's her name."

California showcased the best upcoming new talent once a year, and the concerts always went off. It was a four-hour drive, so Dr. Edwards organized a room for us at a posh hotel next door, and the only reason my dad allowed me to go.

"And what about your..." I cleared my throat, pretending to pass it off as a nasty cough, "... brother?"

"He and Samantha have some event to go to."

Like a couple.

Okay, I'm fucking done.

As much as I hated him right then, there was that tiny part of me that wanted to see him so he could beg me to forgive him. This wasn't the right frame of mind to be in. I had filled out a survey and read numerous articles in *Cosmo* magazine. They all came up with the same answer—he was a fucking jerk, so leave his sorry ass now before you ended up being the fool. Yep, fool me once, shame on you, fool me twice, shame on me. Well, unfortunately, the fool was sitting in Adriana's room still thinking about how much I missed him.

I began flipping through Adriana's magazines, my mind not focusing on them but rather on the bulletin board above her desk. The photographs were scattered everywhere, a ton of us, but it was the ones of Alex which caught my attention. How could one human being be so photogenic in every picture? He was like a goddamn male supermodel. Glancing at the images ignited a spark, one I had been trying to bury along with the hurt and humiliation.

There's one of Alex and Samantha on their wedding day. I felt the knots starting to form in my stomach, reality creeping its way in as I examined his expression. He loved her, right? Otherwise, why would he marry her and fuck her on the piano? There it was again, anger rearing its ugly head.

"I love that photo of them," Adriana sighed.

"How did they meet?"

"In college. First-year, I think. You know my brother, he was a manwhore here in Carmel. I'm surprised he's settled down. I don't know how she did it, but she did."

Way to go for asking that question. Alex was a manwhore. I couldn't say I really paid attention back then, but if I could feel any smaller right now, I'd be a goddamn ant.

"She's nice." It was all I could manage to say.

"Yeah, she is. I mean, don't get me wrong, I like her, but sometimes I think she asks too much of him. Almost like its back to 1950 where women stayed home making pies and leaving them on the windowsills to cool down while the men brought home the bacon."

"Maybe he likes that. You know... that whole I'll-be-the-caveman-you-be-the-cavewoman thing," I mumbled.

"I guess... maybe. It's just that Alex isn't like that. Yes, he's my brother and annoys the fuck out of me, but deep inside, he is such a kind-hearted guy. He'd never hurt anyone intentionally, and he would never treat a woman that way. Sure, he fooled around in high school, but who didn't?" Adriana walked over to her stereo and cranked up the latest Rihanna song.

As we both sang our lungs out, a knock on the door echoed through the room. I was lying on Adriana's bed throwing a rubber ball hitting the ceiling as it rebounded back to me. Yes, I was that frustrated.

"Adriana, you have someone here to see you." His voice made me lose my catch, and the ball rolled over to his feet. "It's Finn."

I sat up as he looked at me, annoyed. *What the fuck did I do?* I wasn't the one fucking my wife on the piano.

"Sweet. Char, grab your things and let's go. I call shotgun," she cheered.

I quietly gathered my things and my phone trying my best not to make eye contact as Alex stood in the doorway blocking the entrance. You could cut the tension with a fucking chainsaw in here. I was praying he'd leave, so I could exit without the drama of having to walk past him.

"C'mon, the concert starts in a few hours, and we need to get a good spot. Thank God, Finn is driving so I can be car DJ."

I was looking forward to Adriana being car DJ, but it annoyed the fuck out of Finn. Their arguments over petty things provided good entertainment while slumming it in the back seat.

Alex stood still by the door, and I had no choice but to walk past him. As I made my way to the door careful not to make any physical contact, he quickly held onto my arm.

"Did you invite him tonight?" he asked, a bitter tone in his deep voice.

"What's it to you? Go back to fucking your wife." I pulled my arm away and bolted down the stairs.

Finn greeted me with a huge grin on his face, pulling me into one of his bear hugs. As he suffocated me in his chest which, by the way, smelled like man sweat, Alex walked slowly down the stairs. With a flat stare, he narrowed his eyes, mumbling something about Adriana using all the soap in the bathroom.

Samantha laughed. "Poor baby. If soap's your biggest problem, I'm sure Mommy can refill the bottle for you next time."

Adriana laughed along with her. I placed my head

down, ignoring the both of them, then encouraged Adriana to leave or we'd be late.

It took exactly five minutes and twenty-one seconds before my phone buzzed. I was sitting in the back of the car by myself. Finn was telling Adriana off for blasting 'Like A Prayer' by Madonna.

Alex: *You didn't answer my question.*

I sat there quiet for a few moments, not knowing how to respond. Outside the window, the freeway appeared like an endless road before us.

Me: *I don't need to explain myself to you. I don't have a ring on my finger. Please stop texting me. I get it, Alex. It was fun while it lasted. Have a nice life.*

"Charlie, c'mon!" Finn shouted.

I shook my head to focus. "What, Finn?"

"Please tell Adriana we aren't listening to 'Immaculate Collection' all the way to the concert," he whined.

I had no say in this matter, and to be honest, I loved that CD. My phone buzzed again. I was nervous to look. I didn't know what I wanted him to say. Was there anything he could say that would change how I felt?

Alex: *We need to talk. I had no choice, Charlotte.*

Sure, he did. You always have a choice. I didn't know what was coming over me, but I wanted to shut it out, just for tonight. To forget I was seeing a married man who also happened to be my best friend's brother, and to forget I told the man who had consumed me to go have a nice life.

It took us a few hours to get there, constant bickering in the car and a thousand pit stops because Finn decided to drink a Big Gulp as we left Carmel.

We met up with Elijah and the rest of the group, and I couldn't have been any happier as the crowds surrounded me, the music playing.

The crowd danced, people cheered, the bands would rotate, and we were having fun—no worries, no drama, just pure unadulterated fun. Finn and I had danced, nothing sexual this time, just laughter and fun, something I had missed over the last year. Senior year had been hard, and it wasn't over just yet.

The concert ended, so we decided to grab a bite to eat, go back to the hotel and change. I shared a room with Adriana but, of course, she bunked with Elijah. If Dr. Edwards found out he'd kill her, and I'd be her accomplice, and therefore, my dad would kill me.

I wore a black dress Adriana picked out a few weeks earlier. I'm not one to wear dresses unless the occasion called for it. To complete my outfit, I paired the dress with some strappy black heels. Dad would kill me if he saw them, hence, shoving them to the bottom of my duffle bag and sneaking them out of the house.

Applying some lip gloss and only a small amount of mascara, I let my hair loose to flow down my back. Staring into the mirror, I begged myself to forget *he* existed, at least for tonight.

The club was packed. Every teenager at the concert was here. It was an under-21 club, so no alcohol of course, but it didn't stop the bumping and grinding that was going on. Adriana was lost somewhere on the dance floor rubbing her ass against Elijah.

Finn was chatting with some other boys from Carmel that had shown up. I hung out with a few girls I knew until a tall, lean guy stood next to me. He was cute and reminded me a bit of Leonardo DiCaprio when he starred in *Romeo and Juliet*.

He smiled at me, I smiled back. Leaning in, he whispered in my ear, "I don't do cheesy lines, but I love this song. You wanna dance?"

Like I said, he was cute, and it was just a harmless dance. It wasn't like I had a ring on my finger and went to bed every night with the person who I made a vow to spend the rest of my life with. I grabbed his hand, and we danced to a few songs. He was a good dancer—smooth—and I moved my body enjoying the thud of the beats.

There was this force that pulled me, and I knew someone was watching me. I searched around the room, the bodies were crammed in tightly, everyone busy in their little world. I tried to focus again without being rude to Leo.

I felt that familiar pull like the floor was about to collapse beneath me, and I was about to be yanked in a different direction, but I couldn't see anything. Once again, my imagination was playing tricks on me.

I continued dancing with Leo until those emerald green eyes found me, standing in the corner, staring at me intently.

He's here.

Quickly excusing myself, Leo graciously moved onto another girl who was eye-fucking him right beside me.

My footsteps were small, yet heavy, with every step I took toward him. Unsure of what to say and also wary of my surroundings, I stopped before him with enough distance not to create any suspicions. His eyes were dark—it didn't matter that the club was too dark to tell for sure. *I could sense it.*

The music blared, so he leaned into my ear. "You didn't answer me."

I sighed, his scent too irresistible and breaking down the walls I had tried to put up. I missed him and wanted to kiss him right here, right now.

Restraint, who would have thought I was so good at it?

"Yes, I invited him. He's my friend. Actually, he is one of my best friends."

"Charlotte, I'm sorry. She kept asking me questions about you, and I panicked. She wanted to know why I hadn't touched her and if it was because of someone else. I didn't want to do it, she made the first move, but I thought it would get her off my back. We didn't continue. I still haven't fucked her since before you. You have to believe me," he pleaded, desperation lacing his voice.

Bowing my head, I let out the long breath I had been holding in. I knew he wouldn't lie to me, but the whole thing still hurt. Adriana had said it loud and clear—he was a manwhore.

So where was that straight-A student brain of mine hiding?

Oh yeah, down his pants.

"I don't know what to say."

Alex stood there, silently staring at me. I didn't know what he was thinking, and it was driving me insane. The DJ mixed songs and started playing music again. The crowd cheered, and the lights dimmed even further. It was dark, people danced, people sang, and I stood still until Alex dragged me to the corner surrounded by strangers. He pulled me in close and started swaying. Placing his hands on my hips, I swayed along with him. I wanted him so bad, I no longer cared who saw us until he pushed me away. As I took several steps away from Alex, I finally crashed into a guy wearing a muscle shirt.

"I'm so sorry," I apologized, clutching his chest. "I tripped."

Adriana was standing where I previously stood, obviously walked in after Alex pushed me out the way, and she was talking animatedly before hugging Alex. Pulling away, they continued talking before both their eyes fell on me.

Upset at his sudden move to push me away, I turned to be greeted by Leo. Just as he was about to say something, Adriana barged between us.

"Char! There you are. Oh, hi, I'm Adriana." She extended her hand which was odd, but being a polite guy he shook it back.

"I'm David."

"You wanna come eat with us, David?" Adriana asked, shooting me a you-can-thank-me- later glare.

"Sounds good."

Adriana linked her arm into mine before whispering, "Char, you're so gonna get laid tonight by him. I can feel it in my bones."

Adriana's bones couldn't have been further away from the truth.

David had no chance.

The only man I wanted was the one staring back at me with an angered gaze, ready to tear David into shreds in one swift movement if he came anywhere near me.

I was going to call this payback, and deep down inside, I loved every minute of it.

THIRTY-SIX

ALEX

Nine Years Ago

"Alex, if you don't want to be here, why the hell did you come?"

Samantha was annoyed by my lack of enthusiasm for baby talk. That's pretty much all we were doing tonight at this stupid dinner party hosted by one of her gallery friends.

"I didn't agree to come to the party so we could talk baby shit all night. You know where I stand on that," I answered back, frustrated.

The whole Finn and Charlotte thing kept replaying in my head. I knew it was an overnight thing, and where the hell would he sleep? There were too many questions, and I had no answers.

Charlotte never answered my question when I texted her which really riled me, not to mention the dozen text messages I had sent her trying to explain what happened last week at my parents' house.

Then I got her text, telling me to go have a *nice life*.

My concentration dwindled to nothing as anger and fear were consuming me. I'd fucked up, big time, and I deserved the cold shoulder. But she could have at least heard me out, but instead, I was standing listening to something I had no interest in whatsoever.

Samantha pulled me aside, digging her nails into my arm. "I'm over this bullshit, Alex. Get your fucking act together and act like my goddamn husband. You're embarrassing me," she spat, clenching her teeth with animosity.

"I'm embarrassing you?" I laughed in her face. "Talking about what position is best to make a baby is what's embarrassing, Samantha."

"What do you want?"

"I don't want to be here." I waved my hands around.

"Then just leave," she shouted and walked away.

I grabbed my keys and left without saying goodbye. On autopilot, I drove my car to exactly where I wanted to be. With Charlotte.

Elijah had texted me earlier to let me know Adriana was okay. But Dad, on the other hand, gave me a long-winded rant about Mom allowing her to go in the first place. On a whim, I called Dad to let him know I'd supervise. He thanked me, then warned me to watch her and make sure Elijah didn't sleep in the same room as her.

I made my way to the club, lucky to get in because I was twenty-five, and it was an underage club.

Charlotte was there on the dance floor, dancing with some dude her own age. At first, I stood at the bar watching them, desperate for a drink, but they weren't serving alcohol.

She finally spotted me and excused herself as she made her way through the crowd of people dancing.

I wanted to tell her how sexy she looked in the dress

and heels, but instead, we fought, both of us frustrated. I led her to a dark corner of the club and pulled her into me. No one could see, and I wanted her so bad that nothing mattered anymore.

We danced and grinded for only a few minutes, but it was enough to have me hard as a fucking rock until I spotted Adriana. I pushed Charlotte aside, hoping she understood. It took her a moment to register before she slipped away. Adriana was happy I came and asked if I had seen Charlotte.

"There she is." Adriana spotted her. "I'm glad she finally met someone... and what a hottie!"

This guy? What the fuck did he think he was doing?

Adriana walked toward Charlotte, leaving me alone with my heated thoughts. He was a jerk, that was all I knew. Adriana motioned for me to follow them, and with every step I took, jealousy shot through me like a thousand bullets.

"Alex, we're going out for a bite to eat. You coming?" Adriana asked.

"Sure, why not."

We left the club and walked over to the hotel which had a restaurant on the lower level. We sat at a booth, Charlotte next to that guy, and Adriana wedged between Elijah and me.

"The mega burger and fries look to die for," Adriana mentioned while reading the menu.

"I know you don't share," Elijah followed. "So, I'll get the turkey burger."

"I'll have the same."

"Charlotte, introduce us to your friend," Adriana insisted, placing the menu down.

His name was David. He talked football with Elijah as

I sat there quietly watching Charlotte without being too obvious. After the most boring conversation about college, we were interrupted by Finn as he walked in and squished himself beside Charlotte at the same time the waiter brought the food over.

"Finn, that was my pickle. I was saving that till last," Charlotte whined.

"Sorry, Charlie... you snooze, you lose," he joked, placing the pickle in his mouth.

"You jerk," she mumbled, knocking his shoulder.

"Thanks, Charlie, I love you, too." He grinned, hugging her tight until she caved and smiled.

My muscles tightened at the sight of them, but this time, the jealousy was over their friendship. How easy it was for them to openly parade their friendship without anyone second-guessing their motives. Well, aside from me, but the more time I spent around Finn, the more I realized he was a protector rather than a potential lover.

"Can you guys get a ride home? Jen's parents had a fight, so she wants to stay over at my place."

"Alex can drive us home," Adriana offered but soon realized we'd have a sleeping arrangement problem. "Shit, Alex, can you get a room? If not, maybe you can crash with Charlie. Or you can stay with Elijah."

Her suggestion was innocent, but the thought of 'crashing' with Charlotte made me think of only one thing.

Throwing some bills on the table telling us they were going for a walk, Adriana and Elijah left the table leaving me alone with Charlotte and David. Fuck, this was awkward. *For him, that is.*

"So, Charlie, did you want to go for a walk as well or something?" he asked, ignoring me sitting right opposite them.

"It's not that I don't want to, but it's been a really long day, and I..." She looked at me, bewildered.

"Sorry, buddy, I can't have her walking around alone with a stranger. Her father would kill me."

"Yeah, I totally get it. Sorry," he sulked.

David grabbed a piece of paper and a pen, jotting down what looked like his phone number, then slid it to her. "Give me a call sometime. We should meet up when you're free." He kissed her on the cheek, said goodbye, and walked out of the restaurant.

"I assume you'll discard that number as soon as we walk outside," I rebuked.

"Excuse me?"

"What? You actually think you'll meet up with him?"

"Screw you, Alex. I'm not the one who said 'I do'!"

Sliding out of the booth, Charlotte raced out of the restaurant leaving me alone.

Burying my head in my hands, I didn't follow her just yet. She had every right to be angry, and if the roles were reversed I'd feel the exact same way.

I walked around the hotel for a while trying to figure out what to do. I decided I would go see her and apologize for trying to stake my claim without actually having anything to back it up with when all along she was right.

I held my hand up against the door, but with fear, I pulled away. If I walked through this door right there, right now, my life would never be the same. There would be no turning back. I'd be sealing our fate.

Bowing my head, I tapped gently. Maybe it was minutes, maybe it was seconds, but she finally opened it.

I could see the turmoil on her face, the apprehension which lingered.

Did she know how much this would mean to me? To us?

I followed her lead, silently, and walked into the dimly lit room. It was just after midnight, the moon shone through the sheer drapes, and the noise of the outside world slowly faded away. Or maybe that was because the only thing I could hear was her heart beating. She was only inches away from me, yet it felt like a mile.

"I'm sorry, Charlotte."

"Alex, I'm scared," she whispered.

I wrapped my arms around her waist and pulled her into me. She smelled heavenly, intoxicating, everything I'd ever need for the rest of my life.

"Scared?"

As much as it wasn't the moment to open up the vault of past sexual escapades, I knew I wasn't her first.

"I don't know if I can stop. I mean this... us. If we take this further, where does it go? Where does it end?"

I placed her hand over her heart. "Just follow this."

"It leads me straight to you," she whispered.

My hands moved upward and settled on her cheeks, bringing her mouth close. Her soft pink lips caressed mine, our movements so slow that every kiss awakened a new sensation I had never felt before. The sound of her soft moans in my mouth aroused me, but I didn't push. I wanted to savor every moment of this night, every part of her. *My Charlotte.*

Without breaking away, I led her to the bed. I held onto her as I laid her down, and gently, I climbed beside her and continued to slowly kiss her lips. Our tongues battled softly, never stopping to catch our breath. I slowly broke the kiss and moved toward her neck, spreading soft kisses as she tilted her head back. She moaned faintly. She was ready, more than ready.

My hands trailed to her stomach, rubbing it as I listened to the sounds her body made. For a moment, I thought she had changed her mind, but she drew away for a mere second to pull her dress over her head. To see her chest only covered in a bra was enough to make me come, but fuck, I needed to remember it was a marathon, not a sprint.

The tips of my fingers grazed her tits, watching them in the moonlight. Making my way around to her back, I undid the clasp and watched it fall around her waist. No words could ever describe how beautiful her tits looked bathed in moonlight, the most perfect natural pair I'd seen in my life.

Resistance was futile. I lowered myself so that I could take them in. She tasted like sweet heaven, and I tried to slow my movements, but I was lost. Lust was taking over, and my tongue sucked on them harder, her pleasure growing as she pulled on my hair whispering slight profanities until she asked me to stop.

"Are you okay?"

She hesitated but only for a moment. "You're wearing too many clothes, and I need you inside me, now."

In the quickest amount of time, my pants and boxers were off as was hers. We both laid there silently admiring each other's bodies.

"Relax. I promise I won't hurt you."

I knew I'd been blessed in the cock department, so I was conscious of taking it slowly. I slid myself in, kissing her shoulder as I waited for her body to relax. She groaned, taking my hips and pushing me in further. I couldn't believe she was in front of me, the girl who meant more to me than anyone in this entire world.

Using the small amount of control I had during this

moment, I tried to be patient and move slow, but like a possessed man, the lust and greed took over. My thrusts became faster, and with every sound she made, I knew she was near. I watched her face desperate for more, the force of her kisses, the way her hips buckled, then slammed harder into mine.

"Alex, I'm sorry. I can't... I'm going to..."

I moved faster, letting her ride out our first orgasm together, and it only took a second later for me to follow her lead. I bit down on her shoulder as I tried to grasp the intensity of it all. Trying to catch my breath, I held onto her tight. Sweat beads had formed on our bodies only adding to the realization of what had just happened.

"Shit, I should have asked you..."

"What is it?" I murmured with my head still buried into her neck.

"To use a condom."

I pulled away and slowly eased myself out of her. Falling on my back, I brought her close to me.

"I'm sorry, you're right. I don't know what I was thinking. I just wanted to feel you. I don't want to sour the mood, but you have nothing to worry about."

"But you're married, which means you sleep with someone else," she lowered her voice.

"Charlotte, look at me." I tilted my head as our eyes met. With a pained expression, I sensed her regret. "Samantha and I haven't had sex in months. I get tested every six months as part of hospital protocol. You're the only one I want to be with, but next time, we can use something if that will ease your mind."

"Next time?"

My ego took a bit of a hit for a moment. *Was it not the same for her?*

"Uh, yeah. Was it not good for you, Charlotte?"

She remained silent. It killed me, but then she spoke the words that were so powerful. Words that drew me to that place again.

"Alex, I've dreamed of this moment since we ran into each other in the kitchen, and nothing could ever compare to how wonderful that felt. Never in my life have I ever felt that way about anyone or shared something so intimate, but it confirmed my fears... I can't stop. I want more. I want all of this with you. I want to feel you inside me, touching and exploring every part of my body. I want to do very dirty things to you that only my imagination has allowed me to experience."

"Well, I think we have a problem." I laughed.

"What's that?"

I grabbed her hand and placed it on my cock which became instantly hard. She moaned, but this time it was different.

"I can take care of that," she murmured as she slid herself down under the sheets.

Oh fuck. Her lips were wrapped around my cock, and damn, my girl gave the best head I had ever experienced in my life. I wanted more, again, begging her to angle herself so I could feel her pussy. She moved slightly to the left within my reach, and I eased my fingers inside making her moans muffled on my cock more arousing. I slid them out rubbing my cum all over her clit. She took me in deeper. I was close, so I warned her because I was some sort of gentleman and didn't know how much she could take.

"I want to taste you."

I was done.

Thrusting my fingers deep inside her one more time, I came as her walls contracted around my fingers. She took all of me, every single drop of fucking cum and she swallowed like a pro. Samantha had never done that, come to think of it, none of the girls I had ever been with had. It was a fucking dream come true, and I was ecstatic that I had experienced it for the first time with my girl.

"Are you okay there, soldier?"

"You're amazing, you know that?"

"Well, it helps that I watch a lot of porn." She grinned proudly.

"Wait! Did you just say what I think you just said?"

"Yes, you heard right. What? My imagination can only think of so much before I need visuals."

My arms wrapped tightly around her, never wanting to let her go. This was perfect, we were perfect. Except for one thing—I was married. And now officially, I had cheated. I was having an affair, and I couldn't turn back. I'd crossed to the dark side, but instead of it being dark, it was warm, sunny, full of rainbows, and naked Charlotte waiting for me with her hair fanned out on a bed of clouds while feeding me grapes.

"I wish we could stay like this forever, but I have to get dressed before Adriana barges in."

She reluctantly untangled herself from me and got dressed. Once she zipped up her dress, I pulled her back onto the bed which was met with a small squeal.

"Alex, you need to go."

"One more minute. Please? Once I walked out that door, you won't be in my arms till God knows when."

It was the truth as much as it hurt.

"We can't be caught. You know that, right?"

Of course, I knew that. I also knew that I wanted her more than ever now, and I didn't know how I'd juggle being married and being with her.

The next morning I was sitting in the lobby with Elijah waiting for the girls to come down. I was nervous. I didn't know how she would react after last night and was hoping that Adriana and Elijah couldn't sense it. The elevator pinged and they walked out. Charlotte bowed her head as Adriana talked a mile a minute.

"C'mon, Charlie, was it the Leo-looking guy? You can tell me. Argh, I'm right, right?"

Charlotte remained silent. Placing their bags down, she finally met my gaze with a small smile.

"What's going on?" Elijah asked.

"Charlie won't tell me who she spent the night with. It's Leo. Just tell me?"

"Adriana! I can't believe you just blurted that out in front of everyone," Charlotte snapped.

"Who's everyone? Elijah and Alex don't care. Stop denying it, you have sex hair."

"Adriana! Leave it alone. *Please*."

I stood there, amused by the argument that was about to go down in front of me. I knew Adriana wouldn't let it go, she was like a dog with a bone, and it was only a matter of time until she started up again.

The car ride was long and, of course, I was the designated driver. We talked about mundane topics like movies, bands, but as I predicted it was only a matter of time until the subject was brought up again.

"Seriously, tell me everything that happened with Leo?" Adriana asked again, the two of them in the back.

"Adriana, drop it," Charlotte answered, exhaustion evident in her voice.

"What's such a secret that you can't tell me?"

"Fine. We did it in his hotel room. We fucked once, then I left because he wanted to go again, and I did not."

"Why not?"

"Why not what?"

"Why didn't you want to go again? I mean, he was smoking hot. Sorry, babe," Adriana apologized, looking at Elijah.

"Because I didn't enjoy it, Adriana. Why would I go back for seconds if I didn't enjoy it the first time?"

"Char, what the hell is going on with you? Finn couldn't make you come either. Are you sure you're doing it right?"

I nearly choked on the piece of gum I was chewing. This conversation had gone from annoying to interesting. Charlotte definitely had no problem climaxing—twice last night in the space of ten minutes to be precise.

"Maybe I just haven't met the right guy yet. The one who pushes all the right buttons to the point that you daydream about fucking him all day every day."

I squirmed in my seat. *Was I that guy?*

"I totally know what you mean," Adriana responded with a grin on her face.

We reached our destination—Charlotte's house. It was torture not being able to kiss her goodbye or even talk to her in the car. She said goodbye to Adriana and Elijah before turning to face me. "Thanks for the ride, Alex," she said with a slight smirk on her face.

"Anytime."

Unable to hide the smile playing on my lips, Elijah turned to look at me with an odd expression. He raised his eyebrow while he rubbed the stubble on his chin.

"You had fun last night, Alex?"

"Yeah, you could say that. Nice to get out for a change,"

I replied, attempting to deflect any further questions as his stare began to bug me.

"Sometimes, you need change. It puts things in perspective," he mumbled.

Once I was home, I parked the car in the driveway, staring at the house for a good ten minutes.

Would I feel different when I walked through those doors?

Would she sense that I had spent the night making sweet love to my girl?

I turned the knob, my heart beating erratically. It was now or never. Scared that the regret would wash over me, I walked in and almost immediately it felt wrong.

It no longer felt like *home*.

THIRTY-SEVEN

CHARLIE

Present

Today is officially known as birthday-hangover day. I have been sitting on my couch for the last three hours watching a show about embarrassing bodies. I'm not really watching it, it's more of a living coma, but every so often something awfully horrendous will come on the screen and I'll be glued to it.

I stare at my phone screen a million times, the same old texts come through from Eric, Nikki, and Adriana, but it isn't what or who I'm waiting for.

Mustering the courage to text him, I thank him for bringing me home in my intoxicated state. It wasn't my finest moment, and lately, there have been too many humiliating moments, all with one thing in common —alcohol.

There's a strange feeling I can't quite put my finger on, the fact that he was here, in my home. Of course, I don't recall anything, and Coco isn't giving anything away either.

The last thing I remember is getting up on stage and

singing to P!nk. I created this terrible habit of using alcohol to avoid reality, and once again, I'm paying the price.

The more I think about last night, the more my head throbs in pain. Not only was the whole party a surprise, I had to deal with both Julian and Lex being there, fucking Lex in the restroom, arguing with Lex in the restroom, dealing with an angry Julian who just upped and left, then the emotions of the gift that Lex gave me which is still sitting heavy on my chest.

Reaching for the pendant, I play with it between my fingers, wondering if I have pushed him away. I recall, once upon a time, being in his exact same position. Praying and wishing he'd leave her just like he's begging me now. The humiliation of being the person on the side isn't something that can easily be ignored. It stays with you for almost a lifetime.

His desperation ran deep, begging me to talk to him. If only it were that easy, if only I could bare my entire soul to him without the aftermath of my emotions driving me to a dark place I refuse to return to.

My phone buzzes beside me, startling a relaxed Coco.

Nikki: *Rocky is dragging me to the Yankees game tonight. Since your so-called 'friend' organized this, you better be at my place at six on the dot.*

Six o'clock *on the dot*, and I'm knocking on the door dressed in my jeans, hoodie, and Converse. The door opens, and an excited Will wraps his small arms around my waist, hugging me real tight. He talks a mile a minute and all I hear are the words 'Yankees,' 'shark project,' and 'rocky road ice cream.' I have no idea how all three of those are linked, but I have a whole night to figure it out.

"Great, Charlie is here. Come on, woman. Let's go." Rocky shoves us out the door impatiently.

Stepping out onto the pavement, my breathing becomes rapid and shallow. My pulse is pounding within my temples, nervous to face Lex again. I have this unwelcoming feeling I said or did something wrong last night. And once again, the only person who can answer that is him.

The black SUV pulls up beside the curb. Rocky jumps in first, much to Nikki's disapproval, ignoring the 'ladies first' rule. Will climbs into the back with Nikki, leaving me to sit beside Lex. As soon as our eyes meet, something pulls me in a different direction. With a welcoming smile, my shoulders relax, releasing the nervous tension I have been carrying.

"Hi." He grins, keeping his hands to himself for once.

He's dressed casually in a pair of jeans, white sneakers, and tee. On his head, he's wearing a Yankees cap. I didn't know he's a fan, but it doesn't surprise me either. Lex has always been athletic and loved all types of sports.

"Hi, yourself."

"Hey, aren't you the guy we ran into at the park? Charlie's friend?" Will questions behind us.

"Yes, you're right," Lex answers politely. "Nice to see you again. Excited about the game, buddy?"

"I am," Rocky roars at the front, twisting the cap on a Budweiser he brought with him.

Everyone laughs, and at times, Will acts more mature than his dad. We talk baseball all the way there, each opinion varying, and the conversation becoming more passionate the closer we get to the stadium.

"Since when did you take an interest in sports? You hated all that." Lex raises his brow, curious.

"Since I was forced to attend every game in college, thanks to Miss Stalker over here."

"There's nothing hotter than watching your man play sports," Nikki quips.

"Mom, what does that mean?"

Rocky laughs, attempting to answer Will. "It means your dad totally rocked the field, and that's why Mommy married me."

"Oh, I thought it was because she got knocked-up," he blurts.

"Will!" the three of us yell, in shock.

"What?" Will lifts his hands, shrugging his shoulders. "Remember that time you and Mommy were fighting because that pretty lady in the coffee shop that used to go to college with you gave you a piece of paper with her phone number? When you were fighting, I heard Mommy say that if she weren't knocked-up, you wouldn't have gotten married. What does knocked-up mean, anyway?"

Lex and I glance at each other wondering how Nikki and Rocky are going to worm their way out of this one.

"You see, Mommy and Daddy were incredibly angry at each other that day and said some mean things. Afterward, we talked and apologized to each other," Nikki says, trying keep her smile pleasant. "I'm sorry you heard that because it was a very silly fight."

Will nods like he understands. "But that doesn't explain the knocked-up part?"

"Look, we're here," Lex announces, pointing to the stadium.

"Oh, wow," Will exclaims, his face flat against the window. "Lex, will you sit next to me during the game? I want to practice my commentating just like Daddy does."

"Sure thing, buddy."

Rocky mouths a 'thank you' to Lex, and typical Nikki says nothing.

The stadium is packed and, of course, Lex made sure we weren't sitting in the regular section, securing us box seats. I sit between Nikki and Will. Rocky is already talking Lex's ear off about stats, but Lex doesn't seem to mind so much. In fact, he actually seems to enjoy it.

We order a ton of food—hot dogs, fries, and nachos—and did I mention that was just for Rocky? Will is also enjoying the game, jumping in his seat at every chance he gets and asking Lex a ton of questions like where he grew up, his favorite color, his favorite team. Even Nikki looks like she's having fun, although her kind of fun is pointing out the hot players. We giggle, and straight away, Rocky knows we're talking about the men.

"He ain't got nothing on me," he yells out every so often.

Sometime during the seventh inning, Rocky takes Will to the bathroom and Nikki joins them, leaving Lex and me alone. I'm determined not to be the so-called cold bitch I have apparently become, welcoming an amicable conversation.

"So..." we both say at the same time, followed by a laugh.

"I'm sorry for last night," I interject, desperate to get things off my chest. "I was drunk, and I don't recall much. But from what I remember, I said some things to hurt you that I shouldn't have."

His expression remains fixed, but upon looking closely, his eyes bear a sign of relief. For the last few hours, he hasn't pushed me with his words or controlled me in ways only he knows how. The Lex I have grown accustomed to the past few weeks isn't the man sitting beside me. Something changed overnight to bring back the old Alex I used to know and love.

"Charlotte, I get it. I honestly do. I hurt you in more ways than I can imagine. I don't know how to make things right anymore. I don't know what you want."

"Everything about us has always been unconventional. We never had a chance to be friends without getting emotions involved. That's what I want."

"Just to be friends?" he asks, a slight hurt registering in his eyes.

"No, I want it to start that way. I can't promise you anything, I can't promise what the future holds, but I just want to get to know you again. I understand if you don't want that."

"Actually, that sounds like a really good idea. So, no more late-night visits to my office?" he teases.

"Mmm... I don't think that's the best idea right now." I smile, not wanting to create an unwarranted argument between us. "It seems to create friction between us."

"Yes, it seems we do get along better when I'm not fucking you on your desk."

I curl my lips, letting out a small laugh. "Yes, it seems that way."

The three of them return, and it isn't long before Lex whisks Rocky away to meet some sports commentators and other big shots in the corporate box. Nikki and I sit there as Will moves a few rows down to wait for the players to come around so they can sign his hat.

"I know I need to talk, Nikki. Long story short, for now, I told him we need a fresh start. We need to learn how to be friends."

"Agreed. I mean, yeah, I get that the sex is hot, and I don't want to admit that he's one hot muthafucker even though he makes my blood boil, but if this is what you want, Charlie, then you need to start with the basics. This isn't high school anymore, you're both adults," she points out, keeping her expression cool. "So, start off with the important questions like how many women has he slept with since he left you?"

I turn to face her—sure she has a pitchfork in hand. "Firstly, that's not an important question. Do you think I have some sort of death wish? And besides, what if he asks me?"

"Then, you tell him."

"Does that include blow jobs?"

"I've never been so technical. I guess so."

"So, what's your magic number?"

"Let's see. There was the guy I lost my virginity to, then I dated him for a year in high school. He cheated on me, so I fucked his best friend. Crude, I know. Then a few guys before I met Rocky. I think six, total."

"And Rocky?"

"Manwhore Rocky? He can't even remember... I think he stopped counting after thirty."

I laugh. "Well, he may have been like that before, but damn girl, you got your man whipped."

"I do know how to keep him entertained." She wiggles her brows.

The men return with Rocky talking Nikki's head off about the sports crew he met and something about having lunch with them on Monday. Walking back to us slowly, Will looks tired with his excitement wearing off.

"You guys take the SUV home. If Lex doesn't mind, I'd like to take him out."

Lex glances at me, tipping his head to the side,

surprised. We say our goodbyes, and I ask Lex if he wants to take a walk through Rockefeller Center.

We take a cab there, talking quietly about the game until we reach our destination.

Lex finds us a bench to sit on near where some performers are playing music. A small crowd gathers, families happily strolling around, and the tourists are snapping anything and everything in sight.

"I love it here," I say, watching the crowds around us. "When I first came to the city, I'd sit here for hours and just watch the people walk by. There's something calming about it."

"I remember once, I think I was twelve or something, Mom and Dad brought us here and we went ice skating. Adriana had the biggest fall... she needed stitches on her head it was that bad. There was blood all over the ice. I can't help but remember that every time I'm here."

"How often do you come to New York?"

"At least once every three months. It depends on work, of course. I've never actually been here for pleasure..." He pauses, then laughs.

"I'd argue that."

"Such a dirty mind, Miss Mason," he teases, averting his eyes back to people walking past us.

"How are your mom and dad? Do they still live in Carmel?"

"They spend the summers there, but most of the time they are on the road. Instead of settling down at the hospital, Dad travels all over the world helping people who don't have the means for medical treatment."

Of the conversations we used to have, the Alex I knew was passionate about being a doctor. He shared similar qualities with his father, often talking about the intensity of practicing medicine and how it changed him in ways he never imagined possible.

"That could have been you," I remind him, gently. "What made you finally quit?"

Shifting on the bench, he places his hands inside the pocket of his jeans, watching a couple in front of us kiss while taking a selfie. My question, raw yet with purpose, pushes the boundary between us. I need to get to know him again because unanswered questions allow my mind to go rampant.

"It was after I found out about Samantha, and the fact that she lied about the baby. I came back from looking for you, and everyone told me to leave you alone, let you live your life the way you deserved. I argued, of course, but in the end I listened, thinking they were right." Closing his eyes momentarily, he pinches the bridge of his nose before opening them wide again. "I couldn't help people, not in the frame of mind I was in. I confronted my grandfather first. He was happy to hand over the reins of his business. I agreed to go back and study, initially only taking on a small portion of work."

"Then what happened?" I ask, trying to process everything.

"I tripled our profits, and the company grew. He was pleased and wanted to hand the rest over to me. I said no, I wanted to focus solely on the part that was mine. My father stopped talking to me then. Eventually, I was doing so well due to not having a life and working twenty-four seven. My grandfather passed away a year later, and the company was left to me."

I'm unable to find the right words to say. So many things hadn't changed, yet so many things were completely different.

"And you're wealthy. It all paid off," I say, admiring his tenacity.

"I was unstoppable," he breathes, almost as if it's a curse. "The money, the power, the control... I lived and breathed it, but there's no denying I was lonely."

"But Lex, look at you..." I turn to face him, tucking my knee under my leg, "... you can have any woman you want. Why didn't you settle down and find someone?"

Cocking his head, he glances at me with a smirk. "That's where you're wrong. I can't have any woman I want. Otherwise, we wouldn't be sitting here as just friends."

I remain silent, pondering his last comment, trying to figure out a way to answer without pushing him away.

"I just need time."

"I'm trying to understand, Charlotte. Believe me."

"I know you are." I bow my head, playing with a loose thread on my jeans. "And I thank you for giving me that."

A cool breeze sweeps past us. Letting out a shudder, Lex warns me he's about to place his arm around me to keep me warm. Good friends would do just that. I laugh at his pathetic excuse but allow him to do it anyway, enjoying how nice it feels.

"So, anything exciting this week?"

"Exciting, no. Busy, yes..." he hesitates, but I'm unsure why. "I'm flying back to London on Monday. I'll be there for two weeks, then back here to work on the opening of the new office."

It makes sense now. The last time he told me he was going to London I acted like a spoiled brat and ran off on him.

"Are you angry with me?"

"No. I'm sorry I behaved like a petulant child the last

time you had to leave. I completely understand your work commitments. There's always email, texting, Facebook, Skype, and tweeting. I'm sure we can find ways to talk to each other."

He chuckles, shaking his head. "I don't have time for social media."

"Well, then, we can stick to good old-fashioned texting."

"Sounds good."

I don't want to end the night, but it's late, and I'm exhausted after last night. The crowds slowly disperse leaving us almost alone to admire the beautiful sight in front of us. The skyscrapers are lit up, and I've never felt so much at home, here, in this big city.

But maybe it isn't the city.

Maybe it's the person beside me.

"Where do you stay when you're here?"

"The Waldorf, my home away from home. When the head chef knows exactly what you eat, you know you have it good."

"Or a lot of money," I add.

"Yes, that, too. Are you free tomorrow for lunch?"

This night is going so well, and I don't want to ruin it. I can lie, but what kind of friendship am I trying to build based on lies and deceit? It's now or never.

"I don't want to fight, Lex," I tread cautiously. "But I'm having brunch with Samantha."

"Samantha. Right." His expression tightens, the sudden crossing of arms a dead giveaway he isn't pleased. "Can I ask why?"

"Business. Confidential matters. Legal... if you can read between the lines."

"Right."

"But I'm free tomorrow night?"

With a promising smile, he drops his hands back into his pockets. "Sounds perfect."

"It's a date. No, sorry, that's the wrong term to use... a friendly catch-up involving something delicious to eat."

Unable to disguise a mischievous grin spreading all over his beautiful face, he drops his head, letting out a small laugh. I can tell he wants to say something until it finally clicks, and my laughter consumes me.

"Okay, I know. I walked right into that one." I smack my forehead, shaking my head, embarrassed. "Nice to see I'm not the only one with the dirty mind, Mr. Edwards."

We stand and walk to the street lined with cabs. I don't want to say goodbye, but I have to, learning to restrain myself. If we are going to be friends, I have to obey my own rules.

Rule number one—avoid all physical contact.

"Thank you, Charlotte. For tonight." He leans in and kisses my cheek softly.

Every part of me wants to grab him, take him back to my place and make sweet love to him. But this 'friends' business, it's imperative to what our future holds.

I can no longer deny that having him back in my life doesn't make me happy.

And that becomes part of a bigger problem.

My happiness has become attached to him, to *us*. Again.

THIRTY-EIGHT

CHARLIE

Nine Years Ago

It had been a month since the night of the concert or to be exact, the night Alex and I finally had sex.

In the space of a month, we fucked God knows how many times in different places and in as many positions that would warrant a Kama Sutra sequel. Alex was insatiable, and every part of me was desperate for more. A few times I was worried we'd be caught, but somehow, we came up with an alibi. That was until the principal contacted my dad about my three absences in two weeks and wanted to make sure I was okay.

"Charlie, can you please explain this?" Dad slid the note across the table. It was a letter addressed to Dad requesting him to authorize my absences at school. "Look, Charlie, what's going on? You're a straight-A student. Is Adriana making you skip school?"

I hesitated, looking for a valid excuse. "It's stupid, and I'm sorry, Dad. There's this guy at school. I like him, and he kinda said some not-so-nice stuff, so I've been avoiding him," I lied.

Shaking his head with disappointment, he bowed his head while pinching the bridge of his nose. "Charlie, since when does a boy do this to you? I've raised you better than this. I see how you are with Finn. No one gives you shit."

"I know, Dad. I'm sorry, it won't happen again. You're right. I need to find my girl power and not let a boy get to me."

He rubbed his beard and gazed at me before leaning down to sign the letter. "I trust you, Charlie, this better not happen again. You understand me?"

"Yes, Dad. I'm sorry."

After lunch was finished and the dishes were done, I told my dad I'd be up in my room studying. I had to admit the constant lying was tiresome, but I had no intention of being caught or giving up Alex. I needed to get in contact with him, just a text would be enough. I used our code in case he was with her.

Me: *Hi Alex, did Adriana ask you for that book we are studying in English? She said you had a spare copy lying around at home.*

I waited impatiently for him to respond, unable to concentrate on studying. I needed him, just for a moment, and then I would finish my history paper.

Alex: *Hi baby, I'm off in an hour. Any chance of meeting up? I miss you.*

A smile graced my lips. I had no idea how I could get

out now with it being a Saturday afternoon and my dad off
for the night.

Me: *Meet me at the back of the library.*

Quickly grabbing my books and backpack, I attempted
to walk like a normal human being and not in a rush to
meet my married boyfriend. The stairs proved tricky as I
nearly fell down the last few steps because my laces were
untied.

"Dad, I'm off to the library for an hour or two before it
closes. I'll pick something up for dinner if you like?" I
yelled from the front door.

He walked into the living room, awkwardly shuffling
his feet. He opened his mouth to say something and then
shut it.

"Yes? No?" I asked, trying to rush.

"I, uh... kinda... uh... have dinner plans tonight," he
mumbled.

"Oh, I see." I chuckled because it was so unlike my dad
to be shy. "Okay. Have fun on your date, Dad."

We met behind the library, but instead, he wanted to
take me somewhere. We hiked about fifteen minutes up a
trail until it unfolded before me—a beautiful clifftop. It was
flat but covered in orchids blooming all around us. The sun
shone perfectly on it, and butterflies flew in the air. It
looked like heaven, it was so surreal.

"Alex, it's beautiful," I gasped.

"Just like you." He stood behind me trailing kisses
down my neck. I closed my eyes, feeling his warm breath
against my skin with the scent of the orchids fresh in the air.
He took me by the hand and laid his jacket on the ground.

As we both sat, he held onto me, humming a tune.

"Baby?" he murmured into my ear.

"Yes?"

He didn't realize that simple gestures like calling me 'baby' awoke things deep inside, things I'd never felt before. Like he was reaching that part of my soul I was desperately trying to hold onto, a part I knew if I let go, it would be with him forever and no one else.

"Turn around, look at me," he begged.

I shifted so my eyes met his. A part of me was terrified he was going to tell me what I dreaded all along, that we needed to stop. His eyes shone a bright, beautiful emerald that mesmerized me every time, pulling me into a trance.

It felt like minutes passed as his eyes gazed into mine like playing a game of who'll blink first, but there was this eerie calm, and neither of us would back down.

"Te amo mi niña, I love you, my girl," he breathed.

With his eyes still fixated on me, my heart stopped because he'd said those words. Those words that no other person had ever said to me, those words which changed everything about us and who we were and what we were doing. I held my breath unaware I was doing so.

"I love you, my girl. I have ever since we ran into each other the night I came back. It's you, it has always been you." He stopped, waiting for me to say something. "You don't need to say anything. I just needed to tell you. I couldn't hold it in anymore."

"I love you, too, Alex."

"You do?"

"I can't deny it anymore. I love you so much that it hurts. I can't sleep, I can't eat, and I can't be a normal human being. It's like it has consumed all of me."

Alex kissed my knuckles with an unassuming grin. He continued to sing, the same song he sang to me that day at the piano. I ignored the painful memories attached to it—it was the day I thought my heart officially stopped beating.

Instead, I allowed the warmth to rush through me as he sang those words, and I couldn't help but sing along with him. The melody only added to this enchanted moment when nothing else mattered in the world, nothing but Alex and me.

It was there, in the middle of the meadow with the sun shining upon us, that the man I loved and he loved me in return, made sweet passionate love to me.

THIRTY-NINE

LEX

Present

There are certain moments in my life I'll never forget, a moment destined to be engrained in my memory, and no measure of time will erase them. This is one of those moments.

Charlotte walks toward me, and almost as if I'm suspended in time, her beauty hypnotizes me. The red dress she's wearing is simple but elegant, accentuating her stunning figure. Her long brown hair flows down and nestles over her shoulder to one side with the soft tendrils framing her beautiful face. Her eyes mirror mine, shining bright as her smile radiates across her face, one that reaches her eyes.

I'm never one to be rendered speechless, but her beauty continues to astound me. For tonight, she'll be mine, although I know I have agreed to be friends.

My desperation to keep her in my life despite the circumstances will prove extremely difficult. I can't reach out and touch her, even though she's beside me. There will be no invading her personal life and asking if she broke it off with him —I'm probably going to bite my way through my lips on that one. I've always controlled what I do, nobody dictates terms for me, but here I am nine years later trying to start a friendship with the girl who is my reason for breathing. How the fuck am I going to get through tonight without mauling her in the car?

"Are you trying to kill me, Charlotte?"

"I'm not sure what you're referring to, but since your eyes have not left this dress, my answer is no. I happen to really like this dress, and a friend wouldn't kill another friend, now would they?" She bats her eyelashes, turning on the charm.

"So, yes, you're trying to kill me."

Inside the car, we sit with the middle seat vacant between us. Every now and then, a soft breeze will come my way, and her scent lingers causing all sorts of discomfort. This is harder than I thought, and it's only been twenty minutes.

"So where are you taking me tonight?"

"You'll see."

I choose to keep our destination a secret, although I know she's desperate to know. Instead, she sits quietly watching the city pass us by. Upon arrival at the dock, she narrows her eyes, grimacing, before turning to me for answers.

"Now, will you tell me?"

The car stops, and I exit to open her door, taking her hand as she climbs out.

"You see that yacht over there?" I point out.

"The one marked with ducks?"

"No, Charlotte. The one behind it."

With a slack mouth, her eyes widen when she finally

sees the yacht. Mr. Vandercamp was kind enough to lend to me on the night of the charity ball as he wasn't sure how much longer he'd have it for.

"OMG, Lex, it's huge!"

"Thanks, I'm glad you think so."

She gently punches my arm, knowing all too well I couldn't let that comment slide.

We walk down to the dock where the captain greets us, then we board the yacht and take a seat by the sail. As we begin to head out to sea, Charlotte relaxes her shoulders, the ocean breeze messing her beautifully styled hair. It doesn't seem to faze her, and I welcome the chilled vibe as we both quietly watch the city pass us by.

The captain finds a spot to dock. With a steady hold of her hand, I lead her to the deck where a dinner table is set up. Okay, so I went a bit overboard and had a candlelit dinner waiting. Money can do wonderful things for your sex life.

"Lex," she gasps.

I usher her to take a seat and slide in her chair. A waiter appears from the lower deck, serving us wine, then reads through the different courses he'll begin serving shortly before scurrying back to the kitchen.

"This is amazing, but you know this seems more like a date than a friendly dinner," she teases.

"Well, you might be my first friend, so I'm not sure what's classified as dating or friendship. I don't date women, and I don't have friends."

"Lex, that's ridiculous. Of course, you have friends, and please... like you haven't dated anyone in eight years."

"I never have time for friends. Work is my life. Yes, there are people who perhaps could be called a friend, but

I'm not running around town with BFFs or whatever you kids call it these days."

"And dating? Surely, you've had sex in eight years."

"I never said I didn't have sex. I said I didn't date."

"Oh."

"Spit it out," I command.

"Spit what out?"

"Whatever it is you're going to ask me because I know you, your face is so obvious."

"It's nothing. It is just something Nikki said, and trust me, it probably isn't something you want to discuss."

"Okay, well, now you have me curious."

"Lex, trust me, you don't want to discuss this."

"No, Charlotte, you said we were friends. Friends share details of matters close to their hearts."

She hesitates while I tap my foot impatiently. We have all night, and isn't the whole point of this 'friends' thing to try to get to know each other again?

"Nikki thought that if we're going to be friends and be open with each other, we should start by giving each other our sexual numbers. This isn't my idea, and I warned you."

Fuck. I didn't see that coming, and now it's all I can think about. I don't even know how many women I've been with, but most importantly, my stomach churns thinking about her number. Charlotte's hot, she can have any man she desires. Of course, her list is massive. No, wait, but she isn't like that.

Why the hell did I push her to open up to me?

"I told you so." She smirks, crossing her arms.

"What's your number?" I ask, gritting my teeth.

What number would make me happy? Fucking zero but fat fucking chance. She's engaged to *him*.

I curl my fist into a ball, trying my best not to smash the bottle in front of me. *Control your anger*.

"I don't have a death wish. We need to get off this topic."

"Answer me, Charlotte," I demand in a low voice. "You want to be honest? This is your chance. Besides, what's the worst I can do?"

The question doesn't have an answer. I've done many things in my life, many of which I am not proud of. I've seen things, know people in the underground world, and if there's a chance I can lose the one thing in my life which means more to me than anything I'll do whatever it takes, whether that be good or bad.

"Not as many as you think, so drop it."

"Number."

"Fine! Five. Are you happy now?"

Anger wells inside my chest. Flexing my fingers, I take a deep breath willing myself to calm down. I can't lose her now, not over my behavior.

"No, I'm not, Charlotte. Why would I ever be happy that someone else had their hands on you?"

"Okay, so give me yours? I can take it. I'm a big girl. Like what? Over a hundred?"

I have no clue because I never cared, I never asked names, never spent the night or cuddled or did any shit like that. I wore fucking condoms and sent them on their merry way. "Let's drop it."

"Bullshit. If I had to tell you then it's only fair."

"Charlotte, I don't know. Sex was just that, meaningless sex. No attachments, no names, no more than one time."

"Wow."

"Wow, what?"

"I don't know." She lowers her head. "I mean, of course, you had sex... but *ouch*."

"Look at me, Charlotte." I cup her chin, raising her eyes to meet mine. "I fucking missed you, and it hurt like hell. I thought they would make me forget, but they didn't. If I could have my way it will only be you for the rest of my life, but I'm not the one calling the shots here."

Charlotte sits in silence, nervously fiddling with the pendant I gave her. The silence is deafening, so I do the only thing a jerk like me would do, I turn the conversation back to her, back to that number five.

"So, five then?"

"Lex, don't... please."

"But we're friends, and there's no point in keeping things from each other. Who were they?"

"Seriously, you're going to turn this on me. I'm not the one who screwed all of the United States."

"Charlotte, please don't. I'm sorry."

"Well, you know what?" she starts, her eyes burn with a raging flame. "Since you asked the question, here goes. It took me two years and twenty-six days after you left me to be able to kiss someone else. Exactly three years and eighty-six days since the day you left me for me to have sex with another man. And even then, every person I was with, the whole five of them, was to escape the very fucking shitty hole you left me in."

Her words cut me deep, all of her actions are premeditated because of me. I want to take her in my arms and kiss away all the scars, but jealousy is a force to be reckoned with. It's ugly, uncontrollable, and in my case—imbedded in me.

Closing my eyes for a brief moment, they spring open

with a clearer vision. "Was Justin Timberlake one of the five?"

It takes her a moment, but eventually, just the corners of her mouth I see a small smile appear.

"If he were, I'd have a ring on my finger, and you would be officially having dinner with Mrs. Timberlake."

"It was a stupid thing for us to bring up, but it's out in the open, and I'm more than happy to place that in the vault of conversations that never should be brought up again," I tell her, politely.

"I'm sorry, too, Lex. You're a guy. I don't know why it would shock me. I mean, Jesus, look at you. It would have been impossible for you to be celibate."

"I'm trying here, Charlotte. This is harder than I thought. I can't deny the fact that I want you, all of you, to be mine." I hold her hand as I say the words, and she lets me do so for a minute before pulling back.

"I need time, Lex. Please don't push me."

I'm a rookie at this relationship stuff. I mean, fuck, I couldn't even hold down a marriage without having a fucking affair. Some things I have no control over.

The waiter appears again with our starter, the two of us eating quietly, engaging in small chit chat before he returns with the entrée.

"So anyway, I wanted to thank you again for my birthday gift. It means a lot to me."

Toying with the pendant between her fingers, her gaze shifts toward the sea, an open stare followed by silence. I'm taken aback that she brought the subject up to begin with. Was she ready to talk about whatever it is that's bothering her?

"I know it means something to you. Otherwise, you wouldn't get it inked on your skin. You hate needles."

Letting out a small chuckle, I remember the time I had to give her a flu shot.

"True, but over time, I got better. I just needed a reminder that no matter what life throws at you, there's always time to be reborn and be the best you can be."

"Well, you're amazing. I mean, at your age to have accomplished so much given what happened..." I hesitate, unsure of what to say next.

Like her mind is distracted with another thought, I give her a moment not wanting to push her. Moments pass with no words, and eventually I suggest we move up to the main deck.

"So, you live in London? What does your place look like? I bet it's all minimalistic and hot." She changes the topic which I welcome.

"It's cold and unlived in. I live in the penthouse of my building. It's big, but honestly, I'm rarely there."

"Okay, so where's the best place you have visited?"

"Mmm, I'd have to say the Greek Islands."

"For holiday or work?"

"Always work. We have a new client based in Greece. When I went over, the CEO ensured the meetings were held on the islands, so I got a taste of the market and culture. The people were extremely friendly, and the food was fantastic."

"Is that why you're so tanned now?" she mocks with a playful grin.

"That would be thanks to a business trip to Thailand a few months back."

She giggles, and I'm not sure what's so funny.

"Um, so Thailand is notorious for ladyboys. They would have been in ladyboy heaven seeing you."

"Charlotte, I don't know what you're implying, but I

don't pay for sex, and I think it's pretty obvious which ones are boys and which ones are girls."

"You'd like to think so, right? Just ask Rocky." She erupts into a ball of laughter holding onto her stomach.

I joined in, but the shock is too much. "No way!"

"He didn't sleep with one, but his close encounter was enough to send him into hiding for days."

The thought is hilarious, and we laugh for what feels like forever.

"It's beautiful out here," she murmurs, gazing at the stars.

The ocean remains calm. The moon shines bright, and the city lights twinkle on the skyline. It's one amazing sight, but her sitting beside me makes it a million times better. She shivers slightly, so I remove my jacket then place it around her shoulders. For a moment, she closes her eyes, and when she opens them, she looks content.

We sit there talking about work, tell more funny stories about Rocky and life in general. It's getting late, and I don't want the night to end, but the yacht needs to sail back and I have a morning flight.

An hour later we're standing at the front of her building attempting to say goodbye. Knowing I won't see her for two whole weeks, I gently tuck a loose curl behind her ear trying to distract myself from the awful feeling forming in the pit of my stomach.

"Thank you for tonight, Lex. I know it didn't start smoothly, but it ended wonderfully."

My hand lingers on her cheek. Is she feeling as desperate as I am? I wait for a sign because I'm one impatient motherfucker.

"Charlotte..."

"I have to go." She hands me my jacket with a smile. "Have a safe trip, Lex."

As she disappears into her building, I walk back to the car with a heavy weight on my shoulders.

This is much harder than I thought.

Three fucking times I jerked off just to fall asleep. My wrist is twisting in pain, but the damn thing wouldn't go down after the first or second time. By the third, I'm spent and fall asleep surrounded in tissues.

But that night, I dreamed of Charlotte, her hair blowing against her skin, lying naked beside me. As I leaned forward to kiss her soft lips, I stop, unaware of an obstruction. Lowering my gaze, her stomach is in full bloom.

She's carrying a baby, and it is mine.

We created a life together.

As the sun rises in the morning, I awake to an empty bed.

Just me, without her, and no closer to the dreams plaguing me in my sleep.

FORTY

CHARLIE

I held onto him, my breaths shallow, head thrown back with my eyes half-closed as he slowly grinded himself against me.

He took his time, savoring every part of my body. His fingers trailed down my body, causing me to shiver. My nipples became erect, I knew he loved that. Like a hungry beast, he slid his hands back up, cupping my breasts then lightly pinching them.

Like my body is possessed, I moved faster, pushing myself down harder and that feeling, it's climbing, soaring high, almost there.

Pulling me down to him, he stopped. Softly caressing my lips, he kissed me like it was our first kiss. His soft tongue rolling over mine, tasting me, and slowly he moved his hips.

The climb started to build again.

He grabbed my hand and entwined his fingers with mine. I held on, and then he kissed me, on my finger where the gold band sat.

"I love you, my wife."

. . .

I wake up startled, drenched in sweat, unable to determine where I am.

It's just a dream.

Shutting my eyes, I try to return to the amazing dream, throwing the blanket over my head looking for that blissful escape. It's pointless. I'm wide awake, and now I am trying to interpret what the dream means.

Marriage and Lex. Is that what I want?

Could I be his girlfriend and be happy with just that?

I'm seriously overthinking this.

After our dinner last night, I left feeling even more conflicted over the situation. Frustrated, I throw my blanket off and head out for a run.

It's five in the morning, quite possibly my earliest workout ever, but I'll be damned if I'd lay there in bed trying to relieve the frustration. After last night's three attempts with a mild and unsatisfying finish, I called it a day after my wrist could no longer physically move, and that damn crystal vibrator was weighing me down.

I have to face the facts that nothing can measure up to the real thing.

I run for an hour straight until my legs feel all wobbly, and my sweats start to stink.

"Charlie... *Charlie,*" I hear my name, slowing down my pace.

It's Kate, and much like me, she's sweating bullets and trying to catch her breath as we catch up.

"Hey, Kate. Sorry, I was off in la-la land again."

We take a seat on the closest bench, both of us letting out a sigh. We laugh as we realize how pathetic we look as the other runners speed by looking so Olympic-medalist like with their fancy running outfits and ridiculous arm weights.

"Oh no, haven't you solved the love triangle yet?" She pants, still trying to catch her breath.

"Argh, I don't know what I'm doing. I'm trying to take the mature road and be friends with one of them, but it's backfiring. I miss him and I'm having withdrawals," I moan.

"Great scx will do that to you."

"I wonder if this is what it's like to be a crack addict in rehab? No wonder they fall off the wagon so many times," I wonder out loud.

"Well, have you fallen off the wagon yet?"

"No, but I was so close to asking him to spend the night last night. I mean the words were there hanging off my tongue. My body was in hell because he looks like a sex god. And all night, the flirting..." I shake my head, trying to clear the image.

"Good for you. A little willpower never hurt anyone. What about the other guy?"

"He gave me the key to his place as a birthday gift. Julian is flawless, you know. I can't ask for a more perfect fiancé than him." Bowing my head, I don't want to admit what I already know.

"But he's not the one who's rocking your world so bad that you can't even get up in the morning without waking up in a pool of sweat because you spent the last eight hours dreaming about him."

Is she seriously psychic?

"You said it, girl. How are things with your honey down under?"

"I'm confused. I thought I trusted him, but I keep hearing stories from friends, and they don't match with what he tells me, and so... I'm not sure." She buries her head into her hands, lifting her gaze moments later, her face troubled. "Like for instance, I called up, and his mom said he was asleep, and then I checked Instagram. One of my friends posted this pic of her at the club with some girls, and in the background, I saw the back of his neck. I knew it was him because the shark tattoo is easy to spot. I tried to call him, and he was like 'yeah, sorry, babe, I had a headache and went to bed.'"

"I'm sorry, Kate. It doesn't sound right. I'd be feeling the exact same way as you. Look, you need to confront him. If he's doing this, then you have to walk away and stop wasting your time."

"I know, but I want to confront him in person. He's coming to the States in three weeks for some surfer convention, so I'll do it then. I'm sick of worrying about this on top of work. Blimey, I need a bloody holiday." Frustrated, she throws her hands in the air.

"Oh, is the bastard boss still acting all weird?"

"Yes, I want to ask him about it. His recent behavior has me all curious, but you don't ask him questions about his personal life. You should have seen him all last week. Screaming down the phone, slamming doors... I swear this bird is riling his feathers, and she must be stupid not to see it."

"Maybe if my love life falls through, you can set me up with him if he's as good-looking as you say." I chuckle.

"Ha! Something tells me he won't stop till she's his. He's that determined. Listen, I've got a few things to do, but I'll be back in the city in a few weeks. Do you want to catch up for a coffee or something?"

"Sounds great."

I give her my number, and she returns hers. We agree to meet up when she's back in the city. I'm looking forward to it. Kate is different from my other friends, not as dramatic. Yes, Nikki, Eric, and Adriana are all drama queens.

"Thanks for listening. Hope you get closer to solving your problem with Mr. Right, who's playing Mr. Wrong but is secretly Mr. Right."

She waves goodbye and runs off.

I try my best to dive into our Monday morning meeting and distract myself with work, but that dream keeps replaying in my mind. After lunch, I cave and text him. I know he'll be on the plane, so I don't expect an instant response, but when his text finally comes through, my heart jumps around like a lovesick moron.

The rest of the day, we text back and forth until he asks me if I miss him. I want to call him and tell him about my dream, how the thought of it becoming a reality sends shivers throughout me but in a good way. Still, I don't know exactly what type of relationship he wants, and so the guard stays up. The one that reminds me every day to be cautious, not to get hurt because if that were to happen again, there's no way I'll ever recover.

After a long day, I head home and fall into bed tossing and turning the entire night, not sure if I actually fell asleep or not. I grab my phone and do what I'm desperate to do—I answer his question and tell him I miss him.

The next few days drag on, but I keep myself as busy as possible. Spending time with Will brightens my mood.

Shopping with Eric proves to be a stress reliever right up until we enter Victoria's Secret with Eric's intention of buying stuff for Lex to see on me.

"Charlie, seriously, you would rock this." He holds up a fluorescent pink thong which actually is just a piece of string.

"Eric, what do you think is the purpose of that?"

"I don't know... to floss the folds?"

I burst out laughing unable to control myself. Eric joins me. He seriously has no clue about women or what goes on down there.

"How about this?" He holds up some lacy number.

"Let's get out of here," I tell him, grabbing the panties and taking them to the counter.

As the days pass, I'm amazed at how much work I achieve. Tate finally closes the Vandercamp case and, of course, Mrs. Vandercamp is elated. Turns out Mr. Vandercamp's mistress left him as well, so she's celebrating for two reasons. I normally don't mix business with pleasure, but when she invites me out for a celebratory drink, I don't hesitate.

It's probably my first weekend in God knows how long where I spend it by myself. Apart from Saturday morning attending Will's ball game, I spend most of the day doing boring stuff. The usual laundry, cleaning the apartment, and so on. By late Saturday afternoon, I'm feeling restless and text Adriana asking her if I can come over.

Dressed in a pair of jeans and my leather jacket, I grab my helmet and make my way downstairs to the garage. I still remember the day when Rocky and Nikki scolded me for purchasing a motorcycle, an impulse buy a year ago when I sold some shares which I had invested in years ago.

During my high school years, I'd jumped on the back of Finn's bike and loved the adrenaline rush. It had always been on my bucket list to own a bike, and I promised Nikki I'd take lessons.

The instructor was smokin' hot, and yes, he was one of my five. It lasted three minutes. Three minutes of my life I'd never get back.

As I rev the bike, the adrenaline runs through me. With my helmet on, I ride out of my garage and through the city then over the Williamsburg Bridge. The thrill of the ride is exactly what I need. I don't know why I don't do it more often—lack of time, I guess.

I park the bike and yank my helmet off, letting my hair loose. Securing the bike, I make my way up the steps, then press the buzzer on the brownstone building to be greeted by Adriana.

"Char, that was quick. How on earth did you... no freaking way!" She races down the steps to my bike. "OMG, I love it! It's so Dylan McKay back in the 90210 days."

She sits on the bike, pretending to ride it. "Take me for a ride, pretty please?"

"I didn't bring my other helmet. Actually, it's permanently in Rocky's closet now. He rides the bike more than me."

Adriana pouts before peeling herself off. Disappointed, she takes me upstairs.

Elijah is on the couch playing some Xbox game. He stops to hug me, then resumes his battle with some ax-wielding lunatic. Adriana leads me to her guest room. Upon entering, I'm not surprised it has been turned into wedding central.

"Okay, so I've narrowed it down to the pale pink or lilac dress. Can you please try them on?"

I don't mind, happy Adriana will finally get her fairy-tale wedding. In true Adriana style, this will be one extravagant event. Every tiny detail is written, drawn, or pictured on her drawing board.

"Where's your dress, Adriana?"

I have been waiting a lifetime to see this. She has been

picking out wedding dresses since we were eight, but I can only assume her taste has changed a lot since then.

"Ahh, yes, all will be revealed. I want you, Eric, and Nikki at the final fitting."

"We'll be there. Wouldn't miss it for the world." I smile.

As I try on both dresses, we agree the pink one is the one, although it's a little tight of course, in the bust area.

"Char, you have a killer body. I'd die to have your boobs. They are so full." She grabs my breasts catching me off guard, so I smack her hands away. "I'm guessing Lex doesn't complain."

"Haha, very funny."

Adriana sits on the floor placing pins in the hem where she'll alter the dress. I stand still, a little caught up in the moment. I wonder what it will be like to be standing one day being fitted for my own wedding dress. It will be lace, something simple yet classic. I'm not one for big weddings, just something intimate with close family and friends.

Shit! Why am I thinking about this again?

"Do you think that one day you will marry him?" she asks, hesitating slightly.

"I don't know. You know I was never one of those chicks who dreamed of their wedding day since they were born like you." I grin at her knowingly. "I didn't think of the future, I only ever thought of that very moment. We were young... well, I was young. Eighteen was too young for me to consider marriage."

"What about now?"

"Adriana, it's complicated."

"What's so complicated? Break it off with Julian. Lex loves you... you love him. You've forgiven him. Time to move on and spend the rest of your life with each other and make beautiful babies that I can spoil rotten."

The weight of her words bares heavy on my soul. It seems too surreal, having this conversation about marriage and babies with Lex. I try to hide my feelings, but the wave of panic rushes through me like a wild storm kickstarting my heart into overdrive.

"Char, are you okay?"

I kneel on the floor and place my hands over my face. The weight of the phoenix is swaying as I rock back and forth. The tears flow, and I beg myself to stop crying, not to break down anymore but the feelings are too forceful.

Adriana drops her sewing kit, holding onto me tight. There are no words, she doesn't ask, and I don't offer. She just holds me. In that moment, I realize how much I've missed and needed her, my best friend, to wash away my anxiety over this whole sorry ordeal.

"I'm so sorry, Adriana," I choke as the tears trickle down my cheeks.

"Charlie, look at me." I gaze into her eyes, praying she understands. Adriana knows me better than I know myself sometimes. "You need to open up. This demon you're carrying, you need to set it free."

"I thought I did. I was fine and had moved on, but then he came back into my life, and I'm a mess. I miss him so much, but I loathe him at the same time. I don't want him to hurt me again."

She holds onto me, quiet for what seems like forever until I manage to compose myself. Passing me a box of tissues, I clean up my face then she tucks my hair behind my ear and smiles.

"I don't mean to push you. I'm sorry. But Charlie, you have to realize Lex knows the mistake he made, and it pains him every day that he put you through that. There's nothing in the world he wouldn't do for you, and hurting you again isn't an option. He loves you way too much."

"But Adriana—"

"Charlie, Lex was a stranger to our family after you left. He barely spoke to us, to anyone for that matter unless it was work-related. He shut himself off from the world. He caused my mother endless worry. Suddenly, you have brought him out whole again, and..." she chokes up, grabbing a tissue, "... I can't thank you enough. We've missed him."

"Your parents know about me?" I ask, shocked at the thought.

It might have been years ago, but I still feel guilty for how I treated them. They were such good people, treating me like their own, and I ruined their family.

"They saw a change in Lex the past few weeks and asked me what's going on. I told them about you."

"And?"

"Mom was happy. She always felt terrible for how she treated you on the street that day. Dad, well, he's very hard to read... much like Lex sometimes."

"Adriana, I don't know if I've fully forgiven him. I'm reminded of the hurt when he's near me. How do I even get past that?"

"You talk to him. You tell him exactly how you feel, exactly how you felt back then. You be one-hundred percent honest with him."

"It's too soon. I can't pour my heart out yet. I'm not ready."

"It's been a month. I don't u-understand..." she stammers.

"Because the moment I do, I'm scared he'll look at me differently. I need to be prepared for that, know that I made the right decision in being honest with him, and be able to handle his reaction." That's the truth. There's so much more he doesn't know, and I'm scared he'll run. I need to be strong, it's the only way I can battle this so-called demon I carry.

"I understand, Char."

We talk more about the wedding, the reception and, of course, the honeymoon. They are staying in a private resort in the Virgin Islands as a wedding present from Lex. Apparently, he is chummy with Richard Branson. Sometimes it's like I don't know him at all. He's some billionaire mogul who mingles with the elite of the world.

"Adriana, is Lex really that wealthy?"

"We lost count years ago. God knows how many properties or investments he owns. We all got a fair share when my grandfather died, but Lex built this empire. He was unstoppable, but in saying that, he never spent his money either. He was either working, or... no wait, he was always working. I don't think in eight years he has even taken a vacation."

"Wow. He was never into that whole money thing before," I mutter.

"No, he wasn't, but it was like it possessed him. Not the money, per se, but the control. It was the only thing he could control in his life."

I change the subject quickly, slightly uncomfortable talking about Lex's wealth even though I'm the one to bring it up. I am not one of those women hung up on money, probably because I have my own. When my grandmother passed away, she left me her house in Connecticut and some money which she inherited from her father. I can never bring myself to sell the house, so I rent it out to a nice family who takes care of the place. I paid for my college and put a deposit on my apartment and used some to start our practice. The rest I placed into a savings account. Most of the time, I forget it's even there. I don't consider myself rich or anything, but I don't have to worry about money either.

"So anyway, I forgot to tell you... one of my designers has a house in The Hamptons which she's offered to let us use next weekend. Are you free? I've already asked Rocky and Nikki, and they are in with Will, of course. Eric has some festival thing on, so he can't make it."

"And Lex?"

I'm desperate to see him, hoping he'll fly in earlier than anticipated. Several times I have contemplated flying to London for a few days, but the mixed messages I would give him could cause more harm than good.

"I haven't been able to reach him this week. He must be busy or something. I'll try again or maybe speak to his assistant. She's my go-to when he ignores me."

"Sounds like fun," I tell her, grinning. "Count me in."

FORTY-ONE

LEX

After a quick session in the hotel gym, I pack my suitcase ready to leave for the airport.

It's a little after nine when our flight takes off. I'm tired from the late night but still check my phone to answer work emails. Kate sits beside me tapping away on her laptop. It lasts about an hour before she shuts it down, obviously frustrated with something.

Normally, I'd ignore her, but I also can't concentrate. Leaving New York no longer provides me with the relief I've grown accustomed to. And this feeling of anxiety is something I'm not comfortable with. Questions, scenarios, past reflections plague my mind. I'm leaving her behind, with *him*. I miss her like fucking crazy, and it will be two weeks until I see her next, and I am already counting down the days.

"Is something wrong?" I ask Kate, the sentiment taking her by surprise.

"It's nothing, sir."

"Look, I know I haven't been the most pleasant person

to be around, but if you need to offload something I can listen. Have you met my sister? Patience is a virtue."

Kate laughs softly, careful not to disrupt the other passengers. Placing her phone into the pocket of the seat in front of her, she wrings her hands nervously.

"It's not like I'm your typical woman. I do believe in trust, but this long-distance thing is hard, and when people start filling your mind with things you question your judgment, especially when you know they've been out on the piss every night."

Her British slang isn't lost on me. I'm not exactly the best person to offer advice, but I'm a man and can offer a male perspective.

"So, you ask him directly if you think he's being dishonest. Tell him that's how you're feeling. Only you will know if he's telling the truth. Go with your instincts."

"Kinda hard over the phone. I'll wait until he comes back. I'd rather do this face to face so I can tell if he's telling porkies."

"Porkies?"

"Pork pies... um, lies," she answers with a smile.

She hesitates again, wanting to say something else, but she remains silent, so I assume the conversation is over.

I close my eyes for a moment trying to gather my thoughts.

"And um... how are things with your... um... lady friend?"

I laugh quietly. I am defeated and delirious from the past week's events, lack of sleep, and jacking off, I think of a reasonable response. "Okay, I guess." I don't feel like elaborating, not when I'm thousands of miles in the air traveling in the opposite direction to where she is. So, I change the subject, needing a distraction. "Do you have friends in New York?"

"A few girls and guys I met on a Contiki tour a few years back. Other than that, I haven't really had time for a social life. I did meet this one woman on my morning run, really nice and so beautiful, but wow, she has one hell of a screwed-up love life."

"Don't we all," I mumble under my breath.

The flight attendant comes around offering us refreshments. We sit there quietly eating before Kate decides to bring up the latest development on the project for Preston Enterprises. We talk for a while on how it's progressing and the new ideas that have been implemented.

"I notice that Ms. Preston sends all meeting requests directly to you rather than via her assistant to me. Is that how she normally works?" she asks, formally.

"Victoria is one of those women who likes to control every situation."

Much like myself, I think, which is why we clash. That, and the fact she's always trying to get her hands on my dick.

The seat belt sign comes on, and we prepare for landing. By the time we land, get out of the gate, and into the car, I decide to send Charlotte a text but am elated to find she has beat me to it.

> **Charlotte:** *I was at lunch today, and my client ordered the lobster. I couldn't help but remember the time we ate at that restaurant in Los Angeles where you teased me with the lobster, and I threw up on the sidewalk.*
> *P.S. Hope you had a safe flight back.*

I laugh to myself, unable to hide my grin from the not-so-fond memory. Adriana, Elijah, Charlotte, and I were having dinner at a restaurant after going car shopping for Adriana. Charlotte told us she'd never had lobster because her mother had an allergic reaction to it. Well, of course, we persuaded her to try, it seemed harmless at the time. Mine and Adriana's arrived first, and I recall grabbing our lobsters and playing a puppet show in front of Charlotte, teasing her, saying, 'please don't eat me.' When hers finally arrived, we gave her instructions on how to eat it. She sat there silently watching the lobster. Adriana and I looked at each other wondering what she was waiting for. Eventually, she found the courage and snapped the lobster in half, but instantly, she ran outside and puked all over the sidewalk.

Me: *I still remember your face, so pale waiting to crack that lobster. Look on the bright side. I actually got to play Dr. Edwards with you, and from what I recall, you were quite the naughty patient.*
P.S. I don't like leaving New York.

Charlotte: *I believe the correct story is that you requested me to strip down to nothing so you could 'examine' me. Considering I was ill, it was very unprofessional of you to take advantage of a poor sick patient.*
P.S. New York misses you too.

Me: *Strictly doctor's orders. I didn't hear you complain once, but then again why would you when you had two orgasms in five minutes?*
P.S. And you?

The rest of the day flies by, last-minute meetings and trying to acclimatize to being back in the London office again. When night falls, it hits me the hardest. Alone, in my apartment, everything feels so cold and lonely. To lay in this huge bed by myself isn't the way I want to live my life anymore.

I need her in my arms every night, and I want to wake up with her every morning. In between, I desperately need to fuck her all night long in every way possible.

Every fantasy needing to be fulfilled involves only her.

My cock starts to ache, but what's new? Jerking off does nothing but subside the ache for like ten minutes before it starts all over again.

It's too late to text her. So, trying to restrain myself, I place my phone on the table beside me until the dark room lights up. Throwing my hand over, the phone slips out of my hand and onto the floor. Flicking the lamp on, I desperately search my surroundings to find it next to the foot of my bed.

Charlotte: *I miss you too.*

I hold onto my phone, rereading the text over and over again.

Until sleep becomes imminent, I drift off again dreaming about her.

The next few days are busy. The board meetings are mundane, nothing exciting is happening. My head clearly isn't in the right place. I mean, how can it be? The girls in the office see a change in me, and I know office gossip is buzzing with talks of me having a girlfriend. It isn't Kate who spilled the beans but some trashy tabloid that took a photograph of Charlotte and I dancing at the charity ball. When I start to see them look at me differently, I pull in the reins and revert back to Mr. Prick CEO. It seems to have worked and balance is restored.

The constant meetings with Preston Enterprises are becoming a drag. When possible, I send my executives over to do the dirty work, but Victoria being the bitch she is, will call me out on it. The so-called dinner work events irritate me, especially when we are having dinner with stakeholders, and Victoria acts like we are some goddamn couple always referring to *we* and *us*.

Get the fucking hint already.

She's playing a nasty game, but I'm always one step ahead of her. You have to be when you're dealing with a shrew with no fucking morals whatsoever.

A week later, I receive a call from Adriana.

"Well, well, well, and where have you been hiding, brother dearest?"

"Well, hello. Yes, I miss you, too, sister dearest."

"I want to let you know that everything is in place. The date has been set. So make sure you get your arse, as you Brits say, back to the States for a fitting in early November."

"November?" I let out an annoyed huff. "Adriana, the wedding isn't until Valentine's Day."

"I kinda changed the date again. December 1st. I've waited nine years to marry the man I love, so why should I wait any longer?"

"Send Kate the details, and I'll have her to schedule in all the dates."

She rambles on for a bit longer about what they have planned, the honeymoon, and her dress. I was only half-listening until she mentions Charlotte as her maid of honor. Of course, she would be, I don't know why it surprises me. My heart sinks for a moment.

Why can't it be us up there at the altar?

Wait! Fuck! Is Lex Edwards talking marriage again?

"Lex, are you listening to me?"

"Sorry, what were you saying?"

"I was telling you that Elijah and I will be in The Hamptons next weekend. It'll be us, Nikki, Rocky, Will, and Charlie. Eric has some festival, so he can't make it."

"Next weekend?"

Saturday is the annual golfing event which is being hosted by Lexed. I have to be there. Shit if that doesn't sour my mood.

"Yes, we're leaving Saturday night because it's a long weekend, and Elijah has a martial arts tournament midday."

"I'm sorry, it's the company's annual golfing event. We have clients and stakeholders there. I have to attend," I answer, disappointed on missing out.

"I understand, Lex. What a shame."

To say my mood went from ordinary to sour would be an understatement. Fucked off that I can't go to The Hamptons, I stomp around the office slamming doors and barking orders at everyone. A few employees who were on my radar for dismissal were instantly terminated on the spot. Fuck patience and wasting my time.

I'm on the warpath, and anyone standing in my way is bound to get hurt.

We are standing on the lawns talking with Mr. Bolton from the Bolton Group, an especially important client of ours. Victoria, again, is going on about us, how lovely it will be if she and I can go out to dinner with him and his wife. I turn to look at her, irked by the fact that she's acting so unprofessional. As I'm about to open my mouth to say something unpleasant, her heel gets caught in the grass, and she falls into me. I hold onto her, and in true Victoria style, she brushes her hand against my cock, excusing her embarrassing fall. *Stupid bitch.*

Kate interrupts us, asking if she can see me in private for a moment. Inside a closed meeting room she demands I listen, much to my annoyance.

"It's quarter past midday now. In exactly fifteen minutes, you'll spend thirty minutes greeting the rest of our shareholders. At exactly one, we'll be unveiling the new business plan which, according to your speech, will take exactly twenty minutes." She takes a deep breath, reading from her phone. "You have a further thirty minutes to walk around and arrange meetings with each person. I'll assist you with this so the clients understand our commitment."

"Kate, I'm not stupid, I know what I need—"

"At two o'clock on the dot, a car will be outside Reception and will take you to the airport. Your flight leaves at two forty-five. You don't need to check anything in, your sister has organized all clothes and necessities for you in New York. The flight arrives just after seven, and your sister will be waiting for you in the terminal. From there, you'll be traveling to The Hamptons, your sister has not confirmed how."

Raising my hand, I beg of her to stop. "Hamptons?"

"Your schedule has been cleared until Wednesday. All relevant members of the board have been notified that your attendance is required in Manhattan, and all matters are to be dealt with from the New York office. IT infrastructure has been fast-tracked and due for completion tomorrow. The Preston's project is on schedule, and Victoria has not requested any meetings until Thursday next week for which I have flights on standby."

My jaw drops, leaving me completely speechless. *So, wait, Kate planned it so I can leave?* I don't know whether I should fire or hug her right now. I rub my chin, unable to process everything she's just told me. The image of Charlotte in a bikini in The Hamptons is enough for me to make my decision.

"Go... be with her," she says in a low but dominant voice.

Without any hesitation, I exit the room to be met by Victoria blocking my way. "You're not leaving," she hisses.

"Victoria. If you'll excuse me, I have clients to mingle with."

"I heard it all, Lex. So what? You almost blew a fifty-million-dollar deal for a woman?"

"My personal life is of no concern to you," I warn her.

"Well, it kind of is, if it affects Preston Enterprises." She softens, and for a moment, I think there might be a compassionate Victoria hidden somewhere.

She places her arms around my neck as we stand in front of the door. As she purrs my name, I reach for her hands, attempting to pull them off before she tightens her grip.

"C'mon, Lex, we could be so good together. You and me, we'd be unstoppable. I know you want me. You've always wanted me. You want control, and Preston Enterprises merged with Lexed would be your dream come true."

I place my hands on her hips for a brief moment. "Victoria, perhaps you misunderstand me. I'm not interested, and the next time you want to act like an overbearing shrew, I'm more than happy to inform Daddy that his precious princess fucked his best friend last year in the back of his Merc, which was the only reason Preston Enterprises won that major tender." With a satisfied smirk, I cup her chin. "Now, if you'll excuse me, I've got a speech to make."

I leave her standing there, mouth wide open, stunned at my words. Yeah, it's times like this it pays to have a private investigator on hand. Victoria is knee-deep in any dick she can get her hands on, and Daddy has no clue his princess is a little *slut*.

I deliver my speech and follow all the instructions Kate gives me. Two hours later, I'm sitting on the plane on my way to see her.

It may have only been ten days, but it's the longest ten days of my life. Closing my eyes, I think about seeing her again, about being honest, and telling her exactly what I want.

No more friend's bullshit.

It's time to give us a chance.

The ache inside my chest can no longer be ignored. I know this ache very well. It's telling me I'm still in love with her, but this time I'm not going to lose her.

No hidden messages, not through a song.

I want the words to leave my lips, watch her face as the words '*I love you*' leave my mouth and maybe, if I'm the luckiest guy who walks this earth, I'll hear those words said in return.

Three simple words to seal our fate.

FORTY-TWO

CHARLIE

We brought in a new major client this week and are inundated with work.

The custody case is messy—two children, a same-sex couple, and sperm donor to add to the mix.

I'm barely functioning, juggling meetings and getting through my caseload, not to mention court hearings. When Friday rolls around I'm beyond exhausted.

As I begin shutting down my laptop and praising the Lord for it being Friday, Julian walks into my office, unannounced. "Charlie." He doesn't call me gorgeous, nor is his tone inviting. Meeting his gaze, I instantly notice the dark circles around his eyes and slightly unkempt hair.

"Julian," I say with a smile.

I stand and walk over, embracing him which seems like the right thing to do. He allows me to hug him before pulling my arms off him.

"Where have you been?"

"At work, at home."

"Why haven't you called me?"

"You said you needed space."

"Charlie, I said *you* needed to think about what it is you want," he corrects me before placing his hand on my chest. He picks up the phoenix sitting on my collarbone. "How did he know to get you a phoenix?"

"Excuse me?" I ask, my pits of my stomach are prickling with nerves.

"You have a tattoo right here," he deadpans, pointing to where I'm inked. "How would he know that?"

My heart beats rapidly, thumping so loud and restricting my ability to breathe.

Think, and do it quickly!

"He doesn't know that. My Facebook profile pic is of a phoenix. That's how he knows," I respond calmly, but my insides are screaming at my vagina to go sit in the naughty corner for fucking Lex behind Julian's back.

"Have you fucked him?"

"You have nothing to worry about," I lie.

I could have easily ended this right now, been honest and moved on with Lex, but I love Julian. He's my fiancé, and Lex is nothing but an ex-boyfriend right now. I'm terrified of making the wrong decision, not wanting to lose either of them. And I hate myself for being selfish, but I don't know what else to do.

With a straight face, I use the tactics I learned in law school. Never show emotion nor let your opponent see your weakness.

Julian pulls my hand toward him, examining the ring. After a few moments, he intertwines his fingers with mine and draws me closer to him. Placing his lips on me, he kisses me deeply, rushed, and with force. I allow him to do so, sucking on his lip gently to ward him off the trail he has been way too close to.

"Gorgeous, I love you. Let's skip this whole wedding thing and take off to Vegas tonight. You and me."

"Julian, don't be ridiculous. We can't just run off and get married tonight."

"Why not?"

"Because we aren't ready. Our friends and family will want to be there. Please just calm down."

"Well, this weekend I want to take you to Vermont. Just you and me."

"I can't, Julian. I have plans."

He withdraws his body, creating a distance as anger smolders across his normally beautiful face. With his jaw clenched and fists tighten into balls, so much so I can almost see his body jittering.

"With Lex?"

"No, he won't be there. I'll be at The Hamptons. How about next weekend?"

He continues to stare at me, waiting for me to crack under the pressure. I spent years learning how not to crack, and it's paying off right now.

With a tight grip on my arm, I'm slightly taken aback by his possessive nature. "I believe you, but you listen to me, Charlie... Lex isn't who you think he is. He's a ruthless man. You don't get where he is today by playing nice. This fifty-million-dollar deal he is wrapped up in right now, there's plenty of strings attached. You think he is the Alex you knew back in high school? Think again, Charlie. I have no doubt he won't stop till he has you, but if you choose him, don't expect to be the only woman in his life."

With that said, he releases his grip on my arm and walks out the door.

Elijah and I are sitting at a coffee shop waiting for Adriana who claims she needs to grab some stuff for our weekend away. I remind her there are shops in The Hamptons, but she's adamant she can only find what she needs in the city. I don't ask any more questions, it's probably some sex toy.

Nikki, Rocky, and Will drove up with a friend of theirs who's staying a few houses away from us, early this morning. Nikki texted me saying the place is gorgeous, and so is the weather considering it's mid-September.

I'm looking forward to a relaxing weekend away, especially after what Julian said to me. I decide to push those thoughts and his threats aside. He's jealous and wants to scare me. At least, that's what I keep telling myself. To give myself a mental break, and choose to leave my engagement ring at home. I don't need a reminder of Julian every single time I look at my hand.

"So, basically, children from the Bronx area, the ones who normally won't be able to afford a class, come by every Friday night. We go through the basics, but I tell you they are extremely talented kids," Elijah mentions.

"I admire you, Elijah, for following your dreams and passion for helping others."

"But you do that as well, Charlie. Don't you love what you do?"

"I do. Family law is hard and emotionally draining, though. It's difficult not to allow emotions to cloud my judgment."

We talk a little while longer, checking our phones to see the time. It's a little after seven, and Adriana has been gone for forty-five minutes. Her lack of consideration for time drives me insane. Some things will never change.

"What on earth is taking your fiancée so long?"

"Me."

The voice sends shivers down my spine but finds its way back up to my heart.

It's him.

We haven't made eye contact, but already I can't hide my happiness. I slowly turn around, and there he stands in front of me, looking as perfect as ever. His eyes soften when he sees me, and I do the most unexpected thing by jumping up and hugging him tight.

"I can't believe you came."

He runs his thumb down my cheek, very un-friend-like, but I don't push him away. I've missed him, and watching the smile grace his beautiful lips I know he feels the same way.

"Let's get this show on the road. Lead the way, Char. Where did you park?"

"You have a car?" Lex asks, confused.

I ignore his question on purpose.

"Behind my building is the parking garage entrance. I'm lucky to get a car spot, but that was a bonus to my apartment," I ramble on then stop myself as Lex gazes at me strangely.

"You have a car here in the city?"

"Yes, Lex. Why is that so hard to believe? It's a twenty-first birthday gift to myself, although I bought it two years ago for my twenty-sixth birthday plus, it's a tax write-off. I have many clients in Long Island, Jersey, and a few in The Hamptons as well, so I often travel out to see them."

He chuckles like a private joke is inside his head. Well, the joke's on him, assuming like every other man, he expects I drive some little pink hatchback with Hello Kitty stickers on the bumper or some shit like that.

As we leave the café with our belongings, we walk to

the parking garage. I press the remote to the main door and motion for them to follow me.

"Bullshit," Lex mouths.

"Oh, Char, super awesomeness. Love, love, love it!"

Adriana jumps up and down, clapping her hands.

Elijah whistles as he runs his hand along the paint job, rambling on about car stats which I already know.

"Cat got your tongue, Lex?" I tease.

"This isn't yours," he says adamantly.

"Would you like to check my license and registration, Officer Edwards?"

"Charlotte, how on earth did you get this car? There was only a limited number of them, and not even I could get one."

"I don't know... batted my eyelashes a little, showed a bit of leg. You know, the usual," I answer, playing dumb.

Okay, I did flirt with the dealer, but nothing happened. He was a naïve, middle-aged man probably going through a mid-life crisis, and so when I worked my magic, my name was bumped to the top of the waiting list.

"But it's a Maserati?"

"Yes, I'm well aware of what brand of car it is."

"Give me the keys. I'm driving." Lex holds out his hand like he expects me just to hand them over.

"Sorry, dude, no one drives my car but me," I tell him, brushing him off.

This is fun. I play it cool, not showing how much I enjoy taunting him.

"Charlotte, come on."

"Charlie, do you want me to move your bike?" Elijah asks.

"Wait! Back the fuck up. That's your bike?" Lex's eyes widen, stunned.

"Yes, Lex, these are both my toys. Now, can we please go? Elijah, do you want to take the bike?"

"I thought you'd never ask." Elijah's eyes light up, and immediately he places the helmet on and grabs a jacket.

"What's wrong? You wanna play with my toys, too?" I joke as Lex stands beside me, speechless.

He breaks out of his trance, trying to snatch the keys from me.

"I'll let you drive on one condition?"

His eyes gaze at me, amused. "What's that?"

My heart is racing, wondering if I even have the confidence to say how I truly feel.

What the hell am I doing? I have no idea.

I'm taking the biggest leap of fucking faith, free-falling again, and praying that down below the safety net is waiting for me, or maybe I won't need one. Maybe this is what it's like to rely on fate.

"This weekend, you and me..." I whisper in his ear. "Nothing's off-limits."

His eyes sparkle as the corner of his lips curve upward into a satisfied smile. Leaning in, he places his lips on mine, soft and loving, making my stomach flutter crazily.

"I missed you," he murmurs.

I dangle my keys before him and watch him take them from me.

It's a symbol—I'm trusting him, not just with my car, but with my heart.

Letting out a sigh, I know there's no turning back

And when I return to the city, I know exactly what I need to do.

I will have to end things with Julian, once and for all.

FORTY-THREE

LEX

The warm breeze filters through the car as we open the windows, enjoying the drive down the Long Island Expressway.

Charlotte's display of toys leaves me absolutely fucking speechless. When she said she has a car, I expected a little bright colored girly piece of plastic with fluffy dice hanging from the rear-view mirror. But no, parked in front of me is a Maserati, the exact model I was trying to get my hands on a year ago but was told it was no longer available. Not that I needed another car for my garage, but I wanted *this* one.

And to add to that, I'm still trying to register what she said.

"This weekend, you and me. Nothing's off-limits."

Bringing her lips to mine, I kiss her as softly as I can, holding back my desperation of wanting more. Aside from our audience, including a misty-eyed Adriana, I don't want Charlotte to think sex is the only thing on my mind. *Your dick will argue that point in a heartbeat.*

For a Saturday night, the traffic is flowing with not too many cars on the road. We'll make it there in an hour and a half, especially the way I'm driving. Adriana and Elijah are taking their time, something about the scenic route. I refuse to ask questions. When anyone takes the 'scenic route,' it's because they are stopping off somewhere to get laid.

"So, Mr. Edwards, how's the drive?" Charlotte teases, connecting her phone to the car while playing Bon Jovi, one of my favorite bands. *If that doesn't bring back memories.*

"Smooth," I say, grinning. I muster up the courage and ask her the question which has been nagging me since we were in the garage. "So, tell me something, Miss Mason, how did you really get this car?"

She hesitates, sending a wave of jealousy to my over-imaginative brain. Charlotte has never been that type of woman. *Get a grip, will you, Edwards?*

"Lex, I'm a lawyer. I argue for a living. I went to the dealer knowing it was a limited production. I did my research, and the salesman tried to take me for a ride. I told him I knew there was a black one left in the Beverly Hills' showroom. I was willing to pay all shipping costs, and full payment for the car. He kept going back and forth to his manager with lame excuses when I demanded to speak to him personally. I read the disclosure to him that where a car remains in another showroom, the dealer has full rights to sell that car to a customer provided all payments are received upfront. Basically, he didn't think I was good for the money."

"But how on earth were you good for the money? I know how much this car is worth?"

I'm hoping I don't offend her. Her silent pauses are dragging out, and I feel myself constantly on edge around her.

She laughs, resting back into her seat with a sigh. "Well, I do make a nice living, but I guess I learned how to invest well. I inherited some property and money from my grandmother when she passed away. I paid off my Yale tuition and put a deposit on my apartment."

"Smart move," I tell her.

"Yes, I agree. I became a bit obsessed with the stock market a few years back, and it paid off. Nikki and I went halves to open the law firm and business has not stopped since we opened. The car came as my present to myself. I never really had a twenty-first birthday, you know, with studying and stuff..." trailing off, she stops mid-sentence. "Anyway, I don't have time to go on vacation, so I don't spend much money. I guess it's there for a rainy day."

There's so much more to Charlotte I don't know. She has always been smart and intelligent, which is a massive turn-on when talking to her. Now, I'm hearing she's into stocks, bonds, and investing, God couldn't have cloned any more of a perfect woman for me.

This weekend, I'm hoping to get to know her better as well as getting my hands on her. I adjust uncomfortably in my seat as mental images of her naked on the hood of this car flash before me. I contemplate reaching over and fingering her tight pussy while I drive, but the car is so precious, plus she's wearing jeans which makes it more difficult.

We spend the rest of the drive talking about the stock market. She knows her stuff, and my dick gets harder the more she speaks.

It's a little after nine when we arrive at the house, and the residence is nothing short of a luxurious Hamptons real estate. Luscious green lawns surround the house, and they're manicured to perfection. The beach sits in front of the property, and toward the back is a massive Olympic-size pool. Hidden in the corner amongst some ferns is a Jacuzzi. *Well, I'll be damned.*

We park toward the rear of the property and grab our bags. The lights are on, so I assume the others are still up. As we pass the pool area, I can't help but point it out.

"Nice Jacuzzi. I hope you brought your bikini, Miss Mason."

Lingering by the door, I pull her into me and take her mouth. All I want to do this weekend is kiss these beautiful lips. Oh, who am I kidding, I want to taste her pussy, fuck her in the pool, on the beach, up the ass, make her blow me... the list goes on and on.

"I didn't think we need it in there."

She pulls away laughing as she enters the front door.

Fuck, if that didn't *kill* me.

As I close the door behind me, I say hello to Rocky and offer the friendliest greeting I can conjure up for Nikki. She does her usual grunt back which is nothing surprising. I turn to look away, my attention focusing on Will and Charlotte. I understand why Charlotte is so in love with him, he's such a great kid, but it's the sight of her with him that captures my attention in an odd way.

His tiny arms wrap around her neck as she holds onto him tight. My mind begins conjuring up our future, imagining her with our child, what that would be like. She's so good with him, and wait! Shit! Did I say with 'our' child? I shake my head trying to clear the thought, jumping the gun when she isn't even my girlfriend yet.

"Will, we allowed you to wait for Charlie and Lex, but now it's bedtime," Nikki scolds in a soft tone.

"Aww, Mom..." He pouts. "Okay. But Cha Cha, can you please read this awesome new book I got? It's about a dinosaur that invades New York City," he pleads, grabbing the book and showing Charlotte.

"Sounds... um... promising."

Charlotte puts her arm around him as Will waves good-night before they disappear up the stairs.

Twenty minutes later, she emerges from Will's room as we meet in the hallway. She places her fingers to her lips, and low and behold, there's a sound-asleep child holding onto his precious dinosaur book.

"You're really great with him, Charlotte," I whisper, taking in the sight of a contented and peaceful child.

"He makes it easy." Her eyes fall downward, only momentarily, before she lifts them with a smile. "So, what's going on downstairs?

"Rocky is organizing poker."

"Well, prepare to get your butt kicked by a girl, Edwards."

I pull her back into me as she attempts to walk away. "Speaking of butts... I can't wait to get my hands on yours. Actually, not just my hands, but to have my cock slide inside your pretty little ass again."

She grinds her ass against my cock, the throbbing becoming increasingly unbearable. "Patience, Mr. Edwards, that cock of yours is going to get a nice little workout this weekend."

Pressing into her, I'm ready to pull her into the room, have my way with her all night long until Rocky, who's standing behind us, clears his throat.

"Strip poker time!"

He failed to mention earlier it would be strip poker.

"Rocky, come on, you always end up losing. So, what's the point?" Charlotte whines, still stuck in my embrace.

Thankfully, it gives me a moment to try to calm my situation down below.

We make our way to the dining area, settling around the table.

"Rocky thinks he's the poker king after a few sessions with some poker hot-shots in Harlem," Nikki moans, grabbing the bottle of tequila and four shot glasses. "Let's at least make this interesting."

An hour later, Rocky is sitting in his underwear.

Why he didn't wear boxers is beyond me.

I've lost my shirt, something which doesn't bother me. Nikki is also shirtless, sitting across from me in her bra and exposing a nice pair of tits.

Then there's Charlotte, looking all smug because she has the highest chip count and is still wearing a tank top and jeans. It's our fourth round of shots, and somehow the game has turned into strip poker combined with truth-or-dare, except it's all truth.

"Okay, my turn. Truth or dare, Lex?" Rocky asks loudly.

"Truth."

Nobody trusts Rocky's dares which is why we always pick truth.

"Age? Who? And where you first fucked a chick."

I nearly choke on a peanut I just threw in my mouth. I don't want to anger Charlotte, but she appears amused by the question, quite possibly because we've never had this conversation when we first started seeing each other.

"I uh... hold on... I was sixteen and the chick, Brittany, I think was her name, was at a party one night. Not much to report. It was the first time I got drunk, and there wasn't much to it. She was some senior from another school, and she got a kick out of preying on the inexperienced."

"Dude, sounds like you were a dud. Did she at least give you head?"

"Yes, she did. I don't know... am I, Charlotte?"

Putting her on the spot, she laughs then purses her lips, remaining silent. We have already smashed the first bottle of tequila, and Nikki's just pulled out the vodka. I can't recall the last time I drank for fun. With my mind already slightly fuzzy, the only times I drink is to escape the sorrow when it overwhelms me.

"Mmm, you'll have to remind me again," she murmurs.

"Woo, go for it! *Go, go, go,*" Rocky chants, fist-pumping the air.

"For Christ's sake, Rocky, they aren't going to do it in front of you," Nikki berates him. "Okay, Charlie, same question."

"I'd answer, but Mr. Possessive over here can't handle sex and my past," she slurs.

She has a point, but if there's any moment to spill the beans it's now, while I'm on the verge of a massive hangover tomorrow. Plus, I know part of her 'dud' sex encounter with Finn.

"I think I can handle it. Finn and his pathetic attempt to get you off," I tell her, uninterested.

She shoots me an annoyed look, so I shut up.

"I was seventeen. Finn and I had been friends for like, forever. One day we decided maybe it was fate, you know, us being together, so we lost our virginities to each other on the beach. It was cold, the sand was gross, and I chaffed because I couldn't get wet. Plus, he was huge."

"How huge?" Nikki raises her brows.

Charlotte holds her shot glass toward her lips with a knowing grin. "Not as big as some."

"Way to go, Edwards!" Rocky holds up his hand to high-five me.

I'm not sure how I'm supposed to react, laughing as I shrug my shoulders. Charlotte slurs something else before bursting out into laughter and accidentally spilling the vodka down her tank top.

"Okay, next question, since Nikki just lost that hand," Charlotte puts her on the spot. "How many guys have you fucked? And I mean fucked, not blow jobs."

Nikki scratches her head trying to think, then she bursts out laughing for no reason.

"I told you six... I think. There was the guy I lost my virginity to then he screwed my best friend, so I fucked his best friend after they won the state championships. Then there was John the science guy—"

"Was he the guy with the funky spunk?" Rocky blurts out.

Charlotte and I cringe in unison.

"Yes, Rocky. Then there was Dave—"

"Small Dick Dave?" Rocky snickers.

"Yes, Small Dick Dave. Then, oh yeah, we can't forget the twins. Michael and Matthew."

"You fucked twins?" Charlotte gasps.

"Yes, but it wasn't... what's the word I'm looking for?"

"Aw babe, not the twin story again," Rocky whines.

"You had an orgy with four girls." Nikki points her finger close to his face. "What the hell are you getting jealous about?"

"Yeah, but they weren't hot like you."

Rocky tries to make kissy sounds toward Nikki, but she pushes him away, stubborn as usual.

"You said it was the greatest experience of your life

because one of them squirted on your face," Nikki reminds him.

I spit out my shot all over my chest and some even through my nose. Unable to contain my laughter, Charlotte joins me as she slaps the table, some poker chips falling to the floor.

An hour later, I'm sitting in my boxers after going all-in, and Nikki calls my bluff.

Charlotte is still winning but has lost one round costing her to lose her tank top. Several times, my eyes wander across to her chest, not that she cares. With the bottle of vodka almost finished, she's determined to win.

Nikki is down to just her underwear, and as much as I detest her, she has an amazing body. Then we are left with Rocky. His stack is gone, and so is his underwear. Sitting on the chair free-balling in all his glory, he's quick to point out the temperature in the room is cold, hence his predicament.

Charlotte grabs my cock then yells, "No, it's not. Lex is as hard as a rock."

With my motor skills compromised, I don't bat her away, wondering why I am hard considering it is cold in the room. Thank fuck I still have my boxers on.

Two bottles of liquor are now finished before Nikki brings out the Sambuca. *Jesus Christ, even I have my limits.* Checking my phone, it's just after midnight, and there's a text from Adriana about stopping off for a late dinner, barely able to read it without squinting my eyes.

"What's wrong, Lex? Got a booty text from your string of skanks?" Nikki chuckles.

"Babe, he got his booty right here." Rocky points to Charlotte, who's attempting to count her stack but keeps stopping at thirteen to start all over again.

She finally catches the conversation, crossing her arms in defiance.

"Yeah, Lex, what... am I your booty on the side? How many booties are you tapping?"

"None at the moment since you won't let me tap yours."

"Oh, *snap!*" Nikki squeaks, covering her mouth in shock.

"Charlie, you're giving the poor guy blue balls. No one wants blue balls, but when you're married, it's—"

Nikki raises her hand, cutting him off. "It's what, Rocky? I fuck you three times a week and blow jobs every other day. What the fuck are you complaining about? Plus, when Flow's in town, I let you fuck me up the ass."

We can't suppress the laughter as we roar in hysterics. This time it takes longer to recover. It isn't even funny, but the damn vodka makes the painting of the trees on the wall hilarious.

"But it's not like every day, you know? I still have to jerk off in between."

"Lex, you don't have regular pussy, so how much do you jerk off?" Nikki questions while attempting to pour shots in all our glasses. She's way off because each glass has spilled over the sides and onto the table.

"I don't know. Before Charlotte it wasn't very often, maybe twice a week. Now like five fucking times a day, and it's still not enough," I say, pouting like it's the saddest thing ever to admit is happening to me.

Rocky is roaring as he bangs his fists on the table. The chips fall over causing Nikki to laugh hysterically, and inadvertently, she spills her Sambuca all over her cards.

"OMG, Lex, that's so sweet of you," Charlotte cries, placing her hand on her heart.

"Fuck, Lex, you're gonna get carpel whatsamajiggy," Nikki slurs, sloshing her glass in the air. "Just marry Charlie already, then you can fuck her twenty-four seven."

"She won't marry me," I deadpan, my expression turning serious. "She's too busy playing the field with Julian."

A small silence falls upon the room, a bit like a tumble-weed rolling by, followed by Nikki and Rocky laughing again.

Charlotte's lips curve upward into a smile as she half-covers her face by holding her cards up. "You've never asked me to marry you. Maybe if you did we could've had nine wonderful years of fucking our brains out. And I'm not playing the field, Julian is my fiancé. You're my friend..."

I can barely string my words together, and I want to say something, but I can't figure out what. I stand, unsteady, and walk as straight as I can to the coffee table, grabbing the keys. Attempting to remove the metal circle loop thing which holds the keys together, I slide it out and walk back to the table.

Kneeling on one knee, in only my boxer shorts, I motion for her to hold out her hand. I slide the ring onto her wedding ring finger.

Charlotte touches the base of her neck, her shoulders loosening as she stares at her hand.

"This weekend you're my wife. You said nothing's off-limits."

We may be overly intoxicated, but there's a mixed emotion coming from her. With a blank stare, I can't figure out whether she's happy or sad. Searching her face for some sort of response, a flush sweeps across her cheeks as her mouth widens into a beautiful smile.

Wrapping her arms around my neck, she places her lips on mine for a brief kiss before mouthing, "I do."

"Are we done with the corny bullshit?" Rocky complains, downing a shot then letting out a loud rasp. "Okay, fuckers, let's play kill, fuck, or marry. Lex, you first."

That's the last thing I remember before it all becomes a blur.

FORTY-FOUR

LEX

I blink my eyes.

It hurts. But why?

I try again.

Fuck, it's the sun causing the pain.

There's a ringing in my ear. I can't figure it out and every muscle hurts when I try.

"Lex... Lex?" The voice is getting closer. The ringing is a voice, and my name is being called. "Lex?"

I open my eyes, barely able to make out that it's my sister. "Adriana?" My voice is hoarse, and when I swallow, my throat burns. Tequila, vodka, strip poker—it's all coming back to me now like a slap between the eyes.

"Yes, it's me. What the hell happened last night?"

I attempt to sit up, only noticing now I crashed on the couch. So much for trying to sneak into Charlotte's room. There's a blanket covering me, my torso exposed, and thankfully, I'm still wearing boxers.

Rubbing my eyes, I open them as wide as I can. "What time is it?"

"Eight. What happened last night?"

"We played poker, drank tequila, and I don't know what else."

"So why are you half-naked?"

"It was strip poker. Rocky's idea." I wince as my head throbs.

Adriana's high-pitched voice isn't helping either.

She laughs before getting up and heading to the kitchen. I can smell some aroma filtering through, and I am hoping Elijah's cooking breakfast. Refusing to waste another minute wallowing in self-pity, I peel myself off the couch and head to my room.

I find some Advil in the bathroom. Thank God because I'm paying for last night's shenanigans. I take the longest shower in the history of mankind, then get dressed in a pair of shorts and a T-shirt.

Back in the kitchen, Adriana pours the strongest coffee I've ever tasted. I welcome it along with a gourmet breakfast Elijah places in front of me. I'm starving.

Ten minutes later, Charlotte drags her hungover ass into the kitchen. She looks like hell. *Gorgeous hell.* She plonks herself on the chair, placing her head down onto her arms. "Don't look at me," she mumbles.

Adriana starts rambling on about the beach while pouring her a coffee. Moments later, Charlotte snaps, threatening Adriana to shut the hell up because her voice is too loud.

It takes over an hour for everyone to be ready for the beach. We're all standing on the porch, towels and gear in tow. Nikki is sporting a massive pair of sunglasses, grumpier than her usual self, and biting everyone's head off for talking.

Rocky is surprisingly normal considering he belittled himself by licking vodka off the table. I have recovered to the best of my ability, and Charlotte, of course, looks like her sexy self again. She's wearing a kaftan, carrying the umbrella and follows the rest of us down to the beach.

We set up all our stuff, and the girls decide to catch some rays. Charlotte pulls her kaftan over her head revealing a skimpy yellow bikini. It looks amazing against her already tanned skin. The fabric barely covers her curvaceous breasts, and the bottoms sit low revealing her tattoo. I can't peel my eyes away from her. She looks like she's just stepped out of a *Sports Illustrated* cover shoot.

The sun is hot, so Rocky decides to take Will in the water. We are running low on drinks, so I offer to get some more and surprisingly, Charlotte offers to come with me.

Back at the house, I know we have ten minutes to spare before someone will come looking for us, so I don't waste any time.

Inside the kitchen she's standing by the fridge with door open while grabbing some water bottles. Her pretty little ass is right there in front of me, and resistance is futile. I lean in, pulling her against me. Without hesitation, I slide my hand down her front and into her bikini bottoms. I begin rubbing my fingers slowly over her pussy, teasing her clit making me so fucking turned on.

Desperately needing to taste her, she lets out a moan, my hands gripping her tight as I spin her around and carry her to the countertop.

Standing in front of her, I use my mouth and tug her bikini top down, exposing her beautiful tits. Her nipples are hard, the desire ravaging within me as I roughly take them in my mouth.

She tugs on my hair, begging me for more. Bending

down, I push her bikini bottoms to the side and plunge my tongue into her drenched pussy. Her moans echo in the room, and with a sense of urgency, she guides me, telling me how she wants to be eaten, exactly how hard she wants me to suck on her clit.

Knowing she's close, I pull away, out of breath.

"Lex..." her breaths are uneven. "Don't stop... please."

I want her like this, begging me for it. I want her to be left in the same agony I felt. When the time is right, I'll make her come, and it will be something she never forgets.

I kiss her shoulder. "Sorry, baby. We've got to get back."

Narrowing her eyes, she mumbles under her breath while fixing her bikini. Stopping mid-foreplay hasn't helped me either. I'm fucking hard and need to blow to release the built-up tension.

My eyes divert to her hand, where the ring I placed on her finger last night sits. I'm thrilled she's still wearing it despite the circumstances of how I placed it on her. It may not have been a real proposal, but it still means something to me.

"Apparently, this is what happens to married couples all the time. Remember you agreed to be my wife for the weekend," I remind her, holding up her hand and kissing her finger.

Charlotte jumps off the countertop, ignoring me as I try to grab her ass one more time.

"Well, honey, if you're my husband for the weekend, watch out because I don't play fair." She grabs the drinks, and I follow her out the door, taking the rest. *Fucking cocktease.*

Back at the beach, we head into the freezing water. Afterward, we lay on our towels drying off and soaking up the sun. As we lay there, we talk about things, life in general. She opens up more about her grandmother and her time at Yale. She tells me stories about people we knew back at home, the ones she still keeps in contact with, mainly Finn.

"So, what, is he still pining after you?"

"He was never pining after me," she says, rolling her eyes. "He married Jennifer. Remember, he was dating her back then? They have four kids. Kasey, Lauren, Jessie, and Milo."

"So, you guys never hooked up after I... you know?"

"No, Lex. We remained incredibly good friends. He even came with Jen to my graduation."

So that explains the photograph I found on Google. I'm relieved. One more question in the big book of Charlotte mysteries answered.

We talk a little more before deciding to head back. It's lunchtime, and we were all famished. Before heading back to the house, Charlotte suggests we take a shower in the outdoor area located on the property. I'm quick to notice it's hidden behind some bushes.

As we stand there under the water washing the sand off us, she leans in to me and places her lips on my mouth, kissing me deeply.

"Since I'm your wife, I guess I should keep up my end of the deal. What was it Nikki said? And blow jobs every other day?"

Hearing her say that she's my wife is enough to send the general out. She places her hands on my chest before sliding them down and into my shorts. Firmly, she wraps her hands around my shaft, stroking it gently all the while kissing my lips. Unable to talk, I groan into her mouth.

She slides down, unbuttoning my shorts. As she squats before me, freeing my cock, I beg for her to take it all in.

With her eyes staring up at me, looking so innocent and pure, I expect her to wrap her mouth around my hard cock. Instead, she latches on, sliding it between her perfect tits. I can barely breathe, cursing under my breath, warning her I can blow any second now.

"You want me to taste you, baby? Is that what you want?"

"Fuck, yes... please," I beg.

She runs the tip of her tongue along the head of my cock. The cold water still falls on us, but for the life of me, I can't feel anything. My skin is burning, and the way she teases me with her tongue is only adding to the fire. I'm close, fucking ready to blow in her mouth when she pulls out, placing my cock in my shorts and standing up with a satisfied smile on her face.

"Charlotte, what the fuck?"

Looking smug, I knew it was coming. "I'm sorry, dear husband of mine. It's time to go have some lunch." She turns off the shower with the biggest smirk playing on her lips. No one leaves me unfinished. As she begins walking away, swaying her hips on purpose, I grab her body, roughly pulling her back to me. Pushing her against the shower wall, I tug her bikini bottom aside, ramming my cock into her. Her groans intensify as I thrust harder.

"It's not nice to leave me hanging," I grit, barely keeping myself together. "If you were my wife, I'd fuck you like this wherever and whenever... in our bed all night long till you begged me to stop."

A few more thrusts, and I pull out. She whimpers, her body collapsing onto mine.

"Lex, nooo. Please... keep fucking me... please."

"I'm sorry, honey. You said it yourself, lunch is ready."

Adjusting her bikini bottoms back in place, I kiss her

shoulder and start walking back to the house. I know I just pissed her off, but she takes it in her stride. She runs to me, jumps on me, and I piggy-back her back to the house. She keeps taunting me and I laugh. She's too cute when she is angry.

We are walking past the pool when she warns me, "Don't you dare, Lex. If I go in, you go in."

I ponder what I should do, but it's too easy to pass up. I jump in the water with her still on my back. She screams, and I accidentally swallow some water from laughing so hard. We swim for a few minutes before Elijah calls out for us.

As we climb out of the pool, I make sure I'm behind her just so I can see her sweet little ass wet in front of me. *She's so fucking sexy in this bikini.*

We sit around the outdoor table as Elijah feeds us. My sister is so lucky to have him, especially because she can't even boil water without burning it. Tonight, we had planned to go to a carnival—typical amusement rides, junk food, and games. Will is excited and wants to go on every ride, begging all of us to join him.

After lunch, we all do our own thing, and when I say we, Nikki asks Charlotte to watch Will, so she and Rocky disappear as do Adriana and Elijah. Those greedy fuckers with their afternoon fucking sessions. What I wouldn't give to be doing that with Charlotte right now. Charlotte, of course, is more than happy to spend some time with Will. We spend the warm afternoon swimming in the pool with Will keen to show off his swimming skills.

"Lex, can you teach me how to dive?" he asks after doing a few laps.

"Sure, buddy." We swim to the edge, and I motion for him to put his hands together and stick his arms out.

Charlotte is sitting on the sideline observing us with this strange look on her face.

He dives in but belly-flops. *Ouch.* He's quick to return to the edge and try again. I love this kid's determination. After the fifth go, he finally gets it causing Charlotte and I both to cheer. I'd never spent any time around kids, but he makes it easy. He's such a laid-back kid, not like those little brats you see in shopping malls.

"Lex, are you Charlie's boyfriend?"

I don't know how to respond to this, and Charlotte simply watches on with amusement. I search my brain for the easiest explanation I can give him, after all, the kid is only seven.

"Uh, not really, buddy. I'm just her friend."

"But you act like Mommy and Daddy. All in love and stuff."

The observation catches me off-guard. Is that how people see us? Well, from my point of view, it's the truth.

"You know what, Will? Sometimes really good friends can love each other, but it's a different type of love," Charlotte intervenes.

"But, Charlie, why don't you marry Lex? Then you can have babies, and I can have someone to play with."

Whoa, kid. *Babies?*

Babies scare me.

So tiny and fragile, and I hear you get no sleep in like forever. Plus, dirty diapers. But then again it will be a tiny piece of Charlotte and me, and there's also the trying to have a baby? That's the fun part, right?

"I'm not sure how to answer that. But look, Will, the sun is going down, and we have a fair to go to. Will you go on the bumper cars with me?"

It's a great distraction and he knows no different.

"Oh, yes! Let's make sure Daddy drives the other car. He can't drive for shit."

"Will," Charlotte and I exclaim in unison.

What do you say to a kid who swears in front of you?

"Sorry." He bows his head, and we try our best to suppress our laughter.

We head back inside and go our separate ways to take showers. I contemplate sneaking into Charlotte's room, but I know she's busy running a bath for Will. Instead, I take a shower by myself and wonder if I should jerk off, but I'd rather blow inside of her.

As we are all dressed for the carnival, I finally get a moment to pull Charlotte aside as the others walk out onto the porch.

"So, why won't you marry me?"

"What?"

"Will asked... why won't you marry me?"

"Lex, he's seven."

"Answer me," I demand in a low voice trying not to cause a scene.

"Well, for starters, we aren't even dating. You've never asked me, and I recall the last time you were married you couldn't stay faithful. What's to say you won't do that to me?"

"I'm not the one seeing two people right now."

"Please don't get into this, Lex."

"So, you don't trust me? Is that it?"

"Lex, it's not just the trust. There are a lot of things."

"Like what? Tell me, Charlotte. How do you expect me to read your mind?"

Will grabs Charlotte's hand saying it's time to go.

The conversation may have been interrupted, but goddammit, I'll find a way to bring this up again. Perhaps later tonight. Maybe I need to get some more alcohol in her to open up to me.

The seven of us walk to the park where the carnival is held. It's your typical rollercoaster, bumper cars, Ferris wheel type of shindig. Charlotte, Adriana, Rocky, Nikki, and Will go on the bumper cars. There's quite a long line, so Elijah and I stand on the sidelines waiting for them to finish.

"So, this weekend is looking promising for you two," Elijah mentions.

"Is it? I can't read her. One minute she hates me, the next minute she wants to be friends. But she's holding back and I don't know why."

"Even though you had your reasons at the time you left her, imagine if the roles were reversed. It's hard to get over the hurt. I'm surprised she has let you get this far. Charlie is one tough woman. Give her time. She needs to make this decision on her own. Don't push her."

"I'm sick of waiting," I utter with frustration. "Plus, I think she's still fucking Julian."

"Honestly, Lex, do you really believe that?"

"I don't know. She hasn't denied it. I need to get rid of him."

"Which you know is wrong because Charlie will hate you for it. Lex, he hasn't done anything wrong. He fell in love with a woman and then in walks her ex. You gotta feel sorry for him."

"Sorry for him?" I let out a ridiculous laugh. "The jerk should know not to mess with me by now."

The rides finish, and the five of them come back laughing, talking about Rocky and his poor driving skills. I didn't hear much of the conversation apart from Rocky whining about a little girl who kept ramming into him which is why he got stuck in the corner for most of the ride.

"Lex, can you play the shooting game with me, please?" Will begs.

"Sure, buddy. Let's go."

We sit down at the stools while the others get food. We gear up to play, and as the buzzer rings, the gun squirts onto the target, and I released my grip every so often so Will can catch up. He wins and happily picks out a large stuffed lion.

"Cha Cha, look... I won!" He jumps up proudly showing off his toy.

"Yay! Did you kick Lex's butt?" She grins, ruffling his hair.

"I sure did."

He runs off to show his parents while Charlotte and I decide to walk around.

"He's such a great kid," I say, watching him as he proudly holds up the lion to Nikki, mimicking his shooting. She hugs him tight before he finds Adriana and does the exact same thing.

"Who? Will? Yeah, I know." Her expression softens as she parts her lips with an adoring smile. "Since the moment I held him for the first time, I knew he was special. There's a reason why he came at that time."

"What do you mean?" I question, confused.

Twisting her neck, she glances in the opposite direction. "I mean, like, you know, a blessing in disguise. Nikki and Rocky weren't ready to be parents, but it worked out. They made it work."

She bows her head, shuffling her feet nervously.

Something is off.

"What's wrong?"

"Nothing."

We're interrupted as Will asks to walk over to this magic show that's about to start. He grabs her hand, and with his other, he grabs mine. He happily chats away, and although the kid can ramble nonstop, I like the thought of having my own son one day.

My phone vibrates in my pocket. Curious to see who's calling me on a Sunday night, I pull it out and check the screen. *Bryce.* Shit! I have missed several of his calls, but something warns me he's trying so desperately to get in touch with me for a reason, so I excuse myself to take the call.

"Mr. Edwards, I've been trying to get a hold of you."

"What's wrong?"

"I managed to get my hands on some personal information regarding Miss Mason."

I move further away from where Charlotte stands, listening to Bryce mention dates.

"She was admitted to a Connecticut private hospital for five days. I'm unable to get any information regarding her illness."

"Okay, so maybe she had appendicitis or something?"

"Mr. Edwards, September 21st was the day Althea Mason passed away."

Her grandmother. So she was admitted to hospital the day her grandmother passed away? Maybe it was the shock of losing a loved one. September 21st is two days away. There's a strong possibility that her moods are up and down due to grieving her grandmother's death anniversary.

"Mr. Edwards, there's one more thing. The reason I was unable to retrieve any further information on her illness was because—" The phone cut out, the crackling sound barreling down the speaker.

"Mr. Edwards, are you there?"

"Yes, Bryce, I didn't get that last part."

"She was in the psych ward."

The words are like dynamite, leaving me stunned and confused. My eyes drift toward where she stands, gazing at her, lost for words.

The psych ward is heavy stuff. I know this back from my medical degree. It's traumatizing, and the grief of losing a loved one can have emotional side effects, but to be placed in the psych ward? I can't get my head around this.

Charlotte is smart. She's headstrong. Something else must have been plaguing her, something else weighing her down for her to break down and be diagnosed that way. My imagination is running wild, but then I think of it logically. Having your boyfriend leave town with a knocked-up wife never to speak to you again, moving across the country to live with someone you barely know and making decisions on which college to attend and what career path to choose, then to have your grandmother pass away suddenly, without any warning. Okay, that's a pretty fucked-up six months she had to endure.

My stare fixates on her face, but something has changed in the few minutes I've been lost in my own thoughts. With a vacant stare, her smile has disappeared. Around her, people are laughing at the magician, but her mouth is set in a hard line, her shoulders slumping while everyone appears relaxed and at ease.

The image looks familiar, and I rack my brain as to why.

Fuck, what the hell is going on here?

Then it clicks.

The photograph of her grandmother and her on the porch swing. How gaunt her face looked, how her eyes had no spark left in them. How she so desperately tried to force a smile for the camera, but it only revealed what was blatantly obvious—she was broken.

I broke her, there's no denying that.

But I have no idea how much.

FORTY-FIVE

CHARLIE

This weekend leaves me questioning everything I believe in, everything I said I wouldn't fall for again.

I know I said nothing's off-limits, but I meant sexually. This other attachment which sort of fell into place I didn't expect that—the hand holding, the tender kissing, stroking of the hair-type gestures, and the constant questions about marriage.

It terrifies me.

I was drunk when he put that ring on my finger, and I was happy to play along with the game, but somewhere in the past few hours it's gone from fantasy to reality.

He asks me if the problem is that I don't trust him. *Do I?* Of course, he can have anyone he wants, and anyone who has a pussy wants him. My insecurities are getting the better of me and I don't like it one bit.

As the magic show plays in the background I stand there dazed, trying to put my thoughts together. My emotions are getting the better of me, and this isn't the place to breakdown. Instead, I put on my best smile and ask

Lex if he wants to go on the Ferris wheel, just him and me. Nothing better than a slow amusement park ride to distract you from asking yourself 'what if.'

We pay for the tickets and jump in the next carriage to arrive. It's a beautiful night with a clear sky. The moon is shining bright, and if you stare long enough, you can catch a glimpse of a shooting star.

There are only a few people riding the wheel, but there's no one in the carriages immediately surrounding us. We sit there silently staring at the view below us, but his stare remains fixated on me.

"Are you okay?"

"I'm fine."

"You know, when a woman says she's fine, she's usually *not* fine," he tells me with a warm smile.

He can't possibly understand the thoughts in my head, so I do the only thing I can to distract him, I run my hand along his thigh stopping in the middle of his legs.

Pulling me close to him, I devour his scent, allowing it to intoxicate my senses. I place my lips on his, kissing him. He returns the kiss until the Ferris wheel stops because more people are getting on. I want more, something dirtier than just kissing on the Ferris wheel.

As if he can read my mind, his hand grazes my thigh, but instead of lifting my dress he slides his hand behind and under my ass. My body shivers in anticipation—the movement of the carriage, the warm breeze, and the loud noises surrounding us—as he moves slowly until he finds what he's looking for. I can see the turmoil in his eyes as he slowly slides a finger inside of me, causing me to gasp when he pushes in deeper. Closing my eyes momentarily, I allow my entire body to feel the rush until his lips brush against my ear.

"Another finger?"

My thoughts are incoherent, and only managing to nod, he slides in another finger. I squeeze my legs tight, adding to the intensity. I want to push the boundaries we never could push before.

"Should I be a nice husband and make you come on the Ferris wheel?"

I turn to look at him, my eyes wild, ready to combust on his fingers. I moan, my breaths deepening, desperate to finish after his incessant teasing all day.

The carriage sways as we sit at the top. I can't even admire the view because it's all a blur. There's no one around us. No one who can see us, anyway.

"Answer me," he demands.

"Yes... please."

I don't care that I'm begging, and my panties are soaked. Just a slight push is all I need as he thrusts his third finger in—the power of his touch barreling through every inch of my body. I'm falling into a beautiful abyss. Struggling to control my body, I buckle in his embrace, bowing my head as I'm consumed by the tingling sensation lingering.

My body starts to gain its composure as I slowly open my eyes. The first thing I notice is his arousal standing up like an eyesore—a beautiful eyesore, mind you.

With a roguish smirk smeared across his face, he demands I open my mouth, forcing me to taste my arousal on his fingers. A spark inside me ignites, and despite my earlier release, I'm back to square one again. *What's he doing to me?*

I attempt to fix my dress, so it isn't obvious I got finger-fucked on the Ferris wheel. If anyone can spot that it will be Nikki. It isn't a surprise when Nikki laughs at me on the way toward the exit, pulling me aside, asking me if I enjoyed my *Mark Wahlberg-Reese Witherspoon* moment. I swear she has some sex radar, it's frightening.

Will begins to get whiny, a sign of his exhaustion. I feel the same after last night's poker game. After Will's sugar rush wore off, he complains about walking home. Lex offers to piggyback him to the house which he gladly accepts. Will went on and on about the magician and how cool it was when the rabbit disappeared. Lex smiles, nodding along with everything Will says.

"I know what you're thinking," I say to Nikki as she watches them.

"Go on then, Charlie. What am I thinking?"

"That I should stop. That he's no good for me."

"I never said that."

"But I know that's what you're thinking."

She remains quiet, her usual judgment expression absent. Nikki has an opinion on everything, and from day one, she disliked Lex and everything about us.

"Charlie... he's not who I thought he was."

"Oh?" Raising my brows, my head jerks back. "Do you care to elaborate?"

Rocky places his arm around Nikki and whispers something into her ear, interrupting us. She giggles, and I refuse to ask what he said. I swore I heard the word strap-on. Again, I didn't want to ask.

Adriana and Elijah make a decision to take a walk along the beach while Nikki and Rocky decide to stay in and watch a movie since Will's gone to bed. Lex asks me if I want to go for a ride on the bike. Of course, I agree. I love to ride, but for once, I'll be the passenger.

We place our helmets on as he starts up the engine. He's beaming from the thrill of it all, racing in and out of the streets. I grip him tight but decide it will be fun to tease him.

As he takes on a straight part of the road, I slide my hands down to the top of his jeans. The moment I do, I'm sure it's no coincidence that I feel the engine roar. Slowly, I slide them into the front of his jeans until his cock is lying firmly in my hands.

I'm obsessed with it.

I want it twenty-four seven—in my mouth, my pussy, my ass, fucking everywhere.

It's incredibly hard, but his skin's so smooth at the same time. I tighten my grip, stroking him.

Driving up through a windy road, we end up at the top of the cliffs in a secluded area. Lex parks the bike, so I pull my hand out of his jeans and jump off, undoing my helmet.

The second I'm able to breathe, he crashes his lips onto mine, thrusting his tongue in my mouth. He never stops even to take a breath, sucking on my bottom lip as I struggle to breathe. The sheer force of it all takes the wind from me, leaving my lips swollen.

"You start it, you finish it," he barks.

He unbuttons his jeans, pushing my head down to his cock. There's no waiting, no more teasing. I take him all in, sucking greedily while he leans against the bike.

My saliva builds up around his cock, making sounds as he arches his back. I take him as deep as I can while he tugs my hair, watching me. His eyes are on fire, his body tense as he struggles to hold on. This time, I'll push him over the edge.

Distancing my mouth, I continue to stroke him. "Should I be a nice wife and make you come here on the bike?"

He groans, nodding his head, unable to form any type

of coherent answer for me. Seconds later, a warm sweet taste hits the back of my throat. I swallow every drop, licking my lips as I finish him off then licking his cock clean.

"Fuck, Charlotte," he grunts, still gripping onto my hair.

I button his jeans, but his hand grips around my wrist. My eyes meet his, and in one glance, I know this is far from over. Lex has the stamina of a wild stallion—he can put porn stars to shame.

"I don't know why you're buttoning my jeans. Get your pussy on this bike and spread your beautiful legs," he demands.

Well, it would be incredibly rude not to follow his instructions. When a gorgeous man like Lex tells you he's going to eat your pussy, you spread your legs faster than the speed of light.

On top of the bike, I sit legs spread, waiting in anticipation. Lex is all about self-gratification, circling his tongue around my clit, taking his fingers and shoving them inside, twisting them, then removing them abruptly to suck on them. Watching him taste me all over his fingers is the icing on the fucking sex cake.

My legs begin to feel like jelly, and I'm barely able to stand. I turn around, so my back is facing him. Leaning my body over the bike, he places his thumb on my asshole rubbing it slightly. With no control, my body begins to cave again. Placing his cock at the entrance, he begins teasing me.

The wait is slowly killing me, and frustrated, I reach around and force him inside me. He grunts as he thrusts, murmuring profanities in my ear. Lex begins to weaken, and my inner self is relishing in this man completely at my mercy.

"Charlotte, I can't take this anymore. You're mine, you understand? It's always been us."

His words resonate with me. I want to be his, but I *need* to be the only woman in his life. I need that promise now more than ever.

I scream his name as my legs start to shake, and every part of me is covered in goosebumps.

One more thrust, deeper and deeper he goes until I come undone. He rides the wave out with me, blowing inside until his body stiffens.

Our bodies slow down, and the slower we go, the more I ache. My muscles tighten, I can barely move. He pulls himself out slowly, kissing my back as he does. Buttoning up his jeans, he leans over and fixes my dress.

Looking into his eyes, something passes between us. No one has fucked me like Lex, and no one has ever made me climax so hard, I swear it's like an out-of-body experience. We are having fun, and I don't want to ruin it by mixing in this emotional bullshit.

As I steady myself, I take in my surroundings. The view is incredible. The ocean is dark, but the sounds of the waves crashing echo through the night.

"Wow, this is amazing. How did you know about this place?"

Lex grins. "Google Maps."

"Oh, I thought this was your go-to-make-out-with-girls place," I tease.

"It is now."

He pulls me into an embrace, kissing me deeply. Afraid, I pull away, unaware if he notices or not.

Lex grabs my hand, walking me toward the edge where we take a seat, admiring the view of the ocean and the lights in the distance. He sits behind me, pulling me in to keep me warm.

"Remember how I promised you on that prom night years ago how we'd watch the sunrise?"

"Yes," I murmur, swallowing the pain caught in my throat.

"Let's do that tonight. Let's stay here and watch the sun rise."

"Lex, I..."

I don't know what to say, not ready for the emotional attachment. He's pushing me, and I don't like to be *pushed*. It frightens me, makes me feel weak, taking me back to that dark place again.

"Charlotte, don't. Just let us have this moment."

I sit there quietly, my mind flashing back to the big fight we had the week before prom.

"Prom, now that was a night to remember..." he trails off.

"I remember our big fight before it, too."

"Charlotte. You know I never slept with Samantha while we were together, right? She told me when she confessed about the baby that I was so wasted that night, she did try, but it was impossible."

"I know."

Samantha and I had come to a truce and sort of became friends not that Lex would ever be happy with that. I know she wouldn't lie about that, but again it boils down to trust. The fact that he stayed married, that he thought he may have slept with her, it was enough to break me, to break us.

"But you still don't trust me?" he huffs, annoyed.

I stare out into the dark night, willing my feelings to come out.

"Lex, my life fell apart when you left. To hear these rumors that she was pregnant, to find out from Adriana that you had left town, and I couldn't contact you. I had no closure. I was left picking up the pieces of what I thought was the greatest love of all time. I felt betrayed. I was the laughing stock of the town, and to have to confront my dad... he literally wanted to hunt you down and kill you." My throat begins to close in, swallowing becoming increasingly hard as my heart rate picks up. "It took me so long to find my grounding, to build my life again, and to be able to trust anyone. It wasn't just you I lost, there was also Adriana. She was my best friend for as long as I can remember. And Finn? You can hate him as much as you want, but he brought me back to life. He made me function as a human being again. Made me laugh for the first time, granted it was a funny situation, but he has always had my back and I love him like a brother. You may not have seen that side of him, but he always takes care of me. My poor grandmother glued me back together as complete as I could be. She taught me about life and moving on to achieve and have the ability to be able to dream and aspire again. I wouldn't be sitting here with you if it weren't for her. As for Julian, for the first time since you left me, he made me realize I could love again."

"So, you still love him?" he interrupts me. Of course, he would.

"He made me smile again. Made me realize that I couldn't go on waiting for a clone of you to walk back into my life. I know you hate him, and I know you want me to end all ties, but Lex, you need to give me time to decide this on my own. Do I trust him? Yes, I do because he hasn't given me any reason not to. But *you* made me lose all trust in *you*, in *us*. You want me, Lex? Then give me time. Don't push me because you might not like the answer."

"And how do you think Mr. Trustworthy will handle knowing you have spent your weekend fucking me?"

"My relationship with Julian is just that, between the two of us. Okay, so yeah, it was my fault for this nothing's off-limits thing, but well..." I search for a reason to justify my impulsive behavior. There's no reason other than the fact that I am a horny little bitch who needs my fix.

"Yeah, I get it. The rabbit broke and you needed cock," he answers, hurt.

"No, Lex, it's not like that. Please don't get me wrong. Oh shit! Let me pull my feet out of my mouth." This is going downhill very fast. "I just need you physically."

"Like I said." He stands, wiping his hands on his jeans.

"Lex, you know it's not like that—"

He cuts me off, handing me the helmet. "Let's head back before sunrise."

"But I thought you wanted to watch it?"

Lex turns to face me, his face void of any loving warmth. His eyes are narrowed, rigid, cold, and hard. In that moment, I know I have hurt him, although it wasn't my intention. I've become the enemy, the woman shredding his heart to pieces.

I have won the game I set out to play.

But revenge isn't gratifying, at all.

Not when I'm about to lose the man I love.

FORTY-SIX

CHARLIE

Nine Years Ago

"Why are you making such a big deal about this? I'm not going to fuck him."

In frustration, I kicked a rock that sat alongside the path next to the back door. Alex stood outside with me, trying to control his temper. It was a Friday afternoon, and Adriana was upstairs trying on her prom dress for Samantha. I didn't know they were coming over together, and boy was I fuming when they did. I mean, it wasn't Samantha's fault she was married to this great guy, and I wouldn't want to let him out of my sight if he were mine.

I had excused myself to grab a drink from the kitchen when really I was going outside to get some fresh air and calm the fuck down. Somehow, he had slipped out and followed me.

"Charlotte, please, the jerk goes around town telling everyone he's going to fuck you on prom night. Like you don't care?"

"I do care, but I'd rather he spread that rumor than the one being spread about a high school girl fucking her best friend's married brother. It's too late now, anyway. I said yes."

"No, it's not too late. Call and tell him you won't go." He motioned for me to take out my phone.

I was just about to tell him where to shove this relationship of ours when Samantha walked outside.

"Is everything okay?" she asked, looking from Alex to me.

"Uh, yeah, Alex just has an attitude with me because I covered for Adriana for prom night. She and Elijah will be staying in a hotel."

Samantha laughed, shaking her head.

"Oh geez, Alex, like you didn't screw around in high school. C'mon, let's go home. You owe me something, remember?" She leaned in and kissed his lips.

I turned away, unable to watch as my heart started to break into a million pieces. It was these moments when the hurt was so deep that it made me question everything about us, about our so-called love. I had a choice. I could break down and cry right in front of them, walk away and act like it didn't bother me, or perform a very sweet act of revenge.

I was eighteen, so, of course, it was revenge. It was always going to be revenge, and it's a dish best served cold.

"Oh, and Alex, don't worry. Adriana will be fine. Carter and I are staying in the room next to hers." I smiled, then with every bit of dignity I could muster, I walked away with my head held high.

Ouch. What the fuck did she think she was doing? Holding it again close to my head, I felt the sting. Damn, did she just burn my scalp? The smell of smoke lingered in the air. I winced as I rubbed the spot where it burned.

"Adriana, you're burning my head," I cried.

"Sorry, Char. It's the bleach in your hair. I'm not a hairdresser, you know. Although I'd be so awesome like in *Steel Magnolias*." She continued using the curling iron, talking to herself in a southern accent.

"Please don't tell me you're comparing yourself to Dolly Parton. She's about a hundred cup sizes ahead of you." Laughing at the comparison, I shook my head which didn't fare too well since the curling iron was still attached.

Damn, karma sure was a bitch tonight.

"Okay, done. Go look."

I stood up and glanced in the mirror. Wow. I had to say even I was amazed. The curls were soft and loosely fell down my back. My hair was naturally wavy, but thanks to the humidity of living by the seaside, it morphed into a ball of frizz every day. I had dyed my hair this week a lighter shade of brown, almost a dark blonde. I was tired of being an ordinary brunette. I don't know what possessed me, but it may have had something to do with the fight Alex and I had last week.

Adriana finished my makeup, not that I wanted much on me. Just a hint of blush, mascara, and some pale pink lipstick to add shine to my dull lips. With all that said and done, I took my dress off the hanger and finally slid it on. It fit perfectly and hugged my body in all the right places.

"Char, you look like a goddess. That shade of green is beautiful on you."

"It's emerald green, actually," I pointed out, happy to find a dress that I loved. It was a beautiful off-the-shoulder design. The satin clung to my body, which I had to thank my lucky stars looked reasonably good considering I hated sports or any form of exercise. It flowed down to the floor with a slight train. Simple, yet classic.

"It reminds me of something, but I can't figure out what. So, anyway, you and Carter, eh?" she teased.

"No. I agreed at the start of the year to go because I needed his notes for geometry, and he agreed to give them to me if I went with him. End of story."

"I don't know what it is about Carter, but he rubs Alex the wrong way."

I quietly sat there trying my best not to show any emotion because I knew why Alex hated Carter. It had been a week, and we hadn't spoken to each other. It didn't stop the fact that I was missing him like crazy and going insane not speaking to him, but I was born a Mason, stubborn as a fucking mule. It was in my blood, and I wasn't giving in. He was being a jerk about Carter, and to top it off, he went home to his wife every night. Nope, I wasn't backing down in this fight.

"You should have seen him this morning at home. When I showed him my dress, he ranted on about how Carter's a jerk and to warn you to watch out, and I'm like 'bro, if she wants to fuck him, then let bygones be bygones.' Seriously, Alex lost it and smashed my mirror."

"What?"

Shocked, I turned around to face her as she nodded her head. I couldn't believe he had done that in front of Adriana. What if she suspected something? I suddenly felt self-conscious and chose my next words very carefully. I couldn't let on.

"He said the jerk keeps talking shit, and he didn't want him to hurt you," she rambled on.

"Well, your brother is one protective guy. He grilled me about you and Elijah, and I'm like 'take a hike, dude.' Seriously, what's his problem, anyway?"

Playing it off, I was hoping she'd believe me. "I don't know, he's always on edge. Something's bugging him, and I think it may have to do with Samantha. I overheard her saying something to my mom, and well, it was kinda gross."

I didn't know if I wanted to know what it was, but curiosity got the better of me. "What could be that gross, Adriana?"

"Oh, some shit about how she wants to try for a baby, but Alex doesn't, and she says he won't even have sex with her. I told you, gross, right?"

I did my best to hide the smile that was dying to burst out of me along with the internal happy dance. My inner self somersaulted across the room.

"You know what?" I laughed, trying to disguise how happy I was to hear he wasn't fucking Samantha. "It's like when you talk about Elijah and shit in front of Alex, and he does the exact same face, it's quite funny watching him cringe. You can so tell you're related."

Adriana finished up and headed back home to get ready. As I sat there staring at myself in the mirror, I wondered how tonight would play out. This wasn't how I envisioned senior prom, going with some jerk when the man I was so desperately in love with sat at home with his wife. Several times, I wanted to back out of it, but I was so frightened someone would catch on. No, I needed to go tonight and act as if there was no Alex, pretend I was an ordinary girl participating in the normal rituals of being a teenager.

I walked down the stairs slowly and found my dad sitting at the dining table with Debbie, his girlfriend, although he loathed that word. He turned to look at me and did a double-take.

"Wow, Charlie. You look beautiful," he said, followed by a scowl. Debbie slightly smacked his arm as he pretended to smile. "So, this Carter kid... I've heard rumors about him."

"That he has a small penis?" I joked.

Debbie laughed out loud, much to Dad's disappointment.

"Dear God, no! But shame for the boy. I heard he has quite the reputation."

"Please, Dad, this was strictly a business deal. He helped me out with geometry, and I agreed to go to prom. Don't worry, I'm not the slightest bit interested in him. Plus, Finn will be there."

"What about that Edwards kid?"

I froze, not expecting him to bring up Alex.

Why the fuck would he bring up Alex? I panicked, trying to find my words.

"Who, Adriana?" I answered, playing dumb.

Debbie made a slight snicker and bowed her head to hide the smirk that formed on her face. *Fuck!* She must've known.

"No, her brother. The other Edwards kid."

"Why would Alex be at prom? He's twenty-five, not a senior."

"I thought he might be chaperoning Adriana."

I snorted, amused by the image. "Yeah, Adriana would die attending prom with her brother. Besides, she has a boyfriend, Elijah."

"Oh yeah, the Morrison kid. Good. Never liked that Edwards boy."

"Why on earth would you not like Alex, Dad? You don't even know him," I said defensively.

"Well, Alex, as you refer to him, was quite a trouble-maker back in the day when he went to Carmel High. Got into all sorts of trouble."

"How do you know that? And what trouble?" I asked.

Alex never came across as a law-breaker type, but then again, he also didn't seem like the I'll-have-an-affair-with-my-sister's-best-friend type either.

"Oh, you know, the usual... reckless behavior, drugs, and alcohol. Your sister used to talk about him all the time to your mother..." he trailed off.

"Drugs?" I repeated, surprised how raised my voice was.

"Geez, Charlie, would you keep it down? Yes, caught smoking marijuana at a local party."

My sister spoke about Alex? I didn't remember any of these conversations, but this was years ago and most likely I also didn't give a fuck, but talking to Mom? I wanted nothing more than to call my sister and ask her about him, but then I remembered she was traveling in a remote part of Africa, so there went that idea.

"Honey, I think Carter is here," Debbie said as the door-bell rang.

Thank God for the interruption. Alex smoking pot wasn't something I really cared about, unless he was still doing it, which would be hypocritical since he was an intern at the local hospital.

Making my way to the front door, I pulled it open to be greeted by an enthusiastic Carter eyeing me up and down. Gross.

"Charliiieee..." He whistled.

My dad cleared his throat, and immediately Carter

regained his posture and extended his hand for Dad to shake. He put on his fake smile, not that it went unnoticed by my dad. "So, anyway, I was thinking of driving you guys to the prom."

"Seriously, Dad?" I groaned.

Like I'd fucking let Carter feel me up in the car.

"That's fine with me, Mr. Mason," Carter agreed.

What a fucking douche.

Dad kissed Debbie goodbye and headed to the car. Just what I had always dreamed about, rolling up to my senior prom in a pickup truck. The drive was in an awkward silence, the arrival even worse. Kids were pulling up in fancy cars, limos, the works. To add insult to injury, Dad spoke to Principal Sinclair to double-check there was no alcohol on the premises. After their combined search came up empty, he decided to leave, but he couldn't resist warning Carter where his hands should remain for the rest of the night.

The gymnasium was immaculately decorated. Adriana was part of the decorating committee. Actually, head of the committee as she referred to herself. The theme was 'A Night in Paris.' The room was strung with fairy lights that sat amongst the artificial trees creating a warm glow. Street signs scattered the room replicating famous Parisian streets. Parisian paintings covered the walls—the attention to detail was astonishing. The most impressive part was the Eiffel Tower. It looked amazing, drawn to perfection. Spotlights were positioned in front of it highlighting its beauty. They did such an amazing job, and for a moment, you could easily forget you were in the gym, not roaming the streets of Paris, the most romantic city on earth.

I sighed as I watched couples entering the hall, carefree, enjoying themselves and probably here with someone they actually liked, while here I stood wishing I had my prom date, my Prince Charming to dance and be silly with, to create memories that would last a lifetime. That's what prom was, right? But instead, I was here alone, not even on good terms with Alex after our huge fight. I was determined to have a good night. One day I'd look back on this night when I'm old and senile in a nursing home and want to smile about it because it was a night to remember. How I'd make it a night to remember was beyond me.

I was minding my own business and enjoying the fashion parade surrounding me until Kaley, the school whore, decided to grace me with her presence. She stood before me dressed in a pale pink ruffle strapless gown. Her boobs barely covered as they popped out and greeted me hello. Her makeup was overkill, but at least her hair looked decent. Yeah, decent for a five-year-old practicing on her Barbie doll.

"So, Charlie, where's the love of your life tonight?"

"I really hope you aren't referring to Carter because I heard you claimed him in the restroom at the truck stop on the interstate," I sneered.

"Funny, Charlie. No, I'm referring to Alex Edwards."

Oh God, why would she think that?

"Um, loser... Alex is Adriana's brother and a good friend. Don't go spreading shit around town. I'm sure your mouth has better use like giving that Ukrainian exchange student a blow job in the janitor's closet."

"You're a bitch, Charlie." Storming off, she walked back to her friends only to trip on her dress. Maybe this wouldn't be such a bad night after all.

I looked at the clock on the wall. It was a little after seven. Where the hell was Adriana? She should have been here an hour ago. I started to worry, but being a typical girl, my damn phone wouldn't fit in my purse, so there was no way I could even call her. Impatiently, I decided to have some punch while chatting with Finn, Jen, and a few of the girls in my class, including Heather, a new student.

Logan and Jen decided to hit the dance floor as Bobby Brown blared through the speakers.

"Oh my God, he's so fucking hot. I can't believe she brought him. Oh my, Charlie, seriously, look at him," Heather gasped.

The other girls in the group were also fluffing their feathers. Who the fuck were they going on about? I turned around and was met by those hypnotic emerald eyes, the ones belonging to *my Alex*. His eyes were already on me, and I had no doubt that I looked just like these girls—jaw-dropping with drool dribbling out of my mouth. He looked like a fucking male model sent from a *GQ* magazine in this flashy-looking black suit and white, collared shirt slightly buttoned. His hair looked different, a little shorter and actually styled with a freshly shaven face.

I couldn't ignore the smile which radiated from his face as soon as his eyes locked with mine. I tried not to smile back only because I didn't want anyone to notice, which only confused him, as the smile faded followed by him whispering into Adriana's ear. Adriana, of course, looked stunning in her short ballerina-style dress matched with an extremely high pair of heels. Her face looked somber, and unfortunately, I had to ask her what happened to Elijah, which meant I needed to be physically near Alex. Restraint had to hold my hand right now because I couldn't go it alone.

"Hey, Char. Sorry I'm so late."

"Um... never mind that. Where's Elijah, and why are you here?"

"Thanks, Charlotte, nice welcome," Alex answered, sarcastically.

"I didn't mean it like that... I uh... was just surprised to see you here since you aren't a senior." I stumbled on my words trying to compose myself as all the girls kept gawking.

From the corner of my eye, I could see Kaley with her big fat you're-in-love-with-him-and- I'm-going-to-spill-it-to-everyone face.

"Elijah came down with that bug that's been going around. He puked up twice before getting in the limo. He looked awful, and he didn't want me to miss out, so he suggested I take Alex."

"Well, you could have gone dateless," I blurted out.

"Wow, Charlotte, anyone would think you didn't want me here," Alex deadpanned, his face annoyed by my hostility to his presence.

Shit! This was all playing out wrong.

"I didn't mean it like that—"

"What the hell's wrong with you two? Oh, that's right, Samantha told me about your big blow-up over covering for me. Well, big bro, since my man is incapacitated, you guys can kiss and make up now. No harm, no foul. Oh my God, someone knocked that street sign over!" Within a flash, she had disappeared, so I stood there, uncomfortable with her suggestion to kiss and make up. If only she fucking knew.

"So now you want to tell me why you so desperately don't want me here?"

"Look, Alex, I just wasn't expecting you."

"No shit. And it's a problem because?"

"Because after a week of you not speaking to me, I'm afraid that people will catch on to the fact that we have some beef with each other. And that beef can be misinterpreted as a lovers' quarrel."

"Well, I didn't see you pick up the phone to text or even email me."

"Maybe because the last conversation we had, you had your wife all over you reminding you of the fantastic sex you were going to have that night!"

Okay, so that was over-the-top melodramatic Charlie at her finest. It didn't erase the hurt I felt that lingered a week later. His silence felt like an admission of what I said. I felt a stab in the heart, a punch in the gut. What did I honestly expect?

"Charlotte, please." He extended his arm to touch me but retracted it almost immediately, aware of the watchful eyes that preyed on gossip. "Samantha was being ridiculous."

"Probably, but for all I know, you welcomed the ridiculousness with your pants down."

"Charlotte, I told you I haven't touched her since we started, nor will I for as long as we're together."

"What does that even mean, for as long as we are together? How long do you expect us to keep up this charade without getting caught?"

I knew there were too many questions in that one sentence, but now they were the burning questions, the ones I had avoided with a passion. The ones I knew had no answer that would erase the ache in my heart. His silence was enough to aggravate me. Thankfully, we were interrupted by Finn and Jen because I was ready to have it out there and then.

"Charlie, you gotta dance. It's prom!"

I laughed at my best friend. "Jen, have you spiked Finn's drink?"

"You know how crazy he is when it comes to music. Sorry, as his best friend, I think you'll have to take over soon. My feet are killing me."

Jen was wearing killer heels, and I didn't blame her. I'd only been standing around, and even my feet hurt. This was why Converse were made, and heels were for the Posh Spice *wannabees* of the world.

"Edwards, what are you doing here?" Finn asked while placing his arm around Jen.

"Long story. I'm sure Adriana will be more than happy to retell the story of Elijah's sick ways," Alex answered lightheartedly.

I had to admit it was kind of nice to see them getting along, but that wouldn't last. Finn would beat the living daylights out of him if he knew something was going on between us.

The silence became awkward even amid the loud music. If I thought that was uncomfortable, I hadn't mentally prepared myself for the shitstorm that was Carter walking my way. His arrogant smirk was enough to make you want to hurl, and on top of that, he had to be the biggest jerk in the world by putting his arm around me in front of Alex like he was trying to stake his claim. I gave him my no-fucking-chance-in-hell glare but, of course, he just laughed it off as usual.

"Wow, Charlie, could you surround yourself with any more losers?"

"Seriously, Carter, grow up."

"What? Edwards and Rodriguez can't speak up for themselves?"

By this point, both Alex and Finn were glaring at Carter. The fuckwit was going to get beaten any second now, and although I'd be more than happy to watch him take one, my dad's voice rang in my head. I couldn't afford to be grounded again. Alex was barely keeping it together.

I made a mental note—*he doesn't like anyone else touching me.*

Okay, yeah, so making him jealous was kind of fun because there was no way he could even let on right now.

"Back off, Reed, or it'll be my fist surrounding you," Finn threatened.

"Fuck you, Rodriguez. Welfare bums like you aren't welcome here. Neither are medical dropouts requiring Daddy's help." Carter snickered as he walked off.

"Charlie, why the fuck did you agree to go with him?" Finn hissed as Jen placed her hand on his chest to calm him down.

"Because I was in shit with my dad for skipping school and missing geometry, and I needed his notes. He may be the biggest douche, but he aces geometry."

"Next time I'll lend you mine," Finn offered.

"Did you not hear my story? He *aces* geometry. I don't need help in flunking, I was managing that just fine by myself." I rolled my eyes, and Finn waved me off before swaying his body to the beat of the Jay-Z song that came on.

Again, I was left alone with Alex.

"You're awfully quiet," I mumbled.

"You're stunningly beautiful tonight, and I have to stand here and pretend you mean nothing to me and allow that lowlife to put his hands on you."

"Alex, I'm sorry."

I ached to touch him, but there was no way.

"No, I'm sorry for not trusting you with that jerk-off. Anyway, from what I've heard, his dick is so tiny he couldn't even get Kaley off."

I laughed so loud. It was true, and there was nothing I

loved more than seeing Alex smile, even if it was about Carter's tiny dick. "That's the rumor. Even my dad has heard it."

"Wow, even Mr. Mason is in the know."

"Sadly, yes. I didn't mean to be so cold back there, but people are catching on. I don't know why but Kaley made a snipe, and I told her she was an idiot, but she's obviously got the impression somehow. I don't know where this is going or what will happen in the future, but I know that right now, we can't be caught."

"We won't, Charlotte. But tonight, I need to get my hands on you somehow, just leave the brainstorming to me." He winked.

It wasn't long before Adriana returned. We danced to a few songs and enjoyed the typical prom fest. An hour or so later, the ceremonies began. In true Carmel High fashion, Carter was named prom king, and Kaley was named prom queen. Of course, she gloated, waving like the fucking diva she was. We all clapped giving her the moment she wanted. I didn't really care because I had no feelings for Carter. They danced the traditional prom king and queen dance. It was all one big hilarious show. It couldn't have been any more stereotypical. They only lasted a few minutes before Kaley stormed off annoyed with something Carter had said.

Walking over to me only moments later, I shuddered at the request I knew was coming.

"Dance with my date?" He held out his hand.

My eyes pleaded with Alex for him to understand why I agreed. Almost like he understood instantly, he stood there with a satisfied smile on his face.

"One dance," I warned him.

We danced for a bit before I started hearing gurgling sounds. I wasn't hungry. I had become BFFs with the waiter who served the mini corn dogs. *Strange*, I thought. Again, I heard the sound. It was quite loud. Carter had this uncomfortable look on his face. I turned to look at him but was distracted by Kaley's interruption.

"You're such a slut trying to have Carter and Alex. Why don't you go fuck them? Hey, have a threesome," she shouted.

The gurgling sound erupted, but this time it was louder. Both Carter and Kaley stood in front of me. Carter immediately excused himself as I watched him run across the gymnasium with his legs squeezed together. *Oh!* I couldn't help but laugh. He must've caught Elijah's bug or something. Totally gross.

"Seriously, Kaley, get a life. I'm not the one flashing my flaps like a winning lottery ticket all over town."

"No, just to Alex?" she asked mockingly.

"What exactly is your fucking problem with him?"

"I have no problem with him, and clearly, you don't either. Otherwise, the two of you wouldn't have been seen fucking on the hood of his car," she sneered.

Oh, holy fuck, so someone had seen.

With my heart pumping loudly in my chest, denial would be my best friend for now. "Yeah, nice try, Kaley. I warned you, don't go making shit up about my friends."

We were both standing there folding our arms in a face-off. Adriana, Alex, Finn, Jen, and a few other guys came over to stop what I thought was just about to happen.

Kaley pushed me back.

So, the little bitch wanted to fight.

I was just about to return the favor when I heard that sound again.

"What the fuck is that?" I asked, looking at Kaley.

Her face contorted as the sound intensified. She

hugged her stomach attempting to run off, but her heel was caught on my dress trailing on the floor. She tugged on my dress with force, attempting to untangle the fabric from her heel.

"Ow, Kaley. Stop fucking moving, you're stuck on my dress!"

"Charlie, let go of me," she screamed.

"Oh my God, Kaley, let me fucking get your heel off."

It was too late.

She covered her face, and the gurgling stopped.

There was a massive eruption of laughter around me, and it was only moments later I realized what had happened. The corners of my lips curled. I fought hard as my cheeks swelled momentarily with the pressure, but it was no use. My laughter erupted, echoing through the crowd as I bent over, slapping my knee repeatedly. "Did you just shart yourself?"

"*Shut up!* Shut the fuck up, you stupid bitch!"

Alex leaned down, unable to contain his laughter as he undid the heel from my dress. A mortified Kaley lifted her dress attempting to cover the brown spot that had formed against the pale pink fabric. The group of us fell to the floor in hysterics.

"Is everything okay?" Principal Sinclair asked.

"Yes, sir," we all said in unison.

We leaned on each other to stand up.

This was a night to remember, all right.

"Char, that was hilarious! I've no idea why she's making up stuff about you and Alex, though?" Adriana asked, looking confused as she attempted to catch her breath.

"Please, like I'd touch this jerk with a ten-foot pole." I chuckled, punching Alex in the arm.

I was worried he'd take offense, but he caught on quickly to the game we were playing.

"Nice, Char," he teased, mimicking Adriana's nickname for me.

"Oh my God, you guys!"

Our heads turned to where Adriana was looking. Standing there at the entrance of the gymnasium was Elijah in his crisp baby blue suit with a black shirt buttoned down. He looked like he belonged in the 1960s, but he rocked that suit. It was a modern take, and no one could have pulled that off except Elijah Morrison.

"Babycakes," Adriana screamed, pulling Elijah into an embrace. She chatted animatedly to Elijah explaining every detail of the night so far. Their long reunion gave Alex a moment to whisper something into my ear.

"Now," were the only words he spoke.

I followed him to the punch table conveniently located next to a hidden exit. Slipping our way through unnoticed, he pulled my hand, and we ended up in a corridor not far from my biology class. "Is this your biology classroom?"

"Yes," I answered, unsure of where he was going with this.

He pulled me to the door and turned the handle. It was unlocked. The room was dark, except for a slight hint of the moon. "Which one is your desk?"

"The one at the back by the window," I responded, still baffled.

He led me to the desk and cupped my face, kissing me hard, our tongues in a frenzy after being apart for a week. I missed him. God, I fucking missed everything about him.

"Charlotte, you look so beautiful tonight, but I need to do filthy things to you right now on your desk."

His lips brushed along my neckline, arousing every inch

of me. Running my tongue along his jaw inhaling his scent as I went then closed my eyes losing myself in this moment. He lifted and placed me on my desk. Spreading my legs wide open, he stood between them, then tilting his head slightly he placed his mouth on my chest, lavishing it with kisses. Hungrily, he unzipped me, exposing my bra that formed no barrier as he pushed it up baring my breasts. Taking each nipple into his mouth, I groaned. This only added to the intensity as he sucked them harder. I arched my back, begging him to enter me.

"You want me to slide my cock in right now?"

I nodded, unable to speak.

"No, Charlotte. You've made my life a living hell this past week. You sent my mind on the wildest goose chase possible, imagining the worst between you and Carter," he continued, taking my nipple in his mouth harder.

I wanted more—his anger was only adding to the pleasure. Sliding my leg up and exposing my ass, he grabbed it tight. Leaning forward, he opened my drawer fumbling for something.

What would he need from my desk?

A ruler.

Exposing my ass, he gently slapped the ruler against my skin while he tugged on my nipples with his teeth. I arched my back, the balance between pleasure and pain overwhelming me. Holy shit, this was so fucking hot. He was spanking me for being naughty. I secretly got off on shit like this.

"Don't ever do that to me again, you understand? You're mine, and I'll not share you with anyone."

I felt the slap of the ruler again, slightly harder this time but even more pleasurable. It may have been dark, but it was impossible not to notice the fire raging in his eyes. This

Alex was different, he was possessive, wild, and dirty, and I fucking loved it.

"Harder," I moaned.

The sound echoed through the room, and I pulled his mouth onto mine to muffle the groan that I let out. He pulled his cock out with no time to waste and slid it inside me. I ached for him, every part of me ready to explode into a blissful orgasm.

"Now, every time you sit here, I want you to remember us and how we are right now. How I'm fucking you. How I am making you feel. How no one else has ever made you feel this way or will ever have the chance to make you feel this way. Nobody touches you but me. Only me..." he faded into a whisper.

I pulled him into me and bit on his shoulder while I rode it out. His body soon followed me as he shuddered, releasing his cum inside me. Our sweaty bodies held onto each other, unable to comprehend what had just happened here, on my desk, in my biology classroom.

I straightened up my dress and attempted to fix my hair as best I could. Alex zipped up his pants before leaning in, this time kissing me softly.

"No podemos estar separados, Charlotte, nunca. We cannot be apart, Charlotte, ever."

There was clear desperation in his voice, pleading with me to feel what he felt. There was no doubt in my mind I felt exactly as he did. I understood, but I didn't understand how it could ever be just him and me one day. I nodded before telling him I loved him. The moment was so overwhelming.

"Charlotte. This dress... your beauty... I can't believe you're mine." His eyes never left me, the emerald green matching the shade of my dress.

"It's my favorite color," I added, still holding his gaze.

"Why, baby?" he asked, nibbling on my collarbone, distracting me from the question.

"It's your eyes, Alex. They do something to me. I can't explain. It's almost like they've cast a spell on me. You must know that since you use them to lure me in anytime we're within a foot of each other."

He lifted his head to face me once again, his face serious. He looked like something was plaguing him, like something he needed to say was on the tip of his tongue, but he didn't say a word until minutes later.

"You're blonde," he said, running his fingers through my hair. "I like you as a brunette."

"Thought I'd change it up a little. Why? Scared you won't be able tell Samantha and me apart?"

Oh, my big fat fucking diarrhea mouth.

His cold stare made me nervous. It didn't last long before his face softened. "I love you, baby, so fucking much I can no longer think straight. I can't live this shitty double life anymore."

He lifted my dress and took me one more time on my desk. This time slower, more agonizing, but it was there staring us both in the face—the love we had for each other. I wanted to ask what that meant, but he was inside me and this wasn't a question and answer time. No, it was time to enjoy my man for a moment, enjoy his touch, and the weight of his body on mine.

Fifteen minutes later, we made our way out separately to the gymnasium. It was nearing the end of the night, and Kaley and Carter were nowhere to be seen. *Thank fuck.* The lights dimmed further for the final song of the night. I stood there dateless as Adriana came to me, dragging Alex with her.

"Okay, can you guys get along enough just to dance one song? Char, you'll never forgive yourself for not having that final dance, even if it's not with your Prince Charming."

How ironic, I thought.

She quickly darted off into the arms of Elijah, who thankfully was at the opposite side of the room.

"Sister's orders." He smirked.

I reached for his hand as he pulled me in, trying his best not to smother me or allow our bodies to touch. The music played allowing me to think too much—about tonight, about us, about our future.

"Are you okay? You're kinda limping," he teased.

"Nice one. At least you don't have cum dripping down your leg."

"If I did, I'd want you on your knees licking it all up."

Oh fuck, now it was worse. Why did this feeling not ease? We'd fucked twice already.

"Thanks. I think I just squirted more out after that comment."

"Wow! You sure know how to make a prom dance romantic."

I grinned and kept my mouth shut. It was time to enjoy the moment. This was the end of an era, time to move on and live life as a woman.

To new beginnings, I thought.

I watched the lights flickering against the Eiffel Tower, my mind lost in the lyrics that consumed me. There couldn't have been a better moment to bring up the question that burned within me, the one question that would make or break us.

"Alex—"

"Shh... one day, my Charlotte, we'll be in Paris dancing with everyone watching. I promise you, one day it will be our turn. I meant what I said in that room... we can't be apart, Charlotte. Never."

And so, in that moment, he promised me a life together, promised me the world.

I closed my eyes, imagining it was now, that people around us meant nothing, and we were free, free to show the world how much we loved each other and that nothing could tear us apart.

FORTY-SEVEN
CHARLIE

Present

The ride back seems fast.

I checked the speedometer a few times, and he was way over the legal limit. When we got back to the property, it's more than obvious Lex has an attitude with me. He told me he's tired and headed to bed. I didn't dare follow him. Instead, I sat on the porch knowing that I'm well and truly in the wrong. Yes, I am still hurt, but I have no right to trample all over his obviously hurt feelings even though I had no idea guys could be offended like that.

Somehow, I have to make this right, but the weight of tonight's events feels enormous. I drag my sorry ass to bed and fall asleep just before sunrise.

I feel my body moving like I'm lying on a trampoline. What the hell is this dream about? It happens again, but this time I open my eyes. There's jumping, and it's waking me up from my deep slumber. I'm just about to yell when it dawns on me that it's Will. No, it's Rocky.

"Rocky, what the fuck?" I groan.

He's standing on my bed jumping like a fucking four-year-old, except he is making moaning sounds and screaming my name.

"Rocky Romano, get the fuck off my bed!"

I'm beyond exhausted, but he continues jumping until I get up, pushing him off the bed.

"Are you kidding me? Plus, I don't sound like that... moron."

He stands up laughing as he walks out of the room scratching his ass.

I decide to have a quick shower to wake myself up, but a quick shower turns into a much longer one as I may have accidentally fallen asleep in there sitting on the floor. I finally get dressed and head to the kitchen.

The house is quiet, and I wonder what everyone is up to.

"Morning, Elijah. Where is everyone? Apart from gorilla over here," I chastise, pointing to Rocky who's doing the maze on the back of the cereal box. He lets out a big, "No," when he realizes it's a dead-end. Seriously, even Will could have done that with his eyes closed.

"Adriana and Nikki went to the markets, and Lex and Will are playing on the beach."

I quickly eat a piece of toast and head out to the beach. A few minutes later, I stand there by the bushes watching Lex play football with Will. He looks so content teaching Will how to kick, the laughter coming off them when Will tackles Lex. At that moment, my heart breaks a little.

Is this all my fault?

Yes, Lex left me, but I made it nearly impossible for him to find me again.

He did what was expected of him back then, and I

acted like a spoiled teen annoyed that he chose someone else.

He's different now, he truly is a man.

A wonderful man.

He has given me no reason at all not to trust him. So why do I still have this nagging feeling inside? Lex catches sight of me as I walk down to where they are playing.

"Hi, Cha Cha! Lex taught me how to tackle."

"I can see. If you go pro, you will make your daddy a very happy man."

He runs off to where the towels are to grab a drink. It gives us a moment together in which I have no idea what to say. I probably should start by saying sorry since I'm in the wrong.

"Lex, about last night—"

"Nothing left to be said, Charlie. You made your feelings perfectly clear. I'm giving you space and time. I'm not pushing you anymore."

"You called me Charlie..."

"That's what everyone else calls you. I'm like everybody else, just a friend," he answers in an uninviting tone.

The words hurt.

No, he isn't pushing me, but why all of a sudden do I want to be pushed?

Why do I want him to tell me I'm his and only his?

And most importantly, why do I crave for him to call me *Charlotte.*

Lex Edwards will never be like everyone else.

Will interrupts us asking to go into the water. I agree, stripping off my clothes wearing only a white ruffled bikini. I catch Lex looking me up and down, admitting it feels nice that he can't completely ignore me.

We jump into the waves. Will is having the time of his

life. Lex piggybacks him, taking him a little further out, which makes me slightly nervous, but there are lifeguards about, so I stop worrying about it. An hour later we decide to head back for lunch. I'm seriously exhausted. I can't shake this tired feeling and know I'll have to sneak in a 'nana nap' sometime today.

Back at the house we jump into the pool while Elijah grills some burgers. Rocky's having swimming races with Will. Nikki and Adriana came back from the markets showing off their new sun hats. I swear it's a hilarious sight, especially because the hats are bigger than the planet Jupiter.

Lex has left, to where I'm not sure.

After lunch, I feel extremely drowsy, so I decide to head to my room to take a nap. I doze off almost instantly only to be awaken by Nikki. It's a little after four when she wakes me.

"Charlie, are you feeling okay?"

I mumble something then open my eyes. "Yeah, just barely any sleep the past two nights."

"Plus, I think you may have sunstroke." She scowls, pulling my tank top aside.

Amid this morning's mayhem, I forgot to put sunblock on. I groan at the sight of the redness. Hopefully, with an overdose of aloe vera I'll tan over.

"Is Lex back yet, from wherever he went?"

"Yes, he is. He's in his room," she tells me before walking out.

I grab the aloe vera and walk over to his room. Knocking on his door, he answers to come in. I open the door gently and find him sitting up in bed with his laptop.

"You have a minute?" I ask with hesitation in my voice.

He closes his laptop, placing it on the nightstand. This

distance thing is as wide as the Grand Canyon, and it's driving me crazy, but I can't jump him, not after he thinks I'm just using him for sex.

"Working while on vacation?"

"Yes, sadly there are certain matters that need to be taken care of." He sounds cold, not the loveable, playful Lex from yesterday.

It pains me that I've caused this. He has climbed back into that cold, lonely shell Adriana said he was living in for years before I came back.

"I need a favor," I ask, trying to lighten the mood. "As you can see my back is burned to a crisp. The girls are out, and well... I don't want to ask Rocky with his lady hands to help me. Would you mind?"

I hold out the bottle, watching him wrestle with the decision, but eventually, he takes the bottle and pats for me to sit down in front of him. I take a seat, removing my tank top revealing just my bikini top. My skin burns like it's on fire, and as soon as the cream touches me, I yelp at the coolness.

Closing my eyes, I focus on his touch. "Lex..." I turn around to face him.

He places the lid on the bottle and gazes into my eyes, distant, and I fucking hate myself for making him feel like this.

"Please listen to me. I'm sorry. I shouldn't have said those things. I don't even mean half of it. I..." I scramble my words, unable to relay what I need to say. "I'm trying so hard here, Lex. Yes, I want you physically, but there's so much more. You aren't just someone I picked up off the street and fucked, so no, I don't only want you for that. I'm sorry that I made you feel that way. I just need—"

"Time, I get it."

He jumps off the bed and announces he's going to help Elijah in the kitchen.

"Rocky, where on earth do you find these jokes?" Adriana cringes while asking the question.

We are sitting on the beach with a bonfire, and Rocky as usual, is making us all laugh with his crude jokes. Thank God, Will chose to stay at a friend's house next door because Rocky holds nothing back. Zero filter when it comes to that man.

"I don't know... somewhere online."

"Oh, that's right. The one you put on there the other day was so gross."

"You liked the status," he roars, calling Adriana out.

We all laugh, but I can't help but notice how quiet Lex is.

"Dude, are you on Facebook?" Rocky turns to Lex.

"No, I don't really have time for that stuff."

"But what about all the hotties in high school? Ya gotta give Charlie a run for her money."

I sit here silently waiting for him to respond to Rocky's question. I'd be surprised if no one else notices the tension between us.

"The girls in my high school were nothing special. The ones in college, no better," he mumbles.

"Then why did you marry Samantha?" I blurt out.

His stare shifts toward me, smoldering with resentment. This isn't the discussion to be having at the bonfire in front of everyone, but I never knew the whole story and now I want to know.

He drops his eyes to the group. "I thought I loved her."

"How long were you guys married?" Nikki questions, her sudden calm demeanor toward him catching me by surprise.

"Married for a year and a half. Together for three years."

"How did you propose?"

I turn to face Nikki, shooting her daggers for the intrusive questions despite my curiosity piquing. Staring blankly at the fire, Lex remains silent. He isn't the type of person to open up about his feelings, so I expect him to tell her to mind her own business.

"She loved animals. She wanted to study to be a veterinarian, but her father disagreed, so he made her study business. A friend of mine knew the owner of the San Diego Zoo. We planned a weekend away, and I organized a private viewing. Her favorite animal was the sloth. We went to the area where they were located, and she was in awe with a baby sloth. It was friendly, and the zookeeper allowed her to hold it. She was happy, but asked why the sloth had to wear a collar if it was in a monitored habitat. She undid the collar, and low and behold, the ring box was attached. I got down on my knee, and the rest is history."

"Dude, that's one rockin' proposal," Rocky cheers.

"Yes, only marginally better than proposing when your girlfriend is riding you in the back of your truck?" Nikki chastises.

"Well, you said yes. Can't have been all that bad." Rocky winks.

It was a beautiful story even though my heart sinks right to the bottom of the ocean as he tells it. Unable to handle my emotions and where they are heading, I excuse myself and walk back to the house.

I find my keys, license, and jacket, then I walk to the

front of the house where my bike is parked. The helmets sit on the handlebars, so I grab one, placing the other on the porch and walk back to my bike, jumping on.

The sound of the engine roaring is enough to soothe me. As I adjust my helmet, arms wrap around me. Without turning around, my heart sinks deeper knowing it's him.

In my rear-view mirror, he has already placed the spare helmet on. With his arms wrapped tight around me, I drive off, choosing another beach to visit and not last night's location.

The speed is ticking over, my anger spiking as the speed is well above the legal limit. Taking a sharp turn, I pull into the beach and stop the bike, abruptly jumping off and ferociously removing my helmet.

"Why the fuck did you get on the bike?" I shout at him.

"Charlotte, please. I'm—"

"No, Lex," I interrupt, pointing my finger at him. "I'm done! I'm so tired. I can't play this game anymore. It's too tiring. Things with Jul..." I trail off not wanting to go there.

"What are you going to say about Julian? Is that what it's come down to now? You can't handle us, so you pick Julian?"

"Lex, we're too complicated."

"And so because it isn't with him, you think that's love?"

"I never said that."

"Well, Charlotte... I. Fucking. Love. You," he yells, raising his hands into the air. "I've always loved you. You know, you have hurt me, too, and here I am trying to fight for us even though you keep pushing me away. You tell me it's between him and me. Well, here I am. Say it once and for all to my face, and I swear if you choose him I'll walk away. You'll never have to see me ever again."

I stand there, silently faced with an ultimatum.

Despite my strength and willingness to hold myself together, the walls crumble, and the tears carelessly fall down my cheeks.

His expression immediately softens, and his arms wrap around me so tight that I can't let him walk away because if he does, I'll blame myself for the rest of my life.

"Lex, I'm so scared of losing you again."

"Charlotte, look at me... *please*."

He cups my chin, lifting my head, so our eyes meet. They shine so brightly, capturing me, taking me to a special place only he can ever do. "You won't. I won't let that happen to us."

Tilting his head, he kisses the tears away from my cheek, making them disappear.

We stand here, for how long, I don't know. Tired, he pulls me along as we sit on the sand, his arms wrapping around me to protect me from the ocean breeze.

"Lex, did you ever think about leaving her for me?"

"All the damn time. I'd replay the conversation in my head, have it all planned out. I was reaching my breaking point. I knew how many lives it would affect but I didn't care. The day I had planned to tell her, she dropped the bombshell." His voice croaks, the memory painful. "I hated her so much at that point. My parents and Adriana were so happy. When she went to the hospital because she was in pain, and after the stories my mother told me about losing a baby, I knew that if anything were to happen it would be all my fault."

I froze, unable to comprehend what he said. With every fiber in my being, I attempt to change the subject. I'm weak, I know that. Life is cruel. I learned that the hard way, but opening up that dark, cruel world is no way to start anew.

"I felt so pressured, Charlotte. No control over my life whatsoever." He held me tighter, brushing his lips against my hair. "I might be controlling now, but the decisions I make are all mine. I have no one to answer to but myself. I thought that was how I wanted to live, but without you, there is no life. You need to know that all I want is you."

Tilting my head to the side, I kiss his beautiful lips. Can I have him forever? Could this finally be it for us? The happily ever after we both are so desperate for?

I know I hold all the cards and this is ultimately my decision.

I need to place all my trust in him, once and for all.

"Marry me, Charlotte."

Stunned, I move my body to face him. His face is deadly serious, and maybe my clouded head is imagining things. He can't have just asked me to marry him. *Did he?*

"Lex, um... what did you just say?"

"I said... marry me, Charlotte. Tonight, here, now."

"But... we can't just get married. Are you crazy?"

"I've never been this sane in my life," he answers calmly.

"It's not even possible. I mean, even if we wanted to."

"Nothing is impossible."

He throws me the helmet, motioning for me to put it on. Jumping on the bike, he starts the engine. Taking out his phone, he types something really fast. I have no idea what he's doing. It isn't like we are in Vegas.

We drive to the next town over as I clutch onto him in a slight panic. Suddenly, he stops in front of a building, jumps off and tells me to wait by the bike. As I wait, I can feel the panic rising and the uncertainty of the situation which is making me start to sweat. A lot.

Trust him, Charlie. Go ahead and trust him, the voices in my head sing.

Lex walks down the path and knocks on the door of the fancy house. A man answers in his robe, taken aback by Lex standing on his porch. He talks, and I can't make out a single word. The man holds his hand up almost like he's refusing to hear something until they both stop, and the man closes the door. Lex continues to wait on the porch, turning around to smile back at me, almost like the smile is saying a thousand words I need to hear right now to ease the trepidation. The door opens again, and the man points to something out back. He closes the door again, and Lex comes running to where I stand.

"Now... will you tell me what's going on?" I ask, panicked.

He grabs my hand and pulls me back toward the house, except we turn the corner, following the rose bushes until we find ourselves standing in the backyard, a few feet away from a gazebo where the man stands, and an older lady beside him.

"Charlotte, marry me. Here. Now."

"Lex, come on... you're joking, right?"

"Marry me, Charlotte," he repeats the words.

I look at the man and woman waiting. Without thinking, I pull Lex toward them until we're standing under the gazebo. I turn to look at the man, Lex giving him a nod before he begins to speak.

"We're gathered here today..." he continues speaking as I stand there dumbfounded, unable to comprehend this moment.

What the hell is happening?

Is this for real?

"Alexander Matthew Edwards, do you take Charlotte

Olivia Mason to be your lawfully wedded wife, to have and
to hold till death do you part?"

"I do."

The lady hands him a gold band, and slowly, he slides it
on my finger. It's slightly tight, but he still manages to get it
on. How on earth did he get rings in five minutes?

"Charlotte Olivia Mason, do you take Alexander
Matthew Edwards to be your lawfully wedded husband, to
have and to hold till death do you part?"

Holy shit! Someone pinch me now.

"I do," I blurt out. "I really do."

I let out a sigh, and at that moment, peace has finally
found me.

The lady hands me another gold band, my fingers trembling as I slide the ring onto Lex's finger.

"By the authority vested in me by the State of New
York, I now declare you husband and wife. You may kiss
your bride."

Lex inches closer, his nose grazing mine gently before
he parts his lips and tenderly kisses mine, soft yet urgent,
desperate yet at ease, under the gazebo as I barely manage
to contain myself. I'm waiting for him to wake me up and
tell me this is all a dream. The most beautiful dream where
I just took the biggest leap of faith known to mankind.

"Are we m... married?" My voice is quivering.

"You better believe it, *Mrs. Edwards.*"

I climbed into his bed that night, and for the first time, he
holds onto me not letting me go. We have never officially
slept together, and this is to new beginnings. A new life for
us, and we're married. The adrenaline refusing to wear off.

Lex Edwards is my husband.

I am married.

As the sun rises in the morning, I wake up with Lex wrapped around my body. It's the most wonderful sleep I have ever had, and I know for now the demons have been set free. We're far from perfect, and there's still so much to overcome, but it's about taking baby steps. Right? *Because getting married on a whim is taking baby steps.*

I lay there for a while, smiling at how happy he has made me. Every part of me knows there's no one else who can make me feel so secure, so content, and so whole. I snuggle into him, not wanting to let go of this perfect man who's now mine. My husband.

Watching him sleep so peacefully, his eyelids flutter every so often. His perfect jaw, his perfect lips, his uncontrollable hair—everything about him makes me smile. So much that my cheeks start to actually hurt.

Reaching over to the nightstand, I grab my phone to see what time it is—seven in the morning—but the text sitting on the main screen catches my attention. It's a link, sent directly to me. I don't recognize the number, and it looks like a spam link, but it's the title that piques my interest.

Billionaire Playboy finally settling down with Heiress to Preston Enterprises

I normally ignore any tabloid trash sent to me, but I click on the link, taken directly to the article on page six of the *New York Times.*

In a move that shocks the business world, entrepreneur and billionaire playboy, Lex Edwards, was seen last week leaving a hotel room while being intimate with heiress to the Preston Enterprises group, Victoria Preston. A source close to the couple says they have been close for a while, but due to business conflicts, the relationship was not made public. Ms. Preston's publicist declines any comments, however, founder of Preston Enterprises, Clive Preston, says that Lex is like a son to him, and any news of a union between the two is great for him as well as the two companies. Photographs have been snapped of them at intimate dinners in New York and London. Ms. Preston has also been caught leaving his apartment dressed casually in the early hours of the morning. The photograph of them intimate at a business function last Saturday is enough to confirm the couple is definitely on.

I click on the pictures and zoom in. *It's him.* My heart stops. Clutching my chest, I'm unable to breathe. I shake my head relentlessly, the shock consuming me.

Barely able to move, my brain is trying to compute what I've read. The pictures don't lie, they are definitely being intimate, his hand is stroking her cheek. You don't do that with business associates. Every image in that article is, in fact, of them being intimate all over the fucking country.

I untangle myself from him, quietly tiptoeing across the room. As I'm about to exit, I catch his phone by the nightstand. I try to ignore it, but I need fucking answers.

I'm so fucking angry at myself for trusting him again.

Quickly grabbing it, I read the message on the screen.

Victoria: *Looks like we made page six, baby. Might as well come out now.*

With shaking hands, I place the phone back and bolt

out of the room. I'm ready to break down, to scream my lungs out, to punch something, do anything to let out the pain. The nausea washes over me. Covering my mouth, I run to the bathroom, barely making it to the bowl. My body is shaking, that familiar feeling is tearing me up inside.

I need to get out of here and fast.

Panicking as I don't want to face him. Scared he'll try to convince me it's all a lie, when, in fact, the damage is done.

He's broken me once again.

Rocky is the only one sitting at the dining table. He has the paper wide open but shuts it closed when he sees me.

"Charlie, do you wanna... look, I saw..."

"Rocky, I need you to do me a favor. I'm packing my bags right now and taking the bike. I don't care how just make sure someone drives my car back. Park it in your garage. I need to get out of here right now. Please, just do this for me?"

He nods as I quickly bolt back to my room shoving everything in my bag. I dump it in the back of the car and run over to my bike. Quickly putting my helmet on, I drive off faster than I ever have before, the noise of the engine echoing through the quiet streets.

I hate myself so much right now.

Why the hell did I ever trust him?

He can't just be with me.

He always has to have his way.

Someone else on the side, and I'm so sick of being that other woman. He's nothing but a fucking liar, a player, and I'm so stupid for believing his lies, *again*, for believing him when he said he loves me.

This anger has taken over, poisoning every positive thought I have of him, of us. No one can understand the outrage I feel right now. How much I hate him for making me love him again. That's the thing that hurts the most. It isn't about loving him again, it's more about awakening the love which never disappeared. Fate has now reared its fucking ugly head and screwed all this shit up. This sick, cruel, twisted game forced upon me and drained me of all my beliefs, all my hopes, telling me that maybe he's my soulmate, and we are meant to live happily ever after.

By the time I reach my building, my phone has twenty-five missed calls and a dozen text messages. I can't bring myself to read the texts.

Throwing the phone against the wall, I watch the screen crack as I scream in the basement, letting out my frustration. Leaning against the wall, I slide down, falling to the hard, concrete floor.

My tears are spilling out, the sobs leaving my chest gut-wrenching, and the pain spreads all over my body. My throat is dry, I am unable to form any words. I have to hide, run away from all this madness. I crawl over to where my phone lays broken on the ground. I can barely make out the numbers as my vision is clouded and the screen has a big crack, but I text his number and wait patiently for him to arrive.

Time is lost, my surroundings unfamiliar, but the voice, the words echo.

I can't understand what's going on.

The faint sight in front of me. What's happening?

The warm arms I feel around me. This is safe, I have nothing to fear.

"Charlie... Charlie... Charlie, please look at me!" The voice is panicked.

I smile as I see his face, now able to focus.

"You came," I mutter, my voice croaking.

"Of course, I did. Please look at me. What happened?"

The pain swells in my chest, the momentary realization knocking me cold.

"What date is it today?" I cry.

"Charlie, it's September twenty-first."

"I need... to... get... out... of... here," I sob.

Placing his arms beneath me, he carries me toward the elevator as I rest my head in his chest.

"Take me somewhere, anywhere but here, anywhere but home. Take away this pain, please? Make it go away. Please? I don't want to go back there. I can't go back to that awful place," I scream.

"Shh. I'll take you away from here. It's okay. It will be okay, Charlie, I promise."

The numbing starts, and I know the protocol. This is the second step of the coping mechanism. The third will be ignorance, and fourth will be the bitterness shown in the light of day. The sweet revenge accompanied by hurtful words that one day will be said, followed by regret.

Her words from long ago keep replaying like a broken record, and somehow, I have to let history repeat itself. I let the big bad wolf—or as my mother referred to them as Dark Angels—strip me bare of everything I have fought so hard to rebuild.

My heart is absolutely broken beyond repair.

He's the most beautiful man you'll ever see. His soul will capture you but don't be fooled, Mi Corazon. He'll use all his powers to draw you in when there's nothing left to do but take the one thing you've been holding on to.

When I was eighteen, I wasn't wise or mature enough to know love is the most powerful thing in the universe, and so I allowed myself to accept it in all its glory. I learned the hard way, it also leads the path to the darkest place that exists.

Now, I believe I have it all figured out. Yes, love is the most powerful thing, I accept that, but this time I'm armed and convinced that I know which path is the road to happiness, *my happily ever after*.

This is no longer the fairy tale my momma read to me. This is the sequel. The story of the *Dark Angel*, who rode back into my sunset disguised as Prince Charming, only this time my armor is shattered, my will to fight obliterated.

The phoenix bird brought back my stolen soul and it lays helpless before me, clipped of its wings, unable to soar, trapped in a cage of my mistakes. The mistake of letting myself love him again, love the man who broke my heart. *Twice.*

Being laid on a warm bed is the last I remember about this day eight years ago almost six months since the day I last saw him. The day when the darkness fell upon me and without any light, I was unable to see, my mind demented by the shadows that lurked.

Like a frightened little girl, I prayed that someone would find me, hold my hand, pull me out of this dark abyss and lead me back into the light.

Alexander Edwards broke me in ways I never imagined possible.

But in the end, it was me who destroyed it all.

I gave up on *us*.

And regret is something I'll have to live with... *forever*.

To be continued...

CHASING US

A Second Chance Love Triangle
The Dark Love Series Book 2

BLURB

I was never supposed to fall in love with a married man.
My best friend's brother.
I'd made too many mistakes in my past.
Like last night—when I married Lex Edwards impulsively.

In a bid to finally find their happily ever after, Lex and
Charlie find themselves on a journey of learning how to
love again. They began a new future to move forward from
a broken past, finally together at last.

They vowed nothing would tear them apart... *again*.
But life's cruel fate destroys their lives, and in desperate
times they tear their love apart grieving over a lost
loved one.

Lex and Charlie find themselves on the verge of finally saying goodbye to each other, until the return of a scorned ex-fiancé who's desperate to claim back what was his.

ALSO BY KAT T. MASEN

The Dark Love Series

Featuring Lex & Charlie

Chasing Love: A Billionaire Love Triangle

Chasing Us: A Second Chance Love Triangle

Chasing Her: A Stalker Romance

Chasing Him: A Forbidden Second Chance Romance

Chasing Fate: An Enemies-to-Lovers Romance

Chasing Heartbreak: A Friends-to-Lovers Romance

The Forbidden Love Series

(Dark Love Series Second Generation)

Featuring Amelia Edwards

The Trouble With Love: An Age Gap Romance

The Trouble With Us: A Second Chance Love Triangle

The Trouble With Him: A Secret Pregnancy Romance

The Trouble With Her: A Friends-to-Lovers Romance

The Trouble With Fate: An Enemies-to-Lovers Romance

Also by Kat T. Masen

The Office Rival: An Enemies-to-Lovers Romance

The Marriage Rival: An Office Romance

Bad Boy Player: A Brother's Best Friend Romance

Roomie Wars Box Set (Books 1 to 3): Friends-to-Lovers Series

ABOUT THE AUTHOR

Born and bred in Sydney, Australia, **Kat T. Masen** is a mother to four crazy boys and wife to one sane husband. Growing up in a generation where social media and fancy gadgets didn't exist, she enjoyed reading from an early age and found herself immersed in these stories. After meeting friends on Twitter who loved to read as much as she did, her passion for writing began, and the friendships continued on despite the distance.

"I'm known to be crazy and humorous. Show me the most random picture of a dog in a wig, and I'll be laughing for days."

Download free bonus content, purchase signed paperbacks & bookish merchandise.

Visit: **www.kattmasen.com**

Made in United States
North Haven, CT
24 April 2023

35813619R00314